Early Evangelicalism

Early Evangelicalism

A Reader

Edited by

Edited by

JONATHAN M.YEAGER

OXFORD
UNIVERSITY PRESS

OXFORD
UNIVERSITY PRESS

Oxford University Press is a department of the University of Oxford.
It furthers the University's objective of excellence in research, scholarship,
and education by publishing worldwide.

Oxford   New York
Auckland   Cape Town   Dar es Salaam   Hong Kong   Karachi
Kuala Lumpur   Madrid   Melbourne   Mexico City   Nairobi
New Delhi   Shanghai   Taipei   Toronto

With offices in
Argentina   Austria   Brazil   Chile   Czech Republic   France   Greece
Guatemala   Hungary   Italy   Japan   Poland   Portugal   Singapore
South Korea   Switzerland   Thailand   Turkey   Ukraine   Vietnam

Oxford is a registered trademark of Oxford University Press in the UK and certain
other countries.

Published in the United States of America by
Oxford University Press
198 Madison Avenue, New York, NY 10016

Library of Congress Cataloging-in-Publication Data
Early evangelicalism : a reader / edited by Jonathan M. Yeager.
pages cm
Includes index. ISBN 978-0-19-991697-9 (pbk. : alk. paper)—ISBN 978-0-19-991695-5
(cloth : alk. paper)   1. Evangelicalism.   2. Christian biography.   3. Evangelicalism—
History.   I. Yeager, Jonathan M.
BR1643.A1E27 2013
280'.4—dc23   2013003239

In recognition of the scholarship of the foremost historians of early evangelicalism, this book is dedicated to David Bebbington and Mark Noll.

Contents

Acknowledgments

MY FIRST ORDER of thanks goes to Cynthia Read for seeing the value of this anthology and giving me the opportunity to publish again with Oxford University Press.

A book like this would be very difficult to produce without the aid of specialists in the field. I am grateful to the following scholars who took time out of their busy schedule to read and comment on portions of the manuscript: Cindy Aalders, Andrew Atherstone, Joel Beeke, Jared Burkholder, Vincent Carretta, Grayson Carter, Chris Chun, Catherine Brekus, John Grigg, Roger Hayden, Bruce Hindmarsh, Peter Jauhiainen, David Ceri Jones, S. T. Kimbrough, Ned Landsman, Gerald McDermott, Richard Newman, Karen Swallow Prior, Isabel Rivers, John Saillant, Darren Schmidt, Patrick Streiff, Robert Strivens, John Tyson, and John Wigger. I also acknowledge the helpful suggestions from David Bebbington, Michael Haykin, Mark Noll, and Doug Sweeney on the prospectus. While I relied heavily on their advice and publications, any remaining errors should be solely attributed to me.

I was fortunate to receive financial support from the Maclellan Foundation and the University of Tennessee at Chattanooga (UTC). Herb Burhenn deserves a special note of thanks for helping me obtain a critical research grant from UTC that allowed me to travel to various archives in Britain and America. In the philosophy and religion department, I have benefited from the encouragement and advice of my colleagues, none more so than Irv Resnick. In a fall 2011 course at UTC titled Religion in the Age of Wesley, Whitefield, and Edwards, I implemented much of the material for this book. The discussions and papers given by the students of this class helped me determine which excerpts to include in the anthology.

In my research for this volume, I have relied on the assistance of librarians at a number of institutions, including the Angus Library at Regent's Park College and the Bodleian Library at Oxford University, Shirley Shire at Bristol Baptist College, the British Library, the Connecticut Historical Society, the Historical Society of Pennsylvania, the Library of Congress, the Andover-Harvard Theological Library, Steven Cox at the Lupton Library, the New Hampshire Historical Society, the New York Public Library, and Elizabeth Frengel at Yale's Beinecke Library. I am also grateful to Penny Jaclyn at the American Antiquarian Society, Callie Stewart at the Bennington Museum, Diana Yount at the Franklin Trask Library, Elizabeth Malloy at the Haddam Historical Society, Hillary Kativa at the Historical Society of Pennsylvania, Rebecca Fawcett at the Hood Museum of Art, the Library of Congress, Rhianydd Davies at the National Library of Wales, the National Portrait Gallery, the New York Public Library, Karen Richter at the Princeton University Art Museum, Lauren Miller at the Spencer Museum of Art, Paula Skreslet at Union Presbyterian Seminary, Jim Gerencser at the Waidner-Spahr Library at Dickinson College, and Ken Minkema and the Yale University Art Gallery for supplying me with the images for *Early Evangelicalism: A Reader*. I owe the greatest debt, however, to my wife, Angela, who once again provided invaluable editorial assistance, and to my sons, Nathan, Nicholas, and Seth, for putting up with their dad's often intense work schedule.

Early Evangelicalism

Introduction

WHAT IS AN evangelical? The answer to this question has been debated, sometimes intensely, over the years. The term *evangelical* means "good news" in the original Greek and was used by New Testament authors to express the salvific benefits of learning that Jesus Christ had come to Earth to rescue humanity from sin. By the time of the Reformation in Europe, the word evangelical came to mean "Protestant" as a way of differentiating one group of people from Roman Catholics. Martin Luther and other reformers stressed the ineffectiveness of works in achieving salvation, arguing that it was solely by divine grace through faith (*sola gratia et fides*) that a person is justified before God. Only by believing on Jesus, and not by good deeds, could a person be liberated from the bondage of sin. A second important principle arising out of the Protestant Reformation was *sola scriptura*. For Protestants, scripture became the major source of authority. No longer would church tradition hold the same weight as the Bible. A third principle emerged during the Reformation: the priesthood of all believers. Whereas previously the priestcraft held a privileged position as educators of Christian beliefs, now all believers were told that they had the right to read and interpret the scriptures. These three pillars—justification by faith, scripture alone, and the priesthood of believers— became the foundation on which Protestantism was built.

All three pillars are present in the movement known as evangelicalism, but with some modifications. In addition to the three previously discussed principles, early evangelicals placed additional emphasis on conversion and missions. To a certain degree the reformers had advocated spiritual rebirth, but in the seventeenth and eighteenth centuries the notion of conversion became more pronounced. Especially at the time of the Great Awakening, evangelicals regularly preached on the necessity of turning away from sin and towards God for divine grace. As an itinerant evangelist in the eighteenth century, George Whitefield consistently declared the need for his audiences to experience a "new birth." Early evangelicals, like many of their Reformation, English Puritan, Scottish Presbyterian, and European Piestist forefathers, insisted that attending church, partaking of communion and baptism, and living morally, while admirable external demonstrations of piety, would not lead to eternal salvation. Rather, most early evangelicals claimed that salvation came only by way of the substitutionary atonement made by Jesus Christ on the cross in place of humanity.

Cross-cultural missions also became tantamount with early evangelicalism. Whereas in the sixteenth and seventeenth centuries, most Protestant Christians proselytized within their own families and regional communities, eighteenth-century evangelicals targeted markets in faraway lands. Taking to heart the Reformation principle of the priesthood of all believers, dedicated laypeople traveled vast distances to preach the gospel. George Whitefield, for instance, crossed the Atlantic some thirteen times during his life, delivering sermons all over colonial America and Britain. Later evangelicals like William Carey traversed even farther to places like India to spread the good news. By the second half of the century, whole denominations—most notably the Baptists and Methodists—were expanding into regions in America and Britain that had been virtually untouched by mainline churches.

Combining the innovations made by early evangelicals with the doctrines of the sixteenth and seventeenth centuries, the British historian David Bebbington, in his book *Evangelicalism in Modern Britain* (1989), has effectively summarized the movement's main characteristics: the need for conversion, a high regard for the Bible, Jesus Christ's death on the cross as the means of salvation, and missionary involvement. Ever since the publication of *Evangelicalism in Modern Britain*, scholars have continually debated Bebbington's so-called quadrilateral of evangelicalism. Certainly not everyone agrees on what constitutes an evangelical or precisely when the movement began, but several historians admit that a new religious entity emerged at the time of the revivals in the early decades of the eighteenth century. Whereas reports of spiritual resurgence were common in the years before the Great Awakening in America and the Evangelical Revival in Britain, the revivals of the eighteenth century were marked by increased frequency and ecumenism to a degree previously unknown. Those who shared convictions on the Bible, the need for conversion, Christ's death on the cross, and a desire to see the gospel proclaimed often willingly crossed denominational boundaries. Evangelical Anglicans, Baptists, Congregationalists, Methodists, Moravians, and Presbyterians worked directly and indirectly to spread the good news. Evangelicalism should be seen as a distinct religious movement within Protestant Christianity that is not tied to one particular denomination. Any person—male or female and regardless of race—holding to the defining characteristics of the Bebbington quadrilateral can rightly be called an evangelical, in the modern sense.

That is not to say that all four noted features should receive the same weight. Most early evangelicals took the Bible for granted as the source for spiritual guidance and the sole text from which to preach. The importance of Christ's death on the cross was also assumed by the majority of evangelical authors in the eighteenth century. In the unpublished and published literature, the dominant characteristic that surfaces again and again is conversion. In their diaries and journals, early evangelicals of diverse backgrounds and denominations fretted whether they had received saving grace, believing conversion to be crucial for authentic Christianity. In hymns and poems, lyricists composed verses on the saving benefits of coming to faith in Jesus. In sermons, ministers heralded the power of the Holy Spirit to transform a person's life for the better, urging listeners to seek divine grace. And in treatises, theologians attempted to elucidate the complexity of soteriology while affirming the need for heartfelt spiritual renewal. If there is a distinguishing mark of evangelicalism in the eighteenth century, it is the promotion of conversion.

Most people today associate eighteenth-century evangelicalism with only a few of its key leaders, usually Jonathan Edwards, John Wesley, and George Whitefield. If pressed, perhaps others like the selfless American missionary David Brainerd, the Baptist missionary William Carey, the celebrated author and playwright Hannah More, the slave trader-turned Anglican clergyman and hymnist John Newton, John Wesley's lyrically talented brother Charles, the abolitionist William Wilberforce, and the patriot and president of the College of New Jersey (Princeton) John Witherspoon could be named. But on the whole, important contributors to early evangelicalism have been largely ignored by scholars, including the diarist Susanna Anthony, the president of the College of New Jersey Samuel Finley, the Methodist exhorter Mary Fletcher, the best-selling author James Hervey, the hymnist Benjamin Ingham, the Glaswegian minister and theologian John Maclaurin, the founding principal of Dickinson College Charles Nisbet, the Scottish minister and revivalist James Robe, the Anglican divine William Romaine, the Baptist minister and intellectual John Ryland, the disciplined Anglican cleric Charles Simeon, the melancholy poet Anne Steele, the Anglican minister and devotional writer Henry Venn, and the founder of Dartmouth College Eleazar Wheelock. While some superb biographies have been written on lesser-known Protestants like the black Methodist leader Richard Allen, the American Methodist Francis Asbury, the grandson of Jonathan Edwards and president of Yale Timothy Dwight, the black author and abolitionist Olaudah Equiano, the black American patriot and theologian Lemuel Haynes, Edwards's disciple Samuel Hopkins, the father of American geography Jedidiah Morse, the Rhode Island small group leader Sarah Osborn, George Whitefield's protégé Gilbert Tennent, and the black poet Phillis Wheatley, their significance has not yet been realized on a popular level.

Besides neglecting important progenitors of the movement, most people know very little about early evangelicalism beyond the middle of the century. There is a wide gap in the literature on evangelicalism between the First and Second Great Awakening. Even when the First Great Awakening is examined, there is usually little or no coverage of the revivals taking place at roughly the same time in Canada, England, Scotland, Wales, and Continental Europe. A few scholars, such as David Bebbington, Mark Noll, and Susan Durden-O'Brien, have shed greater light on the movement's transatlantic nature and on some of its more obscure characters, but much more work needs to be done to preserve the pervasive breadth of early evangelicalism.

Early Evangelicalism: A Reader is designed for people interested in the genesis of this religious movement. The scope of the book is restricted to primary sources published within the eighteenth century or, in a few cases, posthumous writings that can be placed contextually between the years 1700 and 1800. A very good companion piece to this volume is Mark Noll's *The Rise of Evangelicalism: The Age of Edwards, Whitefield, and the Wesleys*, which provides an engaging narrative of the movement and many of its most colorful characters. *Early Evangelicalism* offers over sixty excerpts from a wide range of well-known and lesser-known authors, representing various denominational backgrounds, geographical locations, and underrepresented groups. A variety of genres are represented, including conversion narratives, devotionals, diaries and journals, history, hymns, poetry, ecclesiastical politics, revival accounts, satire, sermons, and theology to produce the most comprehensive anthology of its kind. It would have been impossible to fit in contributions by every notable evangelical of the century within a reasonable length, so some painful cuts had to be made.

There is limited exposure to Jonathan Edwards and John Wesley in *Early Evangelicalism*, partly because of the availability of their printed works. John Smith, Harry Stout, and Ken Minkema have published *A Jonathan Edwards Reader*, which provides a panorama of Edwards's writings. While excerpts from Joseph Bellamy and Samuel Hopkins made it into this volume, the writings of later Edwardsians have been omitted since Doug Sweeney and Allen Guelzo have edited a fine anthology titled *The New England Theology: From Jonathan Edwards to Edwards Amasa Park*. Because of the available resources on the Great Awakening, including Thomas Kidd's *The Great Awakening: A Brief History with Documents* and Richard Bushman's *The Great Awakening: Documents on the Revival of Religion, 1740–1745*, only a portion of *Early Evangelicalism* has selections from this period in American history. Additional recommended books on the subject of early evangelicalism, and specific people within the movement, can be found at the end of this volume.

Early Evangelicalism is organized chronologically. Whenever possible, specific excerpts have been inserted according to the historical context of the passage, and not necessarily when the work was published. The excerpts are intended to be long enough for readers to get a feel for the main argument or narrative of the text. For the most part, the following excerpts are unedited. I have, however, standardized the biblical references and silently amended some of the mispelled words in the excerpts to make the passages more readable, with ellipses used to separate breaks in the text. The hope is that students and scholars interested in early evangelicalism will find the following anthology an interesting and helpful introduction on the primary-source literature of this remarkable religious movement.

A Selection of Hymns

Isaac Watts

LATER DUBBED THE father of English hymnody, Isaac Watts (1674–1748) was born in Southampton, England, and raised by Dissenting parents. His father, a clothier, proudly endured periods of imprisonment during the 1670s and 1680s for not conforming to the Anglican Church. After his education at a free grammar school at Southampton from 1680 to 1690, and a London Dissenting academy in the 1690s, the young Watts took a job as a private tutor before beginning a long career as a Dissenting minister in London. He corresponded with a host of evangelicals, including Philip Doddridge, John Wesley, George Whitefield, and James Hervey in England, and Thomas Prince and Benjamin Colman in America. His excitement for the revivals was somewhat tempered though. Although instrumental in publishing Jonathan Edwards's *A Faithful Narrative of the Surprising Work of God* in 1737, he was somewhat suspicious of Methodism, not wanting to associate with the more emotional forms of evangelicalism.

Unquestionably, Watts's greatest contribution to evangelicalism was as a hymn writer. Displeased that most Anglican and Independent churches at that time sang exclusively the Psalms, he set out to correct the perceived deficiencies in tradition worship services. In the latter half of the seventeenth century, and into the early decades of the eighteenth century, "lining out" was the common practice. A leader in the church would chant a Psalm, one line at a time, and then the congregation would follow in tune. Responding to what he viewed as an archaic method, Watts took the radical step of writing hymns in which he paraphrased scripture passages while experimenting with different tempos. In the prefaces to his *Hymns and Spiritual Songs* (1707) and *The Psalms of David Imitated in the Language of the New Testament* (1719) he explained his intent to compose lyrics that the masses could easily follow and sing. Traditionalists accustomed to singing only the words of scripture deplored Watts's innovations, yet he held his ground that in modernizing hymns he had not betrayed the true spirit of the biblical texts. Despite some initial complaints, Watts's method won the day. His hymns had a direct influence

FIGURE I.I Isaac Watts (Detail), courtesy of the National Portrait Gallery, London.

on the supplemental songbooks published by John and Charles Wesley as well as other early evangelicals who followed Watts's method. His legacy continues today when such hymns as "O God, Our Help in Ages Past," "When I Survey the Wondrous Cross," and "Joy to the World" are sung in churches around the globe.

"Christ Jesus the Lamb of God, Worshiped by All the Creation;" Revelation 5:11–13

1. *Come let us join our cheerful Songs*
       With Angels round the Throne;
   Ten thousand thousand are their Tongs,
       But all their Joys are one.
   "Worthy the Lamb that dy'd," they cried
   "To be exalted thus;"
   "Worthy the Lamb," our Lips reply,
       For He was slain for us.
   Jesus is worthy to receive
       Honour and Power divine;
   And Blessings more than we can give,
       Be, Lord, for ever thine.

2. *Let all that dwell above the Sky,*
       And Air, and Earth, and Seas,
   Conspire to lift thy Glories high,
       And speak thine endless Praise.

3. *The whole Creation join in one,*
       To bless the Sacred Name
   Of him that sits upon the Throne,
       And to adore the Lamb.

"Godly Sorrow Arising from the Sufferings of Christ"

1. Alas! and did my Saviour bleed?
    And did my Sovereign dye?
   Would he devote that Sacred Head
    For such a Worm as I?

2. Thy Body slain, sweet Jesus, thine,
    And bath'd in its own Blood,
   While the firm mark of Wrath Divine
    His Soul in Anguish stood?

3. Was it for Crimes that I had done
    He groan'd upon the Tree?
   Amazing Pity! Grace unknown!
    And Love beyond degree!

4. Well might the Sun in Darkness hide,
    And shut his Glories in,
   When God the mighty Maker dy'd
    For Man the Creature's Sin.

5. Thus might I hide my blushing Face
    While his dear Cross appears,
   Dissolve my Heart in Thankfulness,
    And melt my Eyes to Tears.

6. But drops of Grief can ne're repay
    The debt of Love I owe,
   Here, Lord, I give my self away,
    'Tis all that I can do.

"Crucifixion to the World by the Cross of Christ;"
Galatians 6:14

1. When I survey the wondrous Cross
   Where the young Prince of Glory dy'd,
   My richest Gain I count but Loss,
   And pour Contempt on all my Pride.

2. Forbid it, Lord, that I should boast
   Save in the Death of Christ my God;
   All the vain things that charm me most,
   I sacrifice them to his Blood.

3. See from his Head, his Hands, his Feet,
   Sorrow and Love flow mingled down;

Did e're such Love and Sorrow meet?
Or Thorns compose so rich a Crown?
4. *His dying Crimson like a Robe*
    Spreads o'er his Body on the Tree,
    Then am I dead to all the Globe,
    And all the Globe is dead to me.
5. *Were the whole Realm of Nature mine,*
    That were Present far too small;
    Love so amazing, so divine
    Demands my Soul, my Life, my All.

"Man Frail and God Eternal"

I.

OUR God, our Help in Ages past,
        Our Hope for Years to come,
Our Shelter from the stormy Blast,
        And our eternal Home.

II.

Under the Shadow of thy Throne
        Thy Saints have dwelt secure;
Sufficient is thine Arm alone,
        And our Defence is sure.

III.

Before the Hills in order stood,
        Or Earth receiv'd her Frame,
From everlasting Thou art God,
        To endless Years the same.

IV.

Thy Word commands our Flesh to Dust,
        Return, ye Sons of Men:
All Nations rose from Earth at first,
        And turn to Earth again.

V.

A thousand Ages in thy Sight
Are like an Evening gone;
Short as the Watch that ends the Night
Before the rising Sun.

VI.

The busy Tribes of Flesh and Blood
With all their Lives and Cares
Are carried downwards by thy Flood,
And lost in following Years.

VII.

Time like an ever-rolling Stream
Bears all its Sons away;
They fly forgotten as a Dream
Dies at the opening Day.

VIII.

Like flow'ry Fields the Nations stand
Pleas'd with the Morning-light;
The Flowers beneath the Mower's Hand
Ly withering e'er 'tis Night.

IX.

Our God, our Help in Ages past,
Our Hope for Years to come,
Be thou our Guard while Troubles last,
And our eternal Home.

"The Messiah's Coming and Kingdom"

I.

JOY to the World; the Lord is come;
Let Earth receive her King:
Let every Heart prepare him Room,
And Heaven and Nature sing.

II.

Joy to the Earth, The Saviour reigns;
Let Men their Songs employ;
While Fields & Floods, Rocks, Hills & Plains
Repeat the sounding Joy.

III.

No more let Sins and Sorrows grow,
Nor Thorns infest the Ground:
He comes to make his Blessings flow
Far as the Curse is found.

IV.

He rules the World with Truth and Grace,
And makes the Nations prove
The Glories of his Righteousness,
And Wonders of his Love.

Isaac Watts, *Hymns and Spiritual Songs* (London: John Lawrence, 1707), 60, 86–87, 189.

Isaac Watts, *Psalms of David Imitated in the Language of the New Testament, and Apply'd to the Christian State and Worship* (London: J. Clark, 1719), 229–30, 253.

2

Biography of a Moravian

Nicholas Ludwig von Zinzendorf

IN HIS TWO-VOLUME biography, the Moravian leader A. G. Spangenberg describes the first twenty-seven years of Nicholas Ludwig von Zinzendorf (1700–60), the German count born on May 26, 1700, in Dresden, Saxony. Within weeks of his birth, Zinzendorf's father, Georg Ludwig, Count of Zinzendorf and Pottendorf, died. Young Nicholas and his mother went to live with his maternal grandmother, Henriette Catherine von Gersdorf. Raised in Henriette's Pietist home, the young count began studying at the University of Halle at age ten. While at Halle, the eccentric Zinzendorf penned love letters to Christ and helped to establish "the Order of the Mustard Seed," a society dedicated to fulfilling Christ's teachings. In 1716 he left Halle for further schooling at the University of Wittenberg, where he remained until 1719. Three years later, in 1722, Zinzendorf purchased his grandmother's estate at Berthelsdorf. About the same time, he heard news of a group of Bohemian refugees led by Christian David that were looking for a place to settle. The count offered space on a portion of his estate that was named Herrnhut, or "the Lord's Protection." Removing himself in the late 1720s from his aristocratic duties at the Saxon elector's court, Zinzendorf assumed the position of spiritual leader for the burgeoning community that by 1727 had grown to over two hundred people. Not wanting to start a separate church, Zinzendorf retained the group's historical ties with the Unitas Fratrum (Unity of the Brethren), a religious movement that could trace its history to Jan Hus and his followers. Zinzendorf organized the multifarious refugees into small groups called bands in which members—separated by age, sex, and marital status—were encouraged to confess their sins.

Although a small community, Zinzendorf and the Moravians made a sizeable contribution to early evangelicalism. Beginning in 1732, the Moravians sent missionaries to witness to the slaves of the Danish West Indies. By the time of the count's death in 1760, pockets of Moravians could be found in the Baltics, Egypt, Greenland, North America, South America, and South Africa. In England, the Moravians sought ecumenical relationships with other Christians, including

FIGURE 2.1 Count Zinzendorf (Detail), Emmet Collection, Miriam and Ira D. Wallach Division of Art, Prints and Photographs, the New York Public Library, Astor, Lenox and Tilden Foundations.

Philip Doddridge, John and Charles Wesley, George Whitefield, and the trustees of the newly formed Georgia colony. John Wesley's life was transformed when he attended the Fetter Lane Society in London founded by the Moravian Peter Böhler in the late 1730s. On May 24, 1738, Wesley famously felt his heart "strangely warmed" while listening to a reading of Martin Luther's preface to the book of Romans. Theological differences, however, arose between the Moravians and the Wesleys over matters pertaining to sanctification, with John Wesley arguing for gradual and complete perfection within one's lifetime and Zinzendorf teaching instant regeneration. Later controversies with the Moravians surfaced during the so-called "Sifting Time" of the mid-century when Zinzendorf was known to obsess over the blood and physical wounds of Christ, especially Jesus' outpouring side. Despite his differences with other evangelicals, Zinzendorf viewed all Christian denominations as composing one true church, but each with a distinct Tropus Paideias, or way of teaching, divinely orchestrated to meet the various cultural needs of people around the world at a given time.

The Life of Nicolas Lewis, Count of Zinzendorf and Pottendorf

I WILL here relate something concerning his childlike and early converse with *Jesus Christ* the friend of children. Sometimes when he found a pen, ink, and paper, he would write letters to our dear Saviour, wherein he expressed his heart's situation, and then threw them out of the window, hoping that he would find them. His covenant with our Saviour was this: "Be thou my dear Saviour, and I will be thine." And this he often renewed. About a couple of months before his happy departure, he related to the children in the school at Hennersdorf many circumstances of his life from his third to his tenth year, at which time he thought nothing greater than to be a servant of our Saviour. But the whole scope of the gospel as understood and enjoyed by the children of GOD in this time of grace, was not then clear to him; for if he had rightly apprehended the grace of the following time, which our children now enjoy, and which consists in the tenderest reverence towards the humanity of our Creator and Saviour, from the boy's age, to the full stature of man, then he would have almost been beside himself for joy and awe. That knowledge he attained gradually, which our children now have concentered without prolixity. During his whole life, even in his 60th year, he could recollect every place in the castle of Hennersdorf, where he had tasted and seen the goodness of the LORD, and this he always remembered with peculiar gratitude...

His grand-mother had a general and impartial love for all true servants of GOD, but yet a peculiar confidence in the late professor Herrman Franke. She therefore contrived it so, that her dear grand-son might enjoy his care, with the concurrence and assistance of his mother and father-in-law; and thus he came, August 16, 1710, in his eleventh year, to the Royal Academy in Halle, which, on account of its good regulation, especially with regard to the education of young noblemen, was in universal repute. Here he was treated in a very strict manner, in consequence of a certain idea which professor Franke entertained of him. He had been represented to him as a capable and ingenious young lord, but one who must be kept under, that he might not presume upon his talents. The consequences of this humbling method, occasioned our Count many heavy hours. He was placed in the lowest classes; others, who were his inferiors in learning, were preferred before him; the least mistakes were corrected in an unbecoming manner; such things were often exacted from him, as he could not comply with, without incurring contempt; and he was pointed out in such a light, as rendered him ridiculous to others...

IN the beginning of April, 1716, he removed from Halle, after he had taken leave, in a public oration in the academy, upon this subject, *viz.* The desire which learned men generally have of getting the better in controversy at any rate. After a short stay at Gaverniz with his uncle and guardian, he came to his grand-mother at Gross-Hennersdorf, where he remained eleven weeks. Here he made good use of the library; and especially the writings of Luther, Franke, and other divines, and also composed several poems. His tutor Daniel Crisenius read lectures, and his grand-mother accompanied them with her best admonitions with regard to his academic life. Having spent his time here in a very useful manner, whereof his diary, which he calls the order of his travels gives an account, (for he looked upon his daily procedure as a journey through this world) he returned July 8th, 1716, to his guardian, who read to him the instructions, which his grand-mother had drawn up, and after a few weeks sent him to the university at Wittenberg.

HAD it been left to his own option, he would certainly have preferred Halle to Wittenberg. But his guardian insisted upon the latter, and the more so, because he observed several things in the young Count's way of thinking and acting, on account of which he would fain have him quit Halle and enter into another course. But this was not known at Halle, and therefore his removal to Wittenberg was attributed to his own inclination. He saith himself, "The people at Halle were afraid, when I was unexpectedly sent to Wittenberg, what form of doctrine I might embrace there." ...

FROM what has been related, a judgment may be formed, how far he may be said to have been his own instructor in matters of religion. He had every assistance in *that part*, for which he was educated; but what lay on his heart, what was his final view, and what he thought his peculiar call after many tears and prayers sent up to GOD; *that* he was obliged to study alone. He depended on his parents and guardians, and they opposed his studying divinity farther than as a science. He was therefore under a necessity of learning *his divinity* at the feet of *Jesus*, and not from men.

OUR Count, upon his arrival at Wittenberg, entered directly, according to the instruction of his guardian, upon those other exercises, that are common in the university. I find the following words in a letter under his own hand; "Nothing vexed me more at Wittenberg, than those vain exercises, which mere obedience compelled me to submit to: for they were indeed no pleasure to me, but a trial of my patience." In the above mentioned preface he says further, "At the university I pursued such exercises as I thought useful, but refrained from dancing in company, because I deemed it sinful." He has faithfully noted in his diary his daily lectures and exercises: September the 2d, 1716, he writes, "To-day I was taught the first rudiments of dancing, but with a firm resolution, that I would never practice it, but only make such use of it as far as was conducive to a proper bodily deportment." In another place he mentions, that when once a rapier was presented to him in a fencing-room with a threatening mien, he fell into a passion, and fought with great warmth. This caused him afterwards much grief; he begged our Saviour's pardon, and took the resolution, by the grace of GOD, to be more upon his guard for the future...

[1721] IT would certainly have been a great pleasure to him if his relations had consented to his favourite choice, of becoming a preacher of the gospel. Nothing in his opinion ought to withdraw his attention from this call, which he believed he had received, to be a witness of the sufferings of *Christ*, and to bring souls to him. With this view he seriously recollected the many and strong emotions of grace, which he had experienced in his heart from his tenderest age, and which had increased from year to year, in proportion as the love of *Christ* became more deeply rooted in his heart. This way of thinking was, in itself considered, not wrong, but rather unusual among people of rank in the Protestant church. And because it ran counter to their pre-conceived ideas and expectations, that he should follow the steps of his ancestors, especially his father and uncle, and accept offices of state for the good of his country, therefore his parents could not acquiesce in his desire. They did not indeed absolutely disapprove of his inclination to serve our Saviour, or his zeal for the salvation of souls; for they themselves feared GOD, and loved his word. But they believed, that if he would serve the state, he could, with the gifts bestowed upon him, do much more good than if he commenced a divine, or chose the retired life of a religious lord. Such were the sentiments of his mother, and her consort General Field-marshall de Nazmer, his grand-mother, and all his other relations.

This caused him great perplexity, for he could not well oppose the determination of his dear parents, and yet believed it inconsistent with his call, because it would expose him to danger. He therefore modestly expostulated, and when that was in vain, he prayed and wept.

His grand-mother perceiving his great uneasiness, gave him leave to explain his mind in writing, which he did at large, and humbly remonstrated, that he had a great aversion to the world, was afraid to engage in state-affairs, and at all events never could solicit a worldly employment...

[1722] BEFORE he [Zinzendorf] set out from Dresden for Ebersdorf, he was informed of the arrival of some Moravian exiles in Lusatia...I cannot omit mentioning the occasion thereof, by means of one Christian David. This man born in Senslteben in Moravia was an extraordinary person, whose memory is very dear to me. Being concerned for salvation when but eight years old, he sought rest for his soul, and according to the advice given by those whom he consulted, did all in his power to obtain it, but in vain. At the age of maturity, he travelled abroad as a journeyman carpenter, and arrived at Goerlitz, where he heard the thing named which his soul hungered after.

There he began to read the scriptures diligently, and became a lively witness of the grace of our LORD *Jesus Christ*. At Friedersdorf in Upper Lusatia, a seat of Baron de Schweinitz, he formed his first acquaintance with our Count, to whom he related the oppressed circumstances of the Brethren in Moravia. Perceiving the Count's zeal for the cause of GOD, and his readiness to succor those who suffered for conscience sake, he returned to Moravia, and told his friends, that probably they would find an asylum in the territory of this lord. For he knew very well, that they purposed, if possible, to emigrate to some place where they could serve GOD according to their consciences, and in obedience to the truth, which by his grace they had received. The Brethren in Moravia were glad of this news, for they had entertained thoughts of going to Hungary or Transylvania, but were still undetermined...

[1723] THE views of this little company are set forth in the account of the Four United Brethren as follows: Their first care was that the gospel might be published with all simplicity and plainness of language, without any fear of man, and in full confidence of the blessing of GOD in rendering their labours successful. The bare conviction of their hearers with regard to the truth of the doctrine delivered, did not satisfy them, but they were chiefly concerned to speak the word with the demonstration of the spirit and power of GOD to the heart.

It was the count's principal aim, that they should not dwell upon non-essentials, but only on such points as conduce to the real benefit of the souls. In the next place they also agreed not to lose any opportunity of testifying, in other places, of *Jesus* the only way of life. Whenever any of them took a journey, it was chiefly with a view of promoting the spiritual interest of mankind. And since an acquaintance had commenced with many persons, of high as well as low rank, not only in Germany but also in Holland, France, England, Denmark, Sweden, Switzerland, &c. which was continually increasing, they resolved by means of an epistolary correspondence to make known the mind of *Christ* as contained in the scriptures. Tho' this task was both expensive and laborious, yet in the issue it turned to a blessed account. In this service the Count was indefatigable. Their next step was to select useful pieces of instruction, and to have them printed in the cheapest manner for the benefit of the poor. They did not confine themselves within the sphere of their own denomination, but were desirous to spread a blessing among others likewise. The Count thought himself bound to take an especial care of the exiles, that were settled on his territory; and the more so, as many emigrants have been observed to receive more harm than good for their souls, by leaving their own country, for want of proper instruction. They also consulted about the best method of educating children, according to the mind of *Christ*, and of erecting proper buildings for their oeconomies. The Count thought somewhat different from the others on this point, but condescended to embrace the scheme of his friends, (who were very positive in the matter) and took actual share in the execution thereof; which will be mentioned in its proper place.

IN order to accomplish their laudable intentions these United Brethren found it needful frequently to confer together. When they met for these purposes it was no otherwise than if they thought aloud, that is, they spoke out all their sentiments with the utmost freedom. These deliberations obtained the appellation of conferences, and have continued among the Brethren ever since.

A. G. Spangenberg, *The Life of Nicolas Lewis, Count of Zinzendorf and Pottendorf,* 2 vols. (Bath: T. Mills, 1773), 1:56–8, 1:62–3, 1:84–5, 1:102–05, 2:8–10, 2:46–7, 2:69–71.

3

Justice for the Punishment of Sin

Jonathan Dickinson

OFTEN OVERLOOKED BY scholars of American religious history, Jonathan Dickinson (1688–1747) rivals Jonathan Edwards in importance among early American intellectual evangelicals. In their edited volume, *The Great Awakening: Documents Illustrating the Crisis and Its Consequences,* historians Alan Heimert and Perry Miller described Dickinson as possessing "the most powerful mind in his generation of American divines." Born in Hatfield, Massachusetts, Dickinson graduated from the Collegiate School of Connecticut (renamed Yale College in 1718) in 1706, served the majority of his life as a minister at Elizabethtown, New Jersey, and finished his career as the first president of the College of New Jersey (Princeton University).

Dickinson prefigures Jonathan Edwards in some respects. Both men can rightly be described as moderate evangelicals who supported the Great Awakening while distancing themselves from the excesses of the revivals. Dickinson, like Edwards, promoted a Calvinistic form of evangelicalism that was neither overly rationalistic nor inconsistent with reason. In their quest to understand the faculty of the mind, both concluded that the will and the intellect were not two distinct entities. In an eerie foreshadowing of Edwards's death in 1758 as the newly installed president of the College of New Jersey, Dickinson died in 1747 of smallpox complications, months after being appointed as the first president of the fledgling institution.

One of the challenges for early evangelicals was to answer the criticism posed by deism, which sought to strip Christianity of any vestiges of the supernatural and instead posit a solely rational form of faith. No doubt in response to John Locke's *Reasonableness of Christianity* (1695), Dickinson wrote his own *Reasonableness of Christianity* in 1732, but with a greater emphasis on faith working with reason. In presenting his template for Christianity, Dickinson walked a tightrope, intending to balance the power of human reason with divine inspiration. He wanted to defend traditional Calvinistic doctrines such as the depravity of human nature while at the same time demonstrating that such beliefs were compatible with the newly emerging age of reason.

FIGURE 3.1 Jonathan Dickinson by Edward Ludlow Mooney (Detail), Princeton University, gift of the artist, photo by Bruce M. White.

The Reasonableness of Christianity

UPON the whole, it's most evident, that there are such things in *nature*, as *virtue* and *vice*, right and wrong; this is what our own *consciences* continually remonstrate, and what *all Nations* have always agreed in: Whence that appears agreeable to the very first *dictates* of *reason*, in Genesis 4:7: *If thou doest well, shalt thou not be accepted? And if thou doest not well, sin lieth at the door.*

WE have all a sad experience, that our *first* and *chief* inclinations, are to those ways that are most repugnant unto the *holiness* of the *Divine nature*; and to that *rectitude* that *God* reasonably expects from us.

AS soon as ever we are capable of *action*, the leading *affections* and *passions* of the mind are manifestly *irregular* and *vicious*, the *appetite exorbitant*, and the whole bent of soul after what is most *opposite* to our *duty* and *happiness*: That if our *tender age* were without *restraint* and government, and a *loose* given to our *natural* inclinations; we should be worse than the *wild asses colt*, and be authors of destruction to our selves, and one another. With what *care* and *pains* must our *first* years be cultivated! With what perpetual instructions and admonitions must the seeds of *virtue* be sown in our minds! And with what diligence and vigilance must the poison sprouts of *vice* and immorality be weeded up, in order to prevent our headlong progress in *impiety* towards *God* and *man*!

THUS we begin our course: And in our more *advanced age*, what combat does every thinking person find, between his *reason* and *passions*, whereby he is even distracted with this perpetual struggle and contest for victory! With what difficulty do we form our minds to any *reverence* of our *glorious Creator*, or conformity to His justice, goodness, or holiness! How difficult a task is it to regulate our *appetites*, or to hold the *reins* of our *inordinate* inclinations and desires! This is what the *heathen* World have from the eldest ages observ'd in themselves; whereby they have been fill'd with great *vexation* and *inquietude*; and put upon vain enquiries, after means of composing these *jarring* principles in their minds; which have issued in this *ancient* and common complaint, *Video meliora, proboque, deteriora sequor.* Agreeable to that of the *Apostle, The good I know, I do not; and when I would do good, evil is present with me.* These things lie open to every observer, whereby they cannot but discern, that *the imaginations of the thoughts of their hearts are evil continually*, as Genesis 6:5.

WE cannot but observe, that the greatest part of the World do, against the *light* of their own *reason*, live in courses of *sin* against *God*, and of *disobedience* to Him.

HOW great a part of the World bow down to *stocks* and *stones*, worship the *host of Heaven*, or lie prostrate at the altars of some vile *pagods*; while they *forget the God that made them, and the Rock that formed them!* And tho' *custom* or *education* may so darken their *understandings*, as to satisfy their minds in this *stupid idolatry* yet their own *reason* (were that consulted) would certainly teach them the sin & folly of thus *worshipping and serving the creature, more than the Creator, who is blessed for ever.*

AND besides this *superstition* and *idolatry*, whereby the *Eternal Majesty* is thus dishonour'd, by the much greatest part of mankind; how does *lust* and *passion* get the victory of *reason* and *principle*, even in the most *enlightened* parts of the World? Whence else are the ambition & tyranny, the ravages, massacres, convulsions and confusions, that render the *Earth* an *Aceldama*? Or whence the enormous actions, and flagitious lives, the injustice and fraud, the malice and envy, the luxury, riot and excess; or other like *sinful* and *sensual* pursuits, that the *most* of the *World* are chargeable with? Can the perpetrators of such *impieties* plead *ignorance*? Don't they *sin* against *light*, and against the frequent remonstrances of their *reason* and *consciences*? Yes certainly! *Tho' they know God, they glorify Him not as God, but become vain in their imaginations, until their foolish hearts are darkened*, as Romans 1:21.

IT'S evident that this promptitude to *sin*, flows from the *corruption* and *pollution* of our *natures*.

WHENCE can such *corrupt streams* proceed, but from a *polluted fountain*? And whence such a progress of *impiety*, but from a wicked and depraved *nature*? What reason can be assign'd, why men should choose *irregular* and *sinful*, rather than *innocent* & *rational* pleasures & satisfactions; and gratify their *lusts* at the expence of their comfort, health, reputation, estates, and every thing else that is *pleasant* and *precious*, as we see they do? Why do bold *daring wretches*, without any apparent prospect of *pleasure* or *profit*, with an affronted bravery, defy *Heaven* it self, profane *Divine Attributes*, and curse their *own souls*? And why do they rush on in their *sinful* and *irrational* courses, against contrary convictions, and against all *restraints, Divine* and *humane*? What (I say) can be the cause of all this, but the *depravity* of our *natures*; and the cursed *enmity* of our *hearts* to *God*, and all that is good?

THOUGH there needs no other *Argument* to give us full assurance of this *sad truth*; yet a particular view of the *faculties*, habits and dispositions of our *Souls*, would give us further evidence, that *our hearts are deceitful above all things, and desperately wicked*, as Jeremiah 17:9.

THIS state of *sin* and *pollution*, which we find our selves in, must necessarily be a state of *guilt* and *woe*.

SIN in its formal nature is directly repugnant unto all the *properties* & *perfections of God*; and is the highest *affront* and *indignity* to Him. It is a contempt & denial of His *propriety* in us, and *dominion* over us; as it is a refusing subjection to His known *will*.

IT is a contempt of His *goodness* & *mercy*, in choosing base and brutish *pleasures*, before His *favour*; and refusing to be allur'd to His service; by all the sweet attractives of His *gracious providence*. It is a horrid slight and disregard of His *Omniscience* and *Omnipresence*, that we dare *sin* in His very *presence*, & act contrary to Him, tho' we know that our actions are *open* before Him. It's a daring defiance of His Omnipotence, for such worms as we to oppose, as tho' we could make our party good against the *God* who made the World, and can make us *fuel* to His flaming *vengeance*, at pleasure.

IT is a vile, contempt of His *Holiness* and *Purity*, in preferring the *pollutions* of our own irregular appetites, before the *rectitude* of His *Nature*. In a word, it is a contempt of all His *Attributes*, and direct *enmity* and *rebellion* against Him.

FROM this contemplation, it's most apparent, that we wretchedly *deviate* from the great *end* of our *Creation*, both by the habits and acts of *sin*. For it's the height of *stupidity* to imagine, that *Infinite Wisdom* should make so *noble* a Being, for no higher purposes, than to contemn His *Attributes*, spurn His *Authority*, and maintain a course of *opposition* to Him. And the same consideration lays open before us the *guilt* of a *sinful* state. For if rebellion and treason against an *earthly Sovereign* be by all men voted so *black* a *crime*, as to involve the *rebel* in deepest guilt, and expose him to sharpest *revenges*; how much more *criminal* and *guilty* must he be, that maintains a *rebellion* against the *King of kings*, and lives in a course of open *enmity* & *defiance* both to His *Being* & *Government!* which we have seen to be our case.

WHAT kind or degrees of *punishment*, an offended *Sovereign* will inflict upon such *rebels*, is not so easily discover'd by the *light of nature*. But that we are justly exposed to *punishment*, is visible from the nature of our crimes. None calls in question the equity of *penal* rewards to *traitors* in the *State*: how much less can we reasonably expect to escape *unpunish'd* for our *treason* against *Heaven!* If it be *justice* in man to *punish* the delinquent, it must necessarily be so in *God*; who is the *fountain* of all created *justice*, and whose holy *Nature* is the only pattern of our *virtues* and regular conduct. It is therefore but reasonable to expect, that those who prefer the ways and fruits of *sin*, to the *favour* of God, should be left to their unhappy choice, and be shut out of His *favour* for ever. They may not, they can-not suppose, that such guilty and polluted creatures, such enemies to *God* and *holiness* should be the objects of the *Divine love* and *complacency*; or be admitted to the favourable presence, and delightful fruition of a *holy God*. No! *He is of purer eyes than to behold evil, or to look upon sin with approbation.* Thus we see, that the loss of God's *favour*, and thereby the loss of all happiness (which can only consist in His *favour*) is the natural and necessary result of our state of *sin* and *enmity* to Him. And tho' we cannot discover by *natural light*, to what manner or measure of positive *penalties* our *sins* expose us: Yet we have greatest reason to expect and fear some terrible manifestation of *God's* righteous *displeasure*.

IF it be objected against all this, that the *contrary* is evident, from the *dispensa-tions of Providence*; it being a constant observation, that the most impiously *wicked* and *profane* are often in happy & flourishing circumstances, and seem to be the darling *favourites* of *Heaven*, while the more *holy* and *virtuous* are under great-est *afflictions*, and press'd with many *calamities*, as tho' they were the especial objects of *God's wrath*: I answer, this *Objection* does nothing [to] militate against the *awful* considerations before us, but rather confirms them; For how *dark* and inexplicable so ever the present dispensations of *providence* may be, *God* is a *God of justice*; and *the Judge of all the Earth will do right*. Whence it's a natural conclu-sion, from the present seeming *inequality* in *God's* dealings with us, that this life is not the place of *rewards* and *punishments*; but that there will be a *future retribu-tion*, wherein these crooked things will be made straight, and the flourishing prosperity of *wicked men*, will appear to be but a preparation from their ruin, and a *fatting for the slaughter*. We may reasonably conclude, that *God* will first or last discover the *justice* and *equality* of all His *dispensations*. And since this does not appear from the present face of *providence*, we may look for a *future* season, for the manifestation of His just *aversion* to *sin* and *sinners*, and for the execution of His deserved *wrath* upon them.

THAT we are made for *a future state*, will appear from the contemplation of our own *natures*: Whereby we may certainly find that we have *spiritual* and *imma-terial* substances within us (as I have fully demonstrated in a former *discourse*) and that our *Souls* being *immaterial*, must be likewise incorruptible, & naturally *immortal*; made to survive their earthly tabernacles, and to *live* and act when our *bodies* return to their dust. Now can it be imagin'd that *God* has made so superior a creature as *man*, endow'd him with a *rational* and *immortal Soul*, and with such elevations of mind, only to act a short part in this World, and to just *propagate* his kind, and then return to an eternal state of *insensibility* and inactivity? No surely! these low and mean views are altogether unworthy of *infinite Wisdom*. It's there-fore evident from the *immortal* nature of our *Souls*, and from the *shortness* of our continuance in this World, that we are here but in a state of *probation*; but candi-dates for another World, where we are like to meet with the *rewards* of our present behaviour, whatever it be. And what will be the *reward* of that *sin* and *impiety*, which we are all chargeable with, we have already seen.

THUS we discover our *guilty miserable* state by *sin*, that *God is angry with the wicked every day*, Psalm 7:11. And that *there is destruction to the wicked, and a strange punishment to the workers of iniquity*, Job 31:3.

Jonathan Dickinson, *The Reasonableness of Christianity, in Four Sermons* (Boston: Samuel Gerrish, 1732), 43–53.

4

George Whitefield's Signature Sermon

George Whitefield

THE ANGLICAN ITINERANT George Whitefield (1714–1770) became an international celebrity in the eighteenth century. Born in Gloucester, England, Whitefield matriculated to Pembroke College, Oxford in 1732 where he met John and Charles Wesley, joining them as a member of the "Holy Club," a social organization for students who gathered regularly to pray and study the Bible. After graduating from Oxford in 1736, Whitefield was ordained an Anglican clergyman and within a few years started preaching in the open air. His early studies of plays and acting contributed to his success as an itinerant speaker, particularly during the transatlantic revivals of the early 1740s. He preached an estimated 18,000 sermons in his lifetime, traveling throughout Britain and the American colonies. Utilizing gestures, biblical anecdotes, and well-timed tears, Whitefield captivated audiences wherever he went. During his fifteen-month tour of America between 1739 and 1741, thousands flocked to catch a glimpse of the "boy parson." At an outdoor sermon in Philadelphia, Whitefield's friend and American publisher Benjamin Franklin conducted an experiment on sound, concluding that a crowd of some 30,000 people could in fact hear the bellowing voice of the Anglican evangelical.

Despite Whitefield's popularity as a celebrity preacher, he did not gain the respect of all the clergy. Many of the Anglican ministers in particular were offended by his description of them as unspiritual and worldly. He even had the audacity to state publicly that former Archbishop of Canterbury John Tillotson had no more been a true Christian than Muhammad. A central theme in Whitfield's sermons, and evangelicalism more broadly, was the importance of experiencing a "new birth." In his first publication, *The Nature and Necessity of Our New Birth in Christ Jesus, in Order to Salvation* (1737), Whitefield described the new birth as a life-changing conversion whereby a person is spiritually reborn as an authentic believer. As opposed to many of his Anglican colleagues who taught that church attendance and a general moralism formed the crux of Christianity, Whitefield and other evangelicals spurned these outward manifestations as futile attempts to

FIGURE 4.1 George Whitefield (Detail), courtesy of the National Portrait Gallery, London.

secure eternal salvation. Rather, what a person needed was a spiritual transformation of the heart that could only be obtained by grace through the power of the Holy Spirit. According to Whitefield, anyone who cannot lay claim to the new birth is an "almost," not yet an "altogether," Christian.

The Nature and Necessity of Our New Birth in Christ Jesus

NOW a Person may be said to be *in Christ* two Ways. First, only by an outward Profession. And in this Sense, every one that is called a Christian, or baptized into Christ's Church, may be said to be *in Christ*. But that this is not the sole Meaning of the Apostle's Phrase now before us, is evident, because then "every one that names the Name of Christ," or is baptized into his visible Church, would be a *new Creature*. Which is notoriously false, it being too plain, beyond all Contradiction, that comparatively but few of those that are *"born of Water,"* are *"born of the Spirit"* likewise; or, to use another Scriptural way of speaking, Many are baptized with Water, which were never, effectually at least, baptized with the Holy Ghost.

TO be *in* CHRIST therefore, in the full Import of the Word, must certainly mean something more than a bare outward Profession, or being called after his Name. For, as this same Apostle tells us, "All are not *Israelites* that are of *Israel*," *i.e.* when applied to Christianity, all are not *real* Christians that are *nominally* such. Nay, that is so far from being the Case, that our Blessed LORD himself informs us, That many that have prophesied or preached in his Name, and in his name cast out Devils, and done many wonderful Works, shall notwithstanding be dismissed at the last Day with a "Depart from me, I know you not, ye Workers of Iniquity."

IT remains therefore, that this Expression, *If any Man be in Christ*, must be understood in a second and closer Signification, *viz.* to be *in him* so as to partake of the Benefits of his Sufferings. To be *in him* not only by an outward Profession, but by an inward Change and Purity of Heart, and Cohabitation of his Holy Spirit. To be *in him* so as to be mystically united to him by a true and lively Faith, and thereby to receive spiritual Virtue from him, as the Members of the natural Body do from the Head, or the Branches from the Vine. To be *in him* in such a manner, as the Apostle, speaking of himself, acquaints us he knew a Person was, *I knew a Man in* CHRIST, says he, *i.e.* a true Christian; or, as he himself desires to be *in* CHRIST, when he wishes, in his Epistle to the *Philippians*, that he might be found *in him*.

THIS is undoubtedly the full Purport of the Apostle's Expressions in the Words of the Text; so that what he says in his Epistle to the *Romans* about Circumcision, may very well be applied to the present Subject, *viz.* That he is not a *real* Christian, who is only one *outwardly*; nor is that true Baptism, which is only outward in the *Flesh*. But he is a true Christian, who is one *inwardly*, whose Baptism is that of the *Heart*, in the *Spirit*, and not merely in the *Water*, whose Praise is not of Man, but of GOD. Or, as he speaketh in another Place, Neither Circumcision or Uncircumcision availeth any thing of itself, but a *new Creature*. Which amounts to what he here declares in the Verse now under Consideration, that if any Man be truly and properly *in* CHRIST, he is a *new Creature*.

WHAT we are to understand by being a *New Creature*, was the next and *second* general Thing to be considered.

AND here it is evident at the first View, that this Expression is not to be so explained as tho' there was a Physical Change required to be made in us, *i.e.* as tho' we were to be reduced to our primitive *Nothings*, and then created and formed again. For supposing we were, as *Nicodemus* ignorantly imagined, to enter a "second time into our Mother's Womb, and be born," alas! what would it contribute towards rendering us spiritually *new Creatures*? since that which was born of Flesh would be Flesh still, *i.e.* we should be the same carnal Persons as ever, being derived from carnal Parents, and consequently receiving the Seeds of all manner of Sin and Corruption from them. No, it only means, that we must be so altered as to the Qualities and Tempers of our Minds, that we must entirely forget what manner of Persons we once were. As it may be said of a Piece of Gold that was in the Ore, after it has been cleansed, purified and polished, that it is a new Piece of Gold: As it may be said of a bright Glass that has been covered over with Filth, when it is wiped, and so become transparent and clear, that it is a new Glass: Or, as it might be said of *Naaman*, when he recovered of his Leprosy, and his Flesh returned unto him like the flesh of a young Child, that he was a new Man; so our Souls, tho' still the same as to Essence, yet are so purged, purified and cleansed from their natural Dross, Filth and Leprosy, by the blessed Influences of the Holy Spirit, that they may properly be said to be *made anew*.

HOW this glorious Change is wrought in the Soul, cannot easily be explained. For no One knows the Ways of the Spirit, save the Spirit of God Himself. Not that this ought to be any Argument against this Doctrine; for, as our Blessed LORD observed to *Nicodemus*, when he was discoursing on this very Subject, *The* Wind, says he, *bloweth where it listeth, and thou hearest the Sound thereof, but knowest not whence it cometh, and whither it goeth*; and if we are told of natural Things, and we understand them not, how much less ought we to wonder, if we cannot immediately account for the invisible Workings of the Holy Spirit? The Truth of the Matter is this: The Doctrine of our *Regeneration*, or *New Birth* in CHRIST JESUS, is "dark, and hard to be understood" by the natural Man. But that there is really such a Thing, and that each of us must be spiritually born again, before we can enter into the Kingdom of GOD; or, to keep to the Terms made use of in the Text, must be *new Creatures* before we can be *in* CHRIST . . .

PROCEED we now to the next general Thing proposed, *viz.* To draw some Inferences from what has been delivered.

AND First then, If he that is *in* CHRIST must be a *new Creature*, this may serve as a Reproof for some, who rest in a bare Performance of *outward* Duties, without perceiving any real *inward* Change of Heart.

WE may observe a great many Persons to be very punctual in the regular Returns of public and private Prayer, as likewise of receiving the Holy Communion, and perhaps, now and then too, in keeping a Fast. And so far we grant they do well. But then here is the Misfortune, they rest barely in the Use of the Means, and think all is over, when they have just complied with these sacred Institutions: Whereas, were they rightly informed, they would consider, that all the instituted Means of Grace, as Prayer, Fasting, Hearing and Reading the Word of GOD, Receiving the Blessed Sacrament, and such like, are no further serviceable to us, than as they are found to make us *inwardly* better, and to carry on the Spiritual Life in the Soul.

IT is true, they are *Means*, and *Essential* ones too; but they are *only* Means, they are *Part*, but not the *Whole* of Religion: For if so, Who more religious than the *Pharisee?* who fasted twice in the Week, and gave Tithes of all that he possessed, and yet was not justified, as our Saviour himself informs us, in the Sight of GOD.

YOU perhaps, like the *Pharisee*, may fast often, and make long Prayers; you may, with *Herod*, hear good Sermons gladly; or, as *Judas* himself, in all Probability, did, receive the Blessed Sacrament. But yet, if you continue vain and trifling, immoral or worldly-minded in your Conversations, and differ from the rest of your Neighbours barely in going to Church, or in complying with some outward Performances, are you better than they? No, in no wise: You are by far much worse, because those that wholly neglect the Means, are answerable only for omitting the Use of GOD's Ordinances; whereas if you use them, and at the same time abuse them, by not letting them produce their intended Effect, you thereby encourage others to think there is nothing in them, and therefore must expect to "receive the greater Damnation."

BUT, Secondly, If he that is *in* CHRIST must be a *new Creature*, then this may check the groundless Presumption of another Class of Professors, who rest in the Attainment of some Moral Virtues, and falsely imagine they are good Christians, if they are just in their Dealings, are temperate in their Diet, and do Hurt or Violence to no Man.

BUT if this was all that is requisite to make us Christians, Why might not the Heathens of old be good Christians, who were remarkable for these Virtues? Or St. *Paul*, before his Conversion, who tells us, That then he lived in all good Conscience, and was, touching the Law, blameless? And yet, after his Conversion, we find he renounces all Dependence on Works of this Nature, and only desires to be found *in* CHRIST, and to know the Power of his Resurrection, *i.e.* to have an experimental Proof of receiving the HOLY GHOST, purchased for him by the Death, and insured and applied to him by the Resurrection, of JESUS CHRIST.

THE Sum of the Matter is this: Christianity includes Morality, as Grace does Reason; but if we are only mere *Moralists*, if we are not *inwardly* wrought upon, and changed by the powerful Operations of the *Holy Spirit*, and our Moral Actions proceed from a Principle of a *new Nature*, however we may call ourselves Christians, it is to be feared we shall be found naked at the Great Day, and in the Number of those, who vainly depend on their own Righteousness, and not on the Righteousness of JESUS CHRIST, imputed to and inherent in them, as necessary to their eternal Salvation.

NOR, Thirdly, will this Doctrine less condemn those, who rest in a Partial Amendment of themselves, without going on to Perfection, and experiencing a thorough, real, inward Change of Heart.

A little Acquaintance with the World will furnish us with Instances of no small Number of Persons, who, perhaps, were before openly profane; but seeing the ill Consequences of their Vice, and the many worldly Inconveniences it has reduced them to, on a sudden, as it were, grow civilized; and thereupon flatter themselves that they are very religious, because they differ a little from their former selves, and are not so scandalously wicked as once they were: Whereas at the same time they shall have some secret darling Sin or other, some beloved *Delilah* or *Herodias*, which they will not part with; some hidden Lust, which they will not mortify; some vicious Habit, which they will not take pains to root out. But wouldst thou know, O vain Man! whoever thou art, what the LORD thy GOD requires of thee? thou must be inform'd, that nothing short of a *thorough, sound* Conversion will avail for the Salvation of thy Soul. It is not enough to turn from *Profaneness* to *Civility*; but thou must turn from *Civility* to *Godliness*. Not only *some*, but *all* Things must become *new* in thy Soul. It will profit thee but little to do many Things, if yet some *one Thing* thou lackest. In short, thou must not be only an *almost*, but *altogether* a *new Creature*, or in vain thou hopest for a saving Interest *in* CHRIST.

Fourthly and Lastly, IF he that is *in* CHRIST must be a *new Creature*, then this may be prescribed as an infallible Rule for every Person of whatever Denomination, Age, Degree or Quality to judge himself by. This being the only solid Foundation whereon we can build a well-grounded Assurance of Pardon, Peace and Happiness.

WE may indeed depend on the broken Reed of an external Profession; we may think we have done enough, if we lead such sober, honest, moral Lives, as many Heathens did. We may imagine we are in a safe Condition, if we attend on the public Offices of Religion, and are constant in the Duties of our Closets. But unless all these tend to reform our Lives, and change our Hearts, and are only used as so many Channels of Divine Grace; as I told you before, so I tell you again, Christianity will profit us nothing.

LET each of us therefore seriously put this Question to our Hearts: Have we received the HOLY GHOST since we believed? Are we *new Creatures* in CHRIST, or no? At least, if we are not so *yet*, is it our daily Endeavour to *become* such? Do we make a constant and conscientious Use of all the Means of Grace required thereto? Do we fast, watch, and pray? Do we not only lazily seek, but laboriously strive to enter in at the strait Gate? In short, Do we *renounce* ourselves, take up our Crosses and follow CHRIST? If so, we are in that narrow Way which leads to Life: We are, at least shall in Time, become *new Creatures in* CHRIST. The good Seed is sown in our Hearts, and will, if duly water'd and nourish'd by a regular persevering Use of *all* the Means of Grace, grow up to eternal Life. But, on the contrary, if we have only *heard*, and know not *experimentally*, whether there be any HOLY GHOST; if we are Strangers to Fasting, Watching and Prayer, and all the other spiritual Exercises of Devotion; if we are content to go in the broad Way merely because we see most other People do so, without once reflecting whether it be the right one or not; in short, if we are Strangers, nay, Enemies to the Cross of CHRIST, by leading Lives of Softness, Worldly-mindedness, and sensual Pleasure, and thereby make others think that Christianity is but an empty Name, a bare formal Profession; if this be the Case, I say, then CHRIST is as yet dead in vain as to *us*; we are yet under the Guilt of our Sins; we are unacquainted with that true and thorough Conversion, which alone can entitle us to the Salvation of our Souls.

George Whitefield, *The Nature and Necessity of Our New Birth in Christ Jesus, in Order to Salvation* (London: C. Rivington, 1737), 4–8, 18–24.

5

Calvinism under Fire

John Wesley

JOHN WESLEY (1703–91) rivals Jonathan Edwards as the most recognized evangelical in the eighteenth century. Born on June 17, 1703, in Lincolnshire, England, Wesley believed that he had been snatched from a rectory fire in 1709—as "a brand plucked from the burning"—and set aside for a divine purpose. He was raised by his High Church Anglican parents, John, rector of Epworth, and his wife, Susanna, a disciplined woman, who set up a rigorous course of daily study and personalized religious exercises for her children. In 1720, Wesley entered the prestigious Christ Church, Oxford, graduating with a BA in 1724, and ordained as an Anglican deacon shortly thereafter. In the years following his graduation, he earned a MA, and, after a brief stint as a curate at his father's church at Epworth, Wesley returned to Oxford in 1729 as fellow of Lincoln College. At Oxford he joined the already established intercollegiate piety meetings known collectively as the Holy Club that his brother Charles had been attending, becoming the group's chief organizer and recognized leader.

Seeking to broaden his ministry, Wesley determined to go to the colony of Georgia in 1735 as a missionary on behalf of the Society for the Propagation of the Gospel in Foreign Parts, convincing his brother Charles to accompany him. While traveling to America, Wesley was deeply impressed with a group of Moravians on board the ship who remained unusually calm during a severe storm that seemed life-threatening at the time. When the Moravian leader A. G. Spangenberg took the opportunity to question Wesley if he knew Jesus intimately, he could only respond that he "hoped" that Christ had died to save him. Wesley's time as a minister in Georgia was on the whole disastrous. His pride wounded by a failed attempt to court the niece of a prominent colonist, he refused to administer communion to the girl. As a consequence of his actions, he had to flee the colony in December 1737 having been indicted for abusing his privileges as an officer of the Established Church. In thinking about the time that he had spent in Georgia, Wesley wondered if he was a true Christian.

FIGURE 5.1 John Wesley (Detail), courtesy of the National Portrait Gallery, London.

Arriving in England in February 1738, he reestablished contact with the Moravians, fellowshipping with them at the religious society in London that met at Fetter Lane. On May 24, 1738, Wesley famously recorded his "heart strangely warmed" after hearing a reading from Martin Luther's preface to Romans at a religious meeting on Aldersgate Street. Reflecting on his spiritual journey up to that point, Wesley concluded that he had been naively attempting to acquire salvation by works. He came to believe that divine grace, and more specifically justification, could be received instantaneously, but that a person needed to strive towards a life of holiness. He continued to associate with the Moravians for a while, visiting its leadership in Germany between the months of June and August 1738, but he broke off formal ties with them in 1740 because of theological differences. Wesley could not agree with the Moravian teaching on "stillness" whereby a person was told to wait passively for God to deliver salvation, arguing instead for the active pursuit of conversion using all possible means. By the middle of 1740, Wesley had left Fetter Lane, having set up an alternative headquarters at a remodeled canon factory in London. Now separated from the Moravians, he was positioned to lead what would become one of the largest Christian denominations in the world.

Despite his profound influence, Wesley did not have a monopoly on Methodism. In addition to Wesley's particular brand, there also existed a Calvinistic form of Methodism, led by his friend George Whitefield. Wesley had first come into contact with Whitefield at Oxford where the two participated in the Holy Club. As Wesley developed his talents as an organizer of religious societies, Whitefield was perfecting his rhetoric as a preacher. Whitefield was the first to try his hand at open-air preaching, and, having experienced success, he suggested to Wesley to do the same at Bristol in the spring of 1739. Their willingness to speak anywhere and to anyone, regardless of social rank or gender, became the lifeblood of both varieties of Methodism. But as the movement grew, theological differences became too apparent to ignore. A formal division occurred in the early 1740s initiated by the publication of Wesley's controversial sermon on free grace in which he lampooned the Calvinistic doctrine of election. According to Wesley, scripture could not be clearer in stating that salvation was intended for everyone. He thus could not fathom how the notion of limited atonement, whereby only certain people had been designated to receive divine grace, could be reconciled with Jesus' teachings in which he invited all sinners to come to him for salvation. Wesley reasoned that Calvinism as a theological system deterred a person from living a holy life, for if it did not matter what one did—since God would choose whom he wanted to save regardless of external circumstances and individual effort—why should anyone care about morality and ethics? After a heated exchange, the two men finally agreed to disagree on certain doctrines. Ultimately, two types of Methodism emerged, with Whitefield heading a Calvinistic faction, which grew strongest in Wales, and Wesley firmly in charge of the larger Arminian branch that established its bases of operation in London and Bristol in southern England, and Newcastle upon Tyne in the North.

Free Grace

1. HOW freely does GOD love the World! While we were yet Sinners, *Christ died for the Ungodly.* While we were *Dead in Sin*, GOD *Spared not his own Son, but delivered him up for us all.* And how *freely with Him* does he *give us all things*! Verily Free Grace is all in all!

2. The Grace or Love of GOD, whence cometh our Salvation, is Free in all, and Free for all!

3. *First*, It is Free in all to whom it is given. It does not depend on any Power or Merit in Man: No, not in any Degree, neither in whole, nor in part. It does not in any wise depend either on the Good Works or Righteousness of the Receiver: Not on any thing he has done, or any thing he is. It does not depend on his Endeavours: It does not depend on his good Tempers, or good Desires, or good Purposes and Intentions. For all these flow from the Free Grace of GOD: They are the Streams only, not the Fountain. They are the Fruits of Free Grace, and not the Root. They are not the Cause, but the Effects of it. Whatsoever Good is in Man, or is done by Man, GOD is the Author and Doer of it. Thus is his Grace Free in all, that is, no way depending on any Power, or Merit in Man: But on GOD alone, who freely gave us his own Son, and *with him freely giveth us all things.*

4. But is it Free for All, as well as in All? To this some have answer'd, "No: It is free only for those whom GOD hath ordained to Life; and they are but a little Flock. The greater Part of Mankind GOD hath ordained to Death; and it

is not Free for them. Them GOD hateth; and therefore before they were born, decreed they should die Eternally. And this he absolutely decreed; because so was his good Pleasure: Because it was his sovereign Will. Accordingly, they are born for this, To be destroy'd, Body and Soul, in Hell. And They grow up under the Irrevocable Curse of GOD, without any Possibility of Redemption. For what Grace GOD gives, he gives only for this, To increase, not prevent, their Damnation."

5. This is That Decree of Predestination. But methinks I hear One say, "This is not the Predestination which I hold. I hold only, The Election of Grace. What I believe is no more than this, That GOD, before the Foundation of the World, did elect a certain Number of Men, to be justified, sanctified and glorified. Now all these will be saved, and none else. For the rest of Mankind GOD leaves to themselves. So they follow the Imaginations of their own Hearts, which are only Evil continually, and waxing worse and worse, are at length justly punished with Everlasting Destruction."

5. Is this All the Predestination which You hold? Consider. Perhaps this is not All. Do not You believe, "GOD ordained them to this very thing?" If so, you believe the Whole Decree; you hold Predestination in the full Sense, which has been above described. But it may be, you think you do not. Do not you then believe, GOD hardens the Hearts of them that perish? Do not you believe, He (literally) hardened *Pharaoh's* Heart, and that for this end he rais'd him up (or created him?) Why this amounts to just the same thing. If you believe *Pharaoh*, or any one Man upon the Earth, was created for this End, to be damn'd, you hold all that has been said of Predestination. And there is no need you should add, that GOD seconds his Decree, which is supposed Unchangeable and Irresistible, by hardening the Hearts of those Vessels of Wrath, whom that Decree had before fitted for Destruction.

6. Well; but it may be, you do not believe even this. You do not hold any Decree of Reprobation. You do not think God decrees, any Man to be damn'd, nor hardens, irresistibly fits him for Damnation. You only say, "GOD eternally decreed, That All being Dead in Sin, he would say to some of the Dry Bones, *Live*, and to others, he would not. That consequently, These should be made alive, and Those abide in Death: These should glorify GOD by their Salvation, and Those by their Destruction."

7. Is not this what you mean by *the Election of Grace?* If it be, I would ask one or two Questions. Are any who are not thus Elected, saved? Or were any, from the Foundation of the World? Is it possible any Man should be saved, unless he be thus Elected? If you say *No*, you are but where you was. You are not got one Hair's-breadth further. You still believe, that in consequence of an unchangeable, irresistible Decree of GOD, the greater part of Mankind abide in Death, without any Possibility of Redemption: Inasmuch as none can save

them but GOD: And He will not save them. You believe he hath absolutely decreed, Not to save them; And what is this, but decreeing to damn them? It is, in effect, neither more nor less: It comes to the same thing. For if you are dead, and altogether unable to make yourself alive; then if GOD has absolutely decreed, He will make others only alive and not you; He hath absolutely decreed your Everlasting Death; you are absolutely consign'd to Damnation. So then, tho' you use softer Words than some, you mean the self-same thing. And GOD's Decree concerning the Election of Grace, according to your own Account of it, amounts to neither more nor less, than what others call, "GOD's Decree of Reprobation."

8. Call it therefore by whatever Name you please, "Election, Preterition, Predestination or Reprobation," it comes in the end to the same thing. The Sense of all is plainly this. "By virtue of an Eternal, Unchangeable, Irresistible Decree of GOD, One Part of Mankind are infallibly saved, and the rest infallibly damn'd: It being impossible, that any of the former should be damn'd, or that any of the latter should be saved."

9. But if this be so, then is All Preaching Vain. It is needless to them that are Elected. For they, whether with preaching or without, will infallibly be saved. Therefore the End of Preaching, "To save Souls," is void with regard to them. And it is useless to them that are not Elected. For they cannot possibly be saved. They, whether with Preaching or without, will infallibly be damn'd. The End of Preaching is therefore void, with regard to them likewise. So that in either case, our Preaching is vain, as your Hearing is also vain.

10. This then is a plain Proof, that the Doctrine of Predestination is not a Doctrine of GOD, because it makes void the Ordinance of GOD: And GOD is not divided against Himself. A Second is, That it directly tends to destroy that Holiness, which is the End of all the Ordinances of GOD. I do not say, "None who hold it are Holy." (For GOD is of tender Mercy to those who are unavoidably entangled in Errors of any kind.) But that the Doctrine itself, "That every Man is either Elected or not Elected from Eternity, and that the one must inevitably be saved, and the other inevitably damn'd," has a manifest Tendency to destroy Holiness in general. For it wholly takes away those first Motives to follow after it, so frequently propos'd in Scripture, the Hope of Future Reward and Fear of Punishment, the Hope of Heaven and the Fear of Hell. That *these shall go away into everlasting Punishment, and those into Life Eternal*: Is no Motive to Him to struggle for Life, who believes his lot is cast already: It is not reasonable for him so to do, if he thinks, he is unalterably adjudged either to Life or Death. You will say, "But he knows not, whether it is Life or Death." What then? This helps not the Matter. For if a sick Man knows, that he must unavoidably die, or unavoidably recover, tho' he knows not which, it is not reasonable for him, to take any Physic at all. He might justly say, (and so I have

heard some speak, both in Bodily Sickness and in Spiritual) "If I am ordained to Life, I shall live; If to Death, I shall die. So I need not trouble myself about it." So directly does this Doctrine tend, to shut the very Gate of Holiness in general, to hinder unholy Men from ever approaching thereto, or striving to enter in thereat...

23. This premised, let it be observ'd, That this Doctrine represents our Blessed Lord, *Jesus Christ the Righteous, the only begotten Son of the Father, full of Grace and Truth*, as an Hypocrite, a Deceiver of the People, a Man void of common Sincerity. For it cannot be denied, that he everywhere speaks, *as if he was* willing that all Men should be saved. Therefore to say, *He was not* willing that all Men should be saved is to represent him as a mere Hypocrite and Dissembler. It can't be denied that the gracious Words which came out of his Mouth, are full of Invitations to all Sinners. To say then, He did not *intend* to save all Sinners, is to represent him as a gross Deceiver of the People. You cannot deny, that he says, "*Come unto me all ye that are weary and heavy laden.*" If then you say He calls those that cannot come, those whom he knows to be unable to come, those whom he can make able to come but will not, how is it possible to describe greater Insincerity? You represent him as mocking his helpless Creatures, by offering what he never intends to give. You describe him as saying one Thing, and meaning another: As pretending the Love which he had not. Him *in whose Mouth was no Guile*, you'll make full of Deceit, void of common Sincerity: Then especially, when drawing nigh the City, *He wept over it, and said,* "*O Jerusalem, Jerusalem, Thou that killest the Prophets, and stonest them that are sent unto Thee; How often* wou'd I have gathered thy Children together—and YE wou'd not."... Now if you say, *They wou'd,* but *He wou'd not,* you represent him, (which who could hear?) as weeping Crocodile's Tears, weeping over the Prey which himself had doom'd to Destruction.

John Wesley, *Free Grace. A Sermon Preach'd at Bristol* (London: S. and F. Farley, 1739), 5–12, 22–3.

6

The Conversion of a Welshman

Howell Harris

HEADSTRONG AND CONTROVERSIAL, Howell Harris (1714–1773) was instrumental to the success of the Welsh revival of the 1730s and 1740s. Born on January 23, 1714, in Brecknockshire, Wales, Harris recounted his spiritual journey from the bondage of sin to a spiritual awakening in *A Brief Account of the Life of Howell Harris*, posthumously published in 1791. His conversion experience began with a conviction of his unworthiness to partake of communion at a Palm Sunday Anglican service in 1735. From that point on, Harris made a concerted effort at bettering himself through acts of charity, prayer, fasting, and reading devotional literature. In his diary, he pinpointed 1735 as the date of his spiritual birth, the year when he came to believe that Christ had died for him. But like many early evangelicals of that period, he struggled to obtain assurance of salvation for many years thereafter. He attended St. Mary Hall, Oxford briefly in 1735, but decided very quickly that his time would be better spent in Wales organizing prayer meetings and preaching as a layman. He met the Cardiganshire Anglican curate Daniel Rowland in 1737, and shortly thereafter the two joined forces in order to promote the revival in Wales for the next thirteen years. By December 1740, Harris estimated that he was firmly in control of some sixty-four societies in Wales. A fiery preacher who drew vast crowds, Harris itinerated in England and throughout Wales at the end of the 1730s and into the 1740s. His ministry expanded in 1739 after meeting George Whitefield, who he accompanied to Bristol and London where Harris was introduced to other Methodists and joined the Fetter Lane Society. He worked closely with Whitefield and maintained friendly relations with John Wesley and the Moravians, although Harris preferred Whitefield's Calvinistic Methodism to Wesley's free will Arminianism.

The Welsh revival broke down, however, in the 1740s when Harris and Rowland engaged in a power struggle disguised as a theological dispute over issues related to God's covenant with humanity and whether assurance was necessary for salvation. Harris's theology was further scrutinized by Rowland and others during the

FIGURE 6.1 Howell Harris (Detail), frontispiece from Hugh J. Hughes, *The Life of Howell Harris* (1892).

1740s because of noticeable similarities with the Moravians and their obsession with the wounds of Christ. Although critical of the Moravians, and denying that he had joined them, Harris preached regularly on the topic of the blood of Christ, making him appear as an "enthusiast" to many of his Welsh colleagues. In the years that followed, Harris had difficulty gathering support because of the severe discipline that he exerted over his societies and his harsh criticism towards even the most devout believers. Making matters worse, he controversially befriended a married woman named Sidney Griffith in October 1748. He believed that she was a prophetess with divine insight, and began touring the country with her for weeks at a time. Denying charges of any impropriety, Harris refused to sever the relationship, much to the chagrin of his wife. By 1750 the breach was complete, with the majority of Welsh Methodists siding with Rowland, leaving Harris to retreat with a few followers to Trevecka. But once Griffith died in 1752, and after serving a stint in the militia during the Seven Years' War, Harris reunited with Rowland and his band of Welsh Methodists. A revival at Llangeitho in 1762 brought the two men together and did much to reinvigorate Methodism, even though the height of the Welsh revival never achieved the same success of the mid and later 1730s.

A Brief Account of the Life of Howell Harris

I WAS born at *Trevecka*, in the Parish of *Talgarth*, in the County of *Brecon*, on *January* 23d. 1714. My Parents kept me at School till I was eighteen years old; I made a considerable progress in Learning, my Father then dying, I was so far discouraged, as not to entertain any thoughts of appearing in the world in a public capacity, and therefore undertook to keep a country School: having no serious friends to converse with, and being now without any restraints upon me, I was soon carried away with the stream of vanity, pride, and youthful diversions; which got the ascendant in my soul.

THE many serious thoughts and reflections I before used to be seized with, were now obliged to give way to my pleasures, and yet, having always an habitual conviction in my heart, I was not easy.

MY sphere of acquaintance among my superiors became larger, and I had promising views of preferment in the world; being intended for Holy Orders.

BUT while I was thus about entering more publicly on the stage of life, and while all my corruptions grew stronger and stronger in me, and many providences seemed to concur to raise me in this world; the LORD was pleased to glorify his free Grace in awakening me to a sense of the miserable state I was, and had been in, tho' I knew it not.

ABOUT the one and twentieth year of my Age, on *March* 30th 1735, our Parish Minister was using arguments to prove the necessity of receiving the Sacrament, and in answering objections which people make against going to it, viz. *our being not fit*, &c. I resolved to go to the LORD's Table the following Sunday, being *Easter-day*: And by his saying, "If you are not fit to come to the LORD's Table, you are not fit to come to Church, you are not fit to live, nor fit to die," I was convinced, and resolved to leave my outward vanities; for as yet, I knew and saw but very little of my inward corruption; and as a step to prepare myself (as I thought it) I was immediately in going home from Church reconciled to a neighbour I had some difference with; acknowledging my own fault, and forgiving his. But knowing nothing of the Wedding-garment, being yet an utter stranger to all inward Religion, and the misery of my state by nature; and consequently knowing nothing truly of the LORD JESUS, but only what I learned by reading, and in notions; I had advanced no farther than forming a resolution to lead a new life, tho' I knew not where to begin or what to do.

BUT however, I went to the LORD's Table on *Easter-day*; and by repeating the words in the Confession, "The remembrance of our sins is grievous unto us, the burden of them is intolerable." I began to reflect within me, to search whether this was my case, and soon found my confession was only words, and could not find any inward grief at the remembrance of them, nor indeed was their burden a heavy load to me: I was then convinced it ought to be so, and finding it was not, I saw I was going to the LORD's Table with a lie in my mouth; this, and a sense of the solemnity of the Sacred feast struck me, so that I was much inclined to withdraw; till my mind was quieted, by having determined to lead a new life; and in that resolution I went to the Table, and received the Pledge of GOD's dying love. Then I began that following week, and the week succeeding, to be more serious and thoughtful, and was given to prayer, and strove to keep my heart and thoughts fixed on the Lord, but all in vain; thus I went on for a fortnight, till I had almost lost my convictions.

WHEN on *April* the 20th, providence put a Book in my hand; I looked on the latter part of it, as a help to self-examination, as soon as I began to read it, I was convinced, that in every branch of my Duty to GOD, to myself, and to my neighbours, I was guilty, and had fallen short. I found again the same evening a Book written by *Bryan Duppa*, on the Commandments, which made my convictions somewhat deeper; the more I read, the greater did the spiritual light shone in my mind, by shewing me the extent of the Law of GOD, calling me to account, not only for outward gross sins, but for our looks, aims, and ends, in all we think, say, or do; then I saw plainly and clearly, that if I was to be judged by that Law, I was undone forever.

THUS the more I searched into the nature of things, the more I saw myself, and all others, that I conversed with, in the broad way to destruction. Then I was soon convinced, that I was void of all spiritual life; and came to find I was carnal, and sold under sin; and felt I could no more believe, or mourn for my sins, than I could ascend to heaven. I began to humble myself by fasting, and denying myself in every outward comfort, but knew as yet nothing of the inward self-denial which our SAVIOUR enjoins; I had no knowledge of the Blood of JESUS, the only *Fountain opened for sin and for uncleanness*, Zechariah 13:1, and being a total stranger to the life of faith; and therefore all this while in a damnable state, and in danger of final destruction.

THUS having laid no foundation, I knew not the SAVIOUR's voice, till one day in prayer, I felt a strong impression on my mind to give myself to GOD as I was, and to leave all to follow him. But presently felt a strong opposition to it, backed with reasons, that if I would give myself to the LORD, I should lose my liberty, and would then be not my own, or in my own power; but after a great conflict for some time, I was made willing to bid adieu to all things temporal, and chose the LORD for my portion. I believe, I was then effectually called to be a follower of the LAMB, and had some inward satisfaction in my soul; but had no evidence of my acceptance with GOD, till the following *Whitsunday*, at the Sacrament.

MAY 25, 1735. I went thither, labouring and heavy laden under the guilt and power of my sins; having read in a book, that if we would go to the Sacrament, simply believing in the LORD JESUS CHRIST, we should receive forgiveness of all our sins; and so it was to me: I was convinced by the HOLY GHOST, that CHRIST died for me, and that all my sins were laid on him; I was now acquitted at the bar of Justice, and in my conscience; this evidenced itself to be true faith, by the peace, joy, watchfulness, hatred to sin, and fear of offending GOD, that followed it.

I was then delivered from a grievous temptation, that had followed me ever since I had first given myself to the LORD: before that time I never knew what inward trials, and spiritual conflicts were, only now and then I had some uneasiness from an awakened conscience, which was quite different from those sore trials that I bore from Atheistical thoughts, that made my life a burden to me; for they came with such force and power on my mind, that I could not withstand them. But at the Sacrament, by viewing my GOD on the cross, I was delivered from these temptations; now, the world and all thoughts of human applause and preferment were quite vanished from my sight; the spiritual world, and eternity began (though as yet but faintly) to appear; now I began to have other views and motives, different from what I had; *viz.* I felt some insatiable desires after the salvation of poor sinners; my heart longed for their being convinced of their sins and misery. I also found myself a stranger here; all my heart was drawn from the world and visible things, and were in pursuit of a more valuable riches; I now began to be more happy, and could not help telling in going home from Church, that *Whitsunday*, that I knew my sins were forgiven me; though I had never heard any one make that confession before, or say it could be obtained; but I was so deeply convinced, that nothing could shake my assurance of it. However I knew not whether I should continue in that state; having never conversed with any that had his face towards Sion, and who could instruct me in the way of the LORD; but the cry of my soul being then, "Now or never; If GOD leaves thee now, and thou stiflest these convictions and blessings, thou art undone forever." This fear of losing what I had then, kept me fasting, praying, and watching continually. Though I had peace with GOD; yet I was apprehensive of seeing any of my old companions, lest I should grow cold again; and this also induced me to keep close to him in all duties, and to keep a strict watch over my spirit, heart, and lips, dreading all lightness of mind, and idle words, and foolish jesting, which I was prone to by nature.

JUNE 18th, 1735. being in secret prayer, I felt suddenly my heart melting within me like wax before the fire with love to GOD my SAVIOUR; and also felt not only love, peace, &c. *but longing to be dissolved, and to be with* CHRIST; then was a cry in my inmost soul, which I was totally unacquainted with before, *Abba Father! Abba Father!* I could not help calling GOD my FATHER; I knew that I was his child, and that HE loved me, and heard me. My soul being filled and satiated, crying, "'Tis enough, I am satisfied. Give me strength, and I will follow thee through fire and water" I could say I was happy indeed!—There was in me *a well of water, springing up to everlasting life*—John 4:14. *The love of GOD was shed abroad in my heart by the* HOLY GHOST. Romans 5:5.

BEING still ignorant of GOD's method of bringing the lost sons of Adam home to himself, I did not know in Scripture term, what I had now received; neither did I long retain this immediate fruition of GOD by his Spirit; but as I still kept school (waiting for my call from some near relation to go to *Oxford*) I felt some risings of anger in my heart towards one of the children; the enemy immediately accused me, and alleged to me that I had now forfeited all the happiness, which I had just before enjoyed; and that I was fallen from Grace, and therefore in a

worse condition than ever; this gave me no small pain and confusion, and whilst
I was in this agony (hating myself entirely for sinning against this good GOD, the
SAVIOUR of sinners) on account of the loss of that felicity I had enjoyed, I was
ready to despond; but GOD pitied me, and soon sent that word home to my soul,
I CHANGE NOT. Malachi 3:6. That such word was scriptural I knew not, and how
to apply it to myself was at a great loss; till light broke in upon my soul, to shew
me that my salvation did not depend on my own faithfulness, but on the faithfulness of JESUS CHRIST; therefore, though I change, yet because He changeth not,
I was secure. Then I was entirely freed from all fears, and found uninterrupted
rest in the love and faithfulness of GOD my SAVIOUR...

I was brought more and more to see the deceitfulness that is in man, how
nature may appear like grace, being improved and checked, and seemingly recti-
fied by having the course of it turned from delighting itself in the common way of
the world, of pleasures and honour, &c. to run in a religious channel; now delighting itself in hearing Sermons, and singing Hymns, especially in having the passions enflamed, never considering, whether they were truly rooted and grounded
in CHRIST, but only seemed to be strengthening, establishing, and building each
other up in the faith, and imagined that they were thus growing in grace, &c.
whilst evidently the spirit of their minds stayed behind in the world, had neither
power nor authority over the spirit of the world, nor retained that distance from
it which once they perhaps sought; and yet they shewed the same appearance of
faith, love, and zeal as formerly.

Now seeing things in this light, a necessity was laid upon me to lift up my voice
like a trumpet to all professors to examine their profession, and to make a close
search in what the foundation of their religion and faith was seated: whether in the
outward man, called the flesh or nature, or whether it had indeed penetrated to the
inward man, called the heart or spirit?—I saw clearly that there is such a thing as
knowing CHRIST after the flesh, by a kind of prophetical knowledge and views of
him at a distance, such as *Balaam* had, and from those views, have a certain confidence in him, and a kind of love to him, and seemingly great joy and happiness
(as the seed on the stony ground) and yet the heart be whole, self-righteous, and
worldly amidst all this; and the spirit carnal, asleep, and unawakened, in bondage
to the god of this world; being never convinced of the sin of nature, and the evil of
unbelief, and the difficulty of believing in the SAVIOUR as a sinner, and of obeying the call given to such in the gospel; they look back to something that they done
or felt at different times, and from hence they draw the conclusion, that they are
in the covenant, and belong to GOD, and shall therefore be saved.

I saw plainly that this was the religion of most professors, they formed a faith
to themselves without coming as lost damned sinners to the cross; and looking to
him as the *Israelites* looked to the Brazen-Serpent, fleeing to CHRIST, as the man
fled from the avenger of blood into the City of Refuge. No wonder then, when this

confidence is settled, that the spiritual life, the daily combat, the victory of faith, the feeding on the flesh and blood of GOD our SAVIOUR, the mysteries of his Person, as GOD and Man, opened in all his obedience and humiliation, and the infinite depth of his glorious riches, and the wonders of his Blood and wounds! With the infinite torments which he endured; no wonder, I say, that these mysteries remain a secret to them, and affords no life or entertainment to them;—but become matters of speculation and controversy, if not ridicule,—instead of being their life, delight, and daily food.

Howell Harris, *A Brief Account of the Life of Howell Harris, Esq; Extracted from Papers Written by Himself* (Trevecka: n.p., 1791), 9–17, 68–70.

7

A Selection of Hymns

Charles Wesley

CHARLES WESLEY (1707–1788) has often been overshadowed by his gregarious brother John. Born prematurely as the eighteenth child of Samuel and Susanna Wesley, Charles grew up under the strict guidance of his mother and siblings before entering college in 1727 at Christ Church, Oxford. After a year of card playing, dancing, and attending the theater, he began practicing a spiritual life more consistent with his upbringing. His perceived austerity was such that a fellow student reportedly called him a "Methodist" because of his methodical habits of piety. Soon he joined a fellowship of zealous believers which became known as the "Holy Club." When John Wesley returned to Oxford in 1729 as fellow of Lincoln College, Charles happily submitted to his brother's governance of the club.

As the more introverted sibling, Charles often allowed John to forge the way toward spiritual maturity. Charles, for instance, agreed to accompany John to Georgia in the mid-1730s, despite his initial lack of interest in the American colony. But this is not to say that Charles always gave in to John's demands. For on occasion, he would stubbornly resist the plans his brother laid out. After marrying in 1749, Charles balked at John's insistence that he continue to itinerate as frequently as he did in the early 1740s. Unlike John, Charles enjoyed married life and felt that he owed it to his wife and children to spend as much time with them at home as possible. Charles also had a different perspective on the Wesleyan doctrine of Christian perfection, viewing it as gradual and coming to completion at the end of one's lifetime. John, by contrast, urged his followers to expect a sudden reception of sanctification, which need not come at an elderly age. Although both planned on remaining loyal to the Church of England, Charles held a firmer commitment than his brother, which cost the younger Wesley the admiration of many of the Methodist preachers. Finally, whereas John welcomed laymen into the ranks of the burgeoning movement, Charles was much more cautious in commissioning itinerant preachers. Disgusted with his brother's apparent cavalier attitude toward religion on one occasion, Charles once wrote to a friend that John

FIGURE 7.1 Charles Wesley (Detail), courtesy of the National Portrait Gallery, London.

had turned a tailor into a preacher. Charles confided in his letter that, with the help of God, he would redirect the man back to his former profession. Charles's death in 1788, while officially lamented in the Methodist minutes for that year, opened the door for ambitious preachers in the movement to push John Wesley towards a final break with the Church of England.

Charles's main contribution to Methodism was, of course, as the movement's chief hymn writer. A talented lyricist, he penned an estimated 6,000 to 9,000 hymns and sacred poems during his lifetime. It is difficult to determine exactly how many hymns he composed since he usually published his work jointly with his brother John. Most scholars, however, attribute the majority of early Methodist hymns to Charles, viewing his brother's role as the final editor. The younger Wesley wrote thematically on topics such as "Hymns for Christian Friends," "Hymns for the Persecuted," "Hymns for Children," "Hymns for Families," "Short Hymns on Select Passages of Scripture," and hymns during special seasons like his "Hymn for Easter-Day," better known as "Christ the Lord is Risen Today." After experiencing conversion in May 1738—days before John felt his heart "strangely warmed" at Aldersgate—Charles composed the lyrics that the brothers sang together to mark this joyous event. We don't know for certain which hymn they sang, but it might have been, "And Can It Be," published as "Free Grace" in 1739. Like many of Charles's hymns, "And Can It Be" offered a first-person narrative account of the beloved divine grace that had been given "for me." A second candidate for Charles's conversion hymn is the popular "O for a Thousand Tongues to Sing," composed in 1739 and published in 1740 as, "For the Anniversary of One's Conversion." The inclusion of a "thousand tongues" is said to have come from the Moravian leader Peter Böhler, who once declared, "Had I thousand tongues, I would praise Christ with them all!" The theology behind the words explicitly deferred all power of conversion to divine grace, but encouraged the singer to participate in the narrative of the song.

One of the most powerful hymns in Wesley's corpus is "Wrestling Jacob." When John Wesley announced his brother's death at the 1788 Methodist conference, he noted that this hymn was highly regarded by Isaac Watts who once said, "that single poem, *Wrestling Jacob*, was worth all the verses he himself had written." Originally published in the 1742 edition of *Hymns and Sacred Poems*, "Wrestling Jacob" invites the reader to enter into the story and take the place of the patriarch Jacob who wrestles with God for a blessing. Wesley knew scripture well enough to perform his own exegesis, not needing to rely on commentaries or modern translations like the Authorized Version (King James Bible). Rather than follow the precise order as given in the biblical text, Wesley would often reorder the material to suit his own purposes. In "Wrestling Jacob," there is more of an emphasis on the frailty of the person grappling with God than the actual biblical account. Wesley regularly utilized typology and analogy in his hymns in order to mine biblical passages for deeper meanings that could be given a practical interpretation and theological meaning that conformed to evangelical beliefs. When reading or singing "Wrestling Jacob," one feels the strain of the physical and emotion toll of struggling all night with God. The result is a vivid, first-hand picture of an Old Testament story in which the audience comes to realize that they are incapable of saving themselves from sin. Though humans are weak, Wesley makes the point that they can have strength by faith in God. A glimpse at the following hymns provides a window into the soul of Methodism's lyrical genius.

"Hymn for Easter-Day" ("Christ the Lord is Risen Today")

I.

"CHRIST the LORD is ris'n to Day,"
Sons of Men and Angels say,
Raise your Joys and Triumphs high,
Sing ye Heav'ns, and Earth reply.

II.

Love's Redeeming Work is done,
Fought the Fight, the Battle won,
Lo! our Sun's Eclipse is o'er,
Lo! He sets in Blood no more.

III.

Vain the Stone, the Watch, the Seal;
CHRIST has burst the Gates of Hell!
Death in vain forbids his Rise:
CHRIST has open'd Paradise!

IV.

Lives again our glorious King,
Where, O Death, is now thy Sting?
Dying once he All doth save,
Where thy Victory, O Grave?

V.

Soar we now, where CHRIST has led?
Following our Exalted Head,
Made like Him, like Him we rise,
Ours the Cross—the Grave—the Skies!

VI.

What tho' once we perish'd All,
Partners in our Parent's Fall?
Second Life we All receive,
In our Heav'nly Adam *live.*

VII.

Ris'n with Him, we upward move,
Still we seek the Things above,
Still pursue, and kiss the Son
Seated on his Father's Throne;

VIII.

Scarce on Earth a Thought bestow,
Dead to all we leave below,
Heav'n our Aim, and lov'd Abode,
Hid our Life with CHRIST in GOD!

IX.

Hid; till CHRIST our Life appear,
Glorious in his Members here:
Join'd to Him, we then shall shine
All Immortal, all Divine!

X.

Hail the LORD of Earth and Heav'n!
Praise to Thee by both be giv'n:
Thee we greet Triumphant now;
Hail the Resurrection Thou!

XI.

King of Glory, Soul of Bliss,
Everlasting Life is This,
Thee to know, thy Pow'r to prove,
Thus to sing, and thus to love!

"Free Grace" ("And Can It Be")

I.

AND can it be, that I should gain
  An Int'rest in the Saviour's Blood!
Dy'd He for Me?—who caus'd his Pain!
  For Me?—who Him to Death pursu'd.
Amazing Love! how can it be
That Thou, my GOD, shouldst die for Me?

II.

'Tis Myst'ry all! th' Immortal dies!
  Who can explore his strange Design?
In vain the first-born Seraph tries
  To sound the Depths of Love Divine.
'Tis Mercy all! Let Earth adore;
Let Angel Minds enquire no more.

III.

He left his Father's Throne above,
  (So free, so infinite his Grace!)
Empty'd Himself of All but Love,
  And bled for Adam's helpless Race:
'Tis Mercy all, immense and free!
For O my GOD! it found out Me!

IV.

Long my imprison'd Spirit lay,
  Fast bound in Sin and Nature's Night:
Thine Eye diffus'd a quick'ning Ray;
  I woke; the Dungeon flam'd with Light;
My Chains fell off, my Heart was free,
I rose, went forth, and follow'd Thee.

V.

Still the small inward Voice I hear,
  That whispers all my Sins forgiv'n;
Still the atoning Blood is near,
  That quench'd the Wrath of hostile Heav'n:
I feel the Life his Wounds impart;
I feel my Saviour in my Heart.

VI.

No Condemnation now I dread,
  JESUS, and all in Him, is Mine:
Alive in Him, my Living Head,
  And cloath'd in Righteousness Divine,
Bold I approach th'Eternal Throne,
And claim the Crown, thro' CHRIST, my own.

"For the Anniversary of One's Conversion" ("O for a Thousand Tongues to Sing")

I.

GLORY to GOD, and Praise, and Love
  Be ever, ever given;
By Saints below, and Saints above,
  The Church in Earth and Heaven.

II.

On this glad Day the glorious Sun
  Of Righteousness arose,
On my benighted Soul he shone,
  And fill'd it with Repose.

III.

Sudden expir'd the legal Strife,
'Twas then I ceas'd to grieve,
My Second, Real, Living Life
I then began to live.

IV.

Then with my Heart *I First believ'd,*
Believ'd, with Faith Divine,
Power with the Holy Ghost receiv'd
To call the Saviour Mine.

V.

I felt my LORD's *Atoning Blood*
Close to my Soul applied;
Me, me he lov'd—the Son of GOD
For me, for me He died!

VI.

I found, and own'd his Promise true,
Ascertain'd of my Part,
My Pardon pass'd in Heaven I knew
When written on my Heart.

VII.

O for a Thousand Tongues to sing
My dear Redeemer's Praise!
The Glories of my GOD and King,
The Triumphs of his Grace.

VIII.

My gracious Master, and my GOD,
Assist me to proclaim;
To spread thro' all the Earth abroad
The Honours of Thy Name.

IX.

JESUS the Name that charms our Fears,
That bids our Sorrows cease;
'Tis Music in the Sinner's Ears,
'Tis Life, and Health, and Peace!

X.

He breaks the Power of cancell'd Sin,
He sets the Prisoner free:
His Blood can make the Foulest clean;
His Blood avail'd for me.

XI.

He speaks; and listening to His Voice,
New Life the Dead receive,
The mournful, broken Hearts rejoice,
The humble Poor believe.

XII.

Hear Him ye Deaf, His Praise ye Dumb
Your loosen'd Tongues employ,
Ye Blind, behold your Saviour come,
And leap, ye Lame, for Joy.

XIII.

Look unto Him, ye Nations, own
Your GOD, ye fallen Race!
Look, and be sav'd, thro' Faith alone;
Be justified, by Grace!

XIV.

See all your Sins on JESUS laid;
The Lamb of GOD was slain,
His Soul was once an Offering made
For every Soul of Man.

XV.

Harlots, and Publicans, and Thieves
In holy Triumph join!
Sav'd is the Sinner that believes
From Crimes as great as Mine.

XVI.

Murtherers, and all ye hellish Crew,
Ye Sons of Lust and Pride,
Believe the Saviour died for you;
For me the Saviour died.

XVII.

Awake from guilty Nature's Sleep,
    And CHRIST shall give you Light,
Cast all your Sins into the Deep,
    And wash the Ethiop *white.*

XVIII.

With me, your Chief, you then shall know,
    Shall feel your Sins forgiven;
Anticipate your Heaven below,
    And own, that Love is Heaven.

"Wrestling Jacob"

1. *COME, O Thou Traveller unknown,*
    Whom still I hold, but cannot see,
My Company before is gone,
    And I am left alone with Thee,
With Thee all Night I mean to stay,
And wrestle till the Break of Day.

2. *I need not tell Thee who I am,*
    My Misery, or Sin declare,
Thyself hast call'd me by my Name,
    Look on Thy Hands, and read it there,
But who, I ask Thee, who art Thou,
Tell me Thy Name, and tell me now?

3. *In vain Thou strugglest to get free,*
    I never will unloose my Hold:
Art Thou the Man that died for me?
    The Secret of Thy Love unfold;
Wrestling I will not let Thee go,
    Till I Thy Name, Thy Nature know.

4. *Wilt Thou not yet to me reveal*
    Thy new, unutterable Name?
Tell me, I still beseech Thee, tell,
    To know it Now resolv'd I am;
Wrestling I will not let Thee go,
    Till I Thy Name, Thy Nature know.

5. *'Tis all in vain to hold Thy Tongue,*
       Or touch the Hollow of my Thigh:
   Though every Sinew be unstrung,
       Out of my Arms Thou shalt not fly;
   Wrestling I will not let Thee go,
   Till I Thy Name, Thy Nature know.

6. *What tho' my shrinking Flesh complain,*
       And murmur to contend so long,
   I rise superior to my Pain,
       When I am weak then I am strong,
   And when my All of Strength shall fail,
   I shall with the God-man prevail.

7. *My Strength is gone, my Nature dies,*
       I sink beneath Thy weighty Hand,
   Faint to revive, and fall to rise;
       I fall, and yet by Faith I stand,
   I stand, and will not let Thee go,
   Till I Thy Name, Thy Nature know.

8. *Yield to me Now—for I am weak;*
       But confident in Self-despair:
   Speak to my Heart, in Blessings speak,
       Be conquer'd by my Instant Prayer,
   Speak, or Thou never hence shalt move,
   And tell me, if Thy Name is LOVE.

9. *`Till Love, 'til Love! Thou diedst for Me,*
       I hear Thy Whisper in my Heart.
   The Morning breaks, the Shadows flee:
       Pure UNIVERSAL LOVE Thou art,
   To me, to All Thy Bowels move,
   Thy Nature, and Thy Name is LOVE.

10. *My Prayer hath Power with GOD; the Grace*
       Unspeakable I now receive,
   Thro' Faith I see Thee Face to Face,
       I see Thee Face to Face, and live:
   In vain I have not wept, and strove,
   Thy Nature, and Thy Name is LOVE.

11. *I know Thee, Saviour, who Thou art,*
       JESUS the feeble Sinner's Friend;
   Nor wilt Thou with the Night depart,
       But stay, and love me to the End;
   Thy Mercies never shall remove,
   Thy Nature, and Thy Name is LOVE.

12. *The Sun of Righteousness on Me*
  Hath rose with Healing in his Wings,
Wither'd my Nature's Strength; from Thee
  My Soul it's Life and Succour brings,
My Help is all laid up above;
Thy Nature, and Thy Name is LOVE.

13. *Contented now upon my Thigh*
  I halt, till Life's short Journey end;
All Helplessness, all Weakness I,
  On Thee alone for Strength depend,
Nor have I Power, from Thee, to move;
Thy Nature, and Thy Name is LOVE.

14. *Lame as I am, I take the Prey,*
  Hell, Earth, and Sin with Ease o'ercome;
I leap for Joy, pursue my Way,
  And as a bounding Heart fly home,
Thro' all Eternity to prove
Thy Nature, and Thy Name is LOVE.

John and Charles Wesley, *Hymns and Sacred Poems* (London: William Strahan, 1739), 209–11, 117–19.

John and Charles Wesley, *Hymns and Sacred Poems* (London: William Strahan, 1740), 120–23.

John and Charles Wesley, *Hymns and Sacred Poems* (Bristol: Felix Farley, 1742), 115–18.

8

A Divisive Great Awakening Sermon

Gilbert Tennent

AS A REVIVALIST during the Great Awakening, Gilbert Tennent (1703–64) does not receive nearly the same attention as Jonathan Edwards and George Whitefield. The eldest son of the Scotch-Irish immigrant William Tennent, Gilbert studied under his father's tutorship at the "Log College" seminary in Bucks County, Pennsylvania, receiving additional spiritual guidance from the Dutch pietist Theodorus Frelinghuysen. Both his father and Frelinghuysen trained the young Tennent to appreciate experimental piety whereby a person was spiritually reborn through conversion. The need for the new birth formed the basis for much of Tennent's preaching as an adult. Although conceding that scripture and Christian doctrines conformed to reason, Tennent placed a much greater emphasis on nurturing a practical piety among the laity. For Tennent, the minister had a duty to awaken the unregenerate to the seriousness of their undesirable spiritual state by preaching the terrors of hell in order to spur his listeners to repentance, encouraging them in the process to turn to God for forgiveness and salvation. Clergymen who ignored their responsibility to preach the gospel message thus endangered the spiritual wellbeing of their congregations by inadvertently aiding the devil in populating hell.

When Whitefield arrived at America in October 1739, Tennent found a welcome ally who shared virtually the same opinion on matters pertaining to Christian piety. Like Tennent, Whitefield preached the necessity of the new birth and had no scruples in criticizing the pastors who seemingly cared more about church-going and simple morality than saving souls. Accompanying Whitefield on his preaching tour of the Middle Colonies at the end of 1739, Tennent observed with delight the favorable effects the Anglican itinerant's message had on his audiences. Filling in as a substitute speaker at the Presbyterian Church at Nottingham, Pennsylvania, on March 8, 1740, Tennent delivered a sermon that subsequently went to print in that year as *The Danger of an Unconverted Ministry*. Perhaps emboldened by Whitefield's fearless attacks on his Anglican colleagues, Tennent

FIGURE 8.1 Gilbert Tennent by Jacob Eichholtz (Detail), Princeton University, gift of Miss Smith, photo by Bruce M. White.

issued his own diatribe against local American clergy. In his published sermon, he compared unconverted ministers with the Pharisees of the Hebrew Scriptures who demanded rule keeping over piety. Even more controversial, Tennent suggested to parishioners that they leave a church if their pastor failed to feed them spiritual food. In questioning the ministry of local clerics and proposing that the laity seek alternative spiritual guidance, Tennent contributed to the growing tension brewing between those who accepted and rejected the Great Awakening as the work of God.

The Danger of an Unconverted Ministry

Mark 6:34: *And Jesus, when he came out, saw much People, and was moved with Compassion towards them, because they were as Sheep not having a Shepherd.*

AS a faithful Ministry is a great Ornament, Blessing, and Comfort, to the Church of GOD; even the Feet of such Messengers are beautiful: So on the contrary, an ungodly Ministry is a great Curse and Judgment: These Caterpillars labour to devour every green Thing.

THERE is nothing that may more justly call forth our saddest Sorrows, and make all our Powers and Passions mourn, in the most doleful Accents, the most incessant, insatiable, and deploring Agonies; than the melancholy Case of such, who have no faithful Ministry! This Truth is set before our Minds in a strong Light, in the Words that I have chosen now to insist upon; in which we have an Account of our LORD's Grief, with the Causes of it.

WE are informed, That our dear Redeemer was moved with Compassion towards them. The Original Word signifies the strongest and most vehement Pity, issuing from the innermost Bowels.

BUT what was the Cause of this great and compassionate Commotion in the Heart of Christ? It was because he saw much People as Sheep having no Shepherd. Why, had the People then no Teachers? O yes! they had Heaps of Pharisee-Teachers, that came out, no doubt after they had been at the Feet of *Gamaliel* the usual Time, and according to the Acts, Canons, and Traditions of the Jewish Church. But notwithstanding of the great Crowds of these Orthodox, Letter-learned and regular Pharisees, our Lord laments the unhappy Case of that great Number of People, who, in the Days of his Flesh, had no better Guides: Because that those were as good as none (in many Respects) in our Saviour's Judgment. For all them, the People were as Sheep without a Shepherd...

The Ministry of natural Men is uncomfortable to gracious Souls.

The Enmity that is put between the Seed of the Woman and the Seed of the Serpent, will now and then be creating Jars: And no wonder; for as it was of old, so it is now, *He that was born after the Flesh, persecuted him that was born after the Spirit.* This Enmity is not one Grain less, in unconverted Ministers, than in others; tho' possibly it may be better polished with Wit and Rhetoric, and gilded with the specious Names of Zeal, Fidelity, Peace, good Order, and Unity.

Natural Men, not having true Love to Christ and the Souls of their Fellow-Creatures, hence their Discourses are cold and sapless, and as it were freeze between their Lips! And not being sent of GOD, they want that divine Authority, with which the faithful Ambassadors of Christ are clothed, who herein resemble their blessed Master, of whom it is said, That *He taught as one having Authority, and not as the Scribes.* Matthew 7:29.

And Pharisee-Teachers, having no Experience of a special Work of the Holy Ghost, upon their own Souls, are therefore neither inclined to, nor fitted for Discoursing, frequently, clearly, and pathetically, upon such important Subjects. The Application of their Discourses, is either short, or indistinct and general. They difference not the precious from the vile, and divide not to every Man his Portion, according to the Apostolical Direction to *Timothy.* No! they carelessly offer a common Mess to their People, and leave it to them, to divide it among themselves, as they see fit. This is indeed their general Practice, which is bad enough: But sometimes they do worse, by misapplying the Word, through Ignorance, or Anger. They often strengthen the Hands of the Wicked, by promising him Life. They comfort People, before they convince them; sow before they plow; and are busy in raising a Fabric, before they lay a Foundation. These foolish Builders do but strengthen Men's carnal Security, by their soft, selfish, cowardly Discourses. They have not the Courage, or Honesty, to thrust the Nail of Terror into sleeping Souls; nay, sometimes they strive with all their Might, to fasten Terror into the Hearts of the Righteous, and so to make those sad, whom GOD would not have made sad! And this happens, when pious People begin to suspect their Hypocrisy, for which they have good Reason. I may add, That inasmuch as Pharisee-Teachers seek after Righteousness as it were by the Works of the Law themselves, they therefore do not distinguish as they ought, between *Law* and *Gospel*, in their Discourses to others. They keep Driving, Driving, to Duty, Duty, under this Notion, That it will recommend natural Men to the favour of GOD, or entitle them to the Promises of Grace and Salvation: And thus those blind Guides fix a deluded World upon the false Foundation of their own Righteousness, and so exclude them from the dear Redeemer. All the Doings of unconverted Men, not proceeding from the Principles of Faith, Love, and a new Nature, nor being directed to the divine Glory as their highest End, but flowing from, and tending to Self, as their Principle and End; are doubtless damnably wicked in their Manner of Performance, and do deserve the Wrath and Curse of a Sin-avenging GOD; neither can any other Encouragement be justly given them, but this, That in the Way of Duty, there is a Peradventure or Probability of obtaining Mercy.

And natural Men, wanting the Experience of those spiritual Difficulties, which pious Souls are exposed to, in this Vale of Tears; they know not how to speak a Word to the Weary in Season.

Their Prayers are also cold; little Child-like Love to God, or Pity to poor perishing Souls, runs thro' their Veins.

Their Conversation hath nothing of the Savour of Christ, neither is it perfumed with the Spices of Heaven. They seem to make as little Distinction in their Practice, as Preaching. They love those Unbelievers, that are kind to them, better than many Christians, and choose them for Companions; contrary to Psalm 15:4, Psalm 119:115, & Galatians 6:10. Poor Christians are stunted and starv'd, who are put to feed on such bare Pastures, and such dry Nurses; as the Rev. Mr. *Hildersham* justly calls them. It's only when the wise Virgins sleep, that they can bear with those dead Dogs, that can't bark; but when the LORD revives his People, they can't but abhor them! O! it is ready to break their very Hearts with Grief, to see, how luke-warm those Pharisee-Teachers are in their public Discourses, while Sinners are sinking into Damnation, in Multitudes!...

If it be so, That the Case of those, who have no other, or no better than Pharisee-Teachers, is to be pitied: Then what a Scroll and Scene of Mourning, and Lamentation, and Woe, is opened! because of the Swarms of Locusts, the Crowds of Pharisees, that have as covetously as cruelly, crept into the Ministry, in this adulterous Generation! who as nearly resemble the Character given of the old Pharisees, in the Doctrinal Part of this Discourse, as one Crow's Egg does another. It is true some of the modern Pharisees have learned to prate a little more orthodoxly about the New Birth, than their Predecessor *Nicodemus*, who are, in the mean Time, as great Strangers to the feeling Experience of it, as he. They are blind who see not this to be the Case of the Body of the Clergy, of this Generation. And O! that our Heads were Waters, and our Eyes a Fountain of Tears, that we could

Day and Night lament, with the utmost Bitterness, the doleful Case of the poor Church of God, upon this account.

From what has been said, we may learn, That such who are contented under a dead Ministry, have not in them the Temper of that Saviour they profess. It's an awful Sign, that they are as blind as Moles, and as dead as Stones, without any spiritual Taste and Relish. And alas! isn't this the Case of Multitudes? If they can get one, that has the Name of a Minister, with a Band, and a Black Coat or Gown to carry on a Sabbath-days among them, although never so coldly, and unsuccessfully; if he is free from gross Crimes in Practice, and takes good Care to keep at a due Distance from their Consciences, and is never troubled about his Unsuccessfulness; O! think the poor Fools, that is a fine Man indeed; our Minister is a prudent charitable Man, he is not always harping upon Terror, and sounding Damnation in our Ears, like some rash-headed Preachers, who by their uncharitable Methods, are ready to put poor People out of their Wits, or to run them into Despair; O! how terrible a Thing is that Despair! Ay, our Minister, honest Man, gives us good Caution against it. Poor silly Souls! consider seriously these Passages, of the Prophet *Jeremiah*, c.5:30–31.

We may learn, the Mercy and Duty of those that enjoy a faithful Ministry. Let such glorify GOD, for so distinguishing a Privilege, and labour to walk worthy of it, to all Well-pleasing; lest for their Abuse thereof, they be exposed to a greater Damnation.

If the Ministry of natural Men be as it has been represented; Then it is both lawful and expedient to go from them to hear Godly Persons; yea, it's so far from being sinful to do this, that one who lives under a pious Minister of lesser Gifts, after having honestly endeavor'd to get Benefit by his Ministry, and yet gets little or none, but doth find real Benefit and more Benefit elsewhere; I say, he may lawfully go, and that frequently, where he gets most Good to his precious Soul, after regular Application to the Pastor where he lives, for his Consent, and proposing the Reasons thereof; when this is done in the Spirit of Love and Meekness, without Contempt of any, as also without rash Anger, or vain Curiosity.

Natural Reason will inform us, that Good is desirable for its own sake. Now, as Dr. *Voetius* observes, Good added to Good, makes it a greater Good, and so more desirable; and therefore Evil as Evil, or a lesser Good, which is comparatively Evil, cannot be the Object of Desire.

There is a natural Instinct put even into the irrational Creatures, by the Author of their Being, to seek after the greater natural Good, as far as they know it. Hence the Birds of the Air fly to the warmer Climates, in order to shun the Winter-Cold, and also doubtless to get better Food; *For where the Carcass is, there the Eagles will be gathered together.* The Beasts of the Field seek the best Pastures, and the Fishes of the Ocean seek after the Food they like best.

But the written Word of God confirms the aforesaid Proposition, while God by it enjoins us, *to covet earnestly the best Gifts*; as also *to prove all Things, and hold fast that which is good.* 1 Corinthians 12:31. 1 Thessalonians 5:2. And it is not the Command of God, that we should *grow in Grace*? 2 Peter 3:18 and 1 Peter 2:2. Now, does not every positive Command enjoin the Use of such Means, as have the directest Tendency to answer the End designed? namely, The Duty commanded. If there by a Variety of Means, is not the best to be chosen? else how can the Choice be called rational, and becoming an intelligent Creature? To choose otherwise knowingly, is it not contrary to common Sense, as well as Religion, and daily confuted by the common Practice of all the rational Creation, about Things of far less Moment and Consequence?

That there is a Difference and Variety in Preachers Gifts and Graces, is undeniably evident, from the united Testimony of Scripture and Reason.

And that there is a great Difference in the Degrees of Hearers Edification, under the Hearing of these different Gifts, is as evident to the Feeling of experienced Christians, as any Thing can be to Sight.

It is also an unquestionable Truth, that ordinarily GOD blesses most the best Gifts, for the Hearers Edification, as by the best Food he gives the best Nourishment. Otherwise the best Gifts would not be desirable, and GOD Almighty in the ordinary Course of his Providence, by not acting according to the Nature of Things, would be carrying on a Series of unnecessary Miracles; which to suppose, is unreasonable. The following Places of holy Scripture, confirm what has been last observed. 1 Corinthians 14:12, 1 Timothy 4:14–16, 2 Timothy 1:6, & Acts 11:24.

If God's People have a Right to the Gifts of all God's Ministers, pray, why mayn't they use them, as they have Opportunity? And if they should go a few Miles farther than ordinary, to enjoy those, which they profit most by; who do they wrong? Now, our LORD does inform his people, 1 Corinthians 3:22. That *whether* Paul, *or* Apollos, *or* Cephas; *all was theirs.*

But the Example of our Dear Redeemer, will give farther Light in this Argument. Tho' many of the Hearers, not only of the Pharisees, but of *John the Baptist*, came to hear our Saviour, and that not only upon Week-days, but upon Sabbath days, and that in great Numbers, and from very distant Places; yet he reproved them not: And did not our Lord love the Apostle *John* more than the rest, and took him with him, before others, with *Peter* and *James*, to Mount *Tabor*, and *Gethsemane?* Matthew 17 and c.26.

To bind Men to a particular Minister, against their Judgment and Inclinations, when they are more edified elsewhere, is carnal with a Witness; a cruel Oppression of tender Consciences, a Compelling of Men to Sin: For he that doubts, is damn'd if he eat; and whatsoever is not of faith, is Sin.

Besides it is an unscriptural Infringement on Christian Liberty; 1 Corinthians 3:22. It's a Yoke worse than that of *Rome* itself. Dr. *Voetius* asserts, "That even among the *Papists*, as to Hearing of Sermons, the People are not deprived of the Liberty of Choice." It's a Yoke like that of *Egypt*, which cruel *Pharaoh* formed for the Necks of the oppressed *Israelites*, when he obliged them to make up their stated Task of Brick, but allowed them no Straw. So we must grow in Grace and Knowledge; but in the mean time, according to the Notion of some, we are confined from using the likeliest Means, to attain that End.

If the great Ends of Hearing may be attained as well, and better, by Hearing of another Minister than our own; then I see not, why we should be under a fatal Necessity of hearing him, I mean our Parish-Minister, perpetually, or generally. Now, what are, or ought to be, the Ends of Hearing, but the Getting of Grace, and Growing in it? *Romans* 10:14. 1 Peter 2:2. *As Babes desire the sincere Milk of the Word, that ye may grow thereby.* (Poor Babes like not dry Breasts, and living Men like not dead Pools.) Well then, and may not these Ends be obtained out of our Parish-line? *Faith* is said to come by *Hearing*, Romans 10. But the Apostle doesn't add, *Your Parish-Minister.* Isn't the same Word preach'd out of our Parish? and is there any Restriction in the Promises of blessing the Word to those only, who keep within their Parish-line ordinarily? If there be, I have not yet met with it; yea, I can affirm, that so far as Knowledge can be had in such Cases, I have known Persons to get saving Good to their Souls, by Hearing over their Parish-line; and this makes me earnest in Defense of it.

Gilbert Tennent, *The Danger of an Unconverted Ministry, Considered in a Sermon on Mark VI.34* (Philadelphia: Benjamin Franklin, 1740), 3–4, 8–11, 17–22.

9

Revivals as a Means of Reform

Samuel Finley

AS THE GREAT Awakening heated up in the American colonies, opposition mounted from Old Light ministers who spurned the revivals as disruptive to the traditional religious order. Critics charged evangelical itinerants like George Whitefield and Gilbert Tennent as inciting the passions of crowds and turning parishioners against the established clerical hierarchy. The Presbyterian minister and later president of the College of New Jersey, Samuel Finley (1715–66) responded to some of the accusations by arguing, in his sermon *Christ Triumphing and Satan Raging* (1741), that historically God has often acted unexpectedly when reforming the church, and usually at the darkest hour. The bizarre emotional responses by individuals undergoing conversion did not disqualify the revivals as coming from the hand of God. Rather, evidence that people's lives had changed for the better seemed to verify that the Great Awakening was a divine movement.

Finley pointed out that the "rabble" who the anti-revivalists ridiculed as adherents of the Great Awakening were the same kind of people Jesus called as disciples and targeted for his ministry. From passages in the New Testament, Finley demonstrated that the opposition against Jesus' ministry mirrored the recent hostility levied against the evangelicals. When Jesus' enemies had falsely accused him of serving the devil by casting out demons he responded that exorcisms must be the work of God since demons are the minions of Satan. In the same way that Jesus' ministry had been misinterpreted as demonic, Finley inferred that the current naysayers were just as blind to the benefits of the Awakening as a genuine spiritual renewal that was intended to benefit the church.

Christ Triumphing, and Satan Raging

That there has been a great religious Commotion in the World in our present Day, is so evident, that it cannot be deny'd: But there has been a Murmuring among the

FIGURE 9.1 Samuel Finley by Charles Walker Lind (Detail), Princeton University, gift of Samuel Finley Breese Morse, photo by Bruce M. White.

People; some saying, That GOD is with us of a Truth; that the Day-spring from on high has visited us; and the Day-star has risen in many Hearts: Others saying, Nay, it is all Deceit, or Delusion, or the Work of the Devil. But that CHRIST is come to his Church, will appear, I presume, in the Judgment of any considering Person, if I can make these Things appear:

1. That the Church was in the same Circumstances as when he us'd to visit it.
2. If the Manner of his Coming be in Substance the same.
3. If the Treatment he meets with, be the same.
4. If the Consequences and Effects be the same.
5. If the Attempts and Objections made against him be the same. And, in a Word,

If the Devil be cast out by Means of true Gospel-Doctrine. And

1. As to the Circumstances of the Church; He always came when it needed a Reformation, even in the Judgment of graceless Professors; when Religion dwindled into an empty Form, and Professors had lost the Life and Power of Godliness; in a Word, when there was Midnight-Darkness, and little Faith to be found on the Earth. Thus it was when he came in the Flesh; when he sent St. *Athanasius, Luther* and *Calvin*, and at the Reformation of *Scotland*. We find the graceless *Jews* prayed for the Day of the LORD, in *Amos* 5:18. And hence were our Pulpits filled with seemingly devout Prayers for a Revival of Religion, and Confessions of its decayed State. And what had we lately but a dry Formality? Did not all in general seem to be at Ease in *Zion*, and in much Peace about the

State of their Souls? How few were asking the Watch-men, *What of the Night?*
The Lives of Professors careless, unholy, unguarded; Ordinances attended,
Duties performed, Sermons preached, without Life or Power, and as little
Success. Was not worldly Discourse our mutual Entertainment at our solemn
Assemblies on Holy-days? Thus in Darkness and Security were we: And *like
People, like Priest.*

2. As to the Manner of his Coming; It never was in such a Manner as
carnal Persons imagined; but still unexpected, and out of the common Way.
And this is a necessary Consequent of the State of the Church: For since he
comes in a dark Time, we may easily conclude, that the Manner thereof is
unobserv'd at first. He must needs come unawares, when a carnal World
have forgotten and do not neglect him; and do not know him, or the powerful
Operations of his Spirit until they feel them. For tho' they may pray for the
Day of the LORD; yet they know it not when it comes, and so do not know
what they ask, *Amos* 5:18. Now, by this Means he comes always quite cross to
the Inclinations of the Clergy, who are generally sunk in Carnality, as well as
the People. And as a Consequence of this, the Ministers by whom He works,
have always at first been few: And thus the Work appears the more eminently
to be his own, the less probable that the Instruments appear. Thus it was
when he came in the Flesh. He came indeed out of *Bethlehem*, but in a mean
Condition; and afterwards, unperceivably changing his Place, was mistaken.
When he enter'd on his public Ministry, it was not according to the Traditions
of the Fathers; for we find they were surprised in *Luke* 4 when he began to
expound the Scriptures, being neither a Scribe nor Pharisee. And the People,
not being used with such close and particular Applications, could not bear
his new Methods. Passing by the established, but proud, bigoted, gainsaying
Clergy, he chooses Twelve unlearned, unpolished Men, most of them Fishers;
and gave them a Commission to preach the Gospel, without consulting the
Sanhedrin about such *unprecedented* Proceedings. Thus was his Coming dark
and cross to them. Now, in our Days the Parallel is plain, for supposing the
present Commotion to be the Work of GOD: Every one knows how cross it
is to the Inclinations of the Clergy. Surely, our Opposers will confess, they
neither did, nor do expect Religion to be reviv'd in such a Manner, while there
are so many Things, in their Opinion, wrong. Surely, it is a dark Day to them,
and no Light in it; many of them know not what to make of it, by their own
Confession. We all know how few its Propagators are; and they say, that most
of us are unlearned: But do they not, by the by, betray themselves herein? For,
if unlearned, they must have the less Rhetoric and Oratory; and consequently
the less able to bring such Things to pass. If it were the Work of Man, a superior Power of Man would overthrow it. In a word, the Parallel holds in every
Thing, only our Manner of Licensing is not *unprecedented.*

3. The Treatment he met with; As a native Consequence of his Coming in so dark and mean a Condition, and cross to the Minds of the Clergy; he was rejected by them, and by many of the Noble and Mighty after the Flesh; who embitter'd against him as many People as they could influence. And, as a Consequence of his being disown'd by these, he was chiefly followed by what we call the *Mob*, the *Rabble*, the *common* and *meaner Sort*. And being disown'd by the self-righteous Moralists, was follow'd by the openly Profane, the *Publicans*, and *Harlots*: For he is still set for the *Rise and Fall of many in* Israel; and many who thought themselves *first*, and were esteemed so by others in the Dark, did show themselves to be *last*. Thus it was when he came in the Flesh; rejected by the Clergy so generally, and by the Noble and Wise that it was said, *Have any of the Rulers or Pharisees believed on him?* No: *But this People who know not the Law, are accursed*. Just so is he treated by the same Ranks of Persons at this Day. May I not ask, Have any of the Rulers, have any of the Ministers embraced the present Work? Do they not rather prepossess and embitter the carnal People against it? And many who seemed *first* in Religion, are they not become the very *last*, and the *last, first*? For our Opposers confess of their own Accord, That *it is only the ignorant Rabble that embrace it; many of which never minded any Religion, and so do not know the Law*. Sure they who know the Law might know, that it is a good Proof of a Day of GOD's Power, when *the Poor have the Gospel preach'd to them*, and do receive it, Matthew 11:5. Might they not know that our LORD used this Argument? And also, that *GOD chooses foolish Things to confound the Wise?* But they must confess, that tho' there be not *many*, yet, Glory to GOD! there are *some* of the *Wise*, and *Mighty*, and *Noble*, on our Side.

4. The Effects and Consequences of his Coming; As a Consequence of the strong Opposition of the Clergy, and others of their Adherents, against him. Contrary to their own Intentions, their Speaking of him was a Means of setting the People on the Search; and Numbers flock'd after him, to hear these *new Doctrines*, and *new Methods*; and were then caught in the Gospel-net: *As many as were ordinated to eternal Life, believed*. Thus in *John* 7:2 & *seq.* the Pharisees, speaking against him, put him in the People's Minds, who began to talk of him. His Audiences were often deeply affected, and frequently divided between him and the Clergy: And hence we so often read, that *there was a Division among the People*. He never came to send Peace on the Earth, but a *Sword*, and *Division*. Luke 12:51–58. Just so it has been in our Day. Many can say by Experience, that their Attention and Curiosity was raised by Means of the Contradictions of their Ministers. And hence we have seen unusual Numbers going to hear the Word like thirsty Flocks: And heard a great Mourning, like the Mourning of *Hadadrimmon* in the Valley of *Megiddo*. Also there has been a Division among the People; some praising GOD for what their Eyes have

seen, and their Ears heard, and their Souls felt; others going away mocking, contradicting, blaspheming.

Another Effect was, the Breaking down of Bigotry; partly as a native Consequence of the Attention of all Parties being raised to come and hear; and partly by the Example and Directions of CHRIST and his Followers. Thus he freely conversed, eat, and drank, with different opposite Parties, *Jews* and *Samaritans, Publicans* and *Pharisees*; and justified his so doing from the Need there was of it, that all might come freely, and reap Benefit. And the Apostle, in *Philippians* 3:15–16 advises real Christians, who hold the Foundation, to walk together in such Things as they are agreed in; for in Things wherein they are disagreed they cannot. And just so our Opposers confess it to be now, while they accuse us for holding Communion with different Societies, and would insinuate, that we do so from some politick Design: Indeed there is this Policy in it, To gain some by any Means, and make a Party for JESUS CHRIST.

5. The Attempts; As a Consequence of the People's following CHRIST or his Ambassadors, and disregarding the Clergy, the latter always attempted to overthrow the *new Scheme*: Were (1) unwearied in forming mischievous Devices against him; would tell the People they had an Imposture, and were deluded, and deceiv'd; followed him for no other End but to find something to cavil at; wrested both his Words and Actions to find Matter of Accusation. (2) They were unsatisfied; for after they had been busy all along, they say, *What do we?* q.d. We have been too slack and cowardly; come, let us bestir ourselves, and not suffer all to be overturn'd; we have prevail'd nothing as yet. (3) Their Attempts were still unsuccessful, and always tended to promote the Cause they were set to baffle: Tho' they are still busy, yet are conscious they prevail noth-ing. Thus when the Scribes and Pharisees sought Christ at the Feast, *John* 7:11 they put him in the People's Minds, who straight began to talk of him, some good, some evil: When the Pharisees perceived this, they forbid them to speak of him either good or ill; for so much is imply'd in these Words, *Howbeit no Man spoke openly of him, for Fear of the Jews.* They hoped that the Thoughts of Christ would wear out of the People's Minds thro' Time. Just thus do the Opposers now to a tittle. It can be made appear, how Companies of Ministers and People, have met together in a private Manner, to consult how they might suppress the *new Scheme*, and what they could say against it: And indeed, their Cavils, and the Spirit with which they are urged, do plainly show, that they rather desire Matter of Accusation, than that they really have it. How do they twist and wrest both the Words and Actions, and magnify the Blemishes, of those who stand up for the Work of GOD? If they can find an unguarded Expression, they draw what horrid Consequences from it they can, and then

affirm that this is the Man's Principles. They want some plausible Pretense to blind the People. And they are yet saying, *What do we?* And I could show, were it necessary, how every Instance of Opposition against the present Work, have all been turn'd to its Advantage. Oh that they would consider whom they fight against! For GOD is with us of a Truth. And now some of them beg for Peace, and would have us be silent about these controverted Things, that they may wear out of Mind. Their asking Peace and Quietness has an Aspect pleasing to the Flesh, and looks plausible: But GOD forbid that we should cease to proclaim his wondrous Deeds, to humour the Enemies of his Work! No; let us tell them abroad more loudly, tho' it gall the Consciences, and torment the Minds of all the Opposers on Earth. *Revelation* 11:10. Thus far we are on a straight Parallel, by the Confession of our Opposers.

6. The Objections made against him, are the same as usual. For,

(1) The Pharisees objected Disorder to our LORD and his Apostles. How often are they accused of not walking according to the Traditions of the Elders? And our Opposers say, This cannot be the Work of GOD, because not according to their Order: But they have not proven, that GOD is oblig'd to work by their Rules.

(2) When our LORD and his Apostles pleaded for free Grace, they were called Enemies to *Moses* and the Law; and he was often call'd a Blasphemer. So the present Opposers of GOD's Work, accuse some of us of speaking against the Law, and call us *Antinomians*; and tug and strive, by wresting both the Words and Intentions of some of our Brethren, to prove them Blasphemy. *He hath spoken Blasphemy, why hear ye him?*

(3) It was objected to our LORD and his Apostles, that they held Communion with Persons of different Societies. Hence they stumbled, because he kept Company with *Publicans*, and *Samaritans*, and *Sinners*. And thought, had he been so much as a common Prophet, he would have known better what Company to keep; and hence concluded he could not possibly be the CHRIST. So our Opposers say, that we bring the Church into Confusion by a mixt Communion of different Persuasions; who yet hold the Foundation. And further they ask, Why these who were of no religious Society, are fond of this *new Scheme? Why eateth your Master with Publicans and Sinners?* He that pretends to be so good a Man, why does he keep such bad Company? They seem now to think it unjust, that Persons, who never did so much in Religion as they, should enter into the Kingdom of Heaven before them.

(4) It is objected to us, that this Commotion rends the Church; divides Congregations and Families; sets People at Variance; makes them harsh and censorious. So we hear *Tertullus*, *Acts* 24:5 accuse *Paul* as a *pestilent*

Fellow, a Mover of Sedition, a Profaner of the Temple. The Pharisees, *John* 9:44 ask in a sour Manner, *Are we blind also?* Dost thou judge us to be blind too so rashly? And *Elijah*, because a Son of Thunder, tho' he was the most peaceable, yet he must needs be call'd a *Troubler of Israel*, in 1 *Kings* 18:17. And, in a Word, both they and we are Turners of the World upside down, Subverters of Peace and Church-Government, and the like. Read *Luke* 12:51–57. *Suppose ye*, says Christ, *that I am come to send Peace on the Earth? I came not to send Peace, but a Sword—to divide a Family against itself. Why cannot* our present Opposers *discern the Signs of* THESE TIMES?

(5) The present Opposers say, they do not quarrel with the Work of GOD; no, far be it from them; but only with these Disorders. So, in *John* 10:33 the *Jews* say, *For a good Work we stone thee not*: No; far be it from us, do not so mistake us, we would be ready to encourage every Thing that has the Appearance of Piety; 'tis not for thy good Works, *but for Blasphemy*. But his good Works, instead of procuring their Favour, did raise their Envy: And though they would not be so barefaced before the People; yet they could willingly have imbrued their Hands in his Blood, for no other Crime but his good Works; because he so far out-shined them. But on account of the People, they must first find some plausible Pretense against him. They took no Notice, or laid no Stress on his Miracles; were never satisfied with all the Evidences he gave them; their common Question was, *What Sign shewest thou?* Tho' they seemed resolved not to be satisfied with any Sign. They still found Exceptions against all his Works; and when they could not deny the Matter of Fact, they ascribed it to the Devil sometimes. How often do they ask the Man born blind, how he receiv'd his Sight? And would willingly have deny'd that he was blind: How earnest were they to find some Flaw or other? And when they could find none, they put a Religious face upon their Envy; exhort the Man to give GOD the Glory, but not to mind JESUS; for they were sure he was a Sinner. Just so it is now-a-days to a tittle. Our Opposers have no End of asking for Evidences; without taking Notice of the Power of GOD, that has appear'd in the Assemblies, or on the Lives of Men: They still muster up Objections, and harp only on what they call Disorder. They gather a great many of their Exceptions together, and then ask, if these Irregularities be the Work of GOD. Without observing the deep Concern that Souls seem to be under, they only ask about the *Fits* and *Convulsions* that their Sorrow throws them into; and which they would be ready to allow for, in worldly Respects, as the sudden News of the Death of Friends, or the like. And if some unexceptionable Evidence of the Power of GOD be alleged against them; they strive to evade its Force some Way or other, by saying, That possibly

GOD may bring Good out of Evil; but yet do speak against the Whole, as a Devilish Work. They seem glad to get any Objection against it; not willing that it should be the Work of GOD. They fix their Eyes only on the Failures and Blemishes of those who defend it, and magnify Mole-hills into Mountains: And if they can get nothing that has the Appearance of a Fault, they are industrious to forge and spread slanderous Reports, and false Insinuations; and seem as fond of them, as if they had got a Victory. In a Word; they appear as if their greatest Desire was, to blind their own Eyes, and stop their own Ears, that hearing they might not understand, and seeing they might not perceive, lest they should be *Converts* too, as they call us by way of Ridicule.

Thus the Parallel runs clear and undeniable. The same Attempts and Objections, from the same Ranks of Persons, do prove the same Dispositions to be in graceless Persons now, as formerly; the same Blindness and Enmity. And why should it be thought strange that CHRIST's pretended Ambassadors are his bitterest Enemies, seeing it has been always so? The LORD always reform'd his Church contrary to their Desires. There is the same kind of Opposition, and Opposers too, in *Scotland* and *England* at present, as here in *America*. And had I Time, I could show that all Things, in every Period of the Church, answer and agree with this, as Face answers face in a Glass. But the Coming of CHRIST in the Flesh, will be found to be analogous to his Coming at other Times; and the Parallel from that, is most level to the Capacity of every one; and trac'd with less Difficulty, and more Certainty by common People: And therefore I have chiefly compar'd that Period and our present Day.

Samuel Finley, *Christ Triumphing, and Satan Raging* (Philadelphia: B. Franklin, 1741), 23–32.

10

Diary of Doubts

Hannah Heaton

FOR MANY YEARS Hannah Heaton (1721–94) worried about her salvation. Growing up in Southampton, Long Island, she began penning her thoughts in a diary that she kept from 1741 to 1793. The earliest entries tell of her conversion experience at the height of the Great Awakening. In 1741 she traveled to New Haven, Connecticut, where she felt convicted of her sin and need for Christ after hearing such preachers as George Whitefield and Gilbert Tennent. Initially perceiving God as a wrathful deity who yearned to send her to the pit of hell, she discovered a merciful Christ who welcomed her with open arms and quickly forgave all her past sins. Although she could trace her steps back to the early 1740s as the time of her spiritual birth, Heaton struggled for many years before she found assurance of salvation.

Many of the doubts that crept into her mind stemmed from poor decisions that she deemed to be the root of her problems. She imagined the devil tempting her to doubt God's love or tormenting her with atheistic thoughts. Sometimes God tested her, but on other occasions he punished her for wrongdoings such as her youthful decision to marry an unbeliever. In 1743, Hannah wed Theophilus Heaton, Jr. and moved to North Haven, Connecticut where they raised their two sons, Jonathan and Calvin. Although a moral man who attended a Congregational church, Theophilus did not exhibit signs of experiencing the new birth, and therefore Hannah thought of her husband as an unbeliever. Further, Hannah labeled her husband's minister Isaac Stiles as a "blind guide," an unregenerate clergyman who was leading his congregants to hell. Benjamin Trumbull, who replaced Stiles in 1760, did not rectify the situation. Refusing to attend a church where the minister did not preach the gospel, Hannah threw her lot in with the Separatists who shared a similar conviction that people must seek conversion. Passionate about her faith, and longing for symbiotic closeness with her maker, Hannah Heaton and her diary offers readers a window into the sometimes troubled soul of a pious woman deeply affected by evangelical preaching.

The Diary of Hannah Heaton

Now after a while I went over to New Haven in the fall just before that great work of God began which was in the year 1741. There I heard Mr. Tennent and Mr. Whitefield preach which awakened me much. Mr. Whitefield laid down the marks of an unconverted person. O strange it was such preaching as I never heard before. Don't you said he when you are at the house of God long service should be over that your minds may be about your worldly concerns and pleasures? Is it not a weariness to you said he if one days serving God is so wearisome to you? How could you endure to be in heaven with him forever where nothing but praises are? He said if you was carried to heaven in this condition the first prayer you would make would be that you might go into hell for that would be more agreeable to your natures. O thought I I have found it a weariness to me many a time over and over again. Then I began to think my nature must be changed but how to attain it I knew not. When I was coming from meeting to my quarters which was about 6 miles my company began to worry me to sing. I put them off till I feared they would be offended. At last I sung some verses about a contented me. I thought that was better than to sing a song but O they little thought how I felt. It was hard work for me to sing. I felt in such distress in my mind but I went to frolics all winter and stifled the conviction I had of its being a soul ruining sin. I was much for fine clothes and fashions. In the spring in May I went to Middletown to keep election. One of the days while I was there I was at a tavern in a frolic. Then there come in a young man from Long Island belonging to the society that I did and told me how the work of God was carried on there and of several of my mates that was converted. My sister Elisabeth also sent me a letter. I trembled when I read it. She said her soul magnified the Lord. Her spirit rejoiced in God her Saviour. Her sighs was turned into songs. The comforter is come. I had a strong impression upon my mind to go home which I did in a few days. As soon as I got into my fathers house young people come in and began to talk. Sister Elisabeth began to cry over me because I had no interest in Christ that I wondered at. But the next morning father examined me and I was forced to tell my experiences as well as I could. He told me when I had done what a dreadful condition I was in. It took hold of my heart. I kept going to the meetings and was more and more concerned and O what crying out there was among the people, what shall I do to be saved? Now it began to be whispered in my ear it is too late too late you had better hang your self and when I see a convenient place o how it would strike me. I was afraid to go alone to pray for fear I should see the devil. Once when I was on the ground away alone at prayer trying to give up all to Christ in great distress of soul. I thought I felt the devil twitch my clothes. I jumped up and run in fixed with terror and O how did I look at the wonders in the night to see if Christ was not coming to judgment. O how I did envy toads or any creature that had no souls to perish eternally. Many a time I kneeled down to pray and my mouth was as it were stopped and I did vent out my anguish with tears and groans and a few broken speeches. Now it cut me to think how I had spent my precious time in vanity and sin against God. My not regarding the Sabbath no more was bitter to me now. I thought sometime I could be willing to burn in the flames of fire if I could be delivered from the anger of God or appease his wrath that was out against me. Now my heart and soul and all nature was set against, nay loathed the way of salvation by Christ and it seemed to me if should give up all to Christ he would send me directly to hell. Sometimes my heart would quarrel with God thus why he knows I can't convert myself why then don't he convert me. Now I thought if I knew of any place on earth where I could hide from God O how would I run to it. But them words was terrible to me. In Amos chapter 9 read to the 5th verse, tho' they dig into hell tho' they climb up to heaven tho' they hide in the top of Carmel tho' they be hid in the bottom of the sea &c. O how it cut me to think I could not get away from God but appear before him I must and I lived in daily expectation of it. Now sometimes it would be cast into my mind thus you need not be so concerned you are not so great a sinner as some are. Some have murdered and done dreadful things but you pray and go to meeting and God will not have a heart to send you to hell. This I thought was the devil trying to beat me of. True I had no sense of the justice of God all this while nor could I think what conversion was unless it was this & I fancied it was. I thought a person must be in a sort of a trance and be carried to heaven and see wonders there and then be brought back again, but now them words was terror to me where it says God is angry with the wicked every day and the day cometh that shall burn as an oven and all the proud & them that do wickedly shall be stubble and the day cometh that shall burn them up saith the Lord of Hosts that it shall leave them neither root nor branch. Some years back I used to pray for many things that I was afraid God would hear and answer them. But now I cried for mercy, mercy, mercy Lord O save me from thy wrath, O save me from hell. This my soul wanted. I did not want to go to heaven. I thought I should be tired of singing praises. Nay I felt a hatred against it, and it seemed impossible to me that Christ was willing to save me that I could not believe I such a loathsome sinner and he such a holy God. Sometimes I thought I was willing but he was not. I could hear of others finding mercy but O how it would strike me for I feared greatly that while others was taken I should be left. Now the promises in the scriptures was terror to me for I thought they belonged to the children of God. I had no part in them and I felt such an enmity against the way of salvation by Christ I could see no way to escape damnation. Now I began to feel like one lost in the woods. I knew not what to do nor what course to take for my heart began to grow hard. Now I could not cry and pray as before when I thought of hell. It did not terrify me as before it used to. Me thought I envied the very devils for they believed and trembled but I did not. Nothing now seemed to help me. I grew worse and worse. I thought it must be a gone case with me and I thought so the more because father never spoke one word to me about my soul in particular as I remember after he first examined me till after I had found comfort which was about three weeks after. It being in the year 1741 June 20 I was then I suppose in my twentieth year. It was the Lord's day. I went to our separate meeting in the school house. They I think read a book of Joseph Alleine but I felt so stupid and hardened and shut up that I could not hear nor keep my mind upon anything. I thought if I could have purchased a world by it I could not shed a tear. Now I feared I was hardened & sealed down to damnation with a witness (Jericho was straightly shut up when the walls fell) for I had lost all my concern and felt a heart of stone. Meeting being done I set away to go home. I thought I would not go to the night meeting which was to be at Thomas Sanford's for it would do me no good. I remember in the lot as I went I see strawberries and these thoughts past through my mind. I may as well go to picking strawberries now as not it's no matter what I do it's a gone case with me. I fear I have committed the unpardonable sin and now hardened but as I was going home I considered at last. I turned and went to meeting. Soon after meeting began the power of God come down. Many were crying out the other side of the room, what shall I do to be saved? I was immediately moved to press through the multitude and went to them. A great melting of soul came up on me. I wept bitterly and pleaded hard for mercy, mercy. Now I was brought to view the justice of God due to me for my sin. It made me tremble my knees smote together. Then I thought of Belshazzar when he see the hand writing against him. It seemed to me I was a sinking down into hell. I thought the floor I stood on gave way and I was just a going, but then I began to resign, and as I resigned my distress began to go of till I was perfectly easy, quiet and calm. I could say Lord it is just if I sink in to hell. I felt for a few moments like a creature dead. I was nothing. I could do nothing nor I desired nothing. I had not so much as one desire for mercy left me but presently I heard one in the room say, seek and you shall find. Come to me all you that are weary and heavy laden and I will give you rest. I began to feel a thirsting after Christ and began to beg for mercy, free mercy for Jesus sake. Me thought I see Jesus with the eyes of my soul stand up in heaven. A lovely God-man with his arms open ready to receive me. His face was full of smiles. He looked white and ruddy and was just such a Saviour as my soul wanted every way suitable for me. O how it melted my heart to think he had been willing all this while to save me but I was not willing, which I never believed before now. I cried from the very heart to think what a tender hearted Saviour I had been refusing. How often I turned a deaf ear to his gracious calls and invitations. All that had kept me from him was my will. Jesus appeared altogether lovely to me now. My heart went out with love and thankfulness and admiration. I cried why me Lord and leave so many? O what a fullness was there in Christ for others if they would come and give up their all to him. I went about the room and invited the people to come to him. June 20 1741. About nine o'clock in the evening in the twentieth year of my age I set a way to go home from meeting. It was about a mile, but O me thought the moon and stars seemed as if they praised God with me. It seemed as if I had a new soul & body both. I felt a love to God's children. I thought that night that Jesus was a precious Jesus. It being late our family went to bed, but I sat up and walked about the chamber. It seemed as if I could not sleep while the heavens was filled with praises and singing. That night I was brought into the Lord's Prayer. Before I was afraid to say it, but now it seemed sweet to call God father. Yea my heart could say every word in it.

"Hannah Heaton Autobiography, 1740–1794," MS 73448, Connecticut Historical Society, 3–7.

Racing to Hear Whitefield Preach

Nathan Cole

DURING GEORGE WHITEFIELD'S fifteen-month tour of the American colonies, thousands gathered to see him. Arriving at Delaware on October 30, 1739, he preached in and around Philadelphia and New York before making his way southward until he reached Savannah on January 9, 1740. While in Georgia, he oversaw the foundation of an orphanage, which he named Bethesda, before sailing to Newport, Rhode Island in September 1740. Soon after disembarking, he preached to unprecedented crowds in Boston and then moved inland, reaching Northampton where he delivered four sermons in October 17–20 at Jonathan Edwards's Congregational church. Throughout Whitefield's time in New England, colonists packed into towns where he was scheduled to speak, hoping to hear the man who could reportedly bring an audience to tears simply by pronouncing the word Mesopotamia. A farmer named Nathan Cole (1711–83) recorded in his journal how he and his wife raced to hear Whitefield preach at Middletown, Connecticut, on October 23, 1740, to an estimated 3,000 to 4,000 people. Convicted of sin by the Grand Itinerant's message, Cole wrote in his journal of a lengthy spiritual struggle that culminated in his assurance of salvation. Cole's journal offers a rare glimpse of a common American who was deeply touched by the leading evangelist of the Great Awakening.

"The Spiritual Travels of Nathan Cole"

I was born Feb 15th 1711 and born again October 1741—

When I was young I had very early Convictions; but after I grew up I was an Arminian until I was near 30 years of age; I intended to be saved by [my] own works such as prayers and good deeds.

Now it pleased God to send Mr. Whitefield into this land; and [my] hearing of his preaching at Philadelphia, like one of the Old apostles, and many thousands flocking to hear him preach the Gospel; and great numbers were converted to

Christ; I felt the Spirit of God drawing me by conviction; I longed to see and hear him, and wished he would come this way. I heard he was come to New York and the Jerseys and great multitudes flocking after him under great concern for their Souls which brought on my Concern more and more hoping soon to see him but next I heard he was at Long Island; then at Boston and next at Northampton; then on a Sudden, in the morning about 8 or 9 of the Clock . there came a messenger and said Mr. Whitefield preached at Hartford and Weathersfield yesterday and is to preach at Middletown this morning at ten of the Clock. I was in my field at Work. I dropped my tool that I had in my hand and ran home to my wife telling her to make ready quickly to go and hear Mr. Whitefield preach at Middletown, then run to my pasture for my horse with all my might; fearing that I should be too late; having my horse I with my wife soon mounted the horse and went forward as fast as I thought the horse could bear, and when my horse got much out of breath I would get down and put my wife on the Saddle and bid her ride as fast as she could and not Stop or Slack for me except I bade her and so I would run until I was much out of breath; and then mount my horse again, and so I did several times to favour my horse; we improved every moment to get along as if we were fleeing for our lives; all the while fearing we should be too late to hear the Sermon, for we had twelve miles to ride double in little more than an hour and we went round by the upper house parish and when we came within about half a mile or a mile of the Road that comes down from Hartford [to] Weathersfield and Stepney to Middletown; on high land I saw before me a Cloud or fog rising; I first thought it came from the great River, but as I came nearer the Road, I heard a noise something like a low rumbling thunder and presently found it was the noise of Horses feet coming down the Road and this Cloud was a Cloud of dust made by the Horses feet; it arose some Rods into the air over the tops of Hills and trees and when I came within about 20 rods of the Road, I could see men and horses Slipping along in the Cloud like shadows and as I drew nearer it seemed like a steady Stream of horses and their riders, scarcely a horse more than his length behind another, all of a Lather and foam with sweat, their breath rolling out of their nostrils every Jump; every horse seemed to go with all his might to carry his rider to hear news from heaven for the saving of Souls, it made me tremble to see the Sight, how the world was in a Struggle; I found a Vacancy between two horses to Slip in mine and my Wife said low our Clothes will be all spoiled see how they look, for they were so Covered with dust, that they looked almost all of a Colour Coats, hats, Shirts, and horses: We went down in the Stream but heard no man speak a word all the way for 3 miles but every one pressing forward in great haste and when we got to Middletown old meeting house there was a great Multitude it was said to be—3 or 4000 of people Assembled together; we dismounted and shook off our Dust; and the ministers were then Coming to the meeting house; I turned and looked towards the Great River and saw the ferry boats Running swift backward and forward bringing over loads of people and the Oars Rowed nimble and quick; every thing men horses and boats seemed to be Struggling for life. The land and banks over the river looked black with people and horses all along the 12 miles I saw no man at work in his field, but all seemed to be gone.

When I saw Mr. Whitfield come upon the Scaffold he looked almost Angelical; a young, Slim, slender, Youth before some thousands of people with a bold undaunted Countenance, and my hearing how God was with him every where as he came along it Solemnized my mind; and put me into a trembling fear before he began to preach; for he looked as if he was Clothed with Authority from the Great God; and a sweet, solemn solemnity sat upon his brow and my hearing him preach, gave me a heart wound; By Gods blessing: my old Foundation was broken up, and I saw that my righteousness would not save me; then I was convinced of the doctrine of Election: and went right to quarrelling with God about it; because that all I could do would not save me; and he had decreed from Eternity who should be saved and who not: I began to think I was not Elected, and that God made some for heaven and me for hell. And I thought God was not Just in so doing, I thought I did not stand on even Ground with others, if as I thought; I was made to be damned; My heart then rose against God exceedingly, for his making me for hell; Now this distress lasted almost two years:—Poor—Me—Miserable me.

It pleased God to bring on my Convictions more and more, and I was loaded with the guilt of Sin, I saw I was undone for ever; I carried Such a weight of Sin in my breast or mind, that it seemed to me as if I should sink into the ground every step; and I kept all to my self as much as I could; I went month after month mourning and begging for mercy, I tried every way I could think to help my self but all ways failed:—Poor me it took away most all my Comfort of eating, drinking, Sleeping, or working. Hell fire was most always in my mind; and I have hundreds of times put my fingers into my pipe when I have been smoking to feel how fire felt: And to see how my Body could bear to lye in Hell fire for ever and ever. Now my countenance was sad so that others took notice of it.

Nathan Cole, "The Spiritual Travels, 1741–1765," MSS 12787, Connecticut Historical Society, 2–7.

12

Revival at Cambuslang, Scotland

William McCulloch

IN DECEMBER 1741, the Scottish minister William McCulloch (1691–1771) launched *The Glasgow-Weekly History*, which initially reprinted news of transatlantic revivals appearing in other evangelical magazines. But by May 1742, he could give his readers a firsthand account of an unusual awakening taking place in Scotland. When McCulloch became the minister of Cambuslang in 1731, he could not have expected that his parish would be the site of Scotland's largest revival. Although esteemed by his parishioners, he was hardly a model preacher. In the biographical sketch that prefaced McCulloch's posthumous *Sermons on Several Subjects*, the editor wrote that his subject "was not a very ready speaker: though eminent for learning and piety, he was not eloquent...his manner was slow and cautious, very different from that of popular orators." Yet the combination of McCulloch's sermons on regeneration and George Whitefield's 1741 summer preaching tour in Scotland generated an extraordinary religious awakening at Cambuslang.

By the end of 1741, and into the early months of 1742, several parishioners at Cambuslang were in distress over the spiritual state of their souls. When waves of people flooded into Cambuslang in 1742, the revival intensified, causing McCulloch to enlist the help of ministers at several of the surrounding parish churches. After preaching in London in May, and at the invitation of McCulloch, Whitefield returned to Scotland in June 1742 to join a host of Scottish clergymen in facilitating a communion service that commenced on Friday, July 9 in which an estimated 20,000 to 30,000 people attended and 1,700 qualified (those given a token by their minister) communicants partook of the Lord's Supper. With the success of the first communion, the Edinburgh minister Alexander Webster proposed that a second service be held later that same summer. The crowds at the August 15 communion celebration purportedly surpassed the previous service with estimations in the range of 30,000 to 50,000 people and 3,000 communicants. Considering that the population of nearby Glasgow barely exceeded 17,000 people in 1740, the Cambuslang revival marks the most significant religious event in eighteenth-century Scottish history.

The Glasgow-Weekly History

"Part of a Letter from the Rev. Mr. McC—h"

Cambuslang, July 14, 1742

Our glorious *Emmanuel* is still going on to make numerous Conquests here. It is not yet quite five Months since this Work began in this Place: And in that Time I have reason to think (to his own Praise alone be it spoken who is the Author of this Work) that above 500 Souls have been awakened here, and brought under deep Convictions of Sin, and feeling Sense of their lost and perishing Condition without a Saviour, and are now mostly I believe savingly brought home to God. I do not in this Number include these that have been pretending to be under spiritual Distress, and have been discovered to be mere Counterfeits: Nor these that appeared to have nothing in their Exercise, but a Dread of Hell, which, you know, where it goes no further, never comes to any saving Issue. Some of both these Sorts there have been, but blessed be God, no great Number, so far as I could hitherto discern. Nor do I include these who have been awakened by Means of Mr. *Whitefield's* Sermons in this Place; because I cannot pretend to compute them. He has now preached 17 Sermons here since he came last to *Scotland*. He and Mr. *Webster* assisted at dispensing the Lord's Supper here, last Lord's Day, and the Day before and after, and were both much assisted and countenanced in their Sermons and Exhortations, and a more than ordinary Concern appeared among the People all along: And particularly the Time of Mr. *Whitefield's* Sermon on *Monday*, there was a very great Weeping and Mourning among the *Auditory*. Some reckoned there were more than 30,000 People here on *Sabbath* last: But a more moderate Computation with which Mr. *Wh—d*, who is used to such Things agrees, made them about 20,000. The Tables were below the Brae: The whole Work was without Doors in the open Air. There were two Tents, and two Ministers employ'd in speaking in different Places all Day, except in the Evening, when Mr. *Wh—d* alone preach'd to all the vast Multitude then present. The Tables or Services were 17 in Number, each except the last, which was not quite full, containing about 100 or more. And it appears by the Tokens gathered in from the Communicants at the Tables, that the whole Number of Communicants, was above 1700, I am persuaded that it was a blessed Time to very many. O come and let us sing a new Song to the Lord; for he hath done marvelous Things: His Right-hand and his Holy-arm hath won him the Victory. And yet, I am hopeful that we shall yet see and hear of far greater Things than these.

May the Lord send a plentiful Rain of Divine Influences to *Glasgow* his ancient Heritage, whereby multitudes in it may be made to look to him whom they have pierced and mourn,

W. McC—h

"An Account of the Second Sacrament at *Cambuslang*: In a Letter from Mr. *McCulloch* to a Brother"

Rev. and dear Brother,

YOU know that we had the Sacrament of the Lord's Supper dispens'd here, on the 11th of *July* last. It was such a sweet and agreeable Time to many, that a Motion was made by Mr. *Webster*, and immediately seconded by Mr. *Whitefield*, that we should have another such Occasion again in this Place very soon. The Motion was very agreeable to me, but I thought it needful to deliberate before coming to a Resolution. The Thing proposed was indeed extraordinary, but so had the Work in this Place been for several Months past. Care was therefore taken to acquaint the several Meetings for Prayer with the Motion, who relish'd it well, and pray'd for Direction to these concern'd to determine in this Matter. The Session met next Lord's- Day, and taking into Consideration the Divine Command to celebrate this Ordinance often, join'd with the Extraordinary Work that had been here for some Time past; and understanding, that many that had met with much Benefit to their Souls at the last Solemnity, had express'd their earnest Desires of seeing another in this Place shortly; and hearing that there were many who intended to have join'd at the last Occasion, but were kept back thro' inward Discouragements or outward Obstructions, and were wishing soon to see another Opportunity of that Kind here, to which they might have Access: It was therefore resolv'd (God willing) That the Sacrament of the Lord's Supper should be again dispens'd in this Parish on the 3rd *Sabbath* of *August* then next to come, being the 15th Day of that Month. And there was first one Day, and then another, at some Distance of Time from that, appointed for a general Meeting of the several Societies for Prayer in the Parish, at the Manse, who accordingly met there on the Days appointed, with some other Christians from Places in the Neighbourhood: And when the Manse sometimes could not conveniently hold them, they went to the Church; and at one of these Meetings, when Light failed them in the Church, a good Number, of their own free Motion, came again to the Manse, and continued at Prayers and Praises together, till about one o'clock next Morning.

The Design of these Meetings, and the Business which they were accordingly employ'd in (besides singing of *Psalms* and blessing the Name of God together) was to ask Mercy of the God of Heaven to ourselves: To pray for the *Seceders* and others, who unhappily oppose this Work of God here, and in some other Parts where it takes place; that God would forgive their Guilt in this Matter, open their

Eyes, remove their Prejudices, and convince them that it is indeed his Work, and give them Repentance to the acknowledgement of this Truth: That the Lord would continue and increase the blessed Work of Conviction and Conversion here, & in other Places where it is begun in a remarkable Measure, and extend it to all the Corners of the Land: And that he would eminently countenance the Dispensing of the Sacrament of the Holy Supper a second Time in this Place, and thereby to make the Glory of this Latter Solemnity to exceed that of the Former. Much of the Lord's gracious Presence was enjoy'd at these Meetings for Prayer, Returns of Mercy were vouchsaf'd in Part, and are still further expected and hoped for.

This second Sacrament Occasion did indeed much excel the Former, not only in the Number of Ministers People and Communicants, but, which is the main Thing, in a much greater Measure of the Power and special Presence of God, in the Observation and sensible Experience of Multitudes that were attending.

The Ministers that assisted at this Solemnity were Mr. *Whitefield*, Mr. *Webster* from *Edinburgh*, Mr. *McLaurin* and Mr. *Gillies* from *Glasgow*, Mr. *Robe* from *Kilsyth*, Mr. *Currie* from *Kinglassie*, Mr. *McKnight* from *Irvine*, Mr. *Bonar* from *Torphichen*, Mr. *Hamilton* from *Douglass*, and three of the Neighbouring Ministers, *viz*. Mr. *Henderson* from *Blantyre*, Mr. *Maxwell* from *Rutherglen*, and Mr. *Adam* from *Cathcart*. All of them appear'd to be very much assisted in their Work. Four of them preach'd on the Fast-day, four on *Saturday*, on *Sabbath* I cannot well tell how many, and five on *Monday*, on which last Day it was computed that above 24 Ministers and Preachers were present. Old Mr. *Bonar*, tho' so frail that he took three Days to ride 18 Miles from *Torphichen* to *Cambuslang*, yet his Heart was so set upon coming here, that he could by no Means stay away, and when he was help'd up to the Tent, preach'd three Times with great Life; and return'd with much Satisfaction and Joy. Mr. *Whitefield*'s Sermons on *Saturday, Sabbath and Monday*, were attended with much Power, particularly on *Sabbath* Night about 10, and that on *Monday*, several crying out, and a very great but decent Weeping and Mourning was observable thro' the Auditory. On *Sabbath* Evening while he was serving some Tables, he appear'd to be so filled with the Love of God, as to be in a Kind of Ecstasy or Transport, and communicated with much of that blessed Frame. Time would fail me to speak of the Evidences of the Power of God coming along with the rest of the Assistants: And I am in Part prevented by what is noticed by Mr. *Robe* in his *Narrative*.

The Number of People that were there on *Saturday* and *Monday*, was very considerable. But the Number present at the three Tents on the Lord's-Day was so great, that, so far as I can hear, none ever saw the like since the Revolution in *Scotland*, or even any where else, at any Sacrament Occasion: Some have called them fifty Thousand; some forty Thousand; the lowest Estimate I hear of, with which Mr. *Whitefield* agrees, who has been much us'd to great Multitudes, and forming a Judgment of their Number, makes them to have been upwards of thirty Thousand.

The Number of Communicants appears to have been about three Thousand. The Tables were double, and the double Table was reckoned to contain 114, or 116, or 120 Communicants. The Number of Tables I reckoned had been but 24: But I have been since inform'd, That a Man who sat near the Tables and kept a Pen in his Hand, and carefully marked each Service with his Pen, assur'd that there were 25 double Tables or Services, the last Table wanting only 5 or 6 Persons to fill it up. And this Account seems indeed the most probable, as agreeing nearly with the Number of Tokens distributed, which was about 3,000. And some worthy of Credit, and that had proper Opportunities to know, gave it as their Opinion, that there was such a blessed Frame fell upon the People, that if there had been Access to get Tokens, there would have been a Thousand more Communicants than what were.

This vast Concourse of People, you may easily imagine, came not only from the City of *Glasgow*, and other Places near by, but from many Places at a considerable Distance: It was reckoned there were 200 Communicants from *Edinburgh*, 200 from *Kilmarnock*, 100 from *Irvine*, 100 from *Stewarton*. It was observed, That there were some from *England* and *Ireland* here at this Occasion: A considerable Number of *Quakers* were Hearers: A great many of these that had formerly been *Seceders* were hearing the Word, and several of them were Communicants. A Youth that has a near View to the Ministry, and had been for some Time under great Temptations, that God's Presence was no more to be enjoy'd, either in the Church, or among the *Seceders*, Communicated here, and returned with great Joy, full of the Love of God.

There was a great deal of outward Decency and Regularity observable about the Tables. Public Worship began on the Lord's-day just at half past Eight in the Morning. My Action Sermon, I think, was reasonably short: The third or 4*th* Table was a Serving at 12 o'clock: And the last Table was a Serving about Sun-set, when that was done, the Work was clos'd with a few Words of Exhortation Prayer and Praise, the Precenter having so much Day-light as to let him see to read four Lines of a *Psalm*. The Passes to and from the Tables, were with great Care kept clear, for the Communicants to come and go. The Tables fill'd so quickly, that oftimes there was no more Time between one Table and another, but to sing four Lines of a *Psalm*. The Tables were all serv'd in the open Air, beside the Tent, below the Brae: The Day was Temperate: No Wind or Rain in the least to disturb. Several Persons of considerable Rank and Distinction who were Elders, most cheerfully assisted our Elders in serving the Tables...

But what was most remarkable, was the spiritual Glory of this Solemnity, I mean the gracious and sensible Presence of God. Not a few were awakened to a Sense of Sin, and their lost and perishing Condition without a Saviour. Others had their Bands loos'd, and were brought into the marvelous Liberty of the Sons of God. Many of God's dear Children have declared, That it was a happy Time to their

Souls, where in they were abundantly satisfied with the Goodness of God in his Ordinances, and filled with all Joy and Peace in Believing. I have seen a Letter from *Edinburgh*, the Writer of which says, "That having talk'd with many Christians in that City, who had been here at this Sacrament, they all own'd, That God had dealt bountifully with their Souls at this Occasion." Some that attended here, declared, That they would not for a World have been absent from this Solemnity. Others cry'd, Now let thy Servants depart in Peace, from this Place, since our Eyes have seen thy Salvation here. Others wishing, If it were the Will of God, to die where they were attending God in his Ordinances, without ever returning again to the World or their Friends, that they might be with Christ in Heaven, as that which is incomparably best of all.

I thought it my Duty to offer these few Hints concerning this Solemnity, and to record the Memory of God's great Goodness to many Souls at that Occasion. And now, I suppose you'll by this Time, find yourself dispos'd to sing the 98 *Psalm* at the Beginning, or the Close of the 72 *Psalm*, or some other *Psalm* of Praise. May our exalted Redeemer still go on from Conquering to Conquer, `till the whole Earth be filled with his Glory. *Amen*, so let it be. In him *I am yours, &c.*

William McCulloch, *The Glasgow Weekly History: Or, An Account of the Most Remarkable Particulars Relating to the Progress of the Gospel* (Glasgow: William Duncan, 1743), No. 30, 1–2; No. 39, 1–7.

13

Overcome by the Power of the Spirit

Sarah Pierpont Edwards

DURING THE GREAT Awakening, many people reported experiencing unusual emotional stirrings, including fainting, crying, and other bodily manifestations attributed to the work of the Holy Spirit. Perhaps one of the most surprising accounts came from the wife of Jonathan Edwards, Sarah Pierpont Edwards (1710–58). Sarah Pierpont descended from a distinguished family of ministers in New England. Born in New Haven, Connecticut, her great-grandfather was Thomas Hooker, who helped found the colony of Connecticut and New Haven's first church, where her father, the Reverend James Pierpont, served for thirty years. Deeply impressed by her piety at an early age, Jonathan Edwards eventually wed the girl who had captivated him when she was thirteen. Married in 1727, Sarah Edwards went on to have a total of eleven children, eight girls and three boys within the span of twenty-two years. With Edwards secluded from his family on most days—preparing his sermons, corresponding with friends, reading his Bible and the latest religious texts, composing his many philosophical and theological works, and praying—his devoted wife took charge of the household duties and care of the children.

As Edwards gained a reputation as a revivalist in the early 1740s, churches outside his parish at Northampton began inviting him to come and speak. On one occasion while he was preaching to a congregation in Leicester, Massachusetts in 1742, Sarah Edwards experienced a memorable "season of grace" that her great-grandson, Sereno Edwards Dwight, published later in his *Life of President Edwards* (1830). Overwhelmed with emotion, she recorded fainting in the midst of a rapturous joy and lying on a bed for hours as her body recovered from physical exhaustion. This was not her conversion experience, for that had taken place earlier at age six. Rather, this season is best understood as a spiritual renewal, a time in her life when she had given herself over completely to the will of God while earnestly desiring a revival at Northampton. She had given up the notion of safeguarding her husband's character among the townsfolk, now hoping that an effusion of the

FIGURE 13.1 Mrs. Jonathan Edwards by Joseph Badger (Detail), Yale University Art Gallery, bequest of Eugene Phelps Edwards.

Holy Spirit would come under the auspices of Samuel Buell, the visiting minister who came to Northampton to fill in for her absent husband. Episodes like the one that took place with his wife convinced Jonathan Edwards of the power that religious affections could have on a person overcome by the Spirit.

"Uncommon Discoveries of the Divine Perfections and Glory"

On Tuesday night, Jan. 19, 1742, I felt very uneasy and unhappy, at my being so low in grace. I thought I very much needed help from God, and found a spirit of earnestness to seek help of him, that I might have more holiness. When I had for a time been earnestly wrestling with God for it, I felt within myself great quietness of spirit, unusual submission to God, and willingness to wait upon him, with respect to the time and manner in which he should help me, and wished that he should take his own time, and his own way, to do it.

The next morning, I found a degree of uneasiness in my mind, at Mr. Edwards's suggesting, that he thought I had failed in some measure in point of prudence, in some conversation I had with Mr. Williams of Hadley, the day before. I found, that it seemed to bereave me of the quietness and calm of my mind, in any respect not to have the good opinion of my husband. This, I much disliked in myself, as arguing a want of a sufficient rest in God, and felt a disposition to fight against it, and look to God for his help, that I might have a more full and entire rest in him, independent of all other things. I continued in this frame, from early in the morning until about 10 o'clock, at which time the Rev. Mr. [Peter] Reynolds went to prayer in the family.

I had before this, so entirely given myself up to God, and resigned up every thing into his hands, that I had, for a long time, felt myself quite alone in the world; so that the peace and calm of my mind, and my rest in God, as my only and all sufficient happiness, seemed sensibly above the reach of disturbance from any thing but these two: 1st. My own good name and fair reputation among men, and especially the esteem and just treatment of the people of this town; 2dly. And more especially, the esteem, and love and kind treatment of my husband. At times, indeed, I had seemed to be considerably elevated above the influence of even these things; yet I had not found my calm, and peace and rest in God so sensibly, fully and constantly, above the reach of disturbance from them, until now.

While Mr. Reynolds was at prayer in the family this morning, I felt an earnest desire that, in calling on God, he should say, *Father*, or that he should address the Almighty under that appellation: on which the thought turned in my mind—Why can I say, *Father*?—Can I now at this time, with the confidence of a child, and without the least misgiving of heart, call God my Father?—This brought to my mind, two lines of Mr. [Ralph] Erskine's Sonnet:

> "*I see him lay his vengeance by,*
> *And smile in Jesus' face.*"

I was thus deeply sensible, that my sins did loudly call for vengeance; but I then by faith saw God "lay his vengeance by, and smile in Jesus' face." It appeared to be real and certain that he did so. I had not the least doubt, that he then sweetly smiled upon me, with the look of forgiveness and love, having laid aside all his displeasure towards me, for Jesus' sake; which made me feel very weak, and somewhat faint.

In consequence of this, I felt a strong desire to be alone with God, to go to him, without having any one to interrupt the silent and soft communion, which I earnestly desired between God and my own soul; and accordingly withdrew to my chamber. It should have been mentioned that, before I retired, while Mr. Reynolds was praying, these words, in Romans 8:34, came into my mind, "*Who is he that condemneth; It is Christ that died, yea rather that is risen again, who is even at the right hand of God, who also maketh intercession for us;*" as well as the following words, "*Who shall separate us from the love of Christ,*" etc.; which I occasioned great sweetness and delight in my soul. But when I was alone, the words came to my mind with far greater power and sweetness; upon which I took the Bible, and read the words to the end of the chapter, when they were impressed on my heart with vastly greater power and sweetness still. They appeared to me with undoubted certainty as the words of God, and as words which God did pronounce concerning me. I had no more doubt of it, than I had of my being. I seemed as it were to hear the great God proclaiming thus to the world concerning me; "*Who shall lay any thing to thy charge,*" etc.; and had it strongly impressed on me, how impossible it was for any thing in heaven or earth, in this world or the future, ever to separate me from the love of God which was in Christ Jesus. I cannot find language to express, how *certain* this appeared—the everlasting mountains and hills were but shadows to it. My safety, and happiness, and eternal enjoyment of God's immutable love, seemed as durable and unchangeable as God himself. Melted and overcome by the sweetness of this assurance, I fell into a great flow of tears, and could not forbear weeping aloud. It appeared certain to me that God was my Father, and Christ my Lord and Saviour, that he was mind and I his. Under a delightful sense of the immediate presence and love of God, these words seemed to come over and over in my mind, "My God, my all; my God, my all." The presence of God was so near, and so real, that I seemed scarcely conscious of any thing else. God the father, and the Lord Jesus Christ, seemed as distinct persons, both manifesting their inconceivable loveliness, and mildness, and gentleness, and their great and immutable love to me. I seemed to be taken under the care and charge of my God and Saviour, in an inexpressibly endearing manner; and Christ appeared to me as a mighty Saviour, under the character of the Lion of the Tribe of Judah, taking my heart, with all its corruptions, under his care, and putting it at his feet. In all things, which concerned me, I felt myself safe under the protection of the Father and the Saviour; who appeared with supreme kindness to keep a record of every thing that I did, and of every thing that was done to me, purely for my good.

The peace and happiness, which I hereupon felt, was altogether inexpressible. It seemed to be that which came from heaven; to be eternal and unchangeable. I seemed to be lifted above earth and hell, out of the reach of every thing here below, so that I could look on all the rage and enmity of men or devils, with a kind of holy indifference, and an undisturbed tranquility. At the same time, I felt compassion and love for all mankind, and a deep abasement of soul, under a sense of my own unworthiness. I thought of the ministers who were in the house, and felt willing to undergo any labour and self-denial, if they would but come to the help of the Lord. I also felt myself more perfectly weaned from all things here below, than ever before. The whole world, with all its enjoyments, and all its troubles, seemed to be nothing—My God was my all, my only portion. No possible suffering appeared to be worth regarding: all persecutions and torments were a mere nothing. I seemed to dwell on high, and the place of defence to be the munition of rocks.

After some time, the two evils mentioned above, as those which I should have been least able to bear, came to my mind—the ill treatment of the town, and the ill will of my husband; but now I was carried exceedingly above even such things as these, and I could feel that, if I were exposed to them both, they would seem comparatively nothing. There was then a deep snow on the ground, and I could think of being driven from my home into the cold and snow, of being chased from the town with the utmost contempt and malice, and of being left to perish with the cold, as cast out by all the world, with perfect calmness and serenity. It appeared to me, that it would not move me, or in the least disturb the inexpressible happiness and peace of my soul. My mind seemed as much above all such things, as the sun is above the earth.

I continued in a very sweet and lively sense of divine things, day and night, sleeping and waking, until Saturday, Jan. 23. On Saturday morning, I had a most solemn and deep impression on my mind of the eye of God as fixed upon me, to observe what improvement I made of those spiritual communications I had received from him; as well as of the respect shown Mr. Edwards, who had then been sent for to preach at Leicester. I was sensible that I was sinful enough to bestow it on my pride, or on my sloth, which seemed exceedingly dreadful to me. At night, my soul seemed to be filled with an inexpressibly sweet and pure love to God, and to the children of God; with a refreshing consolation and solace of soul, which made me willing to lie on the earth, at the feet of the servants of God, to declare his gracious dealings with me, and breathe forth before them my love, and gratitude and praise.

The next day, which was the Sabbath, I enjoyed a sweet, and lively and assured sense of God's infinite grace, and favour and love to me, in taking me out of the depths of hell, and exalting me to the heavenly glory, and the dignity of a royal priesthood.

On Monday night, Mr. Edwards, being gone that day to Leicester, I heard that Mr. Buell was coming to this town, and from what I had heard of him, and of his success, I had strong hopes that there would be great effects from his labours here. At the same time, I had a deep and affecting impression, that the eye of God was ever upon my heart, and that it greatly concerned me to watch my heart, and see to it that I was perfectly resigned to God, with respect to the instruments he should make use of to revive religion in this town, and be entirely willing, if it was God's pleasure, that he should make use of Mr. Buell; and also that other Christians should appear to excel me in Christian experience, and in the benefit they should derive from ministers. I was conscious, that it would be exceedingly provoking to God if I should not be thus resigned, and earnestly endeavoured to watch my heart, that no feelings of a contrary nature might arise; and was enabled, as I thought, to exercise full resignation, and acquiescence in God's pleasure, as to these things. I was sensible what great cause I had to bless God, for the use he had made of Mr. Edwards hitherto; but thought, if he never blessed his labours any more, and should greatly bless the labours of other ministers, I could entirely acquiesce in his will. It appeared to me meet and proper, that God should employ babes and sucklings to advance his kingdom. When I thought of these things, it was my instinctive feeling to say, "Amen, Lord Jesus! Amen, Lord Jesus!" This seemed to be the sweet and instinctive language of my soul.

On Tuesday, I remained in a sweet and lively exercise of this resignation, and love to and rest in God, seeming to be in my heart from day to day, far above the reach of every thing here below. On Tuesday night, especially the latter part of it, I felt a great earnestness of soul and engagedness in seeking God for the town, that religion might now revive, and that God would bless Mr. Buell to that end. God seemed to be very near to me while I was thus striving with him for these things, and I had a strong hope that what I sought of him would be granted. There seemed naturally and unavoidably to arise in my mind an assurance, that now God would do great things for Northampton.

On Wednesday morning, I heart that Mr. Buell arrived the night before at Mr. Phelps's, and that there seemed to be great tokens and effects of the presence of God there, which greatly encouraged, and rejoiced me. About an hour and a half after, Mr. Buell came to our house, I sat still in entire resignedness to God, and willingness that God should bless his labours here as much as he pleased; though it were to the enlivening of every saint, and to the conversion of every sinner, in the town. These feelings continued afterwards, when I saw his great success; as I never felt the least rising of heart to the contrary, but my submission was even and uniform, without interruption or disturbance. I rejoiced when I saw the honour which God put upon him, and the respect paid him by the people, and the greater success attending his preaching, than had followed the preaching of Mr. Edwards immediately before he went to Leicester. I found rest and rejoicing in it, and the sweet language of my soul continually was, "Amen, Lord Jesus! Amen, Lord Jesus."

At 3 o'clock in the afternoon, a lecture was preached by Mr. Buell. In the latter part of the sermon, one or two appeared much moved, and after the blessing, when the people were going out, several others. To my mind there was the clearest evidence, that God was present in the congregation, on the work of redeeming love; and in the clear view of this, I was all at once filled with such intense admiration of the wonderful condescension and grace of God, in returning again to Northampton, as overwhelmed my soul, and immediately took away my bodily strength. This was accompanied with an earnest longing, that those of us, who were the children of God, might now arise and strive. It appeared to me, that the angels in heaven sung praises, for such wonderful, free and sovereign grace, and my heart was lifted up in adoration and praise. I continued to have clear views of the future world, of eternal happiness and misery, and my heart full of love to the souls of men. On seeing some, that I found were in a natural condition, I felt a most tender compassion for them; but especially was I, while I remained in the meeting-house, from time to time overcome, and my strength taken away, by the sight of one and another, whom I regarded as the children of God, and who, I had heard were lively and animated in religion. We remained in the meeting-house about three hours, after the public exercises were over. During most of the time, my bodily strength was overcome; and the joy and thankfulness, which were excited in my mind, as I contemplated the great goodness of God, led me to converse with those who were near me, in a very earnest manner.

When I came home, I found Mr. Buell, Mr. Christophers, Mr. Hopkins, Mrs. Eleanor Dwight, the wife of Mr. Joseph Allen, and Mr. Job Strong, at the house. Seeing and conversing with them on the Divine goodness, renewed my former feelings, and filled me with an intense desire that we might all arise, and, with an active flowing and fervent heart, give glory to God. The intenseness of my feelings again took away my bodily strength. The words of one of Dr. Watts's Hosannas powerfully affected me; and, in the course of the conversation, I uttered them, as the real language of my heart, with great earnestness and emotion.

> *"Hosanna to King David's Son,*
> *Who reigns on a superior throne," &c.*

And while I was uttering the words, my mind was so deeply impressed with the love of Christ, and a sense of his immediate presence, that I could with difficulty refrain from rising from my seat, and leaping for joy. I continued to enjoy this intense, and lively and refreshing sense of Divine things, accompanied with strong emotions, for nearly an hour; after which, I experienced a delightful calm, and peace and rest in God, until I retired for the night; and during the night, both waking and sleeping, I had joyful views of Divine things, and a complacential rest of soul in God. I awoke in the morning of Thursday, [January] 28th, in the same happy frame of mind, and engaged in the duties of my family with a sweet consciousness, that God was present with me, and with earnest longings of soul for the continuance, and increase, of the blessed fruits of the Holy Spirit in the town. About nine o'clock, these desires became so exceedingly intense, when I saw numbers of the people coming into the house, with an appearance of deep interest in religion, that my bodily strength was much weakened, and it was with difficulty that I could pursue my ordinary avocations. About 11 o'clock, as I accidentally went into the room where Mr. Buell was conversing with some of the people, I heard him say, "O that we, who are the children of God, should be cold and lifeless in religion!" and I felt such a sense of the deep ingratitude manifested by the children of God, in such coldness and deadness, that my strength was immediately taken away, and I sunk down on the spot. Those who were near raised me, and placed me in a chair; and, from the fullness of my heart, I expressed to them, in a very earnest manner, the deep sense I had of the wonderful grace of Christ towards me, of the assurance I had of his having saved me from hell, of my happiness running parallel with eternity, of the duty of giving up all to God, and of the peace and joy inspired by an entire dependence on his mercy and grace. Mr. Buell then read a melting hymn of Dr. Watts, concerning the loveliness of Christ, the enjoyments and employments of heaven, and the Christian's earnest desire of heavenly things; and the truth and reality of the things mentioned in the hymn, made so strong an impression on my mind, and my soul was drawn so powerfully towards Christ and heaven, that I leaped unconsciously from my chair. I seemed to be drawn upwards, soul and body, from the earth towards heaven; and it appeared to me that I must naturally and necessarily ascend thither. These feelings continued while the hymn was reading, and during the prayer of Mr. Christophers, which followed. After the prayer, Mr. Buell read two other hymns, on the glories of heaven, which moved me so exceedingly, and drew me so strongly heavenward, that it seemed as it were to draw my body upwards, and I felt as if I must necessarily ascend thither. At length my strength failed me, and I sunk down; when they took me up and laid me on the bed, where I lay for a considerable time, faint with joy, while contemplating the glories of the heavenly world. After I had lain a while, I felt more perfectly subdued and weaned from the world, and more fully resigned to God, than I had ever been conscious of before. I felt an entire indifference to the opinions, and representations and conduct of mankind respecting me; and a perfect willingness, that God should employ some other instrument than Mr. Edwards, in advancing the work of grace in Northampton. I was entirely swallowed up in God, as my only portion, and his honour and glory was the object of my supreme desire and delight. At the same time, I felt a far greater love to the children of God, than ever before. I seemed to love them as my own soul; and when I saw them, my heart went out towards them, with an inexpressible endearedness and sweetness. I beheld them by faith in their risen and glorified state, with spiritual bodies re-fashioned after the image of Christ's glorious body, and arrayed in the beauty of heaven. The time when they would be so, appeared very near, and by faith it seemed as if it were present. This was accompanied with a ravishing sense of the unspeakable joys of the upper world. They appeared to my mind in all their reality and certainty, and as it were in actual and distinct vision; so plain and evident were they to the eye of my faith, I seemed to regard them as begun. These anticipations were renewed over and over, while I lay on the bed, from twelve o'clock till four, being too much exhausted by emotions of joy, to rise and sit up; and during most of the time, my feelings prompted me to converse very earnestly, with one and another of the pious women, who were present, on those spiritual and heavenly objects, of which I had so deep an impression. A little while before I arose, Mr. Buell and the people went to meeting.

I continued in a sweet and lively sense of Divine things, until I retired to rest. That night, which was Thursday night, January 28, was the sweetest night I ever had in my life. I never before, for so long a time together, enjoyed so much of the light, and rest and sweetness of heaven in my soul, but without the least agitation of body during the whole time. The great part of the night I lay awake, sometimes asleep, and sometimes between sleeping and waking. But all night I continued in a constant, clear and lively sense of the heavenly sweetness of Christ's excellent and transcendent love, of his nearness to me, and of my dearness to him; with an inexpressibly sweet calmness of soul in an entire rest in him. I seemed to myself to perceive a glow of divine love come down from the heart of Christ in heaven, into my heart, in a constant stream, like a stream or pencil of sweet light. At the same time, my heart and soul all flowed out in love to Christ; so that there seemed to be a constant flowing and reflowing of heavenly and divine love, from Christ's heart to mine; and I appeared to myself to float or swim, in these bright, sweet beams of the love of Christ, like the motes swimming in the beams of the sun, or the streams of his light which come in at the window. My soul remained in a kind of heavenly elysium. So far as I am capable of making a comparison, I think that what I felt each minute, during the continuance of the whole time, was worth more than all the outward comfort and pleasure, which I had enjoyed in my whole life put together. It was a pure delight, which fed and satisfied the soul. It was pleasure, without the least sting, or any interruption. It was a sweetness, which my soul was lost in. It seemed to be all that my feeble frame could sustain, of that fullness of joy, which is felt by those, who behold the face of Christ, and share his love in the heavenly world. There was but little difference, whether I was asleep or awake, so deep was the impression made on my soul; but if there was any difference, the sweetness was greatest and most uninterrupted, while I was asleep.

Sarah Pierpont Edwards, "Uncommon Discoveries of the Divine Perfections and Glory," in Sereno Edwards Dwight, *The Life of President Edwards* (New York: G. & C. & H. Carvill, 1830), 171–79.

14

Revival at Kilsyth, Scotland

James Robe

DURING THE SAME year that the revival at Cambuslang transpired, the town of Kilsyth in western Scotland also witnessed an outpouring of the Spirit in the spring of 1742. The minister of Kilsyth, James Robe (1688–1753), provided a thorough narrative of the "surprising dispensation of grace" at his parish, arguing that it was a continuation of the earlier Cambuslang revival and that it fit within the larger transatlantic awakenings taking place at roughly the same time. In the preface, and subtly throughout his *Faithful Narrative of the Extraordinary Work of the Spirit of God, at Kilsyth*, Robe took great pains to sketch the revival at Kilsyth and the neighboring communities as orderly and free of "enthusiasm." Admitting that several of the awakened trembled, fainted, and convulsed under the work of God's grace, Robe put forward the rejoinder that several others had experienced authentic conversions that exhibited none of the more excessive symptoms.

Robe's *Narrative* paints the picture of a parish in which very few people were interested in godliness prior to 1742 and where brief periods of religious interest soon faded into complacency and indifference. When revival came to Scotland at Cambuslang in the late winter of 1742, and spread to the surrounding communities, Robe could not help but feel disappointed that his church remained stubbornly aloof to the spiritual vibrancy transpiring elsewhere. "It was [a] matter of discouragement to me," he wrote in the *Narrative*, "when I heard that my brethren in Cumbernauld, Kirkintilloch, Calder, and Campsie, had several persons in their parishes awakened at Cambuslang, and that I had not one, so much as the least touched to my knowledge." The situation changed quite dramatically, however, in May 1742 when Kilsyth melted under the same holy fires that had consumed the nearby Scottish towns. Indeed, the awakening at Kilsyth was second only to that at Cambuslang, in terms of the numbers present. George Whitfield boasted to a correspondent that over 10,000 people heard him speak at Kilsyth, a parish numbering slightly more than 1,000 people at that time.

A *Faithful Narrative of the Extraordinary Work of the Spirit of God, at Kilsyth*

THE Town and Parish of *Kilsyth*, formerly, and ordinarily until of late, called *Moniabroch*, are situated between the River of *Kelvin*, running upon the *South* side of the said Parish, and the River of *Carron*, running upon the *North* side, and the Shire of *Sterling* upon the *South* side thereof, where it joins with the Shire of *Dumbarton*. The Town of *Kilsyth* itself, stands at near an equal Distance from the City of *Glasgow* upon the *South-west*, *Falkirk* upon the *East*, *Stirling* upon the *North*, and *Hamilton* upon the *South*; upon the King's Highway where it crosseth to these Towns: Its Distance from them being about *nine Miles*.

THE People of the said Parish, being above *eleven hundred examinable Persons*, are for the most part of a discreet and towardly Disposition. I was settled among them in the Year 1713, they have lived peaceably with, and carried it dutifully towards me. The most part of them have attended upon public Ordinances, and Means of Instruction, as well as any about them. The most of them, who are about, or under 40 Years, have attained such a Measure of Knowledge of the Principles of Religion, as renders them inferior to few of their Station and Education.

FOR several Years they appeared to profit under Gospel Ordinances, by the Blessing of the Lord upon them. In *December*, 1732, and *January*, 1733, the Lord visited us with a distressing Calamity, and heavy Judgments. There were many of the elder Sort carried off by a *Pleuretick Fever*, after a few Days Illness. Upward of 60 were in the Space of *three Weeks* buried in our Church-yard. What made this Dispensation more threatening was, that the most religious and judicious Christians in this Congregation, were removed from us thereby. This made me fear some dreadful Evil to come upon the surviving Generation. I published to the Praise and Glory of God, and with thankful Acknowledgments to his Mercy and Power, that I enjoyed then a State of Health and Strength uncommon to me, as I do at this Time, tho' I travelled from Morning, till late at Night, all the Days of the Week, among the Sick and Dying.

AFTER this the State of Religion declin'd, and grew every Year worse with us. Our *Societies* for Prayer came gradually to nothing. The younger Sort attained indeed to Knowledge took up a Profession, and Numbers of them were yearly added to the Communicants: But I could observe little of the Power of Godliness in their Lives, that was satisfying to me. As to the elder Sort, those of them who were Graceless, and Christless, went on in their former Sins and Carelessness, without any Appearance of a Change for the better: Those who were Professors, seemed sensibly to degenerate into a Negligence, and Indifference, about spiritual Things, and some of them into Drunkenness, and other Vices...

In the Year 1740, I began to preach upon the Doctrine of *Regeneration*. The Method I followed, by the divine Direction, was *first*, to press the Importance and

Necessity of it, which I did from *John* 3:3. *Except a Man be born again, he cannot see the Kingdom of God. Next,* I shewed the Mysteriousness of the Way and Manner of the Holy Spirit in effecting it, from *John* 3:8. *The Wind bloweth where it listeth, and thou hearest the Sound thereof, but canst not tell whence it cometh, and whither it goeth: So is every one that is born of the Spirit.* I proceeded *thirdly,* to explain, and apply the various Scripture Views, and Expressions of it: As (*first*) being born again; from the forequoted, *John* 3:3. (*Secondly*) a Resurrection, from *Revelations* 20:6. *Blessed and Holy is he, that hath part in the first Resurrection.* (*Thirdly*) a new Creation, from *Ephesians* 2:10. *For we are his Workmanship, created in Christ Jesus unto good Works.* (*Fourthly*) Christ's Conquest of the Sinner to himself, from *Psalm* 110:3. *Thy People shall be willing in the Day of thy Power.* (*Fifthly*) the Circumcision of the Heart, from *Ezekiel* 44:9. *Thus saith the Lord God, no Stranger uncircumcised in Heart, nor uncircumcised in Flesh, shall enter into my Sanctuary, of any Stranger among the Children of Israel.* This was also intended to shew the Necessity of Regeneration, in order to the Receiving the Lord's Supper worthily, to be dispensed in the Congregation about that Time. Here this Project was interrupted until the End of the last Year; when I resuming it, preached Regeneration as it is. (*Sixthly*) the taking away the stony Heart, and the giving the Heart of Flesh, from *Ezekiel* 11:19. (*Seventhly*) *The putting God's Law in the Mind, and Writing it in the Heart,* from *Hebrews* 8:10.

I sometimes could observe, that the Doctrine of these Sermons was acceptable to the Lord's People, and that there was more than ordinary Seriousness in hearing them, yet could see no other Fruit. But now I find, that the Lord who is infinitely Wise, and knoweth the End from the Beginning, was preparing some for this uncommon Dispensation of the Spirit *that we look'd not for;* and that others were brought under Convictions, issuing by the Power of the Highest, in their real Conversion, and in a silent Way.

WHEN the News were first brought me, of the extraordinary Out-pourings of the *Holy Ghost* at Cambuslang, I rejoiced at them. I pray'd continually for the Continuance of it there, and that the Lord would thus visit us in *these Bounds* and spake of it sometimes to the Congregation, which was not without some good Fruit, as I have learn'd since. Particularly I was informed by the Minister of *Cambuslang,* and another Reverend, and very dear Brother, that a young Man, from the Parish of *Falkirk,* who had been awakened at *Cambuslang,* and was in a hopeful Condition, said, that the Occasion of his coming there, was his hearing me, the Sabbath immediately preceding, praise the Appearance of the Lord at the foresaid Place, and that this strongly inclined him to go thither.

THERE were few of the People under my Charge, went to *Cambuslang,* notwithstanding of what they heard me say of it. Some of the better Sort went *once* or *twice:* But I scarce heard of any, who needed most of the Work of the *Comforter,* to convince them of Sin, Righteousness, and of Judgment, that went there, until the 13th of *May,* when there were a good many, but came all away (as far as I knew them) without any deep, or lasting Impressions upon them. It was [a] Matter of Discouragement to me, when I heard that my Brethren in *Cumbernauld, Kirkintilloch, Calder,* and *Campsie,* had several Persons in their Parishes awakened at *Cambuslang,* and that I had not one, so much as the least touch'd to my Knowledge. What appeared the most hopeful was, that there appeared a Concern, more than ordinary, among the Hearers of the Gospel, and that there were Proposals for setting up *Societies for Prayer,* which had been long intermitted.

UPON the *Thursday*'s Evening, being the 15th of *April* last, the Rev. *John Willison,* Minister of the Gospel at *Dundee,* came to my House, in his Return from *Cambuslang,* whither he went the *Saturday* before. I desired him to preach to us upon the *Friday* Morning, which he readily complied with; a great Multitude of People met, tho' the Warning was very short. He preached a distinct, plain, and moving Sermon, from *Psalm* 40:2–3. *He brought me up also out of an horrible Pit, out of the miry Clay, and set my Feet upon a Rock, and established my goings. And he hath put a new Song in my Mouth, even Praise to our God: Many shall see it, and fear, and shall trust in the Lord.* Several of those now awakened, date their first serious Concern about their Souls, from their hearing this Sermon, and the Blessing of the Lord upon it.

THE following *Sabbath,* I entered upon the View of *Regeneration,* as it is expressed [in] *Galatians* 4:19. *My little Children, of whom I travail in Birth again, until Christ be formed in you.* I had more than ordinary Tenderness in reading of that Text, and could scarce do it without Tears, and Emotion. I observed much Seriousness among the Hearers.

LAST *Sabbath* of *April,* being the 25th, one Woman was awakened in this Congregation, to a very distressing Sight of her Sin, and Danger thereby. She lived in the Parish of *Campsie,* which lieth to the Westward of this Parish. She was observed by some, under great Uneasiness in the Congregation, but made no Out-cry: She went away when the Congregation was dismiss'd, but was not able to go far, she was found soon in the Field, in great Distress, and crying out *what she should do [to] be saved!* She was brought back to me, and I convers'd with her all that Evening, in the Presence of several judicious Persons. She fainted *once,* or *twice.* I observed every Thing narrowly, and exactly about her, because it was a new Thing to me, and I knew the Objections made against the Work at *Cambuslang.* She seem'd to be a healthy Woman, and about 20 Years of Age; she said that in hearing the Sermon, she was made to see, that she was unlike *Jesus Christ,* and like the *Devil,* and in a *State of Unregeneracy.* She had strong Impressions of the Greatness of the Wrath of God, she was lying under, and liable to. She went away composed and calm, in a hopeful Condition; she continued many Weeks, now and then much distress'd; but hath some Time ago, attained (thro' Grace) to sensible

Relief, and by the Testimony of the Neighbourhood, *her Conversation is such as becometh the Gospel*...

MAY 16th, I preached (as I had done for some Time past) from *Galatians* 4:19. In the *Forenoon*, I insisted upon a Use of Consolation, and in the *Afternoon*, pressed all the Unregenerate to seek to have *Christ formed in them*. An extraordinary Power of the Spirit from on high, accompanied the Word preached. There was a great Mourning in the Congregation, *as for an only Son*. Many cried out, and these not only Women, but some strong, and stouthearted young Men, and some betwixt *forty* and *fifty*.

AFTER the Dismission of the Congregation, an Essay was made to get the distressed into my Barn, but it could not be done; the Number of them, and of their Friends attending them, was so many. I was obliged to convene them into the Church. I sung a Psalm, and prayed with them; but when I essayed to speak to them, I could not be heard, such were their bitter Cries, Groans, and the Voice of their Weeping.

AFTER this, I ordered that they should be brought unto me into my Closet, one by one. I sent also for the Rev. Mr. *John Oughterson*, Minister of the Gospel at *Cumbernauld*, to assist me in dealing with the Distressed that Evening, who readily came. In the mean time, I appointed *Psalms* to be sung with these in the Church, and that the *Precenter*, with *two* or *three* of the *Elders*, should pray with the Distressed; which the Extraordinariness of this Event, seemed to me to warrant. At the same Time, I forbid any to exhort, or speak to them in the Congregation, that I might cut off Occasion of Calumny and Objection, from them who seemed to desire it.

THE Noise of the Distressed was so great, that it was heard from afar. It was pleasant to hear these who were in a State of *Enmity* with God, Despisers of *Jesus Christ*, and *Satan's contented Slaves,* some of them crying out for Mercy! Some that they were lost and undone! Others, *What shall we do to be saved!* Others praising God for this Day, and for awakening them, and others, not only weeping, and crying for themselves, but for their graceless Relations. And yet it would have moved the hardest Heart, that, (as the Children of *Israel* under *Pharaoh's* Oppression) when I spake unto many of them, they hearkened not, for Anguish of Spirit, and the Sense of the cruel Bondage they were under.

THERE appear'd about *thirty* awaken'd this Day, belonging to this, and neighbouring Congregations. About *twenty* of them belonged to this Parish. Some few to the Parish of *Campsie*, and the Remainder to that of *Kirkintilloch*. But I have found since in conversing with the Distressed, that the Number of the awaken'd far exceeds *thirty*...

THERE have been at least *three Hundred* awaken'd in this Parish, since the Beginning of this Work, of which about *two Hundred* belong, or did belong, to this Parish. There were indeed about *fourteen* or *fifteen* of them awaken'd, when Mr. *Whitefield* preached at *Cumbernauld*. In the Parish of *Cumbernauld*, neighbouring with this Parish South-ward, as the Minister informs me, there are above *eighty*.

James Robe, *A Faithful Narrative of the Extraordinary Work of the Spirit of God, at Kilsyth, and Other Congregations in the Neighbourhood, Near Glasgow*, second edition (London: S. Mason, 1742–43), 24–30, 33–35.

15

Jonathan Edwards Assesses a Revival

Thomas Prince

IN ORDER TO document the revivals of the early 1740s taking place throughout America and Britain, Thomas Prince (1687–1758) of Boston and his son established the *Christian History*. The weekly magazine, although lasting only two years from 1743 to 1745, helped to solidify a transatlantic evangelical network. Prince pleaded for ministers throughout the English-speaking world to send news of local revivals that could be published in order to fan into flames the dying embers of the Great Awakening. The front page of the first issue on March 5, 1743, set the agenda for subscribers. The *Christian History* would provide "authentic accounts" from pastors and "other creditable persons," extracts from awakenings in England and Scotland, letters from correspondents in Britain and America, and "give the reader the most remarkable passages historical and doctrinal, out of the most famous old writers both of the Church of England and Scotland from the Reformation, as also the first settlers of New England and their children: that we may see how far their pious principles and spirit are at this day revived." The goal seemed clear: provide evidence that the Great Awakening in America and the Evangelical Revival in Britain represented an extension of God's work that began with the Reformation and had continued with the Puritan settlements in New England.

Between 1743 and 1745, the *Christian History* printed multiple letters and narratives of indigenous revivals, particularly in Scotland and New England. The awakenings at Cambuslang and Kilsyth in Scotland in 1742 featured prominently in the periodical, but there were also significant sections devoted to the defense of religious piety from a host of New England clergymen, including Jonathan Edwards. In a letter to Prince in 1743 Edwards assessed the spiritual vitality of his parish at Northampton, Massachusetts. Edwards compared the spiritual fervor of Northampton in the early 1740s with the earlier period of 1734–35 that he had chronicled in *A Faithful Narrative of the Surprising Work of God* (1737). At the time of his letter to Prince, Edwards believed that the awakenings of the 1740s demonstrated greater stamina than what took place at Northampton in the mid-1730s.

FIGURE 15.1 Thomas Prince by Joseph Badger (Detail), courtesy of the American Antiquarian Society.

The Christian History

Ever since the great Work of GOD that was wrought here about *nine Years ago*, there has been a great abiding Alteration in *this Town* in many Respects. There has been vastly more Religion kept up in the Town, among all Sorts of Persons, in religious Exercises, and in common Conversation, than used to be before: There has remain'd a more general Seriousness and Decency in attending the public Worship: There has been a very great Alteration among the *Youth* of the Town, with Respect to reveling, frolicking, profane and unclean Conversation, and lewd Songs: Instances of Fornication have been very rare: There has also been a great Alteration amongst both *old* and *young* with Respect to Tavern-haunting. I suppose the Town has been in no Measure so free of Vice in these Respects, for any long Time together, for *this sixty Years*, as it has been *this nine Years* past. There has also been an evident Alteration with Respect to a charitable Spirit to the Poor: (tho' I think with Regard to this, we in this Town, as the Land in general, come far short of Gospel Rules). And tho' after that great Work *nine Years ago* there has been a very lamentable Decay of religious Affections, and the Engagedness of People's Spirit, in Religion; yet many Societies for Prayer and social Religion were all along kept up; and there were some few Instances of Awakening and deep Concern about the Things of another World, even in the most dead Time.

In the Year 1740 in the *Spring*, before Mr. WHITEFIELD came to this town, there was a visible Alteration: There was more Seriousness, and religious Conversation, especially among *young* People: Those Things that were of ill Tendency among them were more forborn: and it was a more frequent Thing for Persons to visit their Minister upon Soul Accounts: and in some particular Persons there appeared a great Alteration, about that Time. And thus it continued till Mr. *Whitefield* came to Town, which was about the middle of *October* following: he preached here *four Sermons* in the Meeting-House, (besides a *private Lecture* at my House) one on *Friday*, another on *Saturday*, and two upon the *Sabbath*. The Congregation was extraordinarily melted by every Sermon; almost the whole Assembly being in Tears for a great Part of Sermon Time. Mr. *Whitefield*'s Sermons were suitable to the Circumstances of the Town; containing just Reproofs of our Backslidings, and in a most moving and affecting Manner, making Use of our great Profession and great Mercies as Arguments with us to return to GOD, from whom we had departed. Immediately after this the Minds of the People in general appear'd more engaged in Religion, shewing a greater Forwardness to make Religion the Subject of their Conversation, and to meet frequently together for religious Purposes, and to embrace all Opportunities to hear the Word preached. The *Revival* at *first* appear'd chiefly among *Professors*, and those that entertained the Hope that they were in a State of Grace, to whom Mr. *Whitefield* chiefly address'd himself; but in a very short Time there appeared an *Awakening* and deep Concern among some *young Persons* that looked upon themselves as in a Christless State; and there were some hopeful Appearances of *Conversion*; and some Professors were greatly revived. In about a *Month* or *six Weeks* there was a great Alteration in the Town, both as to the Revivals of Professors, and Awakenings of others. By the *middle* of *December* a very considerable Work of GOD appeared among those that were *very young*; and the Revival of Religion continued to increase; so that in the *Spring*, an Engagedness of Spirit about Things of Religion was become very general amongst *young People* and *Children*, and religious Subjects almost wholly took up their Conversation when they were together.

IN the Month of *May* 1741, a *Sermon* was preached to a Company at a *private House*: Near the Conclusion of the Exercise *one* or *two* Persons that were *Professors*, were so greatly affected with a Sense of the Greatness and Glory of divine Things, and the infinite Importance of the Things of Eternity, that they were not able to conceal it; the Affection of their Minds overcoming their Strength, and having a very visible Effect on their Bodies. When the Exercise was over, the *young People* that were present removed into the other Room for religious Conference; and particularly that they might have Opportunity to inquire of those that were thus affected what Apprehensions they had; and what Things they were that thus deeply impressed their Minds: and there soon appeared a very great Effect of their Conversation; the Affection was quickly propagated through the Room: many of the *young People* and *Children* that were *Professors* appeared to be overcome with a Sense of the Greatness and Glory of divine Things, and with Admiration, Love, Joy and Praise, and Compassion to others, that looked upon themselves as in a State of Nature; and many others at the same Time were overcome with Distress about their sinful and miserable State and Condition; so that the whole Room was full of nothing but *Out-cries, Faintings* and such like. *Others* soon heard of it in several

Parts of the Town, and came to them; and what they saw and heard there was greatly affecting to them; so that many of them were over-power'd in like Manner: and it continued thus for *some Hours*; the Time being spent in *Prayer, Singing, Counseling* and *Conferring.* There seemed to be a consequent *happy Effect* of *that Meeting* to several particular Persons, and in the State of Religion in the Town in general. After this were *Meetings* from Time to Time attended with *like Appearances.* But a little after it, at the Conclusion of the public Exercise on the *Sabbath*, I appointed the *Children* that were *under sixteen Years of Age* to go from the Meeting-House to a *neighbor House*; that I there might further enforce what they had heard in public, and might give in some Counsels proper for their Age. The *Children* were there very generally and greatly affected with the Warnings and Counsels that were given them, and many exceedingly overcome; and the Room was filled with *Cries*: and when they were dismissed, they, almost all of them, *went home crying aloud through the Streets,* to all Parts of the Town. The *like Appearances* attended several such Meetings of *Children* that were appointed. But their Affections appeared by what followed to be of a very different Nature: in many they appeared to be indeed but childish Affections; and in a Day or two would leave `em as they were before: others were deeply impressed; their Convictions took fast hold of them, and abode by them: and there were some that from one Meeting to another seem'd extraordinarily affected for some Time, to but little Purpose, their Affections presently vanishing, from Time to Time; but yet afterwards were seized with abiding Convictions, and their Affections became durable.

About the *middle* of the *Summer,* I call'd together the *young People* that were *Communicants*, from *sixteen to twenty six Years of Age* to *my House*; which proved to be a most happy Meeting: many seemed to very greatly and most agreeably affected with those Views which excited Humility, Self-Condemnation, Self-Abhorrence, Love and Joy: many fainted under these Affections. We had *several Meetings* that *Summer* of *young People* attended with like Appearances. It was *about that Time* that there first began to be *cryings out* in the *Meeting-House*; which several Times occasion'd many of the Congregation to stay in the House, after the public Exercise was over, to confer with those who seemed to be overcome with religious Convictions and Affections; which was found to tend much to the Propagation of their Impressions, with lasting Effect upon many; *Conference* being at these Times commonly joined with *Prayer* and *Singing.* In the *Summer* and *Fall* the *Children* in various Parts of the Town had religious Meetings by themselves for *Prayer,* sometimes joined with *Fasting*; wherein many of them seemed to be greatly and properly affected, and I hope some of them savingly wrought upon.

The Months of August and September were the most remarkably of any *this Year,* for *Appearances* of *Conviction* and *Conversion* of *Sinners*, and great *Revivings, Quickenings,* and *Comforts* of *Professors*, and for extraordinary external Effects of these Things. It was a *very frequent* Thing to see an *House full* of *Out-cries, Faintings,*

Convulsions and such like, both with *Distress*, and also with Admiration and *Joy*. It was not the Manner here to hold Meetings all Night, as in some Places, nor was it common to continue `em `till very late in the Night: but it was pretty often so that there were some that were so affected, and their Bodies so overcome, that they could not go home, but were obliged to stay all Night at the House where they were. There was no *Difference* that I know of here, with Regard to these extraordinary Effects, in Meetings in the *Night*, and in the *Day* Time: the Meetings in which these Effects appeared in the Evening, being commonly begun, and their extraordinary Effects, in the Day, and continued in the Evening; and some Meetings have been very remarkable for such extraordinary Effects that were both begun and finished in the *Day* Time.

There was an *Appearance* of a glorious Progress of the Work of *God* upon the Hearts of Sinners in *Conviction* and *Conversion* this *Summer* and *Fall*; and great Numbers, I think we have Reason to hope, were brought savingly home to CHRIST. But this was remarkable, the Work of GOD in his Influences of this Nature, seem'd to be almost wholly upon a *new Generation*; those that were not come to Years of Discretion in that wonderful Season *nine Years* ago, *Children*, or those that were *then Children*: Others that had enjoyed that former glorious Opportunity without any Appearance of saving Benefit, seem'd now to be almost wholly pass'd over and let alone. But *now* we had the most wonderful Work among *Children* that ever was in NORTHAMPTON. The former great Out-powering of the SPIRIT was remarkable for Influences upon the Minds of *Children*, beyond all that had ever been before; but *this* far exceeded *that*. Indeed as to Influences on the Minds of *Professors*, this Work was by no Means confined to a new Generation: many of all Ages partook of it: but yet, in this Respect it was *more general* on those that were of the *younger Sort*. Many that had formerly been wrought upon, that in the Times of our Declension had fallen into Decays, and had in a great Measure lest GOD, and gone after the World, now pass'd under a very remarkable *new Work* of the SPIRIT of GOD, *as if* they had been the Subjects of a *second Conversion*. They were first led into the Wilderness, and had a Work of *Conviction*, having much greater Convictions of the Sin of both Nature and Practice than ever before, (tho' with some new Circumstances, and something new in the Kind of Conviction) in some with great Distress, beyond what they had felt before their *first Conversion*: under *these Convictions* they were excited to strive for Salvation, and the Kingdom of Heaven suffer'd Violence from some of them in a far more remarkable Manner than before: and after great Convictions and Humblings, and Agonizings with GOD, they had CHRIST discovered to them anew, as an All-sufficient Saviour, and in the Glories of his Grace, and in a far more clear Manner than before; and with greater Humility, Self-Emptiness and Brokenness of Heart, and a purer and higher Joy, and greater Desires after Holiness of Life, but with greater Self-Diffidence, and distrust of their treacherous Hearts.

One Circumstance wherein this Work differed from that which had been in the Town *five* or *six Years* before, was that Conversions were frequently wrought *more sensibly and visibly*; the Impressions stronger, and more manifest by external Effects of them; and the Progress of the SPIRIT of GOD in Conviction, from Step to Step, more apparent; and the Transition from one State to another more sensible and plain; so that it might, in many Instances, be as it were seen by By-standers. The *preceding Season* had been very remarkable on this Account beyond what had been before; but *this* more remarkable than *that*. And in this Season these apparent or visible Conversions (if I may so call them) were more frequently in the Presence of others, at religious Meetings, where the Appearances of what was wrought on the Heart fell under publick Observation.

After *September* 1741, there seem'd to be some Abatement of the extraordinary Appearances that had been; but yet they did not wholly cease, but there was something of them from Time to Time *all Winter*.

Jonathan Edwards to Thomas Prince, December 12, 1743, *Christian History* (1743): 367–73.

16

Piety over Worldly Pleasures

Susanna Anthony

SUSANNA ANTHONY (1726–91) was born at Newport, Rhode Island. Her father, Isaac Anthony, had moved from England to Boston as a youth where he learned the goldsmith trade before marrying Mercy Chamberlin and relocating to Newport. The Anthonys had seven children—all daughters of whom Susanna was the second youngest. Growing up as a Quaker, Susanna stunned her parents when around the age of fifteen she experienced conversion and in 1742 joined the First Congregational Church at Newport pastored by the Puritan Nathaniel Clap. Single throughout her life, the sickly woman made a living in needlework and as a teacher, when her health permitted. Like her close friend Sarah Osborn, Anthony kept a diary of her spiritual progression, a portion of which was later edited and published in 1796 by her pastor at that time, Samuel Hopkins. And like Osborn, but to a greater extent, Anthony had severe bouts of depression over her spiritual state while earnestly seeking assurance of salvation. In her diary, Anthony blamed the devil as the mastermind behind her temptations, fears, and woeful condition. Yet after her conversion, she exhibited signs of hope in her writings as she sought relief from sin through divine mercy.

The Life and Character of Miss Susanna Anthony

Oct. 25, 1743. I am just now entering into the eighteenth year of my age. And does the tempter tell me, that I chose religion when I was a child, and knew no better; when I knew nothing of the pleasures of this world: And that it may be, when these enjoyments and pleasures appear delightful, I shall forsake strict and solid religion, and run with the young, giddy multitude, into the excesses of vanity? Then, O my soul, sit down again, and make another deliberate choice; even now I am entering the prime of all my days: And let me picture the world with its brightest side outmost; and religion in a solitary dress; and then choose my portion. If my former choice has not been free and noble enough; come now, my soul, and make one. Let there be nothing in it mean and low; but let it be great, noble and free.

As to religion: Can I sacrifice my name, and all that the world calls delightful, now in the prime of my age; and be accounted a fool and mad, by the wise, rich and polite world? Can I withstand a thousand temptations to mirth and pleasure; and be a despised outcast among men? Now, if I conform to the world, I shall be a pleasing object to many, and a delight to them, who now despise me. What pleasure that the world can afford shall be withheld from me, if I once give myself up to sensual pleasure, and the gratification of my whole inclination; allowing myself all that mirth and jollity, that my youthful age will now admit of? If I now give a loose to my youthful appetites, and satisfy my carnal desires; what can then deprive me of pleasure, now I am free from pain and the infirmities of old age, which might give a disgust to these pleasures. Now I have life, health and liberty. If I yield to these desires, and seek to satisfy them by a thousand new and fresh delights; take my swing in the world; cast away sorrow, and indulge self in ten thousand new pleasures; what then can cross me?

And, on the other hand, if I choose strict religion now, I may expect reproach, disdain and contempt, from the world, as not fit for common society, or scarce to live. I shall be accounted a poor, mean, ignorant, despicable creature, unworthy the notice of mortals: And, it may be, despised by formal professors, as being religious overmuch: They watching for my halting, and rejoicing at my falls. And besides, I must expect many dark and doubting hours, filled with bitter sighs and groans; denying myself, and taking up my cross; plucking out a right eye, and cutting off a right hand; daily meeting with crosses, and losses, and afflictions; and, it may be, with persecutions, imprisonment, and death, with the utmost distress. While the sensual libertine lives in pleasure, flourishing like a green bay tree, and has no bands in his death.

What a wide difference is here, between the strictly religious, and the sensual worldling! Come, then, my soul, and view them both as far as death; and now make a solemn and deliberate choice, either religion, or carnal pleasure. Come, my soul, and choose for Eternity.

Soul. Upon considering the nature and properties of each, I am brought to a free and full choice. I see nothing in this pleasure that can satisfy an immortal soul; nothing worthy my notice; nothing but an empty sound. Nor can it have any part in my affections, for a portion. They are but mean trifles, unfit to attract and busy an immortal soul. But religion, though it have its troubles with it; yet it hath a sacred sweetness in all. I feel an inward pleasure and satisfaction, which gives a relish, as it were, to this kind of religious pain and sorrow.

Objector. Come, Soul, lay aside prejudice. What! Nothing in all this pleasure, to delight thee. Search a little deeper. Or what can be in this melancholy religion, to allure thee to choose its ways?

Soul. I have found what it is. For in all those pleasures, the soul has no God, and no happiness, suited to its immortal nature; without which, all is but a likening trifle. Wherefore, the soul which hath God for its portion, attended with ever so much sorrow, is unspeakably more happy.

Objector. But if you indulge yourself in pleasures, and strive to divert your company with mirth and jollity, you will gain the esteem of many, and they will greatly prize you, and seek your company.

Soul. I value the approbation of the most high God, before all the esteem of poor mortals; and deliberately make choice of him, and his way of strict religion, for my portion, pleasure and happiness.

I do now, with my whole soul and all my powers, choose God for my portion; taking his cross as well as his crown; esteeming the sorrows of religion greater riches than the pleasures of sin; looking on it a pleasure to be crucified with Christ. I despise every worldly enjoyment, compared with one smile from the lovely Jesus. I do, with my whole heart and soul, choose God and religion, though it may be through a sea of sorrow and distress, rather than the world in all its pomp and splendor, with ten thousand enjoyments. O most great and glorious God, I now choose thee as my sufficient, and every way suitable portion. I solemnly take God, the Father, Son, and Holy Ghost, for my all, in life, death and eternity; and resign myself, soul and body, into thy hands. And I take all the holy angels in heaven; and even the Most High God, the possessor of heaven and earth, himself, to witness that I DO.

And now, Lord, I am thine. Do with me as thou wilt. I am thy clay, feeble, helpless, and hopeless. I throw myself, soul and body, life and health, liberty and pleasure, on thee, the boundless, infinite fullness of heaven, the immutable God. Lord, God, Father, Son and Holy Ghost, I this day and minute subscribe with my heart and hand, to be the Lord's. Even so, Lord Jesus, Amen and Amen.

Susanna Anthony., *The Life and Character of Miss Susanna Anthony ... Consisting of Extracts from Her Writings, With Some Brief Observations on Them. Compiled By Samuel Hopkins* (Worcester: Leonard Worcester, 1796), 50–53.

17

Satan's Strategies of Deception

Thomas Gillespie

AFTER ATTENDING A communion service where he witnessed the persuasive preaching of the elder Thomas Boston, Thomas Gillespie (1708–74) came to faith around the age of twenty. Gillespie began his education at Edinburgh University in 1732, but left the school in 1738 to study briefly at the Secession Church's new divinity school at Perth before completing his theological studies under Philip Doddridge at his academy in Northampton, England. Once licensed as a preacher in October 1740, Gillespie first worked as an Independent pastor in Lancashire before returning to Scotland to become the parish minister at Carnock, Fife in September 1741. Months later, in 1742, western Scotland erupted in revival. Gillespie assisted William McCulloch and James Robe, the pastors of Cambuslang and Kilsyth respectively, by preaching and counseling those who had claimed conversion. Roughly ten years later, in 1752, the inconspicuous Gillespie became the subject of controversy when he refused to settle the unpopular candidate Andrew Richardson as the parish minister at Inverkeithing. Gillespie and other evangelicals on the settling committee would not consent to the General Assembly's demands that they force Richardson upon the unyielding congregation. Members of the liberal faction within the Church of Scotland chose to make an example out of Gillespie by deposing him for disobeying the orders dictated by the highest ecclesiastical court in the land. In the aftermath of his deposition, Gillespie joined the younger Thomas Boston and Thomas Colier to form the Presbytery of Relief in the early 1760s. The members of this new Scottish Church voiced their commitment to evangelical preaching and selecting ministers based on a popular vote by the parishioners, rather than patronage. The Relief Church continued into the mid-nineteenth century, at which time its multiple congregations merged with the United Secession Church.

One of the few works that Gillespie published was his *Treatise on Temptation* (1774). John Erskine, the Scottish evangelical minister who wrote the preface, stated that Gillespie composed the treatise years earlier, at some point after

1744. Erskine remarked that "Gillespie corrected the whole, and caused a small part of it be transcribed; but he was prevented from further revising and completing it, by the hurry and fatigue of body and mind to which his peculiar circumstances after his deposition subjected him." The published version of *A Treatise on Temptation* is made up of six sections in which Gillespie provides a fascinating psychological analysis of the effects of temptations on various age groups, socio-economic conditions, and individual temperaments. But before jumping into the body of the work, he sets the tone for the treatise in his introduction where he identifies Satan and his minions as the primary cause of human sin.

A Treatise on Temptation

I suppose the existence of devils, once holy angels, now apostate spirits, deprived of their original purity, but still possessed of all angelical powers, and also their agency on our spirits and bodies to obstruct us in duty, and lead us into sin. This almost all admit who believe the scriptures; and it will be hard for others to account for several appearances in the course of things, on any other supposition. I believe there is no intelligent person who has carefully observed the frame and posture of his mind at different seasons, and deals candidly, but must own, at one time or other he has felt himself strongly impelled by some external agent to act in such a particular way…

    1. All temptations may be reduced to two kinds; those of allurement, where the object or contrivance by which the devil leads to sin, is in order to attain, increase, secure, what is pleasant or profitable, really or in appearance; and those that are terrifying, where his engine is, to keep from obedience, or engage in transgression, from fear of prejudice or ruin, in person, reputation, estate, friends, advantages possessed or expected, present or future, real or imaginary.

    2. He inverts the order that God and nature have fixed in the operations of the soul of man, if there is a distinction of faculties in it, which has been doubted. However that matter be, it is certain, to act rationally and religiously is, to judge of a thing as directed, whether it is lawful or unlawful, true or false; then having judged, to chose it, or refuse it, as good or evil; next, to have the desire going out towards it, as beneficial in any respect, or to make it, as hurtful, the object of one's aversion. He makes one go the contrary way to work; to apprehend the thing of advantage, as such to choose it as good, then to believe it lawful and true. Thus he makes the affections sway the will, and that to determine the understanding, which should lead all. This appears from his procedure with our first parent. He represented the beauty of the fruit, the happy effects of eating of it, denied the threatening, and questioned the command.

3. His main engine is, to deceive and blind the mind, that it may not be capable to form a right judgment; and also to represent the object in a wrong light, as being desirable, warrantable, or advantageous. He knows, if the command and authority of the Lord, prohibiting the person to act in that manner under pain of his awful displeasure, is duly perceived, there is small probability of obtaining his aim.

4. He proceeds by degrees. He well understands, that if what he points to were at first laid open, the soul would be apt to reject the suggestion with abhorrence. Thus he tempts, first to presume upon duty, or in its performance; then to remissness in it; afterward to indifference about it; next to neglect it; then to nibble and tamper with smaller sins; upon that, to excuse them in others; this done, to commit them one's self; which makes way for a sin or evils of a deeper dye: and in this course he advances, till the soul becomes drenched in evil, if the Lord, by common restraining grace, or that which is saving and special, prevents it not.

5. He insensibly insinuates himself, especially where there is some degree of tenderness of conscience, and one is aware of his devices, and their tendency. This he does by oft presenting the sinful object, the matter of the temptation, to the fancy or apprehension, till the awe with which it was viewed at first, wears off by degrees, and it becomes familiar to the person. In this way the sense of its moral evil and effects is lost altogether, or little of it remains, in many instances where it once was strong, lively, practical, and constant; and as he is aware this is one of the most difficult and ticklish parts of his undertaking, he manages it with suitable address. Nothing is pretended, or appears, but a little innocent amusement to the fancy or apprehension, tired out, perhaps, with serious exercises, or that of one's proper business: but a dismal snare lies at bottom, not to be discovered till it is not to be evited, without immediate interposition of Heaven, or one sees it by being fast held in it. Here, if one discovers his hazardous working under ground, smells the pernicious mine, and takes the alarm, he instantly ceases, as in a fright, and tries every method to make the person think all was a pure conceit, nothing real in the whole transaction; and never gives over soothing till it is forgot. If things go to his mind, he proceeds yet with all caution, and lets even go advantages he might gain, lest the person should be put on his guard: An evidence and caveat with what for an enemy we have to deal.

6. Having presented the alluring and ensnaring object, he tries every expedient to conceal its sinfulness, and the danger of falling in with it in the way proposed. If he cannot represent it as a positive good, of which in the second proposition, he will suggest scruples about its specific nature with astonishing plausibility, and lead the person into a chain of reasoning on that point, throwing and thronging into the mind topics that tend to confound or persuade; by either of which he oft obtains his end...

7. He deals with men in suitableness to the measure of their abilities, natural, acquired, or spiritual. Is a man of a weak understanding, and little firmness of spirit? He will be at small pains with him, and uses common devices in practicing upon him. He is too wise to lose a moment, or employ art without necessity. When one has a solid judgment, a good bodily constitution, and a proper contexture of brain, he attacks him with application of his infernal skill, and weapons of different kind from those used in the case of others some how inferior. Through his singular sagacity, he sees when one improves his advantages against him, and when not, and acts accordingly. He discerns the ideas impressed on the fancy, and the knowledge treasured up in one's mind, very distinctly, and leads the man out of his depth, plies him with a temptation of such kind, or manages one in such a way, that all he knows is of no service to him. If he suspects or concludes one is a Christian, he goes a quite other way to work with him than with another attacked by the same temptation, and acts differently upon a person just set out in the way heavenward, one who has made considerable progress in the narrow way, and one just ready to finish his course with joy.

8. He sets with greatest violence on persons eminent for holiness; tender, exemplary, shining Christians; noted, useful, and able ministers; or those who may hereafter be remarkably successful in that work, or useful in another station. Hence Luther wrote to this effect. "As if he foresaw what he was to suffer by my means, he so raged against me, and used such numberless methods in tempting me, from my very childhood, that I have oft wondered if there was any other of mankind he wanted to destroy." This, with other instances of the same kind, has frequently made me think, that either the Lord, for ends known to himself, reveals to Satan early in one's life, that he is to be employed in the ministry, where somewhat special is intended; or that he suspects it shall be so, from the intention and capacity of the parents to train up their child with that view, and the knowledge he has of his intellectual endowments, disposition, and the capacity he may attain to hurt the kingdom of darkness. His particular efforts against such a one shall perhaps be touched afterwards.

9. He can and does make all that we are, have, can do, hope for, apprehend, might have attained, objects of every kind we are conversant with by our senses or intellectual powers, persons of all denominations we stand related to, see, talk, and have transactions with, temptations to us.

10. He defeats means of conviction as much as possible; uses incredible, numberless contrivances, to divert one from thinking seriously of the nature and consequences of what he is excited to, or engaged in; fills with aversion at perusing the Bible, or leads to be taken up about the historical part of it; instills prejudices against the gospel, the messenger, or particular message, or keeps away from attending the dispensation of it, or fills the mind with

impertinent thoughts; so that all is lost. If a sentence strikes, he will surmise, it is the part of another, not to them, and presents one whom it suits. If there is the least color for it, and even where there is none, he will whisper, one has told the minister, and he wants to affront them, or suspects and singles them out. Does the person purpose to spend time in considering his ways, he will influence one to go to him, and call him to diversion, transact business with him, or to employ him some other way. The moment he enters into his closet, or begins to call his mind to account, the watchful enemy strikes him with the thought of a business neglected, an advantage to be gained, somewhat that must instantly be considered or entered upon; and the person gives over, or his mind is wholly taken up and diverted, which is the same. If the person is determined to go on, he will scar him with dread, the sight of sin shall distract him, or insinuates his mind is not in frame for the duty, it will do better at another season. When the arrow of conviction has pierced, he offers a plaster of his own framing, or pretends the threatening is misunderstood, when still it sticks. He will perhaps gall the spirit by somewhat like conviction, to make the party weary of it, and long to get rid of it at any rate. This of conviction in general, his endeavours to obstruct that previous to conversion shall afterward be touched.

11. He carefully notices, diligently improves all advantages against us. Among these are, a secure frame, a careless temper, a sluggish disposition, a distempered spirit, any how, on whatever account; bodily illness, from the disorder into which it throws one's mind, and the fear flowing from danger that attends it, especially melancholy, which disturbs the imagination and judgment; losses and disappointments; outward prosperity, special manifestations from the Lord, not humbly improved, rendering one liable to be puffed up, exalted above measure; one's walking in darkness; the believer his being at a distance from the Lord, under marks of his displeasure; a person's situation, called to duty, in ordinary way above one's strength, without suitable furniture, or appearance of the Lord's interposition to carry through it; self-confidence, that gives him special advantage over a saint: "Although all shall be offended, yet will not I."

12. When he has tempted one for a time to perpetrate any sin, he waits for a proper conjuncture for accomplishing his design, strangely contributes to, and produces a concurrence of circumstances suiting his end; brings the tempted and the object within view; removes, if he can, and is permitted, obstructions that stood in the way; and hints, "Now you may gratify your inclination without any manner of danger; you are in absolute secrecy; it is certain no discovery shall ever be made; the thing shall be as if not done; if you lose this opportunity, you never shall have such another." He sets all forth in so strong and ensnaring a light, that if the Lord prevents not, when matters are brought to this pass, he is in little hazard of losing his labour.

13. When one is entered into temptation, and it has got hold of him, this cunning enemy gives him no rest, but hurries him perpetually: by night and day, in company and alone, idle or employed, thoughts of his temptation fill his mind. It is vain to think to cast them out. Satan allows him no respite; the ensnaring object is still before the eyes of his mind. Let him endeavour to turn his thoughts which way he will, this he must think of; he ever finds his adversary at his right hand, attacking him, inflaming lust in him. The cursed fiend knows, to allow the person to breathe, would be an opportunity to call in the aid of reason, grace, and Christ, and he might be cut short, and instantly foiled. This he provides against, by keeping the soul ever engaged about his temptation, in order to its further and final prevalence.

14. He presses hardest when one is least capable to make resistance. If the strength of the soul is spent by a long and constant conflict, the spirit is wasted by his fiery darts, or one is willingly carried far by his repeated earnest solicitations; he then makes the utmost efforts, tries all courses to cause the person fall in with the temptation, redoubles his care, and when things are come to extremity with the poor soul, makes a home thrust with all his vigour; sensible, that if then he carries not his point, he probably will fail in the attempt.

15. He tires out a person by frequent false alarms of temptations about prevalence, in which he is not so solicitous; and when one has spent time, thought, and endeavours, in resisting them, and attaining knowledge how to oppose and overcome them, he instantly and violently sets upon him, with what he mainly intended from the beginning, and till then was out of view. The poor soul is in a maze; all is new to him and strange; and ere he knows how to act, probably the temptation shall have got firm footing in him, or prevails over him.

16. Where he cannot think of being disappointed, is determined to run the person down at any rate, will have the vessel of the soul sunk in death or scandal, because perhaps it carries intelligence fatal to the interests of hell, he takes a course somewhat singular; he changes very oft the method and nature of assault, the person is led into a labyrinth, knows not what to think or do, struggling against one temptation, he is surprised into, taken in another, ere he is aware. In prosecution of this stratagem, he tempts to one extreme, that the tempted may fall into another; of which, even though known, he apprehended himself not in the least danger, till the overwhelming shock convinced him to his cost of his mistake. Where his malice is special, and success doubtful, several temptations attack one person, and attend him wherever he is. Sometimes more than one set upon him at once, especially in the morning, at night, when alone, when ensnaring objects are in view, &c. On other occasions they act as several ships fighting with one, give their broadside by turns, and then lie by, one or other still keeping her in play. Thus one temptation assaults the person,

either in company with or after another; and some have thought, that many devils, each with a different temptation, have sometimes joined their efforts against a soul, as it is certain they have united them in bodily possessions.

17. When he finds all ways of assault fail, the person bears every onset, and stands his ground, he gives over a little entirely, and makes a feint that he is defeated. On this the soul thinks he has rode out the storm, and baffled the temptation, and supposes he may rest securely, and lay aside his armour. This done, the enemy sets on him with all his might, and it may be awakens him by a deep wound received, or by bearing him quite down. Thus he learns in sad experience, he is not to be off his guard a moment, nor ever to be without his spiritual armour of every kind while in this world.

18. When solicitation will not do, if the power of God did not restrain, or a sense that it might hurt his interest deter him, he would show himself more openly, and appear in visible shape... If, which is at least generally the case, he is not allowed, or finds it not proper, to show himself openly, he can disturb men exceedingly, as he did Luther, by real or imaginary noises... and in different other ways, making them feel a weight on their bodies and spirits, the case of Paul, in the apprehension of persons of the best judgment. And this agency may be attended with such force, that were it not for the power, care, and immediate interposition of Christ, there would be no refuting; he should certainly carry his point by main force. What affects the senses is not supposed a part of the temptation, but is designed to disturb and make way for it, contribute to its greater efficacy. Mean time his ordinary, chief, and most dangerous agency, is what is not seen or felt, and too often not even suspected to be his agency at all.

19. When a person is in some measure under his power, he does all he can to prevent his escape, shuts up every passage, guards all avenues: he strikes the spirit dead with a fiery dart, a stunning blow. When real or former exercise of grace, and liveliness with fervour, is like to be attained in prayer, he beats the promise out of one's hands, and wrests it from him. When one is on the point of resting on divine faithfulness plighted in it, and finding anchoring ground, he overwhelms with a flood of doubts. If one essays to act faith, by himself, or some egged on by him, he raises a new storm in the mind; when somewhat calmed, and brought to consistence, raises difficulties in one's breast, and aversion at using a mean of whatever kind that may contribute to relief.

20. If he cannot bring the tempted the full length designed, he will be satisfied with small advantages rather than lose all. He greedily catches every opportunity to dishonour the Lord, and hurt men, though in the smallest degree: by it his malice is gratified; and when it is so, he is in his element. He is sensible, a little gained from time to time may be of vast importance to him in the end; is not so foolish as men, to labour in vain, because incapable to

reach their full aim; acts the part of a wise general, wasting the enemy's army by degrees, in cutting off their parties. His cursed pride cannot bear a total defeat. To prevent the shame and torment of this, he snatches even the shadow of victory, and magnifies it to make the person more easily yield. When he is at a stand, ready to be foiled, he will give over the attack as if of his own accord, and as if he chose to push the matter no further.

21. He sometimes offers composition; lets the person understand, if he will go on in such a way, follow a certain course, do one thing and forbear another, he shall not be much disturbed; and gives proof of it, by intermitting that by which the soul was dismally harassed. If this will not take, he will perhaps threaten to bring their secret sins to light, dares them therewith, or that he will bereave them of judgment, waste their bodies and estates. All this is as really transacted as if betwixt two persons; and by this method no doubt he sometimes succeeds.

Thomas Gillespie, *A Treatise on Temptation, Being an Inquiry Why Folly, Wickedness, and Misery, Appear, and Prevail, in Different Forms, Among Various Classes of Men* (Edinburgh: W. Gray, 1774), 3–7, 9–19.

18

Spiritual Devotions for the Soul

Philip Doddridge

PHILIP DODDRIDGE (1702–51) is a veritable bridge between Puritanism and early evangelicalism. The last of twenty children born to the London oil merchant Daniel Doddridge, Philip briefly considered Anglican orders but ultimately sided with the Dissenters. In 1719, at age seventeen, he enrolled in the Dissenting academy of John Jennings. As a student, Doddridge read widely in divinity, philosophy, literature, and history, growing especially fond of the works of Richard Baxter and John Tillotson. Shortly after graduating in early 1723, Doddridge accepted a country pastorate at Kibworth in Leicestershire. As a rural pastor, he continued his studies, purchasing books, joining a literary society, and borrowing heavily from other clergymen. In 1729 Doddridge relocated to Northampton, England to pastor the Independent congregation at Castle Hill. His typical schedule had him preaching extemporaneously twice on Sunday, administering communion once a month, and visiting parishioners during weekday afternoons. His sermons largely focused on traditional themes such as the covenant of grace, the work of the Holy Spirit, and Christology rather than more contemporary topics like natural religion. He usually followed up his homilies with a pertinent hymn that he had composed. Doddridge embodied the ecumenical spirit of early evangelicalism, gladly working with Dissenters, Moravians, and Methodist preachers, including the Arminian John Wesley and Calvinist George Whitefield.

While at Northampton, Doddridge also headed a Dissenting academy. Over the span of twenty-two years, he trained an estimated two hundred students, half of whom entered the ministry. Over four or five years, students honed their skills in biblical and classical languages and were encouraged by their mentor to read a wide range of books, even by deists. Although an orthodox Calvinist, Doddridge did not fear introducing an array of philosophical and theological perspectives, wanting students to form independent opinions on matters of faith. Widely praised for its superior training, Doddridge's academy welcomed not only English Dissenters but also young people as far away as the Netherlands. For his

FIGURE 18.1 Philip Doddridge (Detail), courtesy of the National Portrait Gallery, London.

contributions to divinity, he was granted a doctorate of divinity from Marischal College and King's College, Aberdeen in the 1730s. In his later years, he penned one of his most influential works, *The Rise and Progress of Religion in the Soul* (1745). Dedicated to his friend and fellow Dissenter Isaac Watts, the book brought Doddridge wide acclaim as an important specimen of practical divinity.

The Rise and Progress of Religion in the Soul

WHEN we look round about us with an attentive Eye, and consider the Characters and Pursuits of Men, we plainly see, that tho', in the original Constitution of their Natures, *they only*, of all the Creatures that dwell on the Face of the Earth, be *capable of Religion*, yet many of them shamefully *neglect it*. And whatever different Notions People may entertain of what they call *Religion*, all must agree in owning, that it is *very far from being an universal Thing*.

RELIGION, in its most general View, is such a Sense of God on the Soul, and such a Conviction of our Obligations to him, and of our Dependence upon him, as shall engage us to make it our great Care, to conduct ourselves in a Manner which we have reason to believe will be pleasing to Him. Now when we have given this plain Account of *Religion*, it is by no Means necessary, that we should search among the Savages of the *African* or *American* Nations, to find Instances of those who are *Strangers to it*. When we view the Conduct of the Generality of People *at Home*, in a *Christian* and *Protestant Nation*, in a Nation whose Obligations to God have been singular, almost beyond those of any other People under Heaven, will any one presume to say, that *Religion* has an *universal Reign* among us? Will any one suppose, that it prevails *in every Life*, and much less that it reigns *in every Heart*? Alas! the avowed Infidelity, the Profanity of the Name and Day of GOD, the Drunkenness, the Lewdness, the Injustice, the Falsehood, the Pride, the Prodigality, the base Selfishness, the stupid Insensibility of the Spiritual and Eternal Interests of themselves and others, which so generally prevail among us, loudly proclaim the contrary. So that one would imagine upon this View, that Thousands and Ten Thousands thought the *Neglect*, and even the *Contempt of Religion*, were a Glory, rather than a Reproach. And where is the Neighbourhood, where is the Society, where is the happy Family, consisting of any considerable Number? in which, on a more exact Examination, we find reason to say, *Religion* fills even this little Circle. There is, perhaps, a Freedom from any gross and scandalous Immoralities, an external Decency of Behaviour, an Attendance on the outward Forms of Worship in Public, and here and there in the Family; yet amidst all this, there is nothing which looks like the genuine Actings of the Spiritual and Divine Life. There is no Appearance of Love to GOD, no Reverence for his Presence, no Desire of his Favour as the highest Good: There is no cordial Belief of *the Gospel of Salvation*, nor eager Solicitude to escape that *Condemnation* which we have incurred by Sin; no hearty Concern to secure that *Eternal Life*, which *Christ* has purchased and secured for his People, and which he freely promises to all who will receive him. Alas! whatever the Love of *a Friend*, or even of *a Parent*, can do; whatever Inclination there may be, to *hope all Things*, and *believe all Things* the most favourable; Evidence to the contrary will force itself upon the Mind, and extort the unwilling Conclusion; that, whatever else may be amiable in that dear Friend, in that favourite Child, "*Religion* dwells not in its Breast."

TO a Heart that firmly believes *the Gospel*, and views Persons and Things in the Light of Eternity, *this* is one of the *most mournful Considerations* in the World. And indeed to such a one, all the other Calamities and Evils of Human Nature appear Trifles, when compared with *this*; the Absence of *real Religion*, and that Contrariety to it which reigns in so many Thousands of Mankind. Let *this* be cured, and all the other Evils will easily be borne; nay, Good will be extracted out of them: But if *this* continue, it *bringeth forth Fruit unto Death*; and in consequence of it, Multitudes, who share the Entertainments of an indulgent Providence with us, and are at least allied to us by the Bond of the same common Nature, must in a few Years be swept away into *utter Destruction*, and be plunged beyond Redemption into *everlasting Burnings*...

WHEN I invite you to the *Care* and *Practice of Religion*, it may seem strange, that it should be necessary for me, affectionately to plead the Case with you, in order to your *immediate Regard* and *Compliance*. What I am inviting you to, is so noble and excellent in itself, so well worthy the Dignity of our Rational Nature, so suitable to it, so manly, and so wise, that one would imagine, you should *take Fire*, as it were, at the first Hearing of it; yea, that so delightful a View should presently possess your whole Soul with a Kind of Indignation against yourself, that you pursued it *no sooner*... On this principle, surely, *an immediate Return to* GOD should in all Reason be chosen, rather than to *play the Fool any longer*, and to go on *a little more* to displease GOD, and thereby to *starve* and to *wound* your own Soul; even tho' your *Continuance in Life* were ever so *certain*, and your *Capacity to return* to GOD and your Duty ever so entirely *in your own Power*, now, and in every future Moment, thro' Scores of Years yet to come.

BUT *who*, or *what are You*, that you should lay your Account for *Years*, or for *Months* to come? *What is your Life?* Is it not *even as a Vapour, that appeareth for a little Time*, and then *vanisheth away?* And what is your Security, or what is *your peculiar Warrant*, that you should thus *depend* upon the Certainty of *its Continuance?* and that so absolutely, as venture, as it were, to *pawn your Soul* upon it? Why, you will perhaps say, "I am *young*, and in all my Bloom and Vigour: I see *Hundreds* about me, who are more than *double my Age*; and not a few *of them*, who seem to think it *too soon* to attend to Religion yet." You view *the Living*, and you talk thus. But I beseech you, think of *the Dead*. Return, in your Thoughts, to those *Graves*, in which you have left some of your *young Companions*, and *your Friends*. You saw them *a while ago* gay and active; warm with Life, and Hopes, and Schemes. And some *of them* would have thought a Friend strangely importunate, that should have *interrupted them* in their Business, and their Pleasures, with Solemn Lecture of *Death* and *Eternity*. Yet they were then *on the very Borders* of both. You have *since* seen *their Corpses*, or at least *their Coffins*; and probably carried about with you the Badges of *Mourning*, which you received at their Funerals. Those *once vigorous*, and perhaps *beautiful Bodies* of theirs, *now* lie mouldering *in the Dust*; as senseless, and helpless, as the most *decrepit Pieces* of Human Nature, which *Fourscore Years* ever brought down to it. And, what is infinitely more to be regarded, *their Souls*, whether prepared for this great Change, or thoughtless of it, have *made their Appearance* before GOD, and are, at this Moment, *fixed* either *in Heaven*, or *in Hell*. Now let me seriously ask you, Would it be *miraculous*, or would it be strange if such an Event should *befall you?* How are you sure that some *fatal Disease* shall not *this Day* begin to work in your Veins? How are you sure, that you shall even be *capable* of reading or thinking *any more*, if you do not attend to what you *now* read, and pursue the Thought which is *now* offering itself to your Mind? This *sudden Alteration* may at least *possibly happen*; and if it does, it will be to you *a terrible one* indeed. To be thus *surprised* into the Presence of a forgotten GOD; to be *torn away*, at once, from *a World*, to which your whole Heart and Soul has been riveted; *a World*, which has engrossed all your Thoughts and Cares, all your Desire and Pursuits; and be *fixed in a State*, which you could never be so far persuaded to think of, as to spend so much as *one Hour* in serious Preparation for it: How must you even *shudder* at the Apprehension of it, and with what *Horror* must it fill you? It seems *Matter of Wonder* that, in such Circumstances, you are not *almost distracted* with the Thoughts of the *Uncertainty of Life*, and are not even *ready to die* for *Fear of Death*. To *trifle* with GOD *any longer*, after so solemn an Admonition as this, would be a Circumstance of *additional Provocation* which, after all the rest, might be *fatal*: Nor is there any Thing you can expect in such a Case, but that He should *cut you off immediately*, and teach *other Thoughtless Creatures,* by your Ruin, what a hazardous Experiment they make, when they act as you are acting.

AND will you, after all, run *this desperate Risk?* For what imaginable Purpose can you do it? Do you think, *the Business of Religion* will become *less necessary,* or *more easy,* by your Delay? You know that *it will not.* You know, that whatever the Blessed GOD *demands now,* he will also demand *Twenty or Thirty Years hence,* if you should live to see the Time. GOD hath *fixed the Method,* in which he will pardon and accept Sinners, in His *Gospel.* And will He even *alter that Method?* Or if He will not, can *Men* alter it? You like not to think of *repenting,* and *humbling yourself* before GOD, to receive *Righteousness* and Life from his *free Grace in Christ*; and you above all dislike the Thought, of *returning to GOD* in the Ways of *Holy Obedience.* But will He ever *dispense* with any of these, and publish *a new Gospel,* with Promises of Life and salvation to *impenitent, unbelieving Sinners,* if they will but *call themselves Christians,* and submit to a few *external Rites?* How long, do you think, you might *wait for such a Change* in the Constitution of Things? You know, *Death* will come upon you; and you cannot but know, in your own Conscience, that a general *Dissolution* will come upon *the World,* long before GOD can thus *deny himself,* and contradict all his Perfections, and all his Declarations...

IF after such desperate Experiments you are *ever recovered,* it must be by an Operation of *Divine Grace* on your Soul, yet *more powerful* and *more wonderful,* in Proportion to the increasing *Inveteracy* of your *Spiritual Maladies.* And can you expect, that *the Holy Spirit* should be *more ready to assist you,* in Consequence of your having so shamefully *trifled with him,* and affronted him? He is now, in some Measure, *moving on your Heart:* If you feel any *secret Relentings* in it upon what you read, it is *a Sign* you are not yet utterly forsaken: But who can tell, whether these are not *the last Touches* he will ever give, to a Heart *so long hardened* against him?...

I DO therefore earnestly exhort you, *in the Name of our Lord Jesus Christ,* and by *the Worth,* and, if I may so speak, by *the Blood* of *your immortal and perishing Soul,* that you *delay not* a Day, or an Hour *longer.* Far from *giving Sleep to your Eyes, or Slumber to your Eye-lids,* in the continued Neglect of this important Concern, *take with you* even now *Words, and turn unto the* LORD; and before you quit the Place where you now are, *fall upon your Knees* in his Sacred Presence, and *pour out your Heart* in such Language, at least to some such Purpose, as this...

I NOW consider you, my dear Reader, as *coming to me with the Enquiry,* which *the Jews* addressed to *our Lord; What shall we do, that we may work the Works of* GOD? What *Method* shall I take, *to secure that Redemption and Salvation,* which I am told *Christ has procured for his People?* I would answer it as seriously, and carefully as possible; as one that knows, of *what Importance* it is *to you* to be *rightly informed;* and that knows also, *how strictly he is to answer to* GOD, for the Sincerity and Care with which the Reply is made. May I be *enabled to speak as his Oracle*, that is, in such a Manner, as faithfully to *echo* what *the sacred Oracles* teach!

AND here, that I may be sure to follow the *safest Guides*, and *the fairest Examples*, I must *preach Salvation to you*, in the Way of *Repentance toward* GOD, *and of Faith in our Lord Jesus Christ*: That *good old Doctrine*, which the *Apostles preached*, and which no *Man* can pretend to *change*, but at the Peril of his own Soul, and of theirs who attend to him.

I suppose, that you are, by this Time, *convinced of your Guilt and Condemnation*, and of *your own Inability* to recover yourselves. Let me nevertheless urge you to *feel that Conviction* yet more deeply, and so *impress it* with yet greater Weight *upon your Soul*; that you have *undone yourself*, and that *in yourself is not your help found*. Be persuaded therefore, expressly, and solemnly, and sincerely to *give up all Self-Dependence*; which, you *do not guard against it*, will be ready to *return secretly*, before it is observed, and will lead you to *attempt building up* what you have *just been destroying*.

BE assured, that *if ever you are saved*, you must *ascribe that Salvation* entirely *to the Free Grace of* GOD. If, *guilty* and *miserable* as you are, you are not only *accepted*, but *crowned*, you must *lay down your Crown* with all humble Acknowledgment *before the Throne. No Flesh* must *glory in his Presence; but he that glorieth, must glory in the Lord: For of him are we in Christ Jesus, who of GOD is made unto us Wisdom, and Righteousness and Sanctification, and Redemption.* And you must be sensible, you are *in such a State*, as, having *none of these in* yourselves, *to need them in another.* You must therefore be sensible, that you are *ignorant* and *guilty, polluted and enslaved;* or, as *our Lord* expresses it, with regard to some who were under *a Christian Profession,* that as Sinners, *you are wretched, and miserable, and poor, and blind, and naked.*

IF these Views be *deeply impressed* upon your Mind, you will be *prepared to receive* what I am now to say. Hear therefore in a few Words *your Duty, your Remedy*, and *your Safety*; which consists in *this*, "That you must *turn to Christ*, with *a deep abhorrence* of your former Sins, and *a firm Resolution* of forsaking them; *forming that Resolution* in the Strength of *His Grace*, and *fixing your Dependence on Him* for your *Acceptance with GOD*, even while you are purposing *to do your very best*, and when you have actually *done the best* you ever will do in consequence of that purpose."

THE *first* and most important *Advice* that I can give you in present Circumstances, is, *that you turn yourself to Christ*. And here, *say not in your Heart, Who shall ascend into Heaven, to bring him down to me?* or who shall *raise me up thither* to present me before Him? The blessed *Jesus, by whom all Things consist,* by whom the whole System of them is supported, *forgotten as he is* by most that bear his Name, *is not far from any of us:* Nor could he have *promised* to have been, *where-ever Two or Three are met together in his Name,* but in Consequence of those *truly Divine Perfections* by which he is *every where present.* Would you therefore, Oh

Sinner, *desire to be saved?* Go to *the Saviour*. Would you *desire to be delivered?* Look to *that great Deliverer.* And tho' you should be *so overwhelmed* with *Guilt*, and *Shame*, and *Fear*, and *Horror*, that you should be *incapable of speaking* to him, *fall down* in this speechless Confusion *at his Feet*; and *behold him, as the Lamb of GOD, that taketh away the Sin of the World*...

SUCH as *this* must be *the Language* of *your very Heart* before the Lord. But then remember, it must be *the Language* of *your Life* too. The unmeaning *Words of the Lips* would be *a vain Mockery*. The most affectionate *Transport of the Passions*, should it be *transient* and *ineffectual*, would be but like *a Blaze of Straw*, presented instead of *Incense* at his Altar. With such *Humility*, with such *Love*, with such cordial *Self-Dedication* and *Submission of Soul*, must thou often *prostrate self*, in the Presence of *Christ*; and then thou must *go away* and *keep him in thy View*; must *go away*, and *live unto* GOD thro' him, *denying Ungodliness and worldly Lusts*, and behaving thyself *soberly, righteously, and godly, in this* vain ensnaring *World*. You must make it *your Care*, to *shew your Love* by *Obedience*; *by forming yourself* as much as possible, *according to the Temper* and *Manner of Jesus*, in whom you believe. You must make it *the great Point of your Ambition*, (and a *nobler View* you cannot entertain,) to be *a living Image of Christ*; that so far as Circumstances will allow, *even* those who have *heard* and *read* but *little of him*, may, by *observing you*, in some Measure *see* and *know* what *Kind of a Life* that of *the Blessed Jesus* was. And this must be your *constant Care*, your *prevailing Character*, as long as you live. You must *follow him*, whithersoever he leads you; must *follow*, with *a Cross* on your Shoulder, when he commands you to *take it up*; and so must *be faithful* even *to the Death*, expecting *the Crown of Life*.

Philip Doddridge, *The Rise and Progress of Religion in the Soul: Illustrated in a Course of Serious and Practical Addresses, Suited Persons of Every Character and Circumstance: With a Devout Meditation of Prayer Added to Each Chapter* (London: J. Waugh, 1745), 1–3, 24–7, 29, 77–9, 83–4.

19

A Conversion Story

John Cennick

AFTER COMING TO faith in 1737, the artisan John Cennick (1718–55) turned to the Methodist trio of John and Charles Wesley and George Whitefield for support. John Wesley encouraged Cennick and welcomed his assistance at a revival in Kingswood outside Bristol, England. Exhorting the crowd with an animated style, Cennick discovered that he had a talent for open-air preaching. As the 1740 revivals took shape, Methodism split theologically between those who supported the Arminianism of the Wesleys and those who rallied behind Whitefield's Calvinism. Cennick sided with Whitefield, accepting the Calvinistic doctrine of predestination and denying the Wesleyan notion of Christian perfection. As a result of his decision, Wesley expelled Cennick from the Arminian Methodists in March 1741.

Not deterred, Cennick commenced itinerating as a Calvinistic Methodist preacher along the Welsh border in June 1741, but soon veered toward the Moravian teachings of Count Nicholas von Zinzendorf and his emphasis on personal religious experience. By the close of 1745, Cennick had transferred his allegiance to the Moravians, adopting the view that God offered universal salvation to humanity rather than electing only certain people to heaven. After visiting the Moravians in Germany in December 1745, Cennick received Zinzendorf's approval to itinerate in Ireland. Beginning in June 1746, he traveled throughout the northern parts of Ireland, establishing over 200 Moravian societies in the span of five years. Later, in 1753, Cennick concentrated his efforts in Wales, setting up societies in Leominster and Haverfordwest. As a prolific author of over fifty works, including one of the first hymnbooks produced during the revivals, and as a leading itinerate preacher, Cennick deserves recognition as one of the greatest evangelists of the eighteenth century. The following excerpt from *The Life of Mr. J. Cennick* chronicles his entry into the faith that inspired his ministry.

FIGURE 19.1 John Cennick (Detail), courtesy of the National Portrait Gallery, London.

The Life of Mr. J. Cennick

I. MY Father's Parents, *i.e.* my Grand-father and Grand-mother *Cennick*, were once very great Traders in the Clothier's Way: But when *George Fox* and *Will. Penn* began preaching, they became Quakers, and in the Days of *Oliver Cromwell*, and in part of King *Charles's* Reign they suffer'd *the Loss of all Things*, and were imprison'd in *Reading* Goal, and (I have heard my Mother say) were so far reduced, that my Grand-mother knit, or wove half-penny Laces for her Living, in the Prison; in several Books publish'd by the Quakers of their Sufferings, mention is made of them: But my Father, after he was married to my Mother, was baptiz'd into the Church of *England*: And in that Church I was brought up, and from my Infancy carefully instructed by my Mother in the Principles of Religion; who also kept me strict to Church, and taught me Prayer Morning and Evening, and would not suffer me to play on the LORD's Day, but confin'd me to read, or say Hymns all Day long with my Sisters. This then I counted the worst of Bondage, and indeed Cruelty. So very prone was I to be disobedient and wicked, even when so young; I then envy'd other Children who were not restrain'd as I was, and hoped as I grew up to get their Liberty. When I was very young indeed, I remember my Mother led me to see an Aunt of hers who was then on her Death-bed. I came first into the Room where she lay and heard her saying to the Maid who attended her, Mary, *I have somewhat to say to you, it may be you will think it a Lie, but indeed it is Truth. This Night the Lord stood by me, and invited me to drink of the Fountain of Life freely, and I shall stand before the Lord bold as a Lion.* I found as she spake these Words with uncommon Cheerfulness, my Blood chill'd in my Veins, and I was struck to the Heart! I was set upon praying immediately that before I died I might know (as I thought my Aunt did) that I should go to Heaven. Soon after my

Mother came into the Room, and hearing the dying Woman shout for Joy, and cry out in such Assurance of Faith, she drew near, and said with Tears, *Poor Soul!* My Aunt scarce heard her speak but she cried out, *Who dares call me poor! I am rich in CHRIST! I have got CHRIST! I am rich!* And after this manner she rejoic'd till we left her. The Words she utter'd indeed pierc'd my Soul, so that I could not rest Day nor Night, but was wishing continually after (If I thought of Death, or Sickness) *O that I may be assured of Heaven before I die*, and began to fear to die greatly. These were the most early Convictions I can remember; nor do I know any Time between Whiles till my Conversion, when I did not meditate on my Aunt's last Words; for it was not long after I had seen her that she slept in the Bosom of the Lamb. Now, altho' at times I was inclin'd to be serious, dutiful, &c. till I was about twelve or fourteen Years old, I lived (as other young Children) fond of Play, of fine Clothes, and of Praise, but afraid to swear, or to take GOD's Name in vain.

II. My natural Temper was to be obstinate, and my Lips were full of Lies continually, nor could any one be more furious when provok'd or anger'd, but after my Passion was over, I commonly dreaded to go to Bed, lest I should drop into Hell before Morning. Nor did I dare to sleep till I had said my Prayers, and promis'd GOD how good I would be the next Day. And this was also my Way of buying Pardon from GOD, when I had sinned in any gross Way, as by *Lying, Sabbath-breaking, Stealing from my School-Fellows or Disobedience to my Parents...*

IV. When I came to be near fifteen I began to be very uneasy for want of Employment, and strove to find out a Business in which I might work at Home, and ease myself of so many fruitless Journeys. I began to learn two or three Trades, and long'd to get Money, that I might have wherewith to give to the Poor, and do as I pleas'd. I thought how religious, how thankful, and charitable I would then be; yea, and was so persuaded I should be rich, that I made a Promise, and wrote it down, *To build a Chapel,* and *erect a more strict Order in the Church, wherein People should fast duly according to the Rubric, and set up all Night in Prayer, and go plain in Apparel*; but when I had learnt the Art of Buying and Selling, and laid out much Money, my Heart failed so that I could not consent to set up a Public Shop, tho' my Mother had built one for me; no One can imagine the Fear that came upon me when I thought of it, I tho't if none should buy of me I should be starved; or obliged to run away by Night, and perish in Solitude. Thus restrain'd, I work'd privately, and contented myself with getting just enough for Food and Raiment, and yet keeping more and more to Duties at Church and in the Closet, I said in my Heart, *Here I shall be happy.*

V. From about fifteen I took Delight to see, and read *Plays*, and to look into *Histories*, and *Romances*. And surely had it been in my Power, *Plays* would have had all my Time; and I had forgot JESUS and Everlasting Ages: But being

prevented for want of Money, I delighted myself in reading them, in singing *Songs*, talking of the *Heathen Gods*, of the Wars of the *Jews* and *Greeks*,
of *Alexander* the Great, and in the cursed Delusion of *Card-playing*, in seeing
Sights, in *Horse-Races*, in *Dancing-Assemblies*, *Reveling* and *Walking* with young
Company! *Thus loving Ungodliness more than Goodness, and to talk of Lies more
than Righteousness.*

VI. After this Way I spent my Life till *Easter* (I believe 1735) when as I was
walking hastily in *Cheapside* in *London, the Hand of the* LORD *touched me!* I felt
at once an uncommon Fear and Dejection, and tho' all my Days since I could
remember, had been bitter through the Strength of Convictions, and the Fear
of going to Hell; yet I knew not any Weight before like this...

X. I left off singing Songs, playing at Cards, seeing Plays, and such like;
finding plainly they were *Vanity of Vanities*. And indeed, when I looked into
the World, all Things seemed to be unnatural and unpleasant, as if I had been
banish'd into a Foreign Land; my own Town, House, and Relations being all
Strangers to me. Then I wished strongly to get into a *Romish* Monastery, and
to spend my Life in holy Retirement; but the want of Money for my Journey
seem'd to prevent me from doing it...

XII. All this while I had no Power over Sin, nor the least Strength to resist
Temptations, being carnal, and sold under Sin; I committed it continually, tho'
not in the Eyes of the World. My chief Sins were *Pride, Murmuring against*
GOD, *Blasphemy, Disobedience,* and *Evil Concupiscence*; sometimes I strove
against them, but finding myself always conquer'd, I concluded there was no
Help...

XIX. After I had been thus afflicted, and grieved near two Years, the
Temptation to think *I should never die, or live to a great Age,* so prevail'd upon
me, that instead of asking for Mercy, I asked hourly for Death; yea, and desired
to break into Eternity, tho' at the Hazard of falling into Hell...

XX. When I found any Freedom I read in the Scriptures, and us'd to think
the Testimony of CHRIST, the Promises, &c. were doubtless sweet and precious to Believers, and to such as our SAVIOUR loved, but I thought, *they are
nothing to me, I have no Part in them.* Yea I generally open'd upon such Places
as made most against me, and seem'd to read my utter Condemnation, so
that often I have been afraid to open the Testament, lest I should see more
Threatenings than I had seen already; and sometimes I have thrown down
the Book spitefully (when I saw no Comfort there for me) and own'd, *What
have I to do with thee?* And then in unmeasured Grief look toward Heaven,
and wonder what I was spared out of Hell for! Many Times I have looked on
the Scriptures as very tasteless, insipid, and unpleasant, and thought other
Books better by far; yet believed there were Riches in the Word for others who
had the Spirit of GOD to understand it; but to me, all beside the Law, and the

Judgments, and the Terrors were like a Book seal'd, so that I could not read it (as I thought) to profit by it at all.

XXI. I remember at one Time every Error in Doctrine, or Judgment I heard of stagger'd me, and made me question if it were not right, and ask'd often in my Mind, *How do I know the* Roman Catholics *are wrong? Or, How do I know if the* Jews *be not in the right Way? Or if these are not, for all I know the* Quakers *may.* But yet if any came in my Way, and disputed for their Errors, I had always Words from Scripture to gainsay and withstand their Arguments: Yea I pleaded often for those Truths of which I doubted myself; and could not help mightily defending the Faith of the Church, and of the Scripture, though I stood in Fear lest both shou'd be but Delusion.

XXIII. As I was yet pressed down with Convictions of Sin, and the Fear of GOD's Wrath, and the dreadful Looking for Judgment; *Pride in Apparel* and *Spirit, Lust, Covetousness* and *Passion* still ruled most in my captive Spirit: Against these I strove by *fasting long* and often, and *pray'd kneeling* nine Times a Day; and the Week before the *Communion* I spent as much Time as possible in *Works of Mortification* and *Self-denial*, eating only once a Day, *viz.* in the Evening; and from *Friday* Breakfast I eat not 'till *Sunday* Noon, when I received the *Bread* and *Wine.* Also on some Days I liv'd only upon Bread and Water; and when I thought that was too good for a Christian I would not eat `till the Bread was hard and dry, and at last I thought that was too good, and then I boil'd and bak'd Potatoes, and eat them: Also I eat Acorns, Leaves of Trees, Crabs, and Grass; and wish'd often heartily that I could bring myself to live only upon Roots and Herbs. But when I had done all which was in my Power to do, and found no Relief, I was convinced *Salvation was not of Works.* No *Alms* or *Fastings*, or *Prayers*, or *Watchings* could cover my naked Soul from Almighty Wrath. I hated my *Righteousness*, loath'd my *Prayers*, and could truly say, *I am unprofitable*, and my Righteousness as *filthy-Rags:* Yea, and amidst all my Works such Terror came upon me as made me sweat and quake exceedingly...

XXVII. I envied now more than ever them who were fallen asleep in Death: These I thought are now at rest. They know Sorrow no more, their Tears are wiped away, all their Travail is at an End. If there were Infants or Children where I was, I pitied their Fate, being born into such a World; and rejoiced when I heard they were dead. Yea, when I beheld the State of *Insects, Birds, Beasts,* &c. I wished I was half so happy as them, who, after a short Life, remain in Silence.

XXVIII. Quite forlorn and destitute, finding *Prayers,* and *Tears,* and *Cries* in vain, about the Beginning of *August* 1737, I began to resign myself, in the midst of my Distress, to the wise Disposal of GOD. I gave up my Desires, my Will, and my Remains of Hope; being content to go down to Hell (as GOD should please) either in Life or Death. I found I was willing upon any Terms to be saved, but was convinc'd I deserved Hell, and so bow'd to the Justice of GOD.

XXIX. I waited many Hours silently upon GOD, and if I broke Silence, cried unto JESUS, to remember *His Blood*, and *Tears*, and *Sufferings*; and if there was Room for me in his Favour to reveal it to me. I no more said, LORD *remember how innocent I have lived*; nor *thanked Him because I was better than another*; but pleaded the *great Oblation* and *Sacrifice of* CHRIST *Crucify'd*; I entreated Mercy for His sake alone, I knew my Guilt, and was dumb before my GOD; often repeating these Words of Eli, *It is the* LORD, *let Him do what seemeth Him good.*

XXX. I was still bent to go into some solitary Place, that I might there find the Happiness of waiting on GOD. Tho' I had often before been hindered, I resolved to try once more, and fix'd for it, the 7th Day of *September* 1737. I paid every One to whom I owed any Thing, intending to take a Bible and Common Prayer Book, with *Hugo's* Emblems; and prayed my Journey might be prosperous. As I lay awake on the 6th Day, strange Heaviness came upon me, and when I arose it continued. My Mind was full of Fear and Trouble, and I was, I think more dejected than ever; I purposed notwithstanding to be gone before the next Sun-rising. While I was sitting and reflecting thereon, the Saints Bell rang at St. *Laurence's* Church for Prayers. At first I was careless about going, but after considering what the People would say, and what they would think if I miss'd Church when I was in Town; and that it might stagger some, fearing I was negligent, or gone back; I concluded in my own Breast to go. And when I was risen up, I again thought, *I shall be far enough off about this Time To-morrow, and I may as well forbear to go now; it is but once, and there is no Good there for me, I may as well keep my Place, and be content.* I sat down again, but was so uneasy, that I was obliged to get up and go. I went out like some Outcast into a Foreign Land; my Heart was ready to burst. My Soul [was] at the Brink of Hell, above Measure disconsolate and heavy. Had any met me, my Countenance would have betray'd me, as well as low Voice and Tears. When I had enter'd the Church, and fallen on my Knees, I began murmuring (as I did often) because my Cross seemed more heavy than ever was laid on any one beside; and how untroubled all the Children of GOD pass'd to Heaven, and how full of Terror I must go down to Hell! And I was as if the *Sword of the LORD was dividing asunder my Joints, and Marrow, my Soul and Spirit*; till near the End of the *Psalms*, when these Words were read; *Great are the Troubles of the Righteous, but the* LORD *delivereth him out of them all! And he that putteth his Trust in* GOD *shall not be destitute*: I had just room to think, *Who can be more destitute than me?* When I was overwhelmed with Joy, and I believed there was Mercy. My Heart danced for Joy, and my dying Soul reviv'd! I heard the Voice of JESUS saying, *I am thy Salvation.* I no more groaned under the Weight of

Sin. The Fears of Hell was taken away, and being sensible that CHRIST loved me, and died for me, *I rejoiced in* GOD *my* SAVIOUR.

XXXI. This *Joy* and *Peace in believing*, filled me about three or four Hours; and I began to vow everlasting Obedience, and how faithfully I would stand for the LORD all the Days of my Life. *In this my Prosperity I said, I shall never be moved. Thou LORD hast made my Hill so strong! But it was not long before He hid His Face, and I was troubled.* Satan was suffered to buffet me violently, and to suggest, *Where is now thy GOD? How do I know but this is Delusion? May it not be the* LORD *has shew'd me this as an Aggravation to my Torment, when I am cast away!* My Horrors were so great, that I sweated, pray'd, and cry'd aloud for Mercy! And when I saw no Help, *I drank the Cup which my Father had given me*; and I said (submitting myself to His righteous Will) *If the LORD is pleased to cast me off I am content; I would willingly sit down with the Saints in the Kingdom: But* GOD's *Will be done.*

XXXII. About three Days after I was sitting thoughtful in an inner Room, and in the Multitude of my Temptations, I imagined that the dull Weather might add to my Grief; scarce had I thus thought e're the Sun (which had not shone for some Time) shin'd beautifully from the Clouds; and the Voice of GOD witness'd at that Instant: *"Thus shall the Sun of Righteousness arise on thee."* I believed the Promise, and found the Love of GOD again shed abroad in my Heart; I saw clearly the Will of the LORD in calling me through much Tribulation; and I said gladly, *It is good for me that I have been in Trouble.*

John Cennick, *The Life of Mr. J. Cennick, With an Account of the Trials and Temptations which He Endured Till It Pleased Our Saviour to Shew Him His Love, and Send Him into His Vineyard*, second edition (Bristol: Printed for the Author, 1745), 3–8, 11–12, 18–21, 23–7.

20

A Missionary among Native Americans

David Brainerd

BORN AND RAISED in Haddam, Connecticut, David Brainerd (1718–47) matriculated at Yale in 1739, shortly after he had a conversion experience and around the time that George Whitefield commenced his American tour that launched the Great Awakening. Whitefield's visit to New Haven in October 1740 was followed by the fiery preaching of his protégé Gilbert Tennent, whose published sermon *Danger of an Unconverted Ministry* incited Yale's radicals to question the spiritual state of the local clergy and rebel against the authority of the school's rector, Thomas Clap. To curb the enthusiasm of the revivals on the campus, Clap and the college's trustees issued a statement in late 1741 promising to expel any student who persisted in labeling a member of the faculty or staff as unconverted or a hypocrite. It is within this context that a student overheard Brainerd as saying that Yale's tutor Chauncey Whittelsey had "no more grace" than a chair. Clap demanded a public apology from Brainerd for his remark, and when the young man refused, he was expelled. Although later apologizing for his slanderous comment, and even aided in his defense by Jonathan Edwards and Aaron Burr Sr., Brainerd never earned the degree from Yale that he coveted.

After his expulsion, Brainerd found work as a missionary-pastor to Native Americans. For three years, he had not witnessed very much success as a missionary to the Native Americans of the Delaware River valley. Having been commissioned by the Society in Scotland for Propagating Christian Knowledge (SSPCK) in 1743, first as an interim pastor at Easthampton on Long Island, and then as an apprentice to John Sergeant who had been working with the Mahican Indians at Stockbridge since 1734, Brainerd was instructed to travel to an Indian settlement northeast of Albany where he could support Sergeant's ministry. Brainerd visited Sergeant on March 31, 1743 and from there journeyed eighteen miles to his assignment at Kaunameek, between Albany and Stockbridge. Lonely,

BRAINERD PREACHING TO THE INDIANS.   p. 2

FIGURE 20.1 David Brainerd preaching to the Indians, courtesy of the Haddam Historical Society.

and discouraged by his apparent failure, Brainerd requested that the SSPCK relocate him to southeast Pennsylvania, where, beginning in April 1744, he worked tirelessly for three years. For a time, he held a base at the Forks of the Delaware River, acting as an itinerant to Native Americans and frontier European settlers in the region.

While Brainerd did not make much headway among the Native Americans of the Susquehanna River valley, the Delaware Indians of Crossweeksung, New Jersey greeted him with open arms. In the opening entry of his published journal, Brainerd relayed the story of his contact with the Indians of Crossweeksung, noting gloomily that the audience for his first sermon consisted of women and children. This proved to be a blessing in disguise, however, since the women of the village were so impressed by the foreigner's message that they trekked several miles to invite others to hear Brainerd preach the following day. Another unexpected benefit came when the Native American men killed some deer, which kept the locals in one place, allowing a large proportion of the villagers to hear the gospel from the white man. Probably not feeling threatened by the singular visitor who had not come to swindle them from their land, the Indians of Crossweeksung listened attentively, resulting in a spiritual harvest for the young missionary. With the revival in the village growing in numbers, Brainerd continued to nurture his flock as a missionary-pastor for the surrounding area until his early death of tuberculosis in October 1747.

Mirabilia Dei inter Indicos

Crosweeksung, in New-Jersey, June 19, 1745

HAVING spent most of my Time for more than a Year past amongst the *Indians* in the Forks of *Delaware* in *Pennsylvania*; and having in that Time made two Journeys to *Susquehanna* River, far back in that Province, in order to treat with the *Indians* there, respecting Christianity: And not having had any considerable appearance of *special* Success in either of those Places, which damp'd my Spirits, and was not a little Discouraging to me. Upon hearing that there was a Number of *Indians* in and about a Place call'd (by the Indians) *Crosweeksung* in *New-Jersey*, near *fourscore* Miles Southeastward from the Forks of *Delaware*, I determined to make them a visit, and see what might be done towards the Christianizing of them; and accordingly arrived among them this Day.

I found very few Persons at the Place I visited, and perceived the Indians in these Parts were very much scatter'd, there being not more than two or three Families in a Place, and these small Settlements six, ten, fifteen, twenty and thirty Miles, and some more, from the Place I was then at. However, I preach'd to those few I found, who appear'd well dispos'd, and not inclin'd to object and cavil, as the *Indians* had frequently done otherwise.

When I had concluded my Discourse, I inform'd them (there being none but a few Women and Children) that I would willingly visit them again the next Day. Whereupon they readily set out and travel'd ten or fifteen Miles, in order to give Notice to some of their Friends at that Distance. These Women, like the *Women of Samaria*, seem'd desirous that others might *see the Man that told them what they had done* in their Lives past, and the Misery that attended their *idolatrous* Ways.

June 20. Visited and preach'd to the *Indians* again as I propos'd. Numbers more were gather'd at the Invitations of their Friends, who heard me the Day before. These also appear'd as attentive, orderly and well dispos'd as the others. And none made any Objection, as *Indians* in other Places have usually done.

June 22. Preach'd to the Indians again. Their Number which at first consisted of about seven or eight Persons, was now increased to near Thirty.

There was not only a solemn Attention among them, but some considerable Impressions ('twas apparent) were made upon their Minds by divine Truths. Some began to feel their Misery and perishing State, and appear'd concern'd for a Deliverance from it.

Lords-Day, *June* 23. Preach'd to the *Indians* and spent the Day with them— Their Number still increas'd; and all with one Consent seem'd to rejoice in my coming among them. Not a Word of Opposition was heard from any of them against Christianity, altho' in times past, they had been as opposite to any Thing of that Nature, as any *Indians* whatsoever. And some of them not many Months before, were engaged with my *Interpreter* because he attempted to teach them something of Christianity.

June 24. Preach'd to the *Indians* at their desire and upon their own Motion. To see poor *Pagans* desirous of hearing the Gospel of CHRIST, animated me to discourse to them, altho' I was now very weakly, and my Spirits much exhausted. They attended with the greatest seriousness and diligence; and there was some Concern for their Souls Salvation, apparent among them.

June 27. Visited and preach'd to the *Indians* again. Their Number now amounted to about *Forty* Persons. Their Solemnity and Attention still continued; and a considerable Concern for their Souls became very apparent among sundry of them.

June 28. The *Indians* being now gather'd a considerable Number of them, from their several and distant *Habitations*, requested me to preach twice a Day to them, being desirous to hear as much as they possibly could while I was with them. I cheerfully complied with their motion, and could not but admire at the Goodness of God, who, I was persuaded, had inclin'd them thus to enquire after the Way of Salvation.

June 29. Preach'd again twice to the Indians. Saw (as I thought) the Hand of God very evidently, and in a Manner somewhat remarkable, making Provision for their Subsistence together, in Order to their being instructed in divine Things. For this Day and the Day before, with only walking a little way from the Place of our daily Meeting, they killed *three Deer*, which were a seasonably Supply for their wants, and without which, it seems, they could not have subsisted together in order to attend the Means of Grace.

Lords-Day, June 30. Preach'd twice this Day also. Observ'd yet more Concern and Affection among the poor *Heathens* than ever: So that they even constrain'd me to tarry yet longer with them; altho' my Constitution was exceedingly worn out, and my Health much impair'd by my late fatigues and labours, and especially by my late Journey to *Susquehanna* in *May* last, in which I lodg'd on the Ground for *several Weeks* together.

July 1. Preach'd again twice to a very serious and attentive Assembly of *Indians*, they having now learn'd to attend the Worship of God, with *Christian Decency* in all respects.

There were now between *Forty* and *Fifty* Persons of them present, old and young.

I spent some considerable Time in discoursing with them in a more private Way, enquiring of them what they remembered of the great Truths that had been taught them from Day to Day; and may justly say, 'twas amazing to see how they had receiv'd and retain'd the Instructions given them, and what a Measure of Knowledge some of them had acquir'd in a few Days.

July 2. Was oblig'd to leave these *Indians* at *Crosweeksung*, thinking it my Duty, as soon as Health would admit, again to visit those at the *Forks of Delaware*. When I came to take leave of them, and spoke something particularly to each of them, they all earnestly enquir'd when I would come again, and expressed a great desire of being further instructed. And of their own accord agreed, that when I should come again, they would all meet and live together during my Continuance with them. And that they would do their utmost Endeavours to gather all the other *Indians* in *these Parts* that were yet further remote. And when I parted, one told me with many Tears, *She wished God would change her Heart.* Another, That *she wanted to find Christ.* And an old Man that had been one of their *Chiefs*, wept bitterly with concern for his Soul. I then promis'd them to return as speedily as my Health, and Business elsewhere would admit, and felt not a little concern'd at parting, lest the good Impressions then apparent upon Numbers of them, might decline and wear off, when the Means came to cease; and yet could not but hope that he who, I trusted, had begun a good Work among them, and who I knew did not stand in need of Means to carry it on, would maintain and promote it in the Absence of them, altho at the same Time I must confess, that I had so often seen such encouraging Appearances among the *Indians* otherwhere prove wholly abortive; and it appear'd the Favour would be so great, if God should now, after I had pass'd thro' so considerable a Series of almost fruitless Labours and Fatigues, and after my rising Hopes had been so often frustrated among these poor *Pagans*, give me any *special* Success in my Labours with them, that I could not believe, and scarce dared to hope that the Event would be so happy, and scarce ever found myself more suspended between Hope and Fear, in any Affair, or at any Time than this.

This encouraging Disposition and Readiness to receive Instruction, now apparent among these *Indians*, seems to have been the happy Effect of the Conviction that one or two of them met with some Time since at the Forks of *Delaware*, who have since endeavour'd to shew their Friends the Evil of *Idolatry*, &c. And altho' the other *Indians* seem'd but little to regard, but rather to deride them, yet this, perhaps, has put them into a *thinking* Posture of Mind, or at least, given them some Thoughts about Christianity, and excited in some of them a *Curiosity to bear*, and so made Way for the present encouraging Attention. An Apprehension that this might be the Case here, has given me Encouragement that God may in *such* a Manner bless the Means I have used with *Indians* in other Places, where there is as yet no Appearance of it. If so, may his Name have the Glory of it; for I have learn'd by Experience that he only can open the Ear, engage the Attention, and incline the Heart of poor benighted prejudic'd *Pagans* to receive Instruction...

Aug. 8. In the Afternoon I preached to the *Indians*, there Number was now about Sixty-Five Persons, Men, Woman and Children: I discours'd from *Luke* 14:16-23 and was favour'd with *uncommon* Freedom in my Discourse.

There was much visible Concern among them while I was discoursing publicly; but afterwards when I spoke to one and another more particularly, whom I perceiv'd under much concern, the Power of God seem'd to descend upon the Assembly *like a rushing mighty Wind,* and with an astonishing Energy bore down all before it.

I stood amaz'd at the Influence that seiz'd the Audience almost universally, and could compare it to nothing more aptly, than the irresistible Force of a mighty Torrent, or swelling Deluge, that with its insupportable Weight and Pressure, bears down and sweeps before it whatever is in its Way! Almost all Persons of all Ages were bow'd down with Concern together, and scarce one was able to withstand the *Shock* of this surprising Operation! Old Men and Women who had been drunken Wretches for many Years, and some little Children, not more than Six or Seven Years of Age appear'd in Distress for their Souls, as well as Persons of middle Age. And 'twas apparent these Children (some of them at least) were not *merely* frightened with seeing the general Concern; but were made sensible of their Danger, the Badness of their Hearts, and their Misery without Christ, as some of them express'd it. The most stubborn Hearts was now oblig'd to bow. A principal Man among the *Indians*, who before was most secure and Self-righteous, and thought his State good because he knew more than the Generality of the *Indians* had formerly done, and who with a great Degree of Confidence the Day before, told me, *he had been a Christian more than ten Years*, was now brought under solemn Concern for his Soul, and wept bitterly. Another Man considerable in Years, who had been a *Murderer*, a *Powwow* (or Conjurer) and a notorious Drunkard, was likewise brought now to cry for Mercy with many Tears, and to complain much that he could be no more concern'd when he saw his Danger so very great.

They were almost universally praying and crying for Mercy in every Part of the House, and many out of Doors, and Numbers could neither go nor stand: Their concern was so great, each one for himself, that none seem'd to take any Notice of those about them, but each pray'd as freely for themselves; and (I'm apt to think) were, to their own Apprehension, as much retir'd as if they had been every one by themselves in the thickest Desert: Or, I believe rather, that they thought nothing about *any* but themselves, and their own States, and so were every one praying *a-part*, altho' all *together*.

It seem'd to me there was now an exact Fulfillment of that Prophesy *Zechariah* 12:10-12. For there was now *a great Mourning like the Mourning* of Hadadrimmon.— And each seem'd to *mourn a-part*. Methought this had a near Resemblance to the Day of God's Power, mention'd *Joshua* 10:14. For I must say, I never see *any Day like it* in all Respects: 'Twas a Day wherein I am persuaded the Lord did much to destroy the Kingdom of Darkness among this People.

This Concern in general was most rational and just, those who had been awaken'd any considerable Time, complained more especially of the Badness of their *Hearts*; and those newly awaken'd of the Badness of their *Lives* and *Actions* past; and all were afraid of the Anger of God, and of everlasting Misery as the Desert of their Sins.

Some of the *white* People who came out of Curiosity to *hear what this Babbler would say*, to the poor ignorant *Indians*, were much awakened, and some appear'd to be wounded with a View of their perishing State.

Those who had lately obtain'd Relief, were fill'd with Comfort at this Season; they appear'd calm and compos'd, and seemed to rejoice in *Christ Jesus*: And some of them took their distressed Friends by the Hand, telling them of the Goodness of Christ, and the Comfort that is to be enjoyed in him, and thence invited them to come and give up their Hearts to him. And I could observe some of them in the most honest and unaffected Manner (without any design of being taken Notice of) lifting up their Eyes to Heaven as if crying for Mercy, while they saw the Distress of the poor Souls around them.

David Brainerd, *Mirabilia Dei inter Indicos, or the Rise and Progress of a Remarkable Work of Grace Amongst a Number of the Indians in the Provinces of New-Jersey and Pennsylvania, Justly Represented in a Journal Kept by Order of the Honourable Society (in Scotland) for Propagating Christian Knowledge* (Philadelphia: William Bradford, [1746]), 1–7, 21–4.

21

A Selection of Hymns

Benjamin Ingham

BORN IN OSSETT, Yorkshire, England, the handsome Benjamin Ingham (1712–72) received his education at Queen's College, Oxford, from 1730 to 1734 during which time he met John and Charles Wesley and joined the "Holy Club." After graduating, Ingham and the Wesleys boarded a vessel to Georgia in October 1735. On the voyage, Ingham met a group of Moravians whose piety impressed him greatly. While in Georgia he labored to learn the language of the Native Americans, with the intent of becoming a missionary to the Choctaws, but failed to receive permission from the colonial governor. Returning to England in February 1737, and after a short stint at Ossett, Ingham and John Wesley traveled to Germany in June 1738 where they visited Moravian communities at Marienborn and Herrnhut before returning to England in October of the same year. The following February, Ingham began preaching throughout West Yorkshire, establishing some forty societies, which he later turned over to the Moravians.

Besides being a zealous evangelist, Ingham was a gifted songwriter. In 1748 he published his *Collection of Hymns*, which exhibits a Moravian-type fascination for the blood and wounds of Christ as well as God's grace given to sinners. Although not credited, some of the hymns are believed to be composed by Isaac Watts and Charles Wesley. Ingham officially joined the Moravian Brethren in July 1749, but by February 1753 he had become disillusioned with the religious movement, parting company amicably with them. By 1759 he became interested in the teachings of John Glas and his son-in-law Robert Sandeman, converting his remaining societies into Glasite churches in the early 1760s before his death on December 2, 1772.

FIGURE 21.1 Benjamin Ingham (Detail), Print Collection, Miriam and Ira D. Wallach Division of Art, Prints and Photographs, the New York Public Library, Astor, Lenox and Tilden Foundations.

A Collection of Hymns for Societies

I.

1. *THE Deeds of the Lamb,*
    His Cross, Blood, and Name,
We all are determin'd alone to proclaim.
    2. *When Others relate*
        The Deeds of the Great;
We'll mention his Conquests, and kiss his dear Feet.
        3. *He saw in the Fall*
            The Ruin of all,
The Offences erecting a Partition Wall.
            4. *He saw the drawn Sword*
                Flame forth from the Lord
To slay all the People He made by his Word.
                5. *Then ran He between*
                    The Wrath and the Sin;
And thus to the Father did Jesus begin.
                    6. *My Father revere'd,*
                        Thy People have err'd;
But oh! let thy Creatures in Mercy be spar'd.
                        7. *E'er them Thou consume,*
                            Lo! I thy Son come
To die and be punish'd in poor Sinners Room.

8. *He said; and his Sire*
   Laid by his dread Ire,
Refrain'd to take Vengeance which burnt like a Fire.
9. *Then cried the Lamb;*
   The World's Sin and Shame
Chastise in my Person, and there lay the Blame.
10. *The Father comply'd;*
    Our Lust and our Pride
He charg'd on his Son, who to cancel it died.
11. *This Beelzebub found,*
    Who all Men had bound;
Whose Head the Redeemer by Dying did wound.
12. *This makes him distress*
    And tempt and oppress
The Souls of the Faithful, who firm believe this.
13. *But let him tempt on,*
    He shall not get one
Of those who do trust in the Blood of God's Son.

II.

1. *OF Christ our Righteousness we Sing,*
To Him our hearty Blessings bring;
To Him we Honour give alone,
And chant his Name around the Throne.

2. *On all, besides his precious Blood,*
On all besides the Son of God,
We trample boldly and disclaim
All other Saviours but the Lamb.

3. *The Idol of Self-Righteousness*
We now disown, and now confess
No Righteousness, but His, who died;
By Faith to all his Seed applied.

4. *To Jesus evermore we Sing*
Our crucified exalted King,
And Naught we mention or confess
But Jesu's Blood and Righteousness.

III.

1. *HOW foolish I am,*
     I turn from the Lamb,
And gaze on my Heart, and so nurse my dead Frame.

2. *I often have view'd*
     My Sins Multitude,
And not my dear Saviour all cover'd with Blood.

3. *This keeps me so low;*
     This add to my Woe:
Because to myself, not to Jesus I go.

4. *Look up unto Me*
     Stretched out on the Tree,
Saith Jesus the Saviour, and I will help Thee.

5. *Behold me, and gaze,*
     On my Wounds always:
I've aton'd for thy Sins, and purchas'd thee Grace.

6. *Consider not thou*
     How dead and how low
Thou art in thyself, but thy Saviour view.

7. *O teach me, my GOD,*
     Beneath every Load
To view thee by Faith, and to trust in thy Blood.

VI.

1. *O Thou that hear'st when Sinners cry,*
Tho' all my Crimes before Thee lie,
Behold them not with angry Look,
But blot their Memory from thy Book.

2. *Create my Nature pure within,*
And form my Soul averse to Sin:
Let thy good Spirit ne'er depart,
Nor hide thy Presence from my Heart.

3. *I cannot live without thy Light,*
Cast out and banish'd from thy Sight:
Thine holy Joys, my God, restore,
And guard me that I fall no more.

4. *Tho' I have griev'd thy Spirit, Lord,*
His Help and Comfort still afford:
Heal me with thy precious Blood,
Thou merciful Sin-pardoning God.

XII.

1. BEING of Beings, great I AM,
   Thro' Christ our Father now,
Before thy Foot-stool Mighty God,
   Prostrate ourselves we bow.
   2. God to Perfection who can know?
   Him who has ever seen?
What is his Being, Wisdom, Strength,
   His Majesty or Mien?
   3. In Heaven he dwells in blazing Day,
   In Light so burning bright,
No Creature can approach thereto,
   It blinds the strongest Sight.
   4. Down in the Dust with bended Hearts
   Most willingly we fall;
We are mere Nothings, Worms of Earth,
   And Thou the Mighty All.
   5. Yet, Great I AM, in Jesu's Face
   We know Something of Thee,
Some little we already taste,
   Something we feel and See.
   6. As is thy Majesty most high,
   So is thy Mercy Sweet.
Thee, Lord, we bless, praise, glorify
   And worship at thy Feet.
   7. Hail! holy, holy, holy God,
   Be endless praise to Thee;
Thou art and wert and will be still
   Thro' all Eternity.

XIII.

1. O JESU, Bridegroom of my Soul,
   Make me a broken Vessel whole
   By that sweet Blood which on the Tree
   Was shed for Sinners such as me.
2. Full of Reproach, of Guilt, and Fear
   To Thee, my Saviour, I draw near;
   But tho' I'm naked, sick and blind,
   In Mercy cast me not behind.

3. *Thou, great Physician, cure my Heart,*
   Thy saving Health to me impart;
   Wash every sinful Stain away,
   And let me taste thy Grace to Day.

4. *Hungry and thirsty Lo! I come,*
   O let me in thy Wounds find Room;
   There let me find a sheltering Place
   To hide and screen me from Disgrace.

5. *Do, dearest Lamb, to me apply*
   Thy bloody Sweat and Agony;
   Thy sacred Body slain for me
   From Sin set Soul and Body free.

6. *And from thy Side into my Heart*
   The Seed of Life Divine impart;
   Thy Spirit send to dwell with me
   And form a New Man like to Thee.

7. *Lord Jesus, grant I may abide*
   For ever safe within thy Side;
   In thy dear Side-hole may I dwell
   Secure from all the Powers of Hell.

Benjamin Ingham, *A Collection of Hymns for Societies* (Leeds: James Lister, 1748), 3–6, 13–14.

22

Summarizing God's Law

Joseph Bellamy

THE CONGREGATIONALIST PASTOR Joseph Bellamy (1719–90) ranks as one of the most important evangelical theologians of the eighteenth century. Along with Samuel Hopkins, Bellamy became a disciple of Jonathan Edwards and progenitor of the "New Divinity" movement, a school of ministers who sought to explicate Edwards's theology while dominating the pulpits of New England, which they did from the end of the eighteenth century into the first decades of the nineteenth century. A behemoth of a man, Bellamy reportedly stood over six feet tall and weighed around 300 pounds. After graduating from Yale in 1735, he spent over a year studying under Jonathan Edwards at Northampton, Massachusetts before obtaining a license to preach in 1737 and settling as the minister at Bethlehem, Connecticut in 1740. Bellamy's most influential work is his *True Religion Delineated* (1750), a book prefaced by Jonathan Edwards and described by a character in Harriet Beecher Stowe's novel *Oldtown Folks* as "heedfully and earnestly read in every good family of New England." In it Bellamy outlined the intricacies of what he believed true Christianity depended on, namely obedience to the law.

In the aftermath of the revivals in America in the early decades of the eighteenth century, Bellamy, in a similar way as Jonathan Edwards in his *Religious Affections*, wanted to write a theological work that would help religiously conscious people determine whether they truly had obtained the grace of God. Bellamy aspired to convince his readers that God's moral law, established before creation, remained in force, even after the sacrificial death of Jesus Christ. By the "law," Bellamy did not mean a set of endless legal rules that Christians must follow. Rather, the law could be summed up by the two commands of Jesus: love God with all your heart, soul, and strength, and love your neighbor as yourself. Bellamy asserted that the two decrees formed the heart of what it meant to be an authentic believer. If a person had been given saving grace by God, which resulted in a spiritual new birth, only then could he or she truly love God and others.

True Religion Delineated

It is reasonable and fit, and a Thing becoming and beautiful, that Beings in a State of Probation should be tried: and God looks upon the present outward Ease and Comfort even of his own People, as a Matter of no Importance, compared with Things spiritual and eternal. Eternity, with all its Importance, lies open to his View; and Time appears as a Point, and all its Concerns as Things comparatively of no Worth. If the Wicked are in Prosperity, and the Righteous in Adversity, or all Things come alike to all, God is well-pleased; because Things of Time are of so little Importance, and because such an Administration of Things is suited to a State of Trial. There will be Time enough hereafter, for the Righteous to be rewarded, and the Wicked punished. In this View of Things, we may, in a Measure, understand the darkest, and account for the most mysterious, Dispensations of divine Providence, and discern the Wisdom of the divine Government.

It has doubtless appeared as a Thing strange and dark to many pious Persons, and occasioned not a little Perplexity of Mind, to observe what has come to pass in New-England since the Year 1740. That there should be so general an Out-pouring of the Spirit, so many Hundreds and Thousands awakened all over the Country, and such an almost universal external Reformation, and so many receive the Word with Joy; and yet, after all, Things come to be as they now are: so many fallen away to carnal Security, and so many turned Enthusiasts and Heretics, and the Country so generally settled in their Prejudices against experimental Religion and the Doctrines of the Gospel, and a Flood of Arminianism and Immorality, ready to deluge the Land. But as strange and dark as it may have seemed, yet doubtless if any of us had lived with the Israelites in the Wilderness, or in the three first Ages after Christ, or in the Time of the Reformation from Popery, the Dispensations of divine Providence would upon the whole have appeared much more mysterious than they do now. And yet those were Times when God was doing glorious Things for his Church. And indeed, it has happened in our Day, however strange it may seem to us, no otherwise than our Saviour foretold it commonly would under the Gospel-Dispensation, at least `till Satan is bound, that he may deceive the Nations no more. The Sower goes forth to sow, and some Seed falls by the Way-Side, & some on stony, & some on thorny, and some on good Ground; and while he is sowing good Seed, an Enemy in the Night, the Devil unobserved, sows Tares: Now when the Sun is up, i.e. when new Times come on, and Trials approach, the main of the Seed is lost; not only what fell by the Way-Side, but also what fell on the stony and thorny Ground. And when the good Ground is about to bring forth Fruit, the Tares begin to appear too. Matthew 13. Thus it has always been. This is a State of Trial, and God has permitted so many sad and awful Things to happen in Times of Reformation, with Design to prove the Children of Men, and know what is in their Hearts.

The Young People almost all over New-England professed, they would forever renounce youthful Vanities, and seek the Lord. "Well," God, in the Course of his Providence, as it were, says, "I will try you." Seeming Converts expressed great Love to Christ, his

Truths, and Ministers, and Ways; "Well," says God, "I will try you." Multitudes, being Enemies to all true Religion, longed to see the whole Reformation fall into Disgrace, and Things return to their own Channel; and they sought for Objections and Stumbling-Blocks: "Well," says God, "You may have them, and I will try and see how you will be affected, and what you will say, and whether you will be as glad when the Cause of my SON is betrayed by the Miscarriages of those that profess to be his Friends, as the Jews *of old were, when my SON himself was betrayed into their Hands by* Judas*." Thus God means to try everyone.*

A compassionate Sense of the Exercises, which godly Persons, especially among common People, might be under in these evil Days, while some are fallen away, and others are clapping their Hands and rejoicing with all their Hearts to see Zion *laid waste; while* Arminians *are glossing their Scheme, and appealing to Reason and common Sense, as tho' their Principles were near or quite self-evident to all Men of Thought and Candour; and while* Enthusiasts *are going about as Men inspired and immediately sent by the Almighty, pretending to extraordinary Sanctity, and bold in it that they are so holy in themselves, and so entirely on the Lord's Side, that all godly People must, and can't but, see as they do, and fall in with them, unless they are become blind, dead and carnal, and got back into the World; A compassionate Sense, I say, of the Exercises of Mind, which pious Persons among common People might have, in such a trying Situation of Things, was the first Motive, which excited me to enter upon this Work, which I now offer to the Public. And to make divine Truths plain to such, and to strip Error naked before their Eyes, that they might be established and comforted and quickened in their Way Heavenward, was the End I had in View. And accordingly I have laboured very much to adapt my self to the lowest Capacities, not meaning to write a Book for the Learned and Polite, but for common People, and especially for those that are godly among them.*

To these therefore, that they may read what I have written with the greater Profit, I will offer these two Directions.

(1.) Labour after determinate Ideas of God and a Sense of his infinite Glory. *This will spread a Light over all the Duties and Doctrines of Religion, and help you to understand the Law and the Gospel, and to pry into the Mysteries, and discern the Beauties, of the divine Government. By much the greatest Part of what I have written, besides showing what GOD is, consists in but so many Propositions deduced from the divine Perfections. Begin here therefore, and learn what GOD is, and then what the moral Law is; and this will help you to understand what our Ruin is, and what the Way of our Recovery by free Grace thro'* JESUS CHRIST. *The Bible is designed for rational Creatures, and has God for its Author; and you may therefore depend upon it, that it contains a Scheme perfectly rational, divine & glorious. And the Pleasure of divine Knowledge will a thousand Times more than recompense all your Reading, Study and Pains: Only content not yourselves with a general superficial Knowledge, but enter thoroughly into Things.*

(2.)   Practice, as well as read. *The End of Reading and Knowledge is Practice. And holy Practice will help you to understand what you read.* Love GOD with all your Heart, *and* your Neighbour as your self; *and you can't but understand me, while in the first Discourse I shew what is implied in these two great Commands. And practice* Repentance towards God *and* Faith towards our Lord Jesus Christ; *and the second Discourse, which treats of the Nature of the Gospel and a genuine Compliance therewith, will naturally become plain and easy. And while you daily study divine Truths in your Heads, and digest them well in your Hearts, and practice them in your Lives, your Knowledge and holiness will increase, and God's Word & Providence be better understood, your perplexing Difficulties will be more solved, and you be established, strengthened and comforted, in your Way Heaven-ward; and your Light shining before Men, they will see your good Works, and your Father which is in Heaven will be glorified . . .*

TRUE Religion consists in a Conformity to the *Law* of God, and in a Compliance with the *Gospel* of Christ. The Religion of innocent Man consisted only in a Conformity to the Law; the Law of Nature, with the Addition of one positive Precept: he had no need of Gospel Grace. But when Man lost his Innocence and became guilty and depraved, when he fell under the Wrath of God and Power of Sin; he needed a Redeemer and a Sanctifier: and in the Gospel a Redeemer and a Sanctifier are provided, and a Way for our obtaining pardoning Mercy and sanctifying Grace is opened; a Compliance, with which, does now therefore become Part of the Religion of a fallen Creature. Now if we can but rightly understand the *Law*, and rightly understand the *Gospel*, we may easily see wherein a Conformity to the one, and a Compliance with the other, does consist; and so what *true Religion* is. For the present, let us take the *Law* under Consideration. And it will be proper to inquire into these following Particulars. 1. What Duty does God require of us in his Law? 2. From what Motives must that Duty be done? 3. What is that precise Measure of Duty which God requires in his Law? And a short, but very clear and plain Answer to all these Questions we have before us in our Text; which is the Words of our blessed Saviour, and in which he does upon Design declare what the Sum and Substance of the Law is. He had a Question put to him in these Words; "Master, which is the great Commandment in the Law?" To which he answers— "Thou shalt love the Lord thy God with all thy Heart &c. this is the first. The second is like unto it &c." The ten Commandments are sum'd up in these two, and every Duty enjoined in the Law, and inculcated in the Prophets, are but so many Deductions from these two, in which all are radically contained. A thorough understanding of these two will therefore give us an Insight into all . . .

A true Knowledge of God is implied. For this lays the Foundation for Love. A spiritual Sight of God, and a Sense of his Glory and Beauty, begets Love. When He that commanded the Light to shine out of Darkness, shines in our Hearts, and gives us the Light of the Knowledge of the Glory of God; and when we with open Face behold as in a Glass the Glory of the Lord, then we are changed into the same Image: The Temper and Frame of our Hearts become like God's: (To speak after the Manner of Men) we begin to feel towards God, in a Measure as he does towards himself; i.e. to love him with all our Hearts. 2 *Corinthians* 3:18 & 4:6. For now we begin to perceive the Grounds and Reasons of that infinite Esteem he has of Himself, and infinite Complacency in Himself, and why he commands all the World to love and adore him. And the same Grounds and Reasons which move him thus to love Himself, and command all the World to do so too, do enkindle the divine Flame in our Hearts. When we see God, in a Measure, such as he sees Himself to be, and have a Sense of his Glory and Beauty in being what he is, in a Measure, as he Himself has, then we begin to love him with the same Kind of Love, and from the same Motives, as he Himself does: only in an infinitely inferiour Degree. This Sight and Sense of God, discovers the Grounds of Love to him: We see why he requires us to love him, and why we ought to love him, how right and fit it is; and so we cannot but love him.

This true Knowledge of God supposes, that in a Measure, we see God to be just such a One as he is; and, in a Measure, have a Sense of his infinite Glory & Beauty in being such. For if our Apprehensions of God are not right, it is not *God* we love, but only a false Image of him framed in our own Fancy. And if we have not a Sense of his Glory and Beauty in being what he is, it is impossible we should genuinely love and esteem him for being such. To love God for being what he is, and yet not to have any Sense of his Glory and Beauty in being such, implies a Contradiction. For it supposes, we have a Sense of his Glory and Beauty when we have not: a Sense of the Beauty and Amiableness of any Object being always necessarily implied in Love to it. Where no Beauty or Amiableness is seen, there can be no Love. Love cannot be forced. Forced Love is no Love. If we are obliged to try to force ourselves to love any Body, it is a Sign they are very odious in our Eyes, or at least that we see no Beauty nor Amiableness in them, no Form or Comeliness, wherefore we should desire or delight in them.

Joseph Bellamy, *True Religion Delineated; or, Experimental Religion, As Distinguished from Formality on the One Hand, and Enthusiasm on the Other, Set in a Scriptural and Rational Light* (Boston: S. Kneeland, 1750), iii–4.

23

Revival in the Low Countries

Hugh Kennedy

HUGH KENNEDY'S SHORT *Account of the Rise and Continuing Progress of a Remarkable Work of Grace in the United Netherlands* (1752) provided compelling evidence that America and Britain were not the only places to experience midcentury revivals. Born in Ireland and raised by Scottish parents, Kennedy (1698–1764) studied at Glasgow University before being licensed to preach by the Jedburgh presbytery in 1720. In Scotland, he ministered at Torthorwald and Cavers in the early 1720s and then took a position as a minister at the Scots Church at Rotterdam in 1737, remaining in the Netherlands until his death in 1764. As a clergyman in the Kirk, Kennedy kept abreast of the 1740 revivals in America and Britain through his network of correspondents in Britain. His interest in the religious outpourings in Scotland led him to publish a Dutch translation of James Robe's *Faithful Narrative of the Extraordinary Work of the Spirit of God at Kilsyth* in 1743.

Kennedy argued that the 1742 revivals in Scotland were tied to a larger international upsurge in religious activity that had expanded into the Netherlands. He wrote to his friends about an awakening under the guidance of two Dutch Reformed ministers, Gerard Kuypers and Jacobus Roldanus, at the town of Nieuwkerk (Nijkerk), within the Veluwe region in the province of Gelderland. The revival commenced when an older woman, hearing a sermon by Roldanus, broke out into tears about her sins. Emotions from other congregants flared up later on November 16, 1749 during Kuypers's sermon on Psalm 72:16, and his public catechization the next day. Building on these events, the spiritual resurgence gained momentum and spread to some sixty other locations throughout the Netherlands and western parts of Germany. The Dutch awakening lasted until the autumn of 1752 when the Nijkerk consistory, under pressure from the stadholder William IV of Orange, implemented regulations that curbed religious excessive outbursts within the church services and lay-led meetings.

A *Short Account of the Rise and Continuing Progress of a Remarkable Work of Grace in the United Netherlands*

Rotterdam, October 2, 1750

Reverend Dear Brother,

I BLESS the Lord, I can give you the certain Account of the plentiful pouring out of the Holy Spirit, in several Congregations in the *Veluwe,* one of the Quarters of the Duchy of *Gelderland,* by whose blessed powerful Influences that amiable Kingdom, which consists in *Righteousness and Peace and Joy in the Holy Ghost,* is remarkably advanced. Of this great Event I had some confused Notice before I went to—but thought it my Duty to be silent about a Matter of such vast Importance, till I obtained full and certain Information, knowing well of what pernicious Consequence, groundless precipitant Reports are in most Cases, and especially of this Nature. This Information I have had since my return, and now desire to acknowledge and rejoice in this great Work of God.

This blessed Work begun in a town called *Nieuwkerk,* about ten *English* Miles above *Amersfoort,* and about as many from *Harderwijk* near the Head of the *Zuiderzee,* and from that Town the blessed Wind of the Spirit is blown over to five different Congregations, in the Villages of *Putten, Barneveld, Lunteren, Nunspeet,* and *Soest;* in all of which, especially in *Putten* the *Awakening* has been very great, and Multitudes, according to the best Judgment, brought under the blessed Bond of the everlasting Covenant.

There are two reformed Ministers in the Church of *Nieuwkerk,* the oldest is *J. J. Roldanus;* the other, who was called there [in] 1748, is called *Gerardus Kuypers:* The Lord has honoured them both to be instrumental in carrying on that blessed Work. Mr. *Kuypers* gives this Account of the Work.

It had been in this Place a dead barren backsliding Time for many Years past; conviction and conversion Work was very rare; the Place was full of Infidelity, Carnality, Profanity, and without the Fear of God to that Degree, that it was by other Places reproached, as being an Habitation of People, who by long Prosperity waxed fat and kicked against the Lord, trampling upon his Mercies and Judgments, so that Satan seemed to have established his Throne and Seat there upon Foundations not to be overturned. The small Remnant of the Godly who were in the Place were daily persecuted with bitter Scoffings and Mockings, their righteous Souls were pierced and grieved with the filthy Conversation of the Wicked, and could only look and cry to the Lord for Pity and Mercy, and the Return of his grieved, injured, departed *Spirit.*

In this awful situation of the Place one thing is very remarkable, That the Generality of that spiritually dead, graceless, fearless People, were much set upon fervent earnest Preaching, and loved to have their Ministers speak to them like Men who were seriously and in good earnest concerned about their eternal Welfare. This Temper the Lord seems to have made use of as a Means to bring Mr. *Kuypers* there, who seems to have a good deal of that kind of Talent: He was unanimously chosen and received with all desirable Tokens of Respect by that People, and found no difficulty to recommend himself to their good Opinions. This set something like an open Door before him, and gave some kind of probable Prospect of Usefulness.

The first Means which the Lord was pleased to bless, for awakening that dead secure People to something of Seriousness and Concern about eternal Things, was a public weekly Catechizing, set up with this good Design, that by this plain simple familiar Way of Instruction, ignorant People might be brought to some distinct Knowledge of the Lord in his Righteousness, Holiness, and Hatred of Sin, and in his Love, Grace and Mercy to the chiefest Sinners thro' *Jesus Christ*, and of themselves in their fallen, guilty, corrupt, miserable State and Condition. This Exercise was attended with great Success; many were stirred up to search the Scriptures, and filled with Desires after *the sincere milk of the word*; and the Lord left not himself without a Witness, that the Work was acceptable to him.

Another Thing which the Lord remarkably countenanced as a kind of prelude to and preparation for the great Work of Grace he was about to work among that People, was the setting apart of some Time for a sort of Fellowship Meetings or Christian Conferences, alternately in the Houses of the few among them who seemed to have any Fear of God, and particularly on the Evenings of the Lord's Day, after public Worship was over. Then Mr. *Kuypers* himself inquired particularly at those who were present at the Meetings, what they remembered of the Truths delivered in Public, whether they felt any Impressions, and what Effects were made upon their Hearts by the Word, and what Experience they had of any Progress in the Way of the spiritual Life.

These Meetings both on the Lord's Day and other Days of the Week, whether under the conduct and management of Mr. *Kuypers*, or of the few particular Christians that were in the Place, were immediately much talked of; many frequented them, probably at first out of Curiosity; the Numbers increased daily; Hundreds frequented them after their daily Labour was over (for that was the Time fix'd upon as most convenient) several were brought under some concern about their Souls, and began to see their miserable lost State, and were made to continue earnest in Prayer wrestling at *a Throne of Grace*, and had no Rest till their Eyes were fixed by Faith upon *the Lamb of God who takes away the Sin of the World*, and were brought as weary and heavy-laden Creatures, with the great Burden of all their Guilt, Corruption, Vileness and Unworthiness, to him who is the only appointed Refuge and Redeemer to deliver from the Guilt and Power of Sin, and in whom alone the Soul can find Rest. All this was carried on with little noise, silently as usually in the ordinary Work of the Conversion of particular Persons.

The Number of those who were in Soul-troubles increased, and the Lord made the Arrows of Conviction sharp in the Hearts of many; so that there was generally more than ordinary seriousness and solemnity in Hearing tho' attended with no general Fruit, and tho' some were brought under Convictions that silently issued in their Conversion to God.

In this Way that uncommon Dispensation of the Spirit was usher'd in, which they looked not for; for at last the preaching of the Gospel began to be attended with such awful Power, that several were made to cry aloud with many Tears from a bitter painful Sense of their dreadful Distress and Misery. The first Instance of this kind was under a Sermon of Mr. *Roldanus:* An aged Woman, in the most lamentable manner and with all the signs of Terror and Compunction, cried aloud for pity and mercy from the Lord. The novelty of this Event occasioned a great Commotion in the Congregation, and many were much affected with Distress and Trouble, but were a little calmed by the Minister's telling the Woman gravely and very solemnly, that the Word of Salvation was yet proclaimed to her, that *now* even *now was the accepted Time, the Day of Salvation*; it was not past, and very earnestly called upon all to seek the Lord while he was to be found.

After this all continued quiet for some Days, till the 16th of *November*, 1749, when Mr. *Kuypers* preached upon *Psalm* 72:16: *There shall be an handful of Corn in the Earth, upon the top of the Mountains; the Fruit thereof shall shake like* Lebanon, *and they of the City shall flourish like the Grass of the Earth.* The Spirit of the Lord began to work in an astonishing Manner; all that had past before seemed to have been a Preparation for greater and more glorious Things; for as it plainly appeared afterwards, very many were under that Word awakened, convinced and engaged, with the poor Prodigal, to give up the Husks and Dross of this World for the unsearchable Riches of Jesus Christ: Especially upon *Monday* the 17th, while Mr. *Kuypers* catechized in the Church upon the Subject of the former Day's Sermon, the shaking of that *Lebanon*, (as he expresses it) by the blowings of the Holy Spirit, became astonishing! The Trouble of Conscience and working of Affections was general. There was a great Lamentation, Rivers of Tears gushed out, and several fell trembling and astonished to the Earth, unable to stand by reason of the Agony and Agitation of their Spirits, arising from the sudden strong Impression made upon them of the dreadful State and crying Necessity of their Souls, and of these several called out to those about them, "View in me as in a fearful Glass, and see how bitter a Thing Sin will be at last, and how fearful the Wrath of the great and holy God!"

The troubled and broken in Heart were brought to Mr. *Kuyper's* House, who, upon conversing with them, soon discovered that the Holy Spirit by the Word had begun a Work of Conviction in them; for all their Sins were brought to remembrance and set strongly before them: They saw themselves to be the greatest and vilest Sinners, that by original and actual Sin they were lying under the righteous

Wrath of God: They justified God even thought he should cast them off for ever, and were full of wonder and astonishment that he had so long and so patiently born their horrid Provocations in their dreadful unconverted State. Mr. *Kuypers* finding Things thus with them, began to conceive some Hope that the Lord was coming near to the Congregation in a Way of rich Grace, but yet he stood astonished, conflicting with Doubts and Fears, to see so many Persons so strangely affected in that high measure and degree that all cried out with Sorrow, and made bitter Lamentations. His Doubts and Fears had a good Effect, for they made him very careful and circumspect in examining all these Appearances, and comparing them with the Lord's Word, and determined him to have his Eyes continually to the Throne of Grace for Wisdom to conduct him in this uncommon way the Lord was taking with that People, and Grace to bear up against the Scoffings, Reproaches and Oppositions he foresaw he might expect from those who are only *born of the flesh.* And he found sweet Rest in the believing Consideration of this, that the Lord who gives no account of his Matters, can, in his adorable Sovereignty, work in what way he pleases, and cause the Wind of his Spirit's Influences to blow when, where, and on whomsoever he will. This made him give the whole Work over into the Lord's Hands, who can and will take care of the Event, esteeming it the greatest Honour and dearest Privilege, if the Lord would employ him as a Watchman upon the Mountains of *Ephraim*, to cry, "Arise ye, and let us go up to *Zion* unto the Lord our God."

The next Day there being almost an universal Astonishment and Dejection among the Inhabitants of the Town, Mr. *Kuypers* went early in the Morning to the Houses of such of the awakened and distressed as were best known to him, and the Work being great, he got some private Christians to go to others: They were busy the whole Day, going to innumerable Houses, and every where there was nothing to be heard but bitter Complaints, Lamentations and Cries: Miserable Creatures that we are! What shall we do to be saved?

The following *Thursday* he preached upon *Acts* 16:30–31, where many were brought to a more near and distinct View of their true State and Condition; and *the Arrows of the great King made to stick fast in the Hearts of very many* who had hitherto continued insensible! From that Day the Work increased beyond Description; there is no painting of it to the Life, it was a perfect Commentary upon the second of the *Acts.* Mockers ridiculed, but Multitudes were pricked at their Hearts, and cried, What shall we do? In many Houses where formerly nothing was heard but Profanity and carnal Mirth, and Laughter, there was now nothing to be heard, but the Voice of Weeping, Prayer and Supplication! Mr. *Kuypers* was sent for from all Corners, and his House was continually full of such as came, anxiously inquiring if there was no relief for such miserable Sinners. Next Lord's Day the Lord graciously accompanied the Sermons of both Ministers, with such demonstration of the Spirit and Power, that many more were awakened to see their fearful State under the Curse of the Law and Wrath of God, and the number of the Convinced and Distressed increased more and more.

The Exercises of the most were carried on with a considerable measure of Quietness and Sedateness, who, as far as we may be allowed to judge, are savingly converted. But a great Number were exercised with great bodily Distress and Disorders, so that all that could be said or done to compose the Tumult, was but throwing Oil into a Flame. The Sense they had of the danger they were in every Moment, was too strong, lively and piercing, not to have a mighty and uncommon Influence upon the strongest Constitution. A sudden Surprise, by some interesting temporal Event, has oftentimes given a mortal shock to the human Frame: And may not a sudden Discovery of the dreadful evil of Sin, and of the unsearchable riches of Christ's Grace, meeting as it were in one saving Conviction in the Conscience of a poor awakened Sinner, reasonably be supposed to produce as great effects upon Men's Bodies?

Upon the closest Examination, it was found uniformly true, that this Soul distress and trouble did not flow merely from the fear of Wrath and Punishment, which alone can produce nothing better than *Esau's* Tears, *Ahab's* Fasting, *Nineveh's* Humiliation, or *Judas's* Repentance; but it flowed chiefly and principally from a Sense of the Dishonour and Provocation given to an infinitely good, gracious God, the ruin of his Image in the Sinner, and its loss of Likeness and Conformity to him, and Union to, Communion with, and Enjoyment of God! So that the poor Creatures would mourn over, hate and abhor their Sins and themselves for them, was it even possible that there was no Punishment connected with Sin.

Many in their greatest Distress cried out vehemently thus, Woe's me, what a Monster am I to sin against so gracious and merciful a God, to have injured, provoked, so holy, so good a God! Oh I am ashamed to lift my Face before God or Men! I am unworthy to behold the Heavens! Alas that I have so long been a Slave to Satan, a Servant to the World and Enemy to God! I have broken all his holy Laws, and never done any thing that is good in his Sight! I have despised his Gospel, trampled upon the Blood of his Christ, I have wounded my own Conscience, trod under Foot all my Convictions, and built the House of my Hopes upon the Sand, and upon a vain Imagination that I have little or no Guilt! I have presumptuously called myself one of God's Children tho' I knew him not! I have profanely and unworthily sat down at this Table tho' I loved him not, but had an Heart full of Enmity against him! Oh I have sinned against the Glory of God, and all the great undeniable Obligations that can be laid upon a rational Creature! Alas that I have been so long and so miserably blinded by the Devil, the World and the Flesh! O might I now be delivered from the cruel tyranny of Satan and bondage of Corruption! O I would wish never more to serve Sin nor Satan, tho' there were no Hell nor Punishment; but O how shall I be freed from this cruel hateful Slavery!

In this Way there would have been more than fifty Persons in a Day, at the Houses of the Ministers, struck with so deep a Sense of the exceeding sinfulness of their Sins and dreadfulness of God's Wrath, that they fell upon their Knees and afterwards flat upon the Earth, groaning and sighting out their bitter Lamentations. As the awakened and distressed were many in Number, being several Hundreds; so they were of all Characters and Ages, some Boys and Girls from seven to twelve years old, some that had been virtuously educated, and other that had been entirely neglected and lost in Ignorance and Wickedness, were made to see the Influence of this Work: Young Men and Women in the flower of their Youth and Strength have been made willing to submit to the Redeemer's Scepter! And old Persons of seventy, eighty and ninety Years who spent all their Days in Ignorance of God, deep Forgetfulness of him and Rebellion against him, have been at the eleventh Hour snatched as *brands out of the burning*, and were melted into Tears at the thoughts of the admirable Patience of a Redeemer, to bear so many horrid Provocations from them, and wait so long knocking at their Hearts for Entrance.

Many of the more knowing and learned in the speculative knowledge of Scripture Truths have been deeply and thoroughly convinced of their great Blindness and Ignorance, and have had the light of the Knowledge of the Glory of God in the face of Jesus Christ shining into their Hearts, and those great Things revealed to them of the Father which Flesh and Blood cannot teach: And several of the more virtuous and morally honest have been powerfully awakened out of their dead Formality, their fatal Security and Rest upon their own imaginary Righteousness, happily disturbed and brought to a full Conviction, That all the Morality in the world will not, cannot save a Soul without Union to *Jesus Christ* by the Spirit of Faith, Regeneration and Justification.

The Awakening went on so powerfully all the Months of *June* and *July*, that several hundred Strangers who came from other Places were made to feel its Influence and pricked to the Heart.

Hugh Kennedy, *A Short Account of the Rise and Continuing Progress of a Remarkable Work of Grace in the United Netherlands* (London: John Lewis, 1752), 9–17.

24

Satirical Revenge

John Witherspoon

PRIOR TO HIS installation as the president of the College of New Jersey, John Witherspoon (1723–94) was simply a Scottish minister. Educated at Edinburgh University during the early stages of the Scottish Enlightenment, alongside such luminaries as William Robertson, Hugh Blair, and John Erskine, Witherspoon received his license to preach from the presbytery of Haddington in 1743 before settling as the minister of Beith, Ayrshire, in early 1745. There he served for over thirteen years until he relocated to the prosperous Scottish textile town of Paisley in western Scotland. Gaining a reputation for his theological writings and as a defender of traditional orthodoxy against the more fashionable liberal Christianity of his day, Witherspoon was inundated with pastoral invitations in the late 1750s and 1760s: from the Scots Church at Rotterdam, the Scottish town of Dundee, and a Presbyterian church in Dublin, all of which he declined. He did, however, eventually accept a call from the College of New Jersey to become the school's sixth president, filling the vacancy of an office that had been plagued by the serial early deaths of Jonathan Dickinson, Aaron Burr Sr., Jonathan Edwards, Samuel Davies, and most recently Samuel Finley. Cajoled by Benjamin Rush to take the position, Witherspoon and his family emigrated to America in 1768 where he trained a host of future political leaders, including James Madison. Noted for being the only clergyman to sign the Declaration of Independence and an extremely active politician during the American Revolution, Witherspoon represented New Jersey in Congress from 1776 until 1782.

Witherspoon's *Ecclesiastical Characteristics* (1753) launched his career. One year before its publication, a faction of ministers within the Church of Scotland, known as the Moderate party, and under the leadership of William Robertson, gained control of the General Assembly, the highest ecclesiastical court in the land. Robertson and the Moderates succeeded in deposing the evangelical divine Thomas Gillespie of Carnock for refusing to install an unpopular nominee to the parish of Inverkeithing by force. The issue at stake had to do with patronage, the right of the

FIGURE 24.1 John Witherspoon by an unknown artist (Detail), Princeton University, gift of friends of the University, photo by Bruce M. White.

superior heritor of a parish to present a clergyman to a vacant pulpit regardless of support from the congregation. As a response to the Gillespie case, Witherspoon wrote a satire of his perception of the beliefs and practices of the Moderate party. Initially, written anonymously, Witherspoon's *Ecclesiastical Characteristics* purposely shared a similar title with the earl of Shaftesbury's *Characteristics of Men, Manners, Opinions, Times* (1711). Writing ostensibly as a Moderate minister, Witherspoon parodied the Moderates as valuing virtue over the salvation of souls and catering to the elites of society at the expense of the lower ranks. Witherspoon went on to publish other important works while living in Scotland, notably his *Essay on the Connection between the Doctrine of Justification by the Imputed Righteousness of Christ* (1756) and *A Serious Enquiry into the Nature and Effects of the Stage* (1757), a response to the Moderate minister John Home's play *Douglas*, but his *Ecclesiastical Characteristics* set the chain of events in motion for his later success.

Ecclesiastical Characteristics

Introduction

THE reader will doubtless agree with me, that moderation is an excellent thing, and particularly the noblest character of a church-man. It is also well known, that as all churches have usually in them a moderate, and a zealous, high-flying, wild party; so our church hath, at present, a certain party, who glory in, and fight for moderation; and who (it is to be hoped justly) appropriate to themselves wholly the character of moderate men; neither is it a small presage of a glorious and blessed state of the church, in its approaching periods, that so many of our young men are smitten with the love of moderation, and generally burn with desire to appear in that noble and divine character.

This hath inspired me with the ambition and expectation of being helpful in training up as many as are desirous of it, in this most useful of all sciences: for however perfectly it is known, and however steadily practiced by many who are adepts; and notwithstanding there are some young men, of pregnant parts, who make a sudden and surprising proficiency, with much assistance; yet I have often observed, that there are several persons, who err, in many instances, from the right path, boggle at sundry particular steps of their leaders, and take a long time before they are thoroughly confirmed in their principles and practice. The same persons also, by an unstable conduct, or by an imprudent, or unseasonable discovery of their designs, have brought a reproach upon their party, and been an obstruction to whatever work they had then in hand.

These bad effects, I humbly conceive, flow chiefly, if not only, from the want of a complete system of moderation, containing all the principles of it, and giving a distinct view of their mutual influence one upon another, as well as proving their reasonableness, and shewing, by examples, how they ought to be put in practice.

There is no work of this kind, to my knowledge, yet extant, which renders my present undertaking of it the more laudable, and will, I hope, render it the more acceptable.

I must inform the reader, that after I was fully convinced of the necessity of some such piece as what follows, but before I entered upon it myself, I earnestly entreated several of the most eminent men of the moderate stamp among us, these burning and shining lights of our church, who are, and are esteemed to be, our leaders, that some of them would set about it. However they all devolved it upon me, and made this satisfying excuse for themselves, that they were so busied in *acting* moderation, that they could not have time to *write* upon it. This soon led me to think what would become of many noble designs, and what advantage our discontented zealots might take, if any of the expert steersmen of this ecclesiastical vessel of ours, should retire from the helm but so long time as would be necessary to bring a work of such a nature, to the perfection in strength, symmetry, and elegance, that the reader will perceive, even this of mine is arrived at.

I shall now proceed to the principal part of the work, after I have informed the reader of the plan of it, which is briefly this, to enumerate distinctly, and in their proper order and connection, all the several Maxims upon which moderate men conduct themselves: and forasmuch as the justice of many of them, being refined pieces of policy, is not very evident at first sight, I shall subjoin to each an illustration and confirmation of it from reason, or experience, or both. *N.B.* I shall make but very little use of scripture, because that is contrary to some of the maxims themselves, as will be seen in the sequel.

Maxim I

All ecclesiastical persons, of whatever rank, whether principals of colleges, professors of divinity, ministers, or even probationers, that are suspected of heresy, are to be esteemed men of great genius, vast learning, and uncommon worth, and are, by all means, to be supported and protected.

All moderate men have a kind of fellow-feeling with heresy, and as soon as they hear of any one suspected, or in danger of being prosecuted for it, zealously, and unanimously rise up in his defence. This fact is unquestionable. I never knew a moderate man in my life, that did not love and honour a heretic, or that had not an implacable hatred at the persons and characters of heresy-hunters; a name with which we have thought proper to stigmatize these sons of Belial, who begin and carry on prosecutions against men for heresy in church courts...

Maxim II

When any man is charged with loose practices, or tendencies to immorality, he is to be screened and protected, as much as possible, especially if the faults laid to his charge be, as they are incomparably well termed in a sermon, preached by a hopeful youth, that made some noise lately, good-humored vices.

The reason upon which this maxim is founded, may be taken from the reasons of the former, *mutatis mutandis* there being scarcely any of them that does not hold equally in both cases: a Libertine is a kind of practical heretic, and is to be treated as such. Dr. Tillotson observes, in one of his sermons, that the worst of all heresies is a bad life: now, if instead of *worst*, which is an uncomely expression, you would read *greatest* in that passage, then a Libertine is the greatest of all heretics, and to be honoured in proportion. Even the apostle Paul (who is very seldom of any use to us in our reasonings) seems to suppose, that they are men of most knowledge, who are most free and bold in their practice; and that they are only weak brethren who are filled with scruples. The weak man is restrained and confined by his narrow conscience, but the strong man believeth that he may eat, and, by parity of reason, drink all things.

Let it also be observed, that *good-humored vices* are certainly *social pleasures,* such as flow from, and show benevolence; and this is an affection for which our whole fraternity have the highest regard, insomuch that the very word has become the Shibboleth of our party...

Maxim III

It is a necessary part of the character of a moderate man, never to speak of the Confession of Faith but with a sneer; to give sly hints, that he does not thoroughly believe it; and to make the word orthodoxy *a term of contempt and reproach.*

The Confession of Faith, which we are now all laid under a disagreeable necessity to subscribe, was framed in times of hot religious zeal; and therefore it can hardly be supposed, to contain any thing agreeable to our sentiments, in these cool and refreshing days of moderation. So true is this, that I do not remember to have heard any moderate man speak well of it, or recommend it in a sermon, or private discourse, in my time. And indeed nothing can be more ridiculous, than to make a fixed standard for opinions, which change just as the fashion of clothes and dress. No complete system can be settled for all ages, except the maxims I am now compiling and illustrating; and their great perfection lies in their being ambulatory, so that they may be applied differently, with the change of times...

Maxim IV

A good preacher must not only have all the above and subsequent principles of moderation in him, as the source of every thing that is good, but must, over and above, have the following special marks and signs of a talent for preaching. 1. *His subjects must be confined to* social duties. 2. *He must recommend them only from* rational considerations, *viz. the beauty and comely proportions of* virtue, *and its advantages in the present life, without any regard to a future state of more extended self-interests.* 3. *His authority must be drawn from* heathen writers, NONE, *or as few as possible, from* scripture. 4. *He must be very* unacceptable *to the* common people.

These four marks of a good preacher, or rules for preaching well (for they serve equally for both purposes) I shall endeavour distinctly to illustrate and confirm, that this important branch of my subject may be fully understood.

As to the *first* of these rules, that a preacher's subjects must be confined to *social duties*, it is quite necessary in a moderate man, because his moderation teaches him to avoid all the high flights of evangelic enthusiasm, and the mysteries of grace, which the common people are so fond of. It may be observed, nay, it is observed, that all of our stamp avoid the word *grace* as much as possible, and have agreed to substitute the *moral virtues* in the room of the *graces of the Spirit*, which is the orthodox expression. And indeed it is not in this only, but in all other cases that we endeavour to improve the phraseology, and show, that besides sentiment, even in language itself, we are far superior to, and wiser than our fathers before us...

The *second* rule will be easily confirmed, that duties are to be recommended only from *rational considerations*. What can be imagined more foolish than to contradict this? If there be any thing in a sermon different from rational considerations, it must be irrational, that is to say, absurd. It is in this part of our scheme that we, moderate men, obtain a glorious triumph over our adversaries and despisers. Who but must smile, when they hear the contemptible vulgar, ignorant, hot-headed country elders, or silly women, led captive by them at their will, saying, they do not love this rational way of going to heaven!

But to explain this method a little further, the rational way of preaching is sometimes set in opposition to the pathetic way of raising the passions. This last is what we greatly disapprove of: there is something immoderate in the very idea of raising the passions, and therefore it is contrary to our character: nor was it ever known, that a truly moderate man raised or moved any affection in his hearers, unless perhaps the affection of anger against himself. We leave that to your vehement bawlers, or your whining lamenters, that are continually telling, they will spend and be spent, for the salvation of their hearers, which lord Shaftsbury elegantly derides, by calling it the heroic passion of saving souls. And let any unprejudiced person judge, if there is not something vastly great, something like a heroic fortitude in that man, that can talk of future judgment, heaven and hell, with as much coolness and indifference as if it were a common matter. To say the truth, indeed, we do not often meddle with these alarming themes…

The *third* rule, viz. recommending *virtue* from the authority and examples of the *heathens*, is not only highly proper, because they were very virtuous, but hath this manifest advantage attending it, that it is a proper way of reasoning to two quite opposite kinds of persons. One is, such as are real Christians, who will be shamed by the superior excellence of mere heathens, as they call them, and whom they so much despise. The other is, our present living heathens, who pay no regard to the Christian religion at all, and therefore will only be moved by the authority of the persons they esteem. It is well known, there are multitudes in our island, who reckon Socrates and Plato to have been much greater men than any of the apostles, although (as the moderate preacher I mentioned lately told his hearers) the apostle Paul had an university education, and was instructed in Logic by professor Gamaliel. Therefore let religion be constantly and uniformly called *virtue*, and let the *heathen philosophers* be set up as the great patterns and promoters of it. Upon this head, I must particularly recommend M. Antoninus by name, because an eminent person, of the moderate character, says, his meditations is the BEST book that ever was written for forming the heart.

But perhaps the last part of this third rule will be thought to need most illustration and defence, viz. that NONE at all, or *very little use* is to be made of *scripture*: and really, to deal plainly, the great reason of this is, that very few of the scripture-motives and arguments are of the moderate stamp; the most part of them are drawn from orthodox principles: for example, the apostle Paul cannot even say, *Husbands, love your wives*, but his argument and example comes in these words, *as Christ also loved the church*. The apostle John also speaks in a very mysterious way, of union with Christ, and abiding in him, in order to bringing forth fruit, which is his way of speaking for a virtuous life. Now, let any indifferent person judge, how this kind of expression, and others of the like nature, such as mortifying the deeds of the body through the Spirit, would agree with the other parts of our discourse; they would be like opposite kinds of fluids which will not compound, they would be quite heterogeneous, which is against all the rules of fine writing, and hinders it from being an uniform, beautiful, and comely Whole...

The *fourth* and last rule for a preacher, is, that he must be *very unacceptable to the people.* The Spectator, I remember, somewhere says, that most of the critics in Great Britain seem to act as if the first rule of dramatic writing were, *not to please.* Now, what they make the first rule of writing plays, I make the last rule for composing sermons; not as being the least, but the most important. It is indeed the grand criterion, the most indispensable rule of all...

Maxim V

A minister must endeavour to acquire as great a degree of politeness in his carriage and behaviour, and to catch as much of the air and manner of a fine gentleman, as possibly he can.

This is usually a distinguishing mark between the moderate and the orthodox, and how much we have the advantage in it is extremely obvious. Good manners is undoubtedly the most excellent of all accomplishments, and, in some measure, supplies the place of them all when they are wanting. And surely nothing can be more necessary to, or more ornamental and becoming in a minister: it gains him easy access into the world, and frees him from that rigid severity which renders many of them so odious and detestable to the polite part of it. In former times, ministers were so monkish and recluse, for ordinary, and so formal when they did happen to appear, that all the jovial part of mankind, particularly rakes and libertines, shunned and fled from them; or, when unavoidably thrown into their company, were constrained, and had no kind of confidence to repose in them: whereas now, let a moderate, modern, well-bred minister go into promiscuous company, they stand in no manner of awe; and will even swear with all imaginable liberty. This gives the minister an opportunity of understanding their character, and of perhaps sometimes reasoning in an easy and genteel manner against swearing, which, though indeed it seldom reforms them, yet it is as seldom taken amiss, which shews the counsel to have been administered with prudence.

How is it possible that a minister can understand wickedness, unless he either practices it himself, (but much of that will not yet pass in the world), or allows the wicked to be bold in his presence? To do otherwise, would be to do in practice what I have known narrow-minded bigoted students do as to speculation, *viz.* avoid reading their adversaries books because they were erroneous; whereas it is evident no error can be refuted till it be understood.

The setting of different characters of ministers in immediate opposition, will put this matter past all doubt, as the sun of truth rising upon the stars of error, darkens and makes them to disappear. Some there are, who may be easily known to be ministers, by their very dress, their grave demur looks, and their confined

precise conversation. How contemptible is this! and how like to some of the meanest employments among us; as sailors, who are known by their rolling walk, and
tailors, by the shivering shrug of their shoulders! But our truly accomplished clergy
put off so entirely every thing that is peculiar to their profession, that were you to
see them in the streets, meet with them at a visit, or spend an evening with them
in a tavern, you would not once suspect them for men of that character: agreeably
to this, I remember an excellent thing said by a gentlemen, in commendation of a
minister, that *he had nothing at all of the clergyman about him*...

Maxim VI

*It is not only necessary for a moderate man to have much learning, but he ought to be
filled with a contempt of all kinds of learning but one, which is to understand Leibnitz's
scheme well; the chief parts of which are so beautifully painted and so harmoniously
sung by lord Shaftsbury, and which has been so well licked into form and method, by the
late immortal Mr. H[utcheso]n...*

I shall now subjoin a short catalogue of the most necessary and useful books,
the thorough understanding of which will make a truly learned man: *Leibnitz's
Theodicee, and his Letters, Shaftsbury's Characteristics, Collins' Enquiry into Human
Liberty, all Mr. H[utcheso]n's Pieces, Christianity as Old as the Creation, D[udgeo]n's
best Scheme, and H[ume]'s Moral Essays;* the two last are Scots authors, and it is with
pleasure I can assure my countrymen they are by far the most perfect of them all,
carrying the consequences of the scheme to the most ravishing height...

Maxim VII

*A moderate man must endeavour, as much as he handsomely can, to put off any appear-
ances of devotion, and avoid all unnecessary exercises of religious worship, whether public or private.*

...I must acknowledge, that to be constantly whining and praying, looks so
extremely orthodox-like, that I cannot help conceiving a prejudice at it, for this very
reason; and I doubt not but every moderate man will have the very same fellow-
feeling. In truth, a great abundance of devotion has such a tendency to influence
one with zeal, that any man, who would maintain his moderation, had best keep out
of the reach of such ensnaring influence. Besides, it has been an old remark, and
I begin to suspect there is some ground for it, that let one embrace what system of
divinity he will, it is impossible to pray but according to the orthodox system. And
whatever laudable pains have been taken, by some of our friends, to avoid this inconvenience, yet, from what I have observed, in the most successful of them, I must
own, I can, at present, see no other remedy but to deal as little that way as possible.

Maxim VIII

In church settlements, which are the principal causes that come before ministers for judgment, the only thing to be regarded, is, who the patron, and the great and noble heritors are for; the inclinations of the common people are to be utterly despised.

That this maxim is invariably observed, by all moderate men, is certain, and may be attested by all that ever were present at a General Assembly of this national church. The case is not now as formerly, when presentations were held a grievance; for a presentation is all in all to a moderate man; and when there is no presentation, the greatness and nobility of the heritors upon one side. I was witness once to a cause (which indeed unhappily miscarried) but there was a noble stand made for it by the moderate party, because there was a *lord* upon the side of the *minority*; although he had really *no interest* at all in the parish, but a small bit of ground which he had got from a neighbour, in order to run a dike straight. This appearance greatly rejoiced me, as being a token to what perfection the spirit of moderation was arrived.

There are many reasons upon which this maxim is founded; as the implacable hatred we bear to the elders and common people, and their constant wrong judgment, which has been illustrated above...

Another thing strongly pleads for gentlemen having the chief hand in settling kirks, that now-a-days very few of our principal gentry attend ordinances, or receive any benefit by a minister after he is settled, unless, perhaps, talking of the news at a private visit, or playing a game at back-gammon; and therefore it is but fair, that, in lieu of the edification of the common people, they should have the honour or profit of conferring the benefice. I shall only further add, that having no view of attending upon him for ordinary, they must be the best judges of his preaching-gifts, as being most disinterested: for which reason, non-residing heritors, instead of deserving to be cut out altogether, as the stupid and undiscerning orthodox would have it, are by much to be preferred to those that reside...

Maxim IX

While a settlement is carrying on, the candidate, against whom there is a strong opposition from the people, must be looked upon, and every where declared to be, a person of great worth, and remarkable abilities: provided always, that if ever the same person, after he is settled, be at pains, and succeed, in gaining the peoples affections, he shall then fall as much below the ordinary standard in his character, as before he was raised above it.

Both parts of this maxim will appear very reasonable to all that see with our eyes. The people being against a man is a certain sign of his being a good preacher, as has been proved above: it is also a pretty sure sign of his being of moderate

principles, *which make the comers thereunto perfect*; and these two things are sufficient to justify us in raising his character. It is indeed often absolutely necessary,
when a process is in agitation, that it may help him out with a scanty concurrence,
and have an influence upon the church-courts, which are composed of a mixt multitude. Nor is it easy to conceive, how excellent and well-invented a weapon this
is, the giving a man an extraordinary and high character. It necessarily imprints
a kind of veneration of him on the minds of his judges; and hath this peculiar
advantage, that there is no parrying of it; for whatever some few, of different principles, may think, they dare not plainly contradict it...

As to the other part of the maxim, taking away their character for ability, when
they apostatize to orthodoxy: this will be easily accounted for, if it be remembered
how they came by it. It was freely given them, and therefore it may be taken away
at pleasure: it was given to bring them in as an additional strength to the moderate interest; and therefore, when they forsake that interest, it is but just to deprive
them of it...

Maxim X

*Whenever we have got a settlement decided over the belly of perhaps the whole people in
the parish, by a majority in the General Assembly, the victory should be improved, by
appointing some of the orthodox opposers of the settlement to execute it, especially those
of them that pretend to have a scruple of conscience at having an active hand in any
such settlement.*

They do not deserve a victory who know not how to push it, or to improve the
advantage they have gained. A sentence of the General Assembly, even as of any
other court, signifies nothing if it be not executed. To rest satisfied with the victory
we have gained, by the bare decision, would indeed be yielding it back again, and
losing, in fact, what we gained in appearance. This is self-evident; but the next
point is, who shall be employed in executing it, those who appointed it, or those
who pretend a scruple of conscience at doing what appears to their disordered
intellects to be what they call *sinful*? Now, as to this, allow me only to ask a few
plain questions. Is not every society divided into the governing and the governed,
the masters and the servants? What is the subject of any debate in the Assembly,
that ends in a vote, but to determine who is the one, and who is the other? When
once a vote has made us masters, does not the same vote make the minority servants? And do I need to ask further, if there is any piece of drudgery to be performed, who it belongs to, the masters or the servants? Apply this then to the case
in hand; who would hazard his own life in fording a river if he had a servant, to try
the depth of it before him? Who would choose to go to a pulpit under a shower of

stones, from an enraged populace, if he had others under his authority, whom he could send upon the same ungracious errand?

Now, the usefulness of this conduct is very evident; for, it is plain, they will either obey or disobey: if the first is the case, then we shall have the honour of bringing them, and they themselves the profit and advantage of being brought, into the hatred and abhorrence of the common people; in commendation of which state, enough has been said already. If they disobey, they must be deposed, and cast out as incorrigible, to make way for those that are better than themselves: this will be to the advantage of the church, for young men, *caeteris paribus*, are much better than old…

Maxim XI

The character which moderate men give their adversaries, of the orthodox party, must always be that of knaves or fools; and, as occasion serves, the same person (if it will pass) may be represented as a knave at one time, and as a fool at another.

The justice of this proceeding may be easily made appear. The principles of moderation being so very evident to reason, it is a demonstration, that none, but unreasonable men, can resist their influence. And therefore we cannot suppose, that such as are against us can be so from conscience. Besides, setting aside the superior intrinsic excellence of the one set of principles above the other, there are much stronger carnal motives, to speak in their own style, to act in their way, than in ours; and therefore, there is great ground to conclude, that they act from hypocrisy, but not so of us. They please the people; we please, at least endeavour to please, those of high rank. Now, there are many remarkable advantages they gain by pleasing the people, whereas it is evident, *ex post facto*, that we gain nothing by pleasing the gentry; for they never trampled upon us so much as of late; and have entirely defeated our application to parliament for augmentation of stipend: so far are we from being in any respect the better of the gentry, that we have really great reason to complain of them; for, when we have endeavoured to ingratiate ourselves with them, by softness and complaisance, and by going considerable lengths with them in their freedom, they often-times, most ungenerously, despise us but the more: nay, many of them have first taught us live at a high rate, and then refuse to give us any thing to keep it up. Now, as we men of reason could not but foresee this, it is plain, nothing but the most disinterested virtue could lead us to act as we have done. Whereas, on the other hand, the orthodox have gained, and do possess the esteem of the common people; and so it is plain, they could have no other view in their conduct but to attain it. However, to shew our charity, we allow there are some on their side, who are indifferently honest, but these are men of very weak intellectuals, as is evident from their not thinking as we do…

Maxim XII

As to the world in general, a moderate man is to have great charity for Atheists and Deists in principle, and for persons that are loose and vicious in their practice, but none at all for those that have a high profession of religion, and a great pretence to strictness in their walk and conversation.

This maxim seems to be pretty strongly laid, and yet, upon a strict enquiry, it will be found that we follow it very exactly. That we have charity for the first mentioned sort of persons is evident; for we endeavour to accommodate ourselves to them, and draw as near them as possible we can, insisting upon nothing in our sermons but what may be said to be a part, or an improvement of the law of nature. And as to our having no charity for the other sort it is as evident; witness the odious idea we have affixed to the name of a professor (unless when it is meant of a professor in a college); and witness our ironical way of speaking, when we say of a man he has a *grave sanctified air* nay, even holiness and godliness are seldom taken by us in a very good sense, when we say, *one of the holy brethren*, or a *good godly lady*, they would mistake us very much that would think we had a high opinion of any of these persons.

[John Witherspoon], *Ecclesiastical Characteristics: Or, the Arcana of Church Policy* (Glasgow: n.p., 1753), 7–9, 11–13, 15–21, 23–5, 27–8, 31–7, 45–7.

25

Natural versus Moral Necessity in the Will

Jonathan Edwards

NO AMERICAN THEOLOGIAN has had a greater impact on evangelicalism than Jonathan Edwards (1703–58). Born in East Windsor, Connecticut, on October 5, 1703, Edwards was the only boy of eleven children born to the Reverend Timothy Edwards and Esther Stoddard. After receiving instruction from his father in theology as well as biblical and ancient languages, Edwards entered Connecticut's collegiate school (renamed Yale College in 1718) close to his thirteenth birthday, graduating as the class valedictorian in 1720. He stayed at Yale to study for a MA and then briefly ministered at a Presbyterian church in New York City, from August 1722 to April 1723. After a stint as a pastor in Bolton, Connecticut, he returned to Yale as a tutor and, in 1726, accepted his grandfather's invitation to serve as his clerical assistant at the Congregational church in Northampton, Massachusetts. Edwards's maternal grandfather, Solomon Stoddard, was something of a legend back then. He was one of the most powerful clergymen in New England at that time, reigning over the town for some sixty years until his death in 1729. Given Stoddard's long tenure and the respect he garnered, Edwards had his work cut out for him when he ascended to his grandfather's pulpit.

At the end of 1734, Northampton became the site of a significant revival that lasted into the late spring of 1735. Edwards published an account of the town's spiritual transformation in 1737 as *A Faithful Narrative of the Surprising Work of God*, which brought him international recognition. Despite Edwards's fame, he was deposed from his office in 1750. While unparalleled intellectually, he lacked certain social skills. Rather than making house calls to his parishioners, he preferred studying twelve to fourteen hours a day in solitary confinement. In the time before his dismissal, Edwards attempted to rescind the precedent set by his grandfather, who allowed the baptism and communion of those who had not experienced conversion. More conservative than Stoddard in his ecclesiology, Edwards

FIGURE 25.1 Jonathan Edwards by Henry Augustus Loop (Detail), Princeton University, gift of great-grandsons of Jonathan Edwards, photo by Bruce M. White.

wanted to institute a policy whereby only full members, and upon a declaration of faith, would be able to participate in the Lord's Supper and baptize their children. Out of touch with many of the most important parishioners in his congregation, and without a substantial patron to back his rigid policies, Edwards and his family were forced out of Northampton. After a year of searching, he took a position in 1751 as a minister to a small community of mixed settlers and Native Americans in Stockbridge, Massachusetts. There he stayed until 1758, when he accepted a call by the trustees of the College of New Jersey to fill a vacancy as president of the school, replacing his recently deceased son-in-law, Aaron Burr Sr. Tragically, Edwards died on March 22, 1758 from complications after a smallpox inoculation, barely a month after assuming office.

One of the benefits of living on the frontier in western Massachusetts was that it allowed Edwards more time for research and writing. While at Stockbridge he wrote *Freedom of the Will*, which had an enormous impact on subsequent generations of his admirers. Published in 1754, *Freedom of the Will* was Edwards's attempt to refute contemporary theorists positing that a self-determining will could make choices irrespective of outside circumstances or motives. Edwards argued that the will, which he did not define as a separate faculty from the mind, chooses that which appeals to its strongest desires. Accordingly, no one can make decisions that are completely neutral or unbiased. Edwards called this type of limitation, "moral necessity." When faced with several choices, the will is morally obligated to choose the most appealing option. As this process unfolds, God does not force anyone to act in a certain way. Rather, people choose the deepest desires of their heart. The problem, according to Edwards, is that humanity has an unquenchable thirst for sin, which adversely influences their choices. In addition to the notion of moral necessity, he also introduced "natural necessity," which he tied to the natural laws that govern the universe. Here, a person is physically limited so that, for instance, even if one wanted to jump out of a four-story building and land safety, he or she would be unable to do so because of the laws of gravity. The combination of moral and natural necessity means that although a person is *physically* able to make a number of choices (he or she is not "naturally" inhibited), the outcome of those decisions is certain since one's *moral* proclivity dictates the result. Even though the unregenerate have a natural freedom to love and obey God, they nevertheless lack the moral freedom to do so. While *Freedom of the Will* may come across as too abstract, Edwards had a practical application in mind, for he wanted to prove that humans are hopelessly enslaved to sin unless divine grace is given to counteract their inherent evil cravings.

Freedom of the Will

IT may possibly be thought, that there is no great Need of going about to define or describe the *Will*; this Word being generally as well understood as any other Words we can use to explain it: And so perhaps it would be, had not Philosophers, Metaphysicians and Polemic Divines brought the Matter into Obscurity by the Things they have said of it. But since it is so, I think it may be of some Use, and will tend to the greater Clearness in the following Discourse, to say a few Things concerning it.

And therefore I observe, that the *Will* (without any metaphysical Refining) is plainly, *That by which the Mind chooses any Thing.* The Faculty of the *Will* is that Faculty or Power or Principle of the Mind by which it is capable of *choosing:* An Act of the *Will* is the same as an Act of *Choosing* or *Choice...*

It is sufficient to my present Purpose to say,—*It is that Motive, which, as it stands in the View of the Mind, is the strongest, that determines the Will*—But it may be necessary that I should a little explain my Meaning in this.

By *Motive*, I mean the whole of that which moves, excites or invites the Mind to Volition, whether that be one Thing singly, or many Things conjunctly. Many particular Things may concur and unite their Strength to induce the Mind; and when it is so, all together are as it were one complex Motive. And when I speak of the *strongest Motive*, I have Respect to the Strength of the whole that operates to induce to a particular Act of Volition, whether that be the Strength of one Thing alone, or of many together.

Whatever is a Motive, in this Sense, must be something that is *extant in the View or Apprehension of the Understanding*, or perceiving Faculty. Nothing can induce or invite the Mind to will or act any Thing, any further than it is perceived, or is some Way or other in the Mind's view; for what is wholly unperceived, and perfectly out of the Mind's view, can't affect the Mind at all. 'Tis most evident, that nothing is in the Mind, or reaches it, or takes any Hold of it, any otherwise than as it is perceiv'd or tho't of.

And I think it must also be allowed by all, that every Thing that is properly called a Motive, Excitement or Inducement to a perceiving willing Agent, has some Sort and Degree of *Tendency*, or *Advantage* to move or excite the Will, previous to the Effect, or to the Act of the Will excited. This previous Tendency of the Motive is what I call *the Strength of the Motive*. That Motive which has a less Degree of previous Advantage or Tendency to move the Will, or that appears less inviting, as it stands in the View of the Mind, is what I call a *weaker Motive*. On the contrary, that which appears most inviting, and has, by what appears concerning it to the Understanding or Apprehension, the greatest Degree of previous Tendency to excite and induce the Choice, is what I call the *strongest Motive*. And in this Sense, I suppose the Will is always determined by the strongest Motive.

Things that exist in the View of the Mind, have their Strength, Tendency or Advantage to move or excite its Will, from many Things appertaining to the Nature and Circumstances of the *Thing view'd*, the Nature and Circumstances of the *Mind that views*, and the Degree & Manner of its *View*; which it would perhaps be hard to make a perfect Enumeration of. But so much I think may be determin'd in general, without Room for Controversy, that whatever is perceived or apprehended by an intelligent & voluntary Agent, which has the Nature and Influence of a Motive to Volition or Choice, is consider'd or view'd *as good*; nor has it any Tendency to invite or engage the Election of the Soul in any further Degree than it appears such. For to say otherwise, would be to say, that Things that appear have a Tendency by the Appearance they make, to engage the Mind to elect them, some other Way than by their appearing eligible to it; which is absurd. And therefore it must be true, in some Sense, that *the Will always is as the greatest apparent Good is*. But only, for the right understanding of this, two Things must be well and distinctly observed.

1. It must be observed in what Sense I use the Term *Good*; namely, as of the same Import with *Agreeable*. To appear *Good* to the Mind, as I use the Phrase, is the same as to *appear agreeable*, or *seem pleasing* to the Mind. Certainly, nothing appears inviting and eligible to the Mind, or tending to engage its Inclination and Choice, consider'd as *evil* or *disagreeable*; nor indeed, as *indifferent*, and neither agreeable nor disagreeable. But if it tends to draw the Inclination, and move the Will, it must be under the Notion of that which *suits* the Mind. And therefore that must have the greatest Tendency to attract and engage it, which, as it stands in the Mind's View, suits it best, and pleases it most; and in that Sense, is the greatest apparent Good: to say otherwise, is little, if any Thing, short of a direct and plain Contradiction...

2. When I say, the Will is as the greatest apparent Good is, or (as I have explain'd it) that Volition has always for its Object the Thing which appears most agreeable; it must be carefully observed, to avoid Confusion and needless Objection, that I speak of the *direct* and *immediate* Object of the Act of Volition; and not some Object that the Act of Will has not an immediate, but only an indirect and remote Respect to. Many Acts of Volition have some remote Relation to an Object, that is different from the Thing most immediately will'd and chosen. Thus, when a Drunkard has his Liquor before him, & he has to choose whether to drink it, or no; the proper and immediate Objects, about which his present Volition is conversant, and between which his Choice now decides, are his own Acts, in drinking the Liquor, or letting it alone; and this will certainly be done according to what, in the present View of his Mind, taken in the whole of it, is most agreeable to him. If he chooses or wills to drink it, and not to let it alone; then this Action, as it stands in the View of his Mind, with all that belongs to its Appearance there, is more agreeable and pleasing than letting it alone...

The Phrase, *moral Necessity*, is used variously: sometimes 'tis used for a Necessity of moral Obligation. So we say, a Man is under Necessity, when he is under Bonds of Duty and Conscience, which he can't be discharged from. So the Word *Necessity* is often used for great Obligation in Point of Interest. Sometimes by moral Necessity is meant that apparent Connection of Things, which is the Ground of *moral Evidence*; and so is distinguish'd from *absolute Necessity*, or that sure Connection of Things, that is a Foundation for *infallible Certainty*. In this Sense, moral Necessity signifies much the same as that high Degree of Probability, which is ordinarily sufficient to satisfy, and be relied upon by Mankind, in their Conduct and Behaviour in the World, as they would consult their own Safety and Interest, and treat others properly as Members of Society. And sometimes by moral Necessity is meant that Necessity of Connection and Consequence, which arises from such *moral Causes*, as the Strength of Inclination, or Motives, and the Connection which there is in many Cases between these, and such certain Volitions and Actions. And it is in this Sense, that I use the Phrase, *moral Necessity*, in the following Discourse.

By *natural Necessity*, as applied to Men, I mean such Necessity as Men are under through the Force of natural Causes; as distinguish'd from what are called moral Causes, such as Habits and Dispositions of the Heart, and moral Motives and Inducements. Thus Men placed in certain Circumstances, are the Subjects of particular Sensations by Necessity: They feel Pain when their Bodies are wounded; they see the Objects presented before them in a clear Light, when their Eyes are open'd: so they assent to the Truth of certain Propositions, as soon as the Terms are understood; as that two and two make four, that black is not white, that two parallel Lines can never cross one another: so by a natural Necessity Men's Bodies move downwards, when there is nothing to support them.

But here several Things may be noted concerning these two Kinds of Necessity.

1. Moral Necessity may be as absolute, as natural Necessity. That is, the Effect may be as perfectly connected with its moral Cause, as a naturally necessary Effect is with its natural Cause. Whether the Will in every Case is necessarily determined by the strongest Motive, or whether the Will ever makes any Resistance to such a Motive, or can ever oppose the strongest present Inclination, or not; if that Matter should be controverted, yet I suppose none will deny, but that, in some Cases, a previous Bias and Inclination, or the Motive presented, may be so powerful, that the Act of the Will may be certainly and indissolubly connected therewith. When Motives or previous Bias are very strong, all will allow that there is some *Difficulty* in going against them. And if they were yet stronger, the Difficulty would be still greater. And therefore, if more were still added to their Strength, to a certain Degree, it would make the Difficulty so great, that it would be wholly *impossible* to surmount it; for this plain Reason, because whatever Power Men may be supposed to have to surmount Difficulties, yet that Power is not infinite; and so goes not beyond certain Limits. If a Man can surmount ten Degrees of Difficulty of this Kind, with twenty Degrees of Strength, because the Degrees of Strength are beyond the degrees of Difficulty; yet if the Difficulty be increased to thirty, or an hundred, or a thousand Degrees, and his Strength not also increased, his Strength will be wholly insufficient to surmount the Difficulty. As therefore it must be allowed, that there may be such a Thing as a *sure* and *perfect* Connection between moral Causes and Effects; so this only is what I call by the Name of *moral Necessity.*

2. When I use this Distinction of *moral* and *natural Necessity*, I would not be understood to suppose, that if any Thing comes to pass by the former Kind of Necessity, the *Nature* of Things is not concerned in it, as well as in the latter. I don't mean to determine, that when a *moral* Habit or Motive is so strong, that the Act of the Will infallibly follows, this is not owing to the *Nature of Things.* But these are the Names that these two Kinds of Necessity have usually been called by; and they must be distinguished by some Names or other; for there is a Distinction or Difference between them, that is very important in its consequences. Which Difference does not lie so much in the Nature of the *Connection*, as in the two Terms *connected.* The Cause with which the Effect is connected, is of a particular Kind; viz. that which is of a moral Nature; either some previous habitual Disposition, or some Motive exhibited to the Understanding. And the Effect is also of a particular Kind; being likewise of a moral Nature; consisting in some Inclination or Volition of the Soul, or voluntary Action...

3. It must be observed, that in what has been explain'd, as signified by the Name of *Moral Necessity*, the Word *Necessity* is not used according to the original Design and Meaning of the Word: For, as was observed before, such Terms *necessary, impossible, irresistible*, &c. in common Speech, and their most proper Sense, are always relative; having Reference to some supposable voluntary Opposition or Endeavour, that is insufficient. But no such Opposition, or contrary Will and Endeavour, is supposable in the Case of moral necessity; which is a Certainty of the Inclination and Will it self; which does not admit of the Supposition of a Will to oppose and resist it. For 'tis absurd, to suppose the same individual Will to oppose it self, in its present Act; or the present Choice to be opposite to, and resisting present Choice: as absurd as it is to talk of two contrary Motions, in the same moving Body, at the same Time. And therefore the very Case supposed never admits of any Trial, whether an opposing or resisting Will can overcome this Necessity.

What has been said of natural and moral Necessity, may serve to explain what is intended by natural and moral *Inability*. We are said to be *naturally* unable to do a Thing, when we can't do it if we will, because what is most commonly called *Nature* don't allow of it, or because of some impeding Defect or Obstacle that is extrinsic to the Will; either in the Faculty of Understanding, Constitution of Body, or external Objects. *Moral* Inability consists not in any of these Things; but either in the Want of Inclination; or the Strength of a contrary Inclination; or the want of sufficient Motives in View, to induce and excite the Act of the Will, or the Strength of apparent Motives to the contrary. Or both these may be resolved into one; and it may be said in one Word, that moral Inability consists in the Opposition or Want of Inclination. For when a Person is unable to will or choose such a Thing, through a Defect of Motives, or Prevalence of contrary Motives, 'tis the same Thing as his being unable through the Want of an Inclination, or the Prevalence of a contrary Inclination, in such Circumstances, and under the Influence of such Views.

To give some Instances of this *moral Inability*—A Woman of great Honour and Chastity may have a moral Inability to prostitute her self to her Slave. A Child of great Love and Duty to his Parents, may be unable to be willing to kill his Father. A very lascivious Man, in Case of certain Opportunities and Temptations, and in the Absence of such and such Restraints, may be unable to forbear gratifying his Lust. A Drunkard, under such and such Circumstances, may be unable to forbear taking of strong Drink. A very malicious Man may be unable to exert benevolent Acts to an Enemy, or to desire his Prosperity: Yea, some may be so under the Power of a vile Disposition, that they may be unable to love those who are most worthy of their Esteem & Affection. A strong Habit of Virtue and great Degree of Holiness may cause a moral Inability to love Wickedness in general, may render a Man unable to take Complacence in wicked Persons or Things; or to choose a wicked Life, and prefer it to a virtuous Life. And on the other Hand, a great Degree of habitual Wickedness may lay a Man under an Inability to love and choose Holiness; and render him utterly unable to love an infinitely holy Being, or to choose and cleave to him as his chief Good.

Here it may be of Use to observe this Distinction of moral Inability, *viz.* of that which is *general and habitual*, and that which is *particular and occasional*. By a *general and habitual* moral Inability, I mean an Inability in the Heart to all Exercises or Acts of Will of that Nature and Kind, through a fix'd and habitual Inclination, or an habitual and stated Defect, or Want of a certain Kind of Inclination. Thus a very ill-natur'd Man may be unable to exert such Acts of Benevolence, as another, who is full of good Nature, commonly exerts; and a Man, whose Heart is habitually void of Gratitude, may be unable to exert such and such grateful Acts, through that stated Defect of a grateful Inclination. By *particular and occasional* moral Inability, I mean an Inability of the Will or Heart to a particular Act, thro' the Strength or Defect of present Motives, or of Inducements presented to the View of the Understanding, *on this Occasion*. If it be so, that the Will is always determined by the strongest Motive, then it must always have an Inability, in this latter Sense, to act otherwise than it does; it not being possible, in any Case, that the Will should, at present, go against the Motive which has now, all Things considered, the greatest Strength & Advantage to excite and induce it. The former of these Kinds or moral Inability, consisting in that which is stated habitual and general, is most commonly called by the Name of Inability; because the Word *Inability*, in its most proper and original Signification, has Respect to some *stated Defect*. And this especially obtains the Name of *Inability* also upon another Account: I before observed, that the Word Inability in its original and most common Use, is a relative Term; and has Respect to Will and Endeavour, as supposable in the Case, and as insufficient to bring to pass the Thing desired and endeavoured. Now there may be more of an Appearance & Shadow of this, with Respect to the Acts which arise from a fix'd and strong Habit, than others that arise only from transient Occasions and Causes. Indeed Will and Endeavour against, or diverse from *present* Acts of the Will, are in no Case supposable, whether those Acts be occasional or habitual; for that would be to suppose the Will, at present, to be otherwise than, at present it is. But yet there may be Will and Endeavour against *future* Acts of the Will, or Volitions that are likely to take Place, as view'd at a Distance. 'Tis no Contradiction, to suppose that the Acts of the Will at one Time, may be against the Acts of the Will at another Time; and there may be Desires and Endeavours to prevent or excite future Acts of the Will; But such Desires and Endeavours are, in many Cases, rendered insufficient & vain, thro' Fixedness of Habit: When the Occasion returns, the Strength of Habit overcomes, and baffles all such Opposition. In this Respect, a Man may be in miserable Slavery and Bondage to a strong Habit. But it may be comparatively easy to make an Alteration with Respect to such future Acts, as are only occasional and transient; because the Occasion or transient Cause, if foreseen, may often easily be prevented or avoided. On this Account, the moral Inability that attends fix'd Habits, especially obtains the Name of *Inability*. And then, as the Will may remotely and indirectly resist it self, and do it in vain, in the Case of strong Habits; so Reason may resist present Acts of the Will, and its Resistance be insufficient; and this is more commonly the Case also, when the Acts arise from strong Habit.

But it must be observed concerned moral Inability, in each Kind of it, that the Word *Inability* is used in a Sense very diverse from its original Import. The Word signifies only a natural Inability, in the proper Use of it; and is applied to such Cases only wherein a present Will or Inclination to the Thing, with Respect to which a Person is said to be unable, is supposable. It can't be truly said, according to the ordinary Use of Language, that a malicious Man, let him be never so malicious, can't hold his Hand from striking, or that he is not able to shew his Neighbour Kindness; or that a Drunkard, let his Appetite be never so strong, can't keep the Cup from his Mouth. In the strictest Propriety of Speech, a Man has a Thing in his Power, if he has it in his Choice, or at his Election: And a Man can't be truly said to be unable to do a Thing, when he can do it if he will. 'Tis improperly said, that a Person can't perform those external Actions, which are dependent on the Act of the Will, and which would be easily performed, if the Act of the Will were present. And if it be improperly said, that he cannot perform those external voluntary Actions, which depend on the Will, 'tis in some Respect more improperly said, that he is unable to exert the Acts of the Will themselves; because it is more evidently false, with Respect to these, that he can't if he will: For to say so, is a down-right Contradiction: It is to say, he *can't* will, if he *does* will. And in this Case, not only is it true, that it is easy for a Man to do the Thing if he will but the very willing is the doing; when once he has will'd, the Thing is performed; and nothing else remains to be done. Therefore, in these Things to ascribe a Non-performance to the want of Power or Ability, is not just; because the Thing wanting is not a being *able*, but a being *willing*. There are Faculties of Mind, and Capacity of Nature, and every Thing else, sufficient, but a Disposition: Nothing is wanting but a Will.

Jonathan Edwards, *A Careful and Strict Enquiry into the Modern Prevailing Notions of That Freedom of Will, Which is Supposed to Be Essential to Moral Agency, V[i]rtue and Vice, Reward and Punishment, Praise and Blame* (Boston: S. Kneeland, 1754), 1, 5–7, 21–7.

26

Open Letter to Commit Oneself to God

Sarah Prince Gill

SARAH PRINCE GILL (1728–71) was the fourth of five children born to the Boston minister Thomas Prince and his wife, Deborah. As an evangelical pastor who supported the Great Awakening, Prince associated with other likeminded clergymen in the region, including Jonathan Edwards. Prince's daughter Sarah and Esther Edwards Burr became lifelong friends, maintaining a correspondence even after Esther married the Presbyterian minister Aaron Burr in 1752 and moved away to New Jersey. Encouraged to chronicle her spiritual journey, Sarah began penning her thoughts in a journal as early as 1734 but kept more consistent records from the mid-1750s to 1764. Within the journal she exhibited signs of being well read, no doubt benefiting from access to her father's sizeable library. Yet unlike her childhood friend Esther, Sarah was reluctant to marry. She remained single until her thirty-first birthday, by which time her siblings, parents, and childhood friend had passed away. Perhaps desiring companionship, she married the affluent Boston merchant Moses Gill. This union afforded Sarah the opportunity for more time to read, write, and reflect on spiritual concerns. She died childless on August 5, 1771, at the age of forty-three.

Before grieving over the multiple early deaths of family and friends, Sarah composed a letter entitled "To all my young Acquaintance, into whose hands these lines may come," dated in 1755. The content is presented in the form of an open letter addressed to individuals unwilling to commit their lives fully to God. Within the letter, Sarah pleads for her audience to respond to God's offer of salvation, who earnestly desires to show mercy to sinners. Her message is to give up worldly pursuits, which may appear pleasing at first, but carries no eternal value. Candid in her argument, Sarah warns her readers that God's judgment awaits those who refuse to turn to Christ. Because she left instructions that the letter should not be opened until after her death, the manuscript was not published until 1785.

FIGURE 26.1 Mrs. Gill (Sarah Prince) by John Singleton Copley, courtesy of the Spencer Museum of Art, the University of Kansas, Museum purchase: Letha Churchill Walker Memorial Art Fund, 1973.0092.

"To All My Young Acquaintance, into Whose Hands These Lines May Come"

AS from the invisible world, (that world of spirits into which mine will have entered before this is presented you) I now address you; and I earnestly entreat you to receive my message.

I may now say, since I shall be beyond the sensibilities of this mortal life, that it is a disinterested love and concern for your best good, that prompts me to this. With pity have I often thought on your case: Frequently has my heart bled in secret for those of you who live estranged from God, ignorant of the pleasures of the divine life, unacquainted with the lovely Redeemer, with communion with God, the gracious influences of his Spirit, and the tokens of his love and favour! And while I have seen you engaged in a round of amusements and sensual gratifications, the world smiling on you, and you hearkening to its delusive promises—pleasing yourselves with its airy vanities, have thought you (as you really are), a company of spirits made and bound for eternity, and speedily hastening to it, and uncertain whether you should be happy in the society of perfected spirits, and in the satisfying presence of God for ever, or be miserably fixed in a state of enmity to him, in company with unholy devils: And yet you are diverting on the borders of this eternity, as securely as tho' you could never enter into it. Let me therefore entreat you, by all the motives proper to sway you, as reasonable, as immortal beings, to secure your eternal welfare without any delay—till that is done you are in constant hazard of eternal death: The next hour may be the finishing, the deciding period—can you be easy to stand on the brink of ETERNITY, ready to fall, and not know how your state will be determined at the awful bar of GOD?—Dare you venture into his presence, whose all-seeing eye penetrates the inmost recesses of your hearts, and not know whether he is your FRIEND or your ALMIGHTY ENEMY? Can you think of appearing before him as a JUDGE, and rest till you have secured him as your SAVIOUR?—Are not your souls precious? Do you really see their importance? If you do not, go visit a dying bed—see what that will teach you, read the word of God, and there you will find the Maker of souls tells you, that they are of more worth than a *whole world*.—But this is not all, consider the value Christ set on them; to save souls, the eternal WORD condescended to veil his glory, to take on him the form of a servant, and in that form to suffer and die.— Read the history of his life—his humble state—his hardships and indignities—his painful ignominious death—the agonies of his soul—his bearing the wrath of God—suffering under the immense weight of the divine displeasure.—Read his agony in the garden, and on the cross, and all loudly speak the worth of each of your souls.

Would you be happy in life? The ways of vital godliness are indeed pleasant, and the keeping God's commandments brings a peace passing understanding! Would you be fitted to meet death without terror? Come to Christ, and he will take away the sting of it, and it shall be to you a sweet passage way to glory! Would you be safe for eternity? An interest in Christ will give you such a sure title to eternal life, as nothing can annul!—What pleas shall I use to persuade you to be religious? Shall I tell you *your all* depends upon it; that this is the only way to glorify God, and that you cannot be happy here or hereafter, without it? Shall I allure or terrify you? Shall I tell you that Heaven with all its joys, that God *himself* must be yours, or you must have Hell, with all its amazing terrors, the guilt of sin, the stings of con- science, the wrath of an incensed God, and a slighted Saviour, for your miserable portion to eternity! Can you think of the contrast, and hesitate a moment which to choose!—I speak as from ETERNITY, won't you believe me?—Shall I allure you by the grace of the gospel? Shall I tell you of the amiableness, the transcendent loveliness of the blessed Mediator—That he is altogether glorious in his person, and in his mediatorial character: That he is all-sufficient to save you. Shall I assure you he is now *willing* to do it, offers himself with all his benefits to you, and waits your acceptance—If you will accept him, he will be your almighty Friend, your satisfying Portion, your prevalent Intercessor, and he will be all this, *for ever*.—You shall be filled with love, joy, and peace—Shall see such glories, and feel such hap- piness, as is beyond the conception of the most raised mind on earth to conceive! This is something of the bliss Christ now offers you!—And what answer will you now give him?—Will you accept or refuse?—one or the other you must do.—Do you begin to consider? And are you ready to ask, "What methods shall I use to get into the narrow path which leads to life"—It is, no doubt, your indispens- able duty immediately "to repent and believe the gospel." And, although none but God can give you this repentance and faith, yet, as he usually works through the instrumentality of means, as the most probable method to obtain them, take time for *serious meditation*—let not one day pass without it.—Diligently attend all the means of grace, public, private, and secret—Be much in secret prayer—hear every sermon as for your life, and as though it was the last—Labour to keep eternity in view—labour to realize the eye of God always on you—these are powerful incentives to diligence.—Associate with the fearers of God—seek for proper companions to whom you may open your cases, and do not be afraid or ashamed to do it—O do not be ashamed to appear openly or singularly good;—bear on your minds that you cannot get to heaven without pains, arduous labours, and persevering strivings. Religion is not the work of a day—nor is it a thing to come in by the bye, but it is the one thing necessary, and must be the chief business of your lives;—you must give God your whole hearts.—Do not think you can serve God and sin together—but remember that real religion is a conformity of the soul to God in moral dispositions, and therefore that sin must be forsaken—you must turn from *all sin*, or you will never turn to God —Resolve in a humble dependence on the help of Christ, to delay no longer, but immediately to set about this great work in earnest.

Sarah Prince Gill, "To all my young Acquaintance, into whose hands these lines may come" in *Dying Exercises of Mrs. Deborah Prince: And Devout Meditation of Mrs. Sarah Gill, Daughters of the Late Rev. Mr. Thomas Prince, Minister of the South Church, Boston* (Edinburgh: W. Martin, 1785), 41–4.

27

The Humiliation and Exaltation
of the Cross

John Maclaurin

BORN IN GLENDARUEL, Argyll, John Mclaurin (1693–1754) grew up as the eldest
of two surviving boys. His father, John Maclaurin, was a minister who died in
1698, leaving his widow, Mary, to raise young John and his brother, Colin, until
her death in 1707, after which time the boys were cared for by their uncle, Daniel
Maclaurin, minister of Kilfinan in Argyll. Maclaurin studied at the University
of Glasgow, earning a MA in 1712 before further study at Glasgow's divinity hall
and the University of Leiden. The presbytery of Dumbarton granted Maclaurin a
license to preach in 1717, and close to two years later he was ordained the parish
minister of Luss on Loch Lomond in Dumbartonshire. Maclaurin stayed at Luss
until he translated to the Ramshorn Church in Glasgow in January 1723, remaining there until his death in 1754.

During the 1740s Maclaurin joined William McCulloch and James Robe in support of the awakenings that were taking place in America, Britain, and Continental
Europe. His correspondence with Jonathan Edwards, Thomas Prince, and other
American evangelicals led Maclaurin to help organize a "concert for prayer"
whereby ministers on both sides of the Atlantic agreed to pray regularly for the
continued success of the apparent worldwide spiritual resurgence. Besides his
pastoral work and promotion of the revivals, Maclaurin had a passion for theology. His son-in-law, John Gillies, who compiled his father-in-law's posthumous
sermons in 1755 and wrote a biographical introduction to the work, remarked that
throughout his life Maclaurin read practically every new book of note in addition
to composing his own thoughts on divinity. An example of his mind at work can
be seen in a sermon based on Galatians 6:14, "Glorying in the Cross of Christ,"
in which he declared that eternal salvation is only possible through the death of
Jesus Christ. Fundamental for Maclaurin, the cross paradoxically humiliated and
exalted Jesus. The gruesome and bloody death of Christ glorified God's Son in

what he accomplished: the salvation of those who believe on him. Maclaurin's sermon highlights the fact that Christ's death on the cross has been of central importance to evangelicals of all generations.

"Glorying in the Cross of Christ"

The cross of Christ may signify here, not only his death, but the whole of his humiliation, or all the sufferings of his life and death; of which sufferings, the cross was the consummation: the apostle both here and elsewhere, mentions the Cross, to remind us of the manner of his death, and to strengthen in our minds those impressions which the condescension of that death, had made, or ought to have made in them: that the Author of liberty should suffer the death of a slave; the fountain of honour, the height of disgrace; that the punishments which were wont to be inflicted upon the meanest persons for the highest offences, should be inflicted on the greatest person that could suffer: this is the object that the apostle gloried in.

There are not two things more opposite, than glory and shame; here the apostle joins them together: the cross in it self is an object full of shame; in this case it appeareth to the apostle full of glory: It had been less remarkable, had he only said, he gloried in the Redeemer's exaltation after he left the world, or in the glory he had with the Father, before he came to it, yea, before the world was: but the object of the apostle's glorying is the Redeemer, not only considered in the highest state of honour and dignity, but even viewed in the lowest circumstances of disgrace and ignominy, not only as a powerful and exalted, but as a condemned and crucified Saviour.

Glorying signifies the highest degree of esteem; the cross of Christ was an object of which the apostle had the most exalted sentiments, and the most profound veneration; this veneration he took pleasure to avow before the world, and was ready to publish on all occasions: this object so occupied his heart and engrossed his affections, that it left no room for any thing else; he gloried in nothing else; and, as he telleth us in other places, He counted every thing else but loss and dung, and would know nothing else, and was determined about it. 1 Corinthians 2:2 . . .

To glory in any object includes these two things, first a high esteem of it, and then some concern in it. We do not glory in the things we are interested in unless we esteem them; nor in the things we admire and esteem unless we are some way interested in them. But although all professing Christians are some way concerned to glory in the cross of Christ, because of their outward relation to him, by their baptismal covenant, and because the blessed fruits of his cross are both plainly revealed, and freely offered to them; yet it is those only who have sincerely embraced these offers that can truly glory in that object. Yet what is their privilege, is the duty of all; all should be exhorted to glory in this object, and to have a high esteem of it; because of its excellency in itself; to fix their hearts on it by faith, because it is offered to them; to shew their esteem of it, by seeking an interest in it; and having a due esteem of it, and obtained an interest in it, to study a frame of habitual triumph in it. But the nature of this happy frame of mind, is best understood, by considering the glory of the object of it...

A king which the world admires, is one of extensive power, with numerous armies, a golden crown and scepter, a throne of state, magnificent palaces, sumptuous feasts, many attendants of high rank; immense treasures to enrich them with, and various posts of honour to prefer them to.

Here was the reverse of all this; for a crown of gold, a crown of thorns; for a scepter, a reed put in his hand, in derision; for a throne, a cross; instead of palaces, not a place to lay his head in; instead of sumptuous feasts to others, oft-times hungry and thirsty himself; instead of great attendants, a company of poor fishermen; instead of treasures to give them, not money enough to pay tribute, without working a miracle; and the preferment offered them, was to give each of them his cross to bear. In all things the reverse of worldly greatness from first to last, a manger for a cradle at his birth, not a place to lay his head sometimes in his life, nor a grave of his own at his death.

Here unbelief frets and murmurs, and asks, where is all the glory, that is so much extolled? For discovering this, faith needs only look thro' that thin veil of flesh; and under that low disguise appears the Lord of glory, the King of Kings, the Lord of hosts, strong and mighty, (Psalm 24:8). The Lord mighty in battle; the heavens his throne, the earth his footstool, the light his garments, the clouds his chariots, the thunder his voice, his strength omnipotence, his riches all-sufficiency, his glory infinite, his retinue the hosts of heaven, and the excellent ones of the earth, on whom he bestows riches unsearchable, an inheritance incorruptible, banquets of everlasting joys, and preferments of immortal honour, making them kings and priests unto God, conquerors, yea and more than conquerors, children of God, and mystically one with himself.

Here appears something incomparably above all worldly glory, tho' under a mean disguise. But the objection is still against that disguise; yet even that disguise, upon due consideration, will appear to be so glorious, that its very meanness is honourable: it was a glorious disguise, because the designs and effects of it are so; if he suffered shame, poverty, pain, sorrows and death, for a time, it was that we might not suffer these things for ever. That meanness therefore was glorious, because it was subservient unto an infinitely glorious design of love and mercy.

It was subservient [in] more ways than one, it satisfied the penalty of the law, it put unspeakable honour on the commandments of it. It was a part of Christ's design to make holiness, (that is, obedience to the law) so honourable, that every thing else should be contemptible in comparison of it; love of worldly greatness, is one of the principal hindrances of it: We did not need the example of Christ to commend earthly grandeur to us, but very much to reconcile us to the contrary, and to make us esteem holiness, tho' accompanied with meanness; Christ's low state was an excellent mean for this end. There was therefore greatness, even in his meanness: other men are honourable by their station, but Christ's station was made honourable by him; he has made poverty and meanness joined with holiness, to be a state of dignity.

Thus Christ's outward meanness, that disguised his real greatness, was in itself glorious, because of the design of it. Yet that meanness did not wholly becloud it; many beams of glory shone through it...

The glory of the cross of Christ, which we are chiefly to esteem, is the glory of God's infinite perfections displayed in the work of redemption, as the apostle expresses it, *the glory of God in the face of Christ Jesus*, (2 Corinthians 4:6). *Even of Christ crucified*, 1 Corinthians 2:2. It is this which makes any other object glorious, according as it manifests more or less of the perfections of God. This is what makes the works of creation so glorious; the heavens declare God's glory, and the firmament, his handy-work. And we are inexcusable for not taking more pains to contemplate God's perfections in them, his almighty power, and incomprehensible wisdom, and particularly his infinite goodness. But the effects of the Divine goodness, in the works of creation are only temporal favours; the favours purchased to us by the cross of Christ are eternal. Besides, although the works of creation plainly shew that God is in himself good; yet they also shew that God is just, and that he is displeased with us for our sins; nor do they point out to us the way how we may be reconciled to him: they publish the Creator's glory, they publish at the same time his laws and our obligations to obey them. Our consciences tell us we have neglected these obligations, violated these laws, and consequently incurred the lawgiver's displeasure: his works declaring his glory, shew that in his favour is life, and consequently that in his displeasure is death and ruin; yea they lay us in some measure under his displeasure already. Why else do natural causes give so much trouble in life, and pain in death? From all quarters the works of God revenge the quarrel of his broken law: they give these frail bodies subsistence for a time, but it is a subsistence embittered with many vexations, and at last they crush them, and dissolve them in dust.

The face of nature then is glorious in it self, but it is overcast with a gloom of terror to us; it shews the glory of the judge to the criminal; the glory of the sovereign to the guilty rebel: this is not the way to give comfort and relief to a criminal; it is not the way to make him glory and triumph: accordingly the enemies of the cross of Christ, who refuse to know God, otherwise than by the works of nature, are so far from glorying in the hopes of enjoying God in heaven, that they renounce all those great expectations, and generally deny that there is any such blessedness to be had. Conscience tell us, we are rebels against God: and nature does not shew how such rebels may recover his favour; how in such a well-ordered government, as the divine government must be, the righteous judge and lawgiver may be glorified, and the criminal escape; much less how the judge may be glorified, and the criminal obtain glory likewise.

The language of nature, tho' it be plain and loud in proclaiming the glory of the Creator, yet it is dark and intricate as to his inclination towards guilty creatures: it neither assures peremptorily that we are in a state of despair, nor gives sure footing for our hopes. If we are favourites, whence so many troubles? If we are hopeless criminals, whence so many favours? Nature shews God's glory, and our shame; his law our duty, and consequently our danger: but about the way of escape, it is silent and dumb: it affords many motives for exciting desires after God; but it shews not the way to get these desires satisfied. Here in the text is an object which gives us better intelligence. It directs us not merely to seek by feeling in the dark (Acts 17:27) if haply we may find, but to seek him so, as certainly to find him. Unlikely doctrine to a carnal mind: that there should be more of God's glory manifested to us in the face of Christ crucified, than in the face of heaven and earth; the face of Christ, in which sense discovers nothing but marks of pain and disgrace; that bloated, mangled visage, red with gore, covered with marks of scorn, swelled with strokes, and pale with death, that would be the last object in which the carnal mind would seek to see the glory of the God of life; a visage clouded with the horror of death it; would with more pleasure and admiration, view the same face when transfigured, and shining like the sun in its strength. Divine glory shone indeed then in a bright manner in that face on the mount; but not so brightly, as on mount Calvary: this was the more glorious transfiguration of the two. Tho' all the light in the world, in the sun and stars were collected together, into one stupendous mass of light, it would be but darkness to the glory of this seemingly dark and melancholy object: for it is here, as the apostle expresses it, 2 Corinthians 3:18. *We all as with open face may behold the glory of God.*

Here shines spotless justice, incomprehensible wisdom, and infinite love all at once: none of them darkness or eclipses the other, every one of them gives a lustre to the rest. They mingle their beams, and shine with united eternal splendor: The just Judge, the merciful Father, and the wise Governor. No other object gives such a display of all these perfections, yea all the objects we know, give not such a display of any one of them. No where does justice appear so awful, mercy so amiable, or wisdom so profound...

When God gave us his Son, he gave us an infinitely greater gift than the world; the Creator is infinitely more glorious than the creature, and the Son of God is the Creator of all things. God can make innumerable worlds by the word of his mouth; he has but one only Son, and he spared not his only Son, but gave him to the death of the cross for us all.

God's love to his people is from everlasting to everlasting: but from everlasting to everlasting there is no manifestation of it known, or conceivable by us, that can be compared to this. The light of the sun is always the same, but it shines brightest to us at noon: the cross of Christ was the noon-tide of everlasting love; the meridian splendor of eternal mercy; there were many bright manifestations of the same love before, but they were like the light of the morning, that shines more and more unto the perfect day; and that perfect day was when Christ was on the cross, when darkness covered all the land.

John Maclaurin, "Glorying in the Cross of Christ" in *Sermons and Essays. By the Late Reverend Mr John McLaurin, One of the Ministers of Glasgow* (Glasgow: James Knox, 1755), 59–60, 62–5, 67–71.

28

Determining Divine Grace

Sarah Osborn

THE CONTRIBUTION OF Sarah Osborn (1714–96) to evangelicalism has gone largely unnoticed despite her importance as a spiritual mentor and devout Christian. Born in England in 1714, young Sarah and her family emigrated to Boston in the early 1720s before finally settling at Newport, Rhode Island, in 1730. In her teens, she was captivated by the Puritan-style preaching of Nathaniel Clap, pastor of the city's First Congregational Church. Her devotion to Calvinism continued after her marriage at age seventeen to Samuel Wheaten, who died at sea shortly after the birth of their son, and her second marriage in 1742 to widower Henry Osborn. With the failure of her second husband's business ventures, Osborn made amends as a schoolteacher and performing odd household chores for other families.

Prior to the time of the Great Awakening, Osborn wrestled on and off again with her spiritual state. She found relief for her soul after hearing the evangelical preaching of George Whitefield and Gilbert Tennent in the early 1740s. From this point on, Osborn ceased to doubt her beliefs and became an ardent supporter of the Great Awakening. In the wake of the revivals in Newport, she organized a women's society for the females in the First Congregational Church. Its popularity led to prayer meetings in her home during the week that admitted all ages: adults, young men and women, free blacks, and slaves. At its peak in January 1767, Osborn recalled that over 500 people gathered on a weekly basis. Wanting to strengthen this renewal of Christian piety, Osborn and other women at the First Congregational Church successfully campaigned to bring Samuel Hopkins to Newport in 1770 as their pastor. Osborn respected the theology of Jonathan Edwards and the New Divinity and saw Hopkins as a welcome instructor of evangelical Calvinism.

Besides leading prayer meetings and mentoring, Osborn spent much of her time writing. Her memoir, diaries, and letters provide a window into her soul and commitment to evangelical doctrines. In appreciation of her piety, Hopkins edited some of her manuscripts, posthumously publishing *Memoirs of the Life of Mrs. Sarah Osborn* in 1799. According to Hopkins, Osborn penned more than fifty volumes of diaries in addition to roughly one hundred letters. One of her letters to a friend was published within her lifetime in 1755 as *The Nature, Certainty, and Evidence of True Christianity*. In it she related some of her former struggles while affirming her certainty of being born again as a result of the "evidences of a work of grace."

The Nature, Certainty and Evidence of True Christianity

But now perhaps you'll say, Aye, *but how do I know this God is mine; and that I myself am not deceived?* I *answer*, by the *Evidences* of a *Work of Grace* wrought in my Soul. And now as God shall enable me, *my dear Friend*, I'll tell you truly what GOD has done for my Soul, and what I call *Evidences* of a *Work of Grace*. This *Question* I could never fully verbally answer, when with you, which makes me now attempt to explain myself.

First, then, I do know that God has by his *Word* and *Spirit*, convinced me of *Sin*, *Original* and *Actual*; that I was by Nature a Child of Wrath, an Heir of Hell, an Enemy to Him, and his Ways, yea, Enmity itself; *Dead in Trespasses and Sins*; and that I was both utterly, *unable*, and *unwilling* too, to help myself out of this miserable State, being averse to the Gospel-Way of Salvation, wrought out by *Christ*. I plainly see the Cause of the Complaint, *Ye will not come to me, that ye might have Life*. God convinced me also that *by the Deeds of the Law, no Flesh living should be justified*, and that He and his Throne would be spotless forever tho' He should cast me off, and condemn me to the hottest Hell: Since He ow'd me nothing nor was any Way bound to bestow his Grace upon me; and if he did, it would be absolutely free and sovereign. GOD shew'd me I was utterly unworthy that he should help me.

Nevertheless, tho' I had thus destroyed myself, yet in *Him* was my Help. Yea He *discover'd to me*, that *he had laid Help* upon ONE who is *mighty to save to the uttermost all that come to God by Him*; even a glorious CHRIST the Great EMMANUEL God-Man, even one Co-equal with Himself, *the express Image of his Person, in whom dwells, all the Fullness of the Godhead bodily*; One every Way complete and suited to all my wants; and that He was not only thus qualify'd and sealed and sent by the FATHER, but that he was absolutely *willing* as well as *able* to accomplish the great Work; and would by no means cast out any that come to him.

Well upon *this Discovery* of the amiable and lovely JESUS, if I know that I have a Being, I do know that God compell'd or *sweetly constrained me* to *throw down* the Weapons of my Rebellion and to *submit* to HIM as *Prince* and *Saviour*, and *consent* to be saved by him in his own way, and upon his own Terms; that he should be the *Alpha* and *Omega*, the Foundation and the Topstone in my Salvation. Yea, God caus'd *my Heart to go out after Him* in strong and *vehement Desires*, and to *choose Him* in *all his Offices*, with *all his Benefits*, to be *my Portion* forever. Yea *He appear'd to me* to be *in Himself the most lovely and desirable Object*, the fairest of ten thousand Fairs: and God enabled me to *give myself*, my *whole Soul and Body* with *all my Concerns* for Time and Eternity into his merciful and faithful Hands: and had I a thousand precious Souls, I would gladly venture them all with him; for *I am persuaded* he will keep by his mighty Power what I have committed to his Charge; nor shall all the Hosts of Hell, ever be able to pluck me out of his Hands.

But to proceed; upon *this choice*, and *surrender* to CHRIST as *Mediator*, GOD the FATHER *manifested* himself to me, as my reconciled GOD and *Father*; the *blessed* SPIRIT took up his abode with me, afforded me his Influences and Assistance daily; and God made with me an *everlasting Covenant*, never to be forgotten, *Even the sure Mercies of David*: and *I solemnly gave myself up*, all I have, am, or can do, both in Life and Death, in Time and for Eternity, to GOD the FATHER, SON and HOLY GHOST, to be his own, in a Covenant Way, to be disposed of as shall most consist with his Glory; and chose the glorious TRINITY for my *Portion* forever, in opposition to all Others, even a GOD of infinite Perfections. Oh happy Choice! Oh happy I, that I liv'd to see that Day where God betroth'd me to himself in loving Kindness and tender Mercy!

Thus I was *effectually called* and *made willing* in the Day of GOD's Power to *receive* Him: and *to as many as receiv'd Him to them gave He Power to become the Sons of God, even to those that believe on his Name*.

And now the *Foundation* of my *Hopes* are laid upon the *Rock of Ages*. And agreeable to those covenant Engagements, a faithful GOD, has ever since dealt with me. And surely I can say; whereas I was born blind, now I can see; *old Things are done away, all Things become new*. Now thro' Grace I dare appeal to a Heart-searching GOD and say; that none of his Commands are grievous; I esteem them all *holy, right, just,* and *good*; and long to yield a *universal Obedience* to them all: yea GOD does excite in me strong and *vehement Desires* after an *entire Conformity* to his *Law*, as tho' my whole Salvation depended thereon: while at the same Time, he will not suffer me to depend on any thing but CHRIST alone; notwithstanding a strong *Propensity* to cleave to the *Covenant of Works*; but enables me to *account all Things as Loss and Dung and filthy Rags, in point of Justification*; nor would I for a Million Worlds appear before GOD, in the best Performance I ever did: No 'tis in *that spotless Righteousness*, which CHRIST has wrought out, imputed to me, and in that only I dare appear before GOD. But he gives me to see a *Beauty* in *Holiness*, which far exceeds the Lustre of all created Things. Nor do I know what Desire means, after any, or all the *Enjoyments* of *Time* and *Sense, compar'd* with those ardent *Longings*, and *Pantings*, which He at sometimes excites in my Soul, after the *Enjoyment of Himself*; and for *sanctifying Grace*.

And tho' Grace is not always alike in Exercise; (no I am sometimes dull and lifeless as to Exercise) yet blessed be GOD it has been the habitual, and settled Bent of my Soul for many Years; to choose GOD, his CHRIST, and *Grace* for my Portion in all Conditions, both adverse and prosperous. Blessed be GOD, my Faith has not been stagger'd. Sometimes He has bereav'd, cut off the Streams of earthly Comforts, one after another; and then caused me to justify him, and fly to *Him* as my all. Sometimes He has hid his Face, and caused me to mourn after *Him*, and refuse all Comfort till *He* return'd. Sometimes He has permitted *Satan* to tempt and tyrannize over me for a Season; and many a precious *Jewel* has he stolen from me by clouding my Evidences and insinuating that all was Delusion and Hypocrisy; and how many distressing gloomy Days I have had GOD only knows: but *Satan* could not keep *them*; for a faithful GOD would not suffer me to be tempted above that I was able, but made way for my escape.

Sometimes He has permitted the *Remains* of *indwelling Corruption* to rally all its Force and strive for Mastery; but at the same time stir'd up an inveterate Hatred and an Abhorrence of it, and myself for it, because 'tis the abominable Thing which His Soul hates. And sometimes *Unbelief*, has so far prevailed, that I have cry'd out *I shall one Day perish by the Hands of these Enemies*, or I shall at least fall *foully* to the Dishonor of the dear Name by which I am called, if not *finally*: But for *more than Sixteen Years* has GOD preserv'd me from open scandalous Sins. (Yea, blessed be *God*, thro' restraining Grace, all my Life long) and from ever making a League with Sin, since I have thro' Grace proclaim'd War with it: And by grace assisting I am determin'd never to lay down my Arms, but to fight till I die, under the Banner of *the great Captain of my Salvation*: Yea, and Truth and Veracity itself has said, *Sin shall not have Dominion over you*, and *my Grace shall be sufficient for you*. And here (my Dear) my great Strength lies: For *all the Promises are Yea and Amen in* CHRIST JESUS: And since *my* LORD is mine, *all* is mine, and I shall come off more than a Conqueror thro' Him that has loved me and given himself for me. Tho' now I groan under *a Body of Sin and Death*; and may I never cease to mourn, but daily look on Him whom I have pierc'd: Oh it was *Sin, my Sin*, that pierc'd his sacred Head and Side, that put all the bitter Ingredients into the Cup, that extorted that heart-piercing Cry from him, *My God my God, why hast thou forsaken me*: And never does it appear more odious, than when I am well satisfied it never will prove my Ruin. God disposes me to choose any Affliction, or all the Afflictions in this World rather than *Sin*. I do esteem it the worst of Evils; yea I had rather have all the Furies of Hell let loose to perplex me, than to be given over to the *Tyranny* of *my own* inbred *Lusts*, and *Corruptions*. O thanks be to GOD, He has said, *I will subdue your Iniquities!* Oh how sweet here to consider CHRIST as my *King*, that will e're long set his Foot on the Necks of these Enemies! How sweet to espouse his Cause! Bring forth the Traitors, and entreat him to slay every one that says they will not have him to reign over them! Oh that CHRIST would entirely possess his rightful Throne in my Soul, wholly sway the Scepter there, fill every Room; that not a Lust, a Usurper, might ever dare to lift up its venomous Head again! O transporting Thought; one Everlasting Day, this shall be the happy Case!

Again, GOD causes me *to love his Image* wherever I see it; in *Strangers*, in *Rich*, in *Poor*, in *Bond* or *Free*, of *what Denomination soever.* Surely I do *esteem* the *Saints,* the *excellent of the Earth,* and *they are my Delight.* Again, God enables me to *love my Enemies,* to forgive Injuries, and earnestly to pray that God would forgive them also. But I must not innumerate more.

But *these,* my dear Friend, are what I call *Evidences* of a *Work of Grace*: and for my part I had rather be able to read them, than to hear a Voice from Heaven telling me, *I am a Child of GOD.* If you ask again, *if I can always, or of myself read them to my Satisfaction?* I *answer,* without CHRIST I can do nothing; I am not sufficient for one good Thought; all my sufficiency is of GOD: But GOD has taught me to live *more* by *Faith,* and *less* by *Sense,* than I us'd to do; and therefore if he hide his Face, I do not immediately raze Foundations as formerly; and draw up hard Conclusions against myself: But having treasur'd up the *Experiences of many Years,* I repair to them in a dark and cloudy Day, and find, *thus, and thus, GOD has done for me, and appear'd for my Help in Times past*: and this as an Anchor holds me sure, and He will in his own time return, and revive me; He has begun that good Work in me, that he will carry on till the Day of JESUS; HE was the *Author,* and he will be the *Finisher* of *my Faith*: And so he makes me hang on the *Faithfulness* of *a Covenant*-GOD, who will not deceive nor make any ashamed of their Hope, that put their Trust in him.

[Sarah Osborn], *The Nature, Certainty and Evidence of True Christianity. In a Letter from a Gentlewoman in New-England, to Another Her Dear Friend, in Great Darkness, Doubt and Concern of a Religious Nature* (Boston: S. Kneeland, 1755), 3–10.

29

Eloquent Calvinism

James Hervey

THE ANGLICAN CLERGYMAN James Hervey (1714–58) made a name for himself writing books that appealed to elite tastes while teaching evangelical doctrines. Born on February 26, 1714, Hervey grew up in a village near Northampton, England. He entered Lincoln College, Oxford, in 1731, soon uniting with John Wesley and other Methodists in their religious activities. After graduating in 1736, Hervey was ordained a deacon and, in 1739, an Anglican minister. Between 1736 and 1743 he held curacies at two parishes before moving back home to assist his father, the rector of Collingtree and Weston Favell. When his father died in 1752, he took his place as senior pastor. Throughout his life, Hervey maintained friendships with evangelicals inside and outside the Established Church. He counted Anglicans like George Whitefield, John Wesley, the Countess of Huntingdon, and Lady Frances Shirley as his friends along with Dissenters such as Philip Doddridge and John Collett Ryland. But in terms of his beliefs, Hervey held firmly to a moderate form of Calvinism, which can be seen in his publications.

As a writer, he sought to promote evangelical Calvinism using polite rhetoric that would charm the educated and affluent. Drawing from classical and modern poets like Homer, Virgil, and Milton, Hervey fashioned his prose to mimic the mannered style of Lord Shaftesbury and other widely read authors. Hervey's most important works were his *Meditations and Contemplations* (1746–47), which surpassed one hundred editions during the eighteenth century, and *Theron and Aspasio* (1755), a much more theological enterprise that went through twenty-six editions by 1800. The latter was presented in the form of seventeen dialogues and twelve letters between the genteel Theron, who is shepherded to conversion by his grave acquaintance, Aspasio. Within the series of dialogues, Hervey intended to defend the Calvinistic notion of imputed righteousness and uphold Christianity as a rational religion suitable to polite standards. While many contemporary evangelicals praised *Theron and Aspasio*, others, like John Wesley, were quick to point out its faults. In Wesley's case, he disapproved of Hervey's blatant preferment of

FIGURE 29.1 James Hervey (Detail), courtesy of the National Portrait Gallery, London.

Reformed theology, which he feared would encourage antinomianism. When the unresponsive Hervey disregarded Wesley's initial suggestions on how to improve *Theron and Aspasio*, the Methodist leader decided to publish his formerly private letter as *A Preservative against Unsettled Notions in Religion* (1758). Wesley's caustic comments deeply wounded Hervey, who spent his dying days composing an answer to his former mentor. Unfortunately, Hervey died on Christmas Day, 1758, before completing his response. Even though he entrusted his manuscript to his brother with clear instructions that it should not be published, Hervey's *Eleven Letters from the Late Rev. Mr Hervey, to the Rev. Mr John Wesley* appeared in print in 1765, with some subsequent editions retitled as *Aspasio Vindicated*. Hervey's *Theron and Aspasio*, and posthumous reply to Wesley, sparked heated debates among evangelicals in the last quarter of the century on the validity of imputed righteousness and Calvinism in general.

Theron and Aspasio

THERON, was a Gentleman of fine Taste; of accurate, rather than extensive Reading; and particularly charmed with the Study of Nature. He traced the Planets in their Courses, and examined the Formation of the meanest Vegetable; not merely to gratify a *refined* Curiosity, but chiefly to cultivate the *nobler* Principles of Morality. Several Discoveries He made, and every Discovery He improved, to this important End—to raise in his Mind, more *exalted* Apprehensions of the SUPREME Being—and to enlarge his Affections, with a *disinterested* Benevolence; conformable, in some Degree, to that boundless Liberality, which pervades and animates the whole Creation.

ASPASIO, was not without his Share of polite Literature, and philosophical Knowledge. He had taken a Tour through the Circle of the Sciences; and, having transiently surveyed the Productions of *human* Learning, devoted his final Attention to the *inspired* Writings. These He studied, with the unbiased Impartiality of a Critic; yet with the reverential Simplicity of a Christian. These He regarded, as the *unerring* Standard of Duty—the *authentic* Charter of Salvation— and the *brightest* Mirror of the DEITY; affording the most satisfactory and sublime Display of all the divine Attributes.

Theron, was somewhat *warm* in his Temper; and would, upon Occasion, make Use of a little innocent Raillery; not to expose his Friend, but to enliven the Conversation. Sometimes *disguising* his real Sentiments; in order to sift the Subject, or discover the Opinion of others.—*Aspasio* seldom indulges the humorous or satirical Vein, but argues with *Meekness of Wisdom*. Never puts on the Appearance of Guile, but always speaks the Dictates of his Heart.

Aspasio was on a Visit at *Theron's* Seat.—One Evening, when some neighbouring Gentlemen were just gone, and had left them alone, the Conversation took the following Turn.

Aspasio. I would always be ready, both to acknowledge and applaud, whatever is amiable in the Conduct of Others. The Gentlemen, who gave Us their Company at Dinner, seem to be all of a *different* Character. Yet each, in his own Way, is extremely *agreeable.*

Lysander has lively parts, and is quick at Repartee. But He never abuses his Wit, to create Uneasiness in the honest Heart, or flush the modest Cheek with Confusion.—What Solidity of Judgment, and Depth of Penetration, appear in *Crito!* Yet, how free are his Discourses, from the magisterial Tone, or the dictatorial Solemnity!—*Philenor's* Taste in the polite Arts, is remarkably correct: yet, without the least Tincture of Vanity, or any weak Fondness for Applause. He never interrupts the Progress, or wrests the Topic of Conversation; in order to shine in his particular Province.—*Trebonius*, I find, has signalized his Valour, in several Campaigns. Though a Warrior and a Traveler, He gives Himself no overbearing or ostentatious Airs. In *Trebonius*, You see the brave Officer, regulated by all the Decency of the Academic, and sweetened with all the Affability of the Courtier.

No one affects a *morose* Silence, or assumes an *immoderate* Loquacity. To engross the Talk is tyrannical: to seal up the Lips, is monkish. Every one, therefore, from a Fund of good Sense, contributes his Quota: and each speaks, not with an Ambition to *set off* Himself, but from a Desire to *please* the Company.

Theron. Indeed, *Aspasio*, I think myself happy, in this accomplished Set of Acquaintance. Who add all the Complaisance and Politeness of the Gentleman, to the Benevolence and Fidelity of the Friend.

Their Conversation is as innocent, as their Taste is refined.—They have a noble Abhorrence of *Slander*, and detest the low ungenerous Artifices of *Detraction.*—No *loose Jest*, has either the Service of their Tongue, or the Sanction of their Smile. Was

You to be with them, even in their freest Moments; You would hear Nothing, that borders upon *Profaneness*, or is in the least injurious to *Purity* of Morals.

Aspasio. There is but *one* Qualification wanting, to render your Friends completely valuable; and their social Interviews a continual Blessing.

Theron. Pray, what is that?

Aspasio. A Turn for *more serious* Conferences.—Their literary Debates are beautiful Sketches, of whatever is most curious in the Sciences, or most delicate in the Arts. From their Remarks on our national Affairs, and on foreign Occurrences, a Person may almost form a System of Politics. But, they never touch upon any Topic of *Morality*; never celebrate the *sublime Perfections* of the DEITY; never illustrate the Beauties, nor enforce the Truths.—

Theron. Fie upon You, *Aspasio*, for your impolite Hint! Who can forbear interrupting an Harangue, that pleads for such an outrageous Violation of the *Mode*? Would introduce *edifying* Talk into our *fashionable* Assemblies!—How is it that You, who, in other Instances, are a Gentleman of Refinement, can be so strangely inelegant in this Particular?

Aspasio. For such a Practice, *Theron*, We have no inconsiderable Precedents.— Thus *Socrates*, the wisest of the *Athenian* Sages, thus *Scipio*, the most accomplished of the *Roman* Generals, conversed.—Thus *Cicero*, the Prince of Orators, improved his elegant Retirement at the *Tusculan* Villa.—And *Horace*, the brightest Genius in the Court of *Augustus*, formed the most agreeable Hours of his Conversation, upon this very Plan.

Was I to enumerate all the Patrons of this, forgive me if I say, *more honourable* Mode; the most illustrious Names of Antiquity, would appear on the List.

Theron. This Practice, however extolled by the philosophic Gentry of ancient Times; would make a very *singular* Figure, in the present Age.

Aspasio. And should not the *Copy*, after which the Generality of Mankind write, be *singularly correct*? Persons of exalted Fortune, are the Pattern for general Imitation: are the Copy, in Conformity to which, the inferior World adjust their Manners, and regulate their Behaviour. *They*, therefore, are under the strongest Obligations, not to give a *contemptible* Stamp to the Fashion.—Benevolence to their Fellow-creatures calls loudly upon them, a Concern for the public Good challenges it at their Hands, that *they* signalize themselves by a Pre-eminence in all that is excellent.

Theron. Away, away with these *austere* Notions! Such a Strain of Conversation, would *damp* the Gaiety of our Spirits, and *flatten* the Relish of Society. It would turn the Assembly into a Conventicle, and make it Lent all the Year round.

Aspasio. Can it then be an austere Practice, to cultivate the Understanding, and improve the Heart?—Can it damp the Gaiety of our Spirits, to refine them upon the Plan of the highest Perfection?—Or, will it flatten the Relish of Society, to secure and anticipate everlasting Delights?

Thereon. Everlasting Delights, Aspasio!—To talk of such a Subject, would be termed, in every Circle of Wit and Gallantry, an Usurpation of the Parson's Office. A *low* Method, of retailing by Scraps, in the Parlour; what the Man in Black, vends by wholesale, from the Pulpit.—It would infallibly mark Us out for *Pedants*. And, for aught I know, might expose Us to the Suspicion of *Enthusiasm*.

Aspasio. Your Men of Wit must excuse me, if I cannot persuade myself to admire, either the *Delicacy* of their Language, or the *Justness* of their Opinion.

The first, be it ever so *humane* and *graceful*, I resign to themselves.—As for the other, I would beg Leave to inquire; "Are the Clergy, then, the *only* Persons, who should act the *becoming* Part, and converse like *rational* Beings? Is solid Wisdom, and sacred Truth, the Privilege of their Order? While nothing is left for You and me, but the Play of Fancy, or the Luxuries of Sense."

I would farther ask the Circles of Gallantry; "Where is the Impropriety, of interweaving the *noble* Doctrines, displayed by the Preacher, with our common Discourse? Or, what the Inconvenience, of introducing the *amiable* Graces, recommended by his Lectures, into our ordinary Practice?"

Will *such* an Exercise of our Speech, rank Us among Pedants? Is *this* the Badge of Enthusiasm? A splendid and honourable Badge truly! Such as must add Weight to any Cause, and Worth to any Character.

Theron. This would curb the sprightly Sallies of *Wit*; and extinguish that engaging Glow of *Good-humour*, which enlivens our genteel Intercourses. Accordingly, You may observe, that if any *formal Creature*, takes upon Him to mention, in polite Company, a religious Truth, or a Text of Scripture; the pretty Chat, though ever so profusely flowing, stagnates in an Instant. Each voluble facetious Tongue seems to be struck with a sudden Palsy. Every one wonders at the strange Man's Face; and they all conclude Him, either *mad*, or a *Methodist*.

Aspasio. Agreeable Strokes of Wit, are by no Means incompatible with useful Conversation. Unless we mistake an *insipid* Vivacity, or *fantastic* Levity, for Wit and Facetiousness.—Neither have I heard, that, among all our Acts of Parliament, any one has passed to *divorce* Good Sense and Good-humour. Why may they not both reside on the same Lips, and both circulate through the same Assembly?—For my own Part, I would neither have our Discourse *soured* with Austerity, nor *evaporate* into Impertinence: but unite (as a judicious Ancient advises) the Benefits of Improvement, with the Blandishments of Pleasantry.—And as to your polite People; if they can find more Music, in the *Magpie's* Voice, than in the *Nightingale's* Note; I must own myself as much surprised at *their* Ears, as they are at the strange Man's Face.

Theron. With all your grey-headed Authorities, I fancy, You will find very few Proselytes, among the Professors of modern Refinement. *Fashion* is, with the World, the Standard of Morals, as well as of Clothes. And He must be of a very *peculiar* Turn indeed, who would choose to be ridiculous in either.

Aspasio. Rather, *Theron*, He must be of a very *pliant* Turn, who tamely delivers up his Conduct, to be moulded by a Fashion; which has neither true Elegance to dignify it, nor the least Usefulness to recommend it.

And which, I beseech You, is most ridiculous?—He, who servilely imitates every *idle* Fashion, and is the very *Ape* of corrupt Custom?—Or He, who asserts his native Liberty; and resolutely follows, where *Wisdom* and *Truth* lead the Way...

Aspasio. [speaking of God's order in the beauty of nature] But, my dear *Theron*, is not this apparent, in a much more wonderful Manner, throughout the whole Oeconomy of REDEMPTION?—It were a small Thing for this inferior Class of *unintelligent* Creatures, to be continually employing themselves for our Benefit. Even the *Son of the most High GOD*, through all his incarnate State, acted the very same Part.—He took Flesh, and bore the Infirmities of human Nature, not for Himself, but *for Us Men, and our Salvation*. He suffered Want, and endured Misery in all its Forms; that *We* might possess the Fullness of Joy, and abound in Pleasures for evermore.—When he poured out his Soul in Agonies, under the Curse of an *avenging* Law; what other End had He in View, but to make *Us* Partakers of eternal Blessedness? When He fulfilled, perfectly fulfilled the whole *commanding* Law; was it not on purpose, that his Merits might be imputed to Us? That *We*, by *his* Obedience, might be made righteous?

_____ *For Us He liv'd*
Toil'd for our Ease, and for our Safety bled.

Nothing in the whole Course—

Theron. Pardon me for interrupting You, *Aspasio*. I have no Objection to the general Drift of your Discourse. But that particular Notion of *imputed Righteousness*, has always appeared to me in a very ridiculous Light. And I must say, that such a *Puritanical Nostrum* makes a very unbecoming Figure, amongst your other manly and correct Sentiments of Religion.

Aspasio. You know, *Theron*, I have long ago disavowed that *ignoble* Prejudice, which rejects Doctrines, or despises Persons, because they happen to be branded with contemptible Names. 'Tis true, the Writers styled *Puritans*, are remarkable for their Attachment to this *Peculiarity* of the Gospel. It runs through all their Theological Works; and very eminently distinguishes them, from the Generality of our modern Treatises.—But, must it *therefore* be wrong, because maintained by that particular Set of People? Or, are they the *only* Advocates for this important Truth?...

Aspasio. To conceive a Dislike of any Doctrine, only because Persons of a particular Denomination, have been very officious to promote its Reception; this is hardly consistent with an *impartial* Inquiry after Truth.

Theron. I grant it, *Aspasio.* And I should be ashamed of my Opposition, if it was founded on so slight a Bottom. But, abstracted from all *Party-Considerations,* I can see nothing in this supposed Article of our Faith, that may recommend it to the unprejudiced Inquirer.—What can be more *awkward* than the Term, or more *irrational* than the Sentiment?

Aspasio. The Word *imputed,* when used in this Connection, may possibly convey a disagreeable Sound to the Ears of some People. Because, they look upon it, as the peculiar Phraseology of a few *superstitious Sectarists*; and reject it, merely on the Foot of that unreasonable Surmise.—But, how can *You* be disgusted at the Expression, *Theron*; who have so often read it, in the most approved and judicious Writers? St. *Paul,* who might affirm with Relation to his Epistles, much more truly than the Painter concerning his Portraits, *I write for Eternity*; scruples not to use this awkward Language, several Times in the same Chapter [Romans 4]. *Milton,* the Correctness of whose Taste, and the Propriety of whose Style, no Person of Genius will ever question; delights to copy, in various Parts of his incomparable Poem, the Apostle's Diction.—Authorized by *such* Precedents, it is superior to Cavil, and warranted beyond all Exception.

As to the *Sentiment,* I take it to be the *very fundamental* Article of the Gospel: and I believe, whoever is acquainted with ecclesiastical History, will allow, that it bore the *principal Sway,* in extricating Us from Popish Darkness, and introducing the *Reformation.*—What says our LORD, with regard to the Love of GOD, and the Love of our Neighbour? *On these two Commandments hang all the Law and the Prophets.* Much the same would I venture to say, concerning the Imputation of our Sins to *CHRIST,* and the Imputation of *CHRIST*'s Righteousness to Us: On *these two* Doctrines, hang all the Privileges and the whole Glory of the Gospel.

Theron. In our last Conversation, I must own, I saw a strong Resemblance between the *Works* and the *Word* of GOD. But I never observed any Thing in Nature, that bore the least *Analogy* to imputed Sin, or imputed Righteousness.— To me your two Doctrines seem very unaccountable and irrational.

Aspasio. That our Sins should be charged upon the only begotten Son of GOD, and that his Righteousness should be made over to sinful Worms, is strange, exceeding strange. The Psalmist calls it, *marvelous Loving-Kindness* [Psalm 17:7]. The Apostle styles it, *Love that passeth Knowledge* [Ephesians 3:19]. And it has sometimes, I must freely confess, been almost ready to stagger my Belief.—However, I have found myself relieved in this Perplexity, not only by the *Testimonies* of *Scripture,* but even from the *Contemplation* of *Nature.* All Nature is full of strange and mysterious Effects; consequently, is a Voucher for the mysterious Truths of Christianity...

Theron. Two of your Terms want some further Explication. What do You understand by *CHRIST*'s Righteousness? And what is the Meaning of *imputed*?

Aspasio. By *CHRIST*'s *Righteousness* I understand, *all* the various Instances of his *active* and *passive* Obedience; springing from the perfect Holiness of his Heart;

continued through the whole Progress of his Life; and extending to the very last Pang of his Death. By the Word *imputed* I would signify, That this Righteousness, though performed by our LORD, is *placed to our Account*; is reckoned or adjudged by GOD as *our own*. Insomuch, that We may *plead* it, and *rely* on it, for the Pardon of our Sins; for Adoption into his Family; and for the Enjoyment of Life eternal.— Shall I illustrate my Meaning by a well attested Fact?

Theron. Nothing gives Us so easy a Conception of any difficult Point, as this Method of explaining, by *parallel* Facts, or proper Similitudes.

Aspasio. I don't say the Case is parallel. I only produce it, to aid our Conceptions.—*Onesimus*, You know, was *Philemon's* Slave. He had perfidiously deserted his Master's Service, and still more perfidiously stole his Goods. The Fugitive, in his guilty Rambles, providentially meets with St. *Paul*. He is charmed and captivated with that gracious Gospel, which proclaims Mercy even for the vilest of Sinners. He becomes a thorough Convert to the Religion of *JESUS*, and is received into the spiritual Patronage of the Apostle. Who, learning his criminal Conduct, and obnoxious State, undertakes to bring about a Reconciliation, with his offended Master: dispatches Him, for this Purpose, with a Letter to *Philemon*: and amongst other Persuasives, writes, thus in the poor Criminal's Behalf; *If He hath wronged Thee, or oweth Thee aught, put that on mine Account. I Paul have written it with mine own Hand; I will repay it.*

That, which the zealous Preacher of Christianity *offered*, the adored Author of Christianity *executed*.—*We* had revolted from the LORD of all Lords, and broke his holy Commandments. The Son of GOD, infinitely compassionate, vouchsafes to become our Mediator. That nothing might be wanting, to render his Mediation successful, He places Himself in our Stead. The Punishment, which *We* deserved, *He* endures. The Obedience, which *We* owed, *He* fulfils.—Both which, being imputed to Us, and accepted for Us, are the Foundation of our Pardon, are the procuring Cause of our Justification...

Theron. If People may be safe, and their eternal Interests secure, without any Knowledge of these Particularities; why should you offer to puzzle their Heads, about a few unnecessary *scholastic* Terms?

Aspasio. Scriptural Terms, You should have said, *Theron.*—However, We are not very solicitous, as to the Credit, or the Use, of any particular Set of Phrases. Only let Men be humbled, as *repenting Criminals*, at the REDEEMER's Feet: Let them rely, as *devoted Pensioners*, on his precious Merits: and they are undoubtedly in the Way to a blissful Immortality.—Yet, will their Way be less clear, and their Steps more embarrassed, by not distinctly understanding the benign Genius of the Gospel. A proper Information in this Important Point, would shed *Light* upon their Paths, and *encourage* them in their Journey; would further their Progress in vital Holiness, and increase their Joy to the LORD.

Theron. The Followers of your Opinion, I have observed, are perpetually dwelling upon this *one favourite* Topic; to the Exclusion of that grand and truly essential Part of Christianity, *Sanctification.*

Aspasio. If You have ever taken notice of such a Conduct, You are unquestionably right, in with-holding your Approbation. It is a manifest *Incongruity*, and deserves your *Censure.* But, assure Yourself, it proceeds from a Misapprehension in the Persons, and has no Connection with the Nature of the Doctrine.

I am far, very far from reducing the *various* Parts of Christianity, (which, when connected, make up so well-proportioned a System) to this *single*, however distinguished Branch. Sanctification is *equally necessary*, both to our present Peace, and to our final Felicity. Indeed, they are as reciprocally necessary, for the Purposes of *intellectual* and *eternal* Happiness; as the *Heart* and the *Lungs* are, to the Subsistence of the animal Oeconomy. The former must transmit, the latter must refine, the vital Fluid; or else, Disease will take Place, and Death will ensue. My Intention is, that those *fundamental Truths* of the Gospel, like these *Master-Organs* in the Body, may have *each* its proper Office assigned; each concur to support the better Health, and to promote the spiritual Growth, of the Christian.

James Hervey, *Theron and Aspasio: Or, a Series of Dialogues and Letters, upon the Most Important and Interesting Subjects*, volume 1 (London: Rivington, 1755), 1–10, 5–51, 54–7, 59–61, 65–7.

30

Life as the Wife of a College President

Esther Edwards Burr

ESTHER EDWARDS BURR (1732–58) was the third child of Jonathan Edwards and Sarah Pierpont Edwards. She grew up in Northampton, Massachusetts, at the height of the Great Awakening, hearing the preaching of such evangelists as George Whitefield, and witnessing ecstatic religious behavior, including her mother's in 1742. In the wake of her father's dismissal as pastor at Northampton, Esther married Aaron Burr in 1752, a Presbyterian minister in Newark, New Jersey, who also served as the second president of the fledgling College of New Jersey. Moving to Newark after her wedding, and later relocating to Princeton in 1756, Esther had to make due with her new life as the wife of a college president, a role in which she felt obliged to feed and entertain house guests at a moment's notice. Although happily married, Esther complained of her husband's frequent absences and often felt alone without the company of familiar friends and family. Her children, Sally and Aaron Burr Jr., provided some comfort, but also brought with them the challenges of rearing in an age without modern medicine. The end of her life was marked with tragedy. Her husband passed away on September 24, 1757 after battling a fever, and her father, who had agreed to replace Burr as the president of the College of New Jersey, died months later in March. Within weeks of her father's death, Esther developed a fever that led to her demise on April 7 of the same year. Esther's brother, Timothy Edwards, took care of the orphaned Sally and Aaron Burr Jr., who would later become vice president of the United States under Thomas Jefferson in 1800 and famously kill Alexander Hamilton in a duel in 1804.

In 1754, Esther started a journal that she kept for almost three years. It consisted of a chain of letters addressed to her intimate childhood friend, Sarah Prince Gill, the daughter of the Boston minister Thomas Prince. The letters reveal much about Esther's personality, way of life, reading habits, and faith. She candidly expressed her struggles with depression, bemoaned her house duties, questioned her parenting skills, worried about her family's safety, and wrestled over spiritual matters. The journal offers a firsthand perspective of the day-to-day life of a prominent woman living in eighteenth-century America.

"The Journal of Esther Edwards Burr"

Friday [October 11, 1754]

It is a great comfort to me when my friends are absent from me that I have em some where in the World, and you my dear for *one* not of the least for I esteem you one of the best, and in some respects nearer than any Sister I have. I have not one Sister I can write so freely to as to you the Sister of my heart. There is a friend nearer than a brother, *Certainly*... That old Proverb is not a true one, out of sight out of mind...

Thursday, October 17 [1754]

I did not write yesterday because I felt so dull that I knew that what I should write would not be worth reading... Don't you want to know how I spend my time Now Mr. Burr is gone? I [imagine that] you do in reason. In the forenoon my Brother reads loud to me. In the P.M. we commonly Ride out frequently on business if I have not company. Eve My Brother reads again. We generally Sit and chat a little after dinner about Mr. Burr and you and the rest of Boston good friends, Northampton and Stockbridge which has no Small Share in our conversation as well as thoughts. Poor people! I fear they suffer a great deal! I wish they were some where else out of danger! You can't conceive the distress I have been in on their account... It is late so a good Nights rest to you My dear...

Saturday P.M. [November 2, 1754]

There is so much goodness, kindness, openness with every other good quality, savoured with piety in your Letters that when I am read I am always charmed. Now don't Say this is a compliment. I Shall dislike it if you do, for I abhor em among friends and such a friendship as ours. I have such a *Duke of a pen* that I must be obliged to leave off, pray be so good as to Send me Some, for them you was so kind as to leave me when you went home, Suited me the best that ever any did... I am of your mind, it is very needful, this private way of corresponding, (I mean our billets to be burnt) we can no other way be let into one another's circumstances, which would give us both much distress, but tis very hard to commit any thing of so dear a friends to the flames, it grieves me so I can hardly bare it. I have promised and will not break my word, nor give you uneasiness...

Friday [November 8, 1754]

Am a little better. A gentleman from Albany has been here today and brings the Certain news that all the Indians in Stockbridge have left the place except two or three families, he Say they are much disgusted, and Say the white people are jealous of em and they will not live among em any longer, he Said farther that they had a mind to Send for a neighbouring Tribe to assist em to kill all the people in

Stockbridge. O my dear what a dismal aspect things have! I am almost out of my wits! What will become of my Dear father and his afflicted family! O help me to commit em to God who orders all things in mercy, and don't willingly afflict nor grieve any of his Children! I am ready to Say Some times, why is it? Why does God Suffer his own most dear children to be hunted about in this manner! But this is a very wrong temper of mind. I hope I may be enabled to crush it by divine assistance. This day was our preparation day for a reception of the holy ordinance of the Lords Supper...

Tuesday Eve [December 10, 1754]

Know Sooner is the house emptied but filled again. Just now came in Mr. [William] Tennent of Freehold and his Wife, and two Sons that he has brought to put under Mr. Burr's care. I am of the mind that my days are to be Spent in a hurry of business. Such Sort of business as this that I have mentioned...

Monday Eve [January 6, 1755]

...I feel too Silly to write anymore, so I think I'll leave off—No I won't neither. Pray why do you think every body marries in, or about Winter for? Tis quite merry, is not it? I really believe tis for fear of laying cold, and for the want of a bedfellow. Well, my advice to Such is the Same with the Apostles, Let them Marry—and you know the reason given by him, as well as I do—Tis better to marry then to—

I always Said I would never be married in the Fall nor Winter, and I did as I Said, and am glad of it (I have been reading over my Scrawls—And I don't know *what's the matter*. It did not use to be just so bad I think)...

Monday [January 13, 1755]

I wonder what Sort of Ideas you have of Mrs. [Elizabeth] *Rowe*, I believe the same that I have. I have been reading Some of her Real Letters, they are very fine. I wish I could See and converse with her. She was, to my notion hardly a mortal although She did die. She Seemed to live among the dead, and Angels and departed spirits (I wish She and Doctor [Isaac] Watts had got together and had one Child that [we] might see what they could do)...

Friday [January 17, 1755]

I don't know but I write the Same thing *over* and *over again*, and again, for as Soon as I have laid down my pen, I have perfectly forgot what I have been writing about, and I dare not read it over, for it appears so *Silly* that I can't bare to Send it out of my hands, and I hate to have Such a mean opinion of my Self—I believe if I Should read all over, I Should not find but about one fourth part fit to Send to you...Our house is very gloomy, as tis *always* when Mr. Burr is gone. I am ready to imagine the *Sun* does not give so much light as it did when my best Self was at home, and *I* am in the glooms two, half *dead*, my *Head* gone, *behead* a person and they will Soon *die*...Strange tis no Vessels come, nor go, to Boston. I am really impatient. You want to hear from me too...

Sabbath Eve [February 2, 1755]

Two excellent Sermons My dear I must Say from Deuteronomy the 21 chap, 18. 19. 20. 21. verses. Pray my dear be so good as to turn to the passage tis so remarkable a paragraph that I think no one can read it and not feel moved. Tis true, lamentably true that we have many of these Rebellious Stubborn Sons, and Daughters too, amongst us. Never did our young people get to Such a height of wickedness as now, they are come to that, to go to pulling down buildings in the day time, and then so daring as to Say in excuse for them selves, O we were drunk—Drunkenness and uncleanness prevail abundantly. O my dear I am Sick of this World!...

Saturday [February 15, 1755]

How *vain and empty* is the World and all its enjoyments—tis enough to make one weary of life and all its charms, but just now it hasn't many charms to me, altho' few have so many of its comforts and conveniences allotted to 'em as I have, nay I believe nobody. I am Sure I would not change my circumstances for any one living, do you think I would change my *good Mr. Burr* for any person, or thing, or all things on the Earth? *No Sure!* Not for a Million Such Worlds as this that had *no Mr. B—r in it*. But I must ask your pardon, you will think I am not so very indifferent to everything in the world neither, but to tell the truth when I Speak of the *world*, and the things that are in the *World*, I don't mean *friends*, for *friendship* does not belong to the *world*, *true friendship* is first enkindled by a Spark from *Heaven*, and *heaven* will never Suffer it to go out, but it will *burn* to all *Eternity*. I am apt to think that the *indifference* I feel, is not from a weanedness from Sensual enjoyment, no I am not in so good a frame, but arises from bodily disorder, and a degree of low Spiritedness, tho' I am better than I was yesterday...

Friday P.M. February the last Day [February 28, 1755]

...I had almost forgot to tell you that I have begun to govern Sally. She has been Whip'd once on *Old Adams* account, and She knows the difference between a Smile and a frown as well as I do, when She has done any thing that She Suspects is wrong, will look with concern to See what Mama Says, and if I only knit my brow She will cry till I Smile, and altho' She is not quite Ten months old, yet when She knows so much, I think tis time She Should be taught. But none but a parent can conceive how hard it is to chastise your *own most tender Self*. I confess I never had a right idea of the mother's heart at Such a time before. I did it my Self too, and it did her a vast deal of good, if you was here I would tell you the effect it had on her...

Monday P.M. [March 10, 1755]

Phoo, folks always coming. Eve. I have borrowed [Samuel Richardson's] Pamela and am reading it now. I fancy I Sha'nt like it so well as I did Clarissa, but prejudice must have its weight. I remember you Said that in your opinion it did not equal her. Your judgment my dear has a very great influence on mine, nay I would venture to report that Such a Book Surpassed Such an one, if you Said so, if I had never laid my Eyes on 'em—but for all I intend not to be so complaisant but I will have a judgment of my own. Tis quite late may guardian angels protect my dear friend this night..

Tuesday P.M. [March 11, 1755]

...Eve. Pray my dear how could Pamela forgive Mr. B.—all his Devilish conduct so as to consent to marry him? Certainly this does not well agree with so much virtue and piety, nay I think it a very great defect in the performance, and then isn't it Setting up Riches and honour as the great essentials of happiness in a married State? Perhaps I am too rash in my judgment for I have not read it half out tho' I have enough to See the Devil in the Man...

Sabbath—19 [September 19, 1756]

Last eve I had Some free discourse with My Father on the great things that concern my best interest—I opened my difficulties to him very freely and he as freely advised and directed the conversation has removed some distressing doubts that discouraged me much in my Christian warfare—He gave me Some excellent directions to be observed in Secret that tend to keep the Soul near to God, as well as others to be observed in a more public way—What a mercy that I have Such a Father! Such a Guide!...

Sabbath Jan—2 day [January 2, 1757]

I long to begin this year with God—O for God's presence through this year! When I look back on the year past and take a view of the Numberless Mercies I have been the Subject of, I Stand amazed at God's goodness to Such an Ill deserving Hell deserving Creature I am—Why am I thus distinguished from the greater part of the World—What obligations am I under to Spend the remainder of my time for God—I don't want to live unless I can live more to the glory of God and do more good...

Tuesday A.M. 10 o'Clock [April 12, 1757]

I have had a Smart Combat with Mr. [John] Ewing about our Sex—he is a man of good parts and Learning but has mean thoughts of Women—he began the dispute in this Manner, Speaking of Miss [Annis] Boudinot [Stockton] I Said She was a Sociable friendly creature, a Gentleman Sitting by joined with me, but Mr. Ewing Says—*She and the Stocktons are full of talk about Friendship and Society and Such Stuff—and made up a Mouth as if much disgusted*—I asked what he would have 'em talk about—whether he chose they Should talk about fashions and dress—*he Said things that they understood, he did not think women knew what Friendship was, they were hardly capable of anything so cool and rational as friendship* (My Tongue, you know, hangs pretty loose, thoughts Crowded in—so I Sputtered away for dear life). You may Guess what a large field this Speech opened for me—I retorted Several Severe things upon him before he had time to Speak again, he Blushed and Seemed confused, the Gentleman Sitting by Said little but when did Speak it was to my purpose and we carried on the dispute for an hour—I talked him quite Silent. He got up and Said your Servant and went off.

Esther Edwards Burr, "The Journal of Esther Edwards Burr, 1754–1757," MS. Z117 39e, Burr Family Papers, Beinecke Library, Yale University, Letters 9–11, Letter 25, Letter 1, Letter 3.

31

Report on African American Religion in Virginia

Samuel Davies

SAMUEL DAVIES (1723–61) received his education from Samuel Blair, a notable evangelical Irish emigrant who had studied with William Tennent Sr. at the so-called Log College in Bucks County, Pennsylvania. Davies went on to become a prominent Presbyterian minister in Hanover County, Virginia. In 1753, Davies and Gilbert Tennent traveled to Britain to raise money for the fledgling College of New Jersey. When Jonathan Edwards died unexpectedly in 1758, the trustees of the college turned to Davies to fill this vacancy in 1759, which he did until his untimely death in 1761.

While ministering in Virginia, Davies noted the religious zeal of the African slave community. He found southern blacks to have as much interest in the Bible and Christianity (if not more) as the "respectable" members of society. In his letter on April 1, 1755 to a representative of the Society in London for Promoting Religious Knowledge among the Poor, Davies expressed compassion for enslaved Africans and a desire for them to learn how to read religious books donated by the society. Throughout many of his letters, Davies complained about the spiritual neglect of slaves by their masters. He submitted that such a workforce should be treated humanely—preferring that slaves be viewed as members of a family who needed the same kind of care as children—but more importantly that they hear the gospel. Although a slave owner himself whose paternalism is evident, Davies was a pioneer of religious equality in the South, teaching Christianity to anyone willingly to listen.

FIGURE 31.1 Samuel Davies, courtesy of Union Presbyterian Seminary.

Letters from the Rev. Samuel Davies

Though there are very few of the white people in this Colony in abject poverty, yet there are many in such low circumstances, that they cannot *spare* money to purchase good books. And there are many more, who might indeed spare so much, without injury to their temporal affairs; but as they are stupidly insensible of their *Want* of Instruction, and do not form so high an estimate of the Means of Grace, as of the Necessaries, or even Conveniences of this moral Life; they are willing to excuse themselves from it, as a piece of *needless* expence.

On one or other of these accounts, there are few houses in *Virginia* well furnished in this important respect; and multitudes are grossly ignorant, and consequently careless, about the concerns of Immorality. To some of these I have distributed *The Compassionate Address, Baxter's Call to the Unconverted, the Sabbath-breaker's Monitor*, &c. with the best Advice I could give them, and I hope I shall be able hereafter to give you an agreeable account of the happy effects of the distribution.

But the poor neglected NEGROE SLAVES, who are so far from having money to purchase books, that they themselves are the property of others; who were originally *African Savages*, and never heard of JESUS and his Religion, until they arrived on the land of their slavery in *America*; whom their masters generally neglect, as though Immorality was not the privilege of their souls, nor the religion of JESUS their concern! These *poor Africans* are the principal objects of compassion; and, I think, the most proper objects of the SOCIETY's Charity.

The inhabitants of *Virginia* are computed to be about three hundred thousand; and one half of them are supposed to be Negroes. The number that attend upon my ministry at particular times, is uncertain; but, I think, there are about *three hundred* that give a stated attendance. And never have I been so much struck with the appearance of an assembly, as when I have glanced my eyes to one part of the Meeting-house, adorned (so it has appeared to me) with so many black countenances, eagerly attentive to every word they heard, and some of them washed with tears.

A considerable number of them (about an hundred) have been *baptized*, after they had been Catechumens for some time, and given credible evidence, not only of their acquaintance with the important doctrines of the Christian Religion, but also of a deep sense of these things upon their spirits, and a life of the strictest Morality and Piety. As they are not sufficiently polished to dissemble with a good grace, they express the sensations of their minds so much in the language of simple nature, and with such genuine indications of Sincerity, that it is impossible to suspect the profession of some of them, especially when attested by a regular behaviour in common life.

My worthy friend Mr. *Todd*, Minister of the next congregation, has near the same number of negroes under his Pastoral charge; and some of them, he tells me, discover the same serious turn of mind. In short, there are multitudes of them in various parts, who are willing, and even eagerly desirous to be instructed, and to embrace every opportunity for that end. They have generally but very little help to learn to read; and yet, to my agreeable surprise, sundry of them, by the dint of application in their leisure hours, have made such progress, that they can intelligibly read a plain author, particularly the *Bible*.

Some of them have the misfortune of irreligious masters; and hardly any of them are so happy, as to have masters, that will be at the expence of furnishing them with *Bibles*, *Psalm Books*, &c. Before I had the honour of joining as a Member of the Society, they were wont frequently to come to me with such moving accounts of their necessity in this respect, that I could not help supplying them with books to the utmost of my small ability; and when I distributed those among them which my Friends with you sent over, I had reason to think that I never did a charitable action in all my life, that met with *so much Gratitude* from the receivers. I have already distributed all the books which were suitable to them, particularly *Bibles, Testaments, Watts's Songs for Children*, &c. but on Saturday evening, the only leisure time they can redeem, my house is still crowded with them; and their very countenances carry the air of *importunate Petitioners* for the same favours with those that came before them. But alas! I must send them away grieved and disappointed.

Samuel Davies, *Letters from the Rev. Samuel Davies, Shewing the State of Religion in Virginia, Particularly among the Negroes* (London: n.p., 1757), 4–7.

32

Praising the Ineffable

Anne Steele

THE POET AND hymnist Anne Steele (1717–78) grew up in the village of Broughton, in Hampshire, England. Her father, William Steele, was a wealthy timber merchant who moonlighted as the pastor of a local Particular Baptist church. Throughout her life, Steele was plagued by health problems—headaches, digestive problems, and fits of "the ague"—and forced to deal with the death of beloved family members, including her mother Anne Froude in 1720, her stepmother Anne Cator in 1760, her father in 1769, and scores of uncles, aunts, nieces, and cousins. Perhaps helping her cope with life's difficulties, the remarkably literate Steele developed a talent for poetry as a youth. Her poems reveal a bias for Calvinism that stems from her Particular Baptist upbringing. Anne's family, recognizing her literary talents, made arrangements for two volumes of her poetry and hymns to be published in 1760 as *Poems on Subjects Chiefly Devotional* under the pseudonym Theodosia. In 1780, two years after her death, the same work was republished with the addition of a third volume entitled *Miscellaneous Pieces, in Verse and Prose*, which included a preface by the Baptist minister Caleb Evans. Although largely ignored in the twentieth century, Steele was one of the most popular hymn-writers of her day.

Her poetry does not carry the upbeat tempo that one finds in the hymns of Charles Wesley. Within her writings, Steele exhibited signs of self-doubt, uncertainty, depression, and suffering. Stanza after stanza, she struggled to find words to express her feelings, especially towards an indescribable God. For her, God is beyond explanation because human language spews out of the mouths of fallen creatures that are tainted by sin. When measuring her own success as a writer, she felt the effects of inherent sin. While submitting that the Almighty had blessed her with certain literary "powers," she doubted her abilities to reach her God-given potential. Yet she rarely ended her poems in complete despair. More often than not, she looked to God as the source of hope that greater joy awaited her in the future, if not in this life, then in the next. Regardless of her own sufferings, Steele willingly resigned her life to God's will, which she assumed to be benevolent and flawless. Her message, although often painted in gloomy colors, is that God ultimately does what is good and right.

Poems on Subjects Chiefly Devotional
"Desiring to PRAISE GOD"

I.

ALMIGHTY author of my frame,
To thee my vital powers belong;
Thy praise, (delightful, glorious theme!)
Demands my heart, my life, my tongue.

II.

My heart, my life, my tongue are thine:
Oh be thy praise their blest employ!
But may my song with Angels join?
Nor sacred awe forbid the joy?

III.

Thy glories, the seraphic lyre
On all its strings attempts in vain;
Then how shall mortals dare aspire
In thought, to try th' unequal strain?

IV.

Yet the great Sovereign of the skies
To mortals bends a gracious ear;
Nor the mean tribute will despise,
If offer'd with a heart sincere.

V.

Great God, accept the humble praise,
And guide my heart, and guide my tongue,
While to thy name I trembling raise
The grateful, though unworthy song.

"Imploring DIVINE INFLUENCE"

I.

MY God, whene'er my longing heart
The praiseful tribute would impart,
In vain my tongue with feeble aim,
Attempts the glories of thy name.

II.

In vain my boldest thoughts arise,
I sink to earth and lose the skies;
Yet I may still thy grace implore,
And low in dust thy name adore.

III.

O let thy grace my heart inspire,
And raise each languid weak desire;
Thy grace, which condescends to meet
The sinner prostrate at thy feet.

IV.

With humble fear let love unite,
And mix devotion with delight;
Then shall thy name be all my joy,
Thy praise, my constant blest employ.

V.

Thy name inspires the harps above
With harmony, and praise, and love;
That grace which tunes th' immortal strings,
Looks kindly down on mortal things.

VI.

O let thy grace guide every song,
And fill my heart and tune my tongue;
Then shall the strain harmoniously flow,
And heaven's sweet work begin below.

"HOPE in DARKNESS"

I.

GOD is my sun, his blissful rays
Irradiate, warm, and guide my heart!
How dark, how mournful, are my days,
If his enlivening beams depart!

II.

Scarce through the shades, a glimpse of day
Appears to these desiring eyes!
But shall my drooping spirit say,
The cheerful morn will never rise?

III.

O let me not despairing mourn,
Though gloomy darkness spreads the sky;
My glorious sun will yet return,
And night with all its horrors fly.

VI.

Hope, in the absence of my Lord,
Shall be my taper; sacred light,
Kindled at his celestial word,
To cheer the melancholy night.

V.

O for the bright the joyful day,
When hope shall in assurance die!
So tapers lose their feeble ray,
Beneath the sun's refulgent eye.

"Mourning the ABSENCE of GOD, and Longing for His Gracious PRESENCE"

I.

MY God, to thee I call—
Must I for ever mourn?
So far from thee, my life, my all?
O when wilt thou return!

II.

Dark as the shades of night
My gloomy sorrows rise,
And hide thy soul-reviving light
From these desiring eyes.

III.

My comforts all decay,
My inward foes prevail;
If thou withhold thy healing ray,
Expiring hope will fail.

IV.

Away distressing fears,
My gracious God is nigh,
And heavenly pity sees my tears,
And marks each rising sigh.

V.

Dear source of all my joys,
And solace of my care,
O wilt thou hear my plaintive voice
And grant my humble prayer!

VI.

These envious clouds remove,
Thy cheering light restore,
Confirm my interest in thy love
`Till I can doubt no more.

VII.

Then if my troubles rise,
To thee, my God, I'll flee,
And raise my hopes above the skies,
And cast my cares on thee.

"GOD the ONLY REFUGE of the TROUBLED MIND"

I.

DEAR refuge of my weary soul,
On thee, when sorrows rise:
On thee, when waves of trouble roll,
My fainting hope relies.

II.

While hope revives, though prest with fears,
And I can say, my God,
Beneath thy feet I spread my cares,
And pour my woes abroad.

III.

To thee, I tell each rising grief,
For thou alone canst heal;
Thy word can bring a sweet relief
For every pain I feel.

IV.

But oh! when gloomy doubts prevail,
I fear to call thee mine;
The springs of comfort seem to fail,
And all my hopes decline.

V.

Yet, gracious God, where shall I flee?
Thou art my only trust,
And still my soul would cleave to thee,
Though prostrate in the dust.

VI.

Hast thou not bid me seek thy face?
And shall I seek in vain?
And can the ear of sovereign grace
Be deaf when I complain?

VII.

No, still the ear of sovereign grace
Attends the mourner's prayer;
O may I ever find access,
To breathe my sorrows there.

VIII.

Thy mercy-seat is open still;
Here let my soul retreat,
With humble hope attend thy will.
And wait beneath thy feet.

"SUBMISSION to GOD under AFFLICTION"

I.

PEACE, my complaining, doubting heart,
    Ye busy cares be still;
Adore the just, the sovereign Lord,
    Nor murmur at his will.

II.

Unerring wisdom guides his hand;
    Nor dares my guilty fear,
Amid the sharpest pains I feel,
    Pronounce his hand severe.

III.

To soften every painful stroke,
    Indulgent mercy bends,
And unrepining when I plead,
    His gracious ear attends.

IV.

Let me reflect with humble awe
    Whene'er my heart complains,
Compar'd with what my sins deserve,
    How easy are my pains!

V.

Yes Lord, I own thy sovereign hand,
    Thou just, and wise, and kind;
Be every anxious thought supprest,
    And all my soul resign'd.

VI.

But oh! indulge this only wish,
    This boon I must implore!
Assure my soul, that thou art mine,
    My God, I ask no more.

"RESIGNATION"

I.

WEARY of these low scenes of night,
My fainting heart grows sick of time,
Sighs for the dawn of sweet delight,
Sighs for a distant, happier clime!

II.

Ah why that sigh?—peace, coward heart,
And learn to bear thy lot of woe:
Look round—how easy is thy part,
To what thy fellow-sufferers know.

III.

Are not the sorrows of the mind
Entail'd on every mortal birth?
Convinc'd, hast thou not long resign'd
The flattering hope of bliss on earth?

IV.

'Tis just, 'tis right; thus He ordains,
Who form'd this animated clod;
That needful cares, instructive pains,
May bring the restless heart to God.

V.

In him, my soul, behold thy rest,
Nor hope for bliss below the sky:
Come Resignation to my breast,
And silence every plaintive sigh.

VI.

Come Faith, and Hope, celestial pair!
Calm Resignation waits on you;
Beyond these gloomy scenes of care,
Point out a soul-enlivening view.

VII.

Parent of good, 'tis thine to give
These cheerful graces to the mind:
Smile on my soul, and bid me live
Desiring, hoping, yet resign'd!

VIII.

Thy smile,—sweet dawn of endless day!
Can make my weary spirit blest;
While on my Father's hand I stay,
And in his love securely rest.

IX.

My Father, dear, delightful name!
Replete with life, and joy sincere!
O wilt thou gracious, seal my claim,
And banish every anxious fear!

X.

Then, cheerful shall my heart survey
The toils, and dangers of the road;
And patient keep the heavenly way,
Which leads me homewards to my God.

[Anne Steele], *Poems on Subjects Chiefly Devotional*, 3 Vols (Bristol: W. Pine, 1780), I.1–3, I.126–7, I.143–6, I.148–9, II.9–11.

33

Before Dartmouth College

Eleazar Wheelock

ALTHOUGH A NOTED evangelist during the Great Awakening, Eleazar Wheelock (1711–79) is best known for founding Dartmouth College. Born in Windham, Connecticut, Wheelock attended Yale College before his appointment in 1735 as the pastor of the Second Congregational Church in Lebanon, Connecticut. Supplementing his salary as a minster, Wheelock began training youths for college, including the Mohegan Samson Occom who began his studies in 1743. Encouraged by Occom's progress, Wheelock determined to educate additional Native Americans, both male and female. The men learned English, Latin, Greek, and arithmetic, with the expectation that they would return to their people as teachers and missionaries. Females were taught writing and "housewifery."

Wheelock campaigned heavily to raise funds for the education of Native Americans. One of the earliest patrons, Colonel Joshua Moor of Mansfield, donated land and buildings for the aptly named Moor's Indian Charity School. Wheelock paraded his prized student Samson Occom in order to generate money for the school. In the mid-1760s, Occom toured throughout Great Britain, collecting some £12,000 and increasing the awareness of Wheelock's educational endeavors. But Wheelock grew dissatisfied with the results of his efforts since many of his pupils had taken ill and died or returned to their native customs. To Occom's dismay, in the late 1760s Wheelock turned his attention to establishing a new college that would train white missionaries separately from Native Americans. The money that Occom had raised on his expedition to Britain for the expressed purpose of educating young Indians became the seed money for Dartmouth College, which relocated from Lebanon, Connecticut, to Hanover, New Hampshire, in 1770.

FIGURE 33.1 The Reverend Eleazar Wheelock (Detail), 1st President of Dartmouth College (1769-1779) by Joseph Steward, courtesy of the Hood Museum of Art, commissioned by the trustees of Dartmouth College.

A *Plain and Faithful Narrative*... *of the Indian Charity-School at Lebanon, in Connecticut*

AFTER the Trial I made of this Nature some Years ago, by the Assistance of the Honourable LONDON Commissioners, in the Education of Mr. *Samson Occom*, one of the *Mohegan* Tribe, who has several Years since been a useful School-Master and successful Preacher of the Gospel to the *Indians* at *Montauk* on *Long-Island*, where he took the Place of the Rev. Mr. *Horton*, Missionary; and was, under God, instrumental to cure them, in a good Measure, of the Wildness they had been led into by some Exhorters from *New-England*, and in a Judgment of Charity was the Instrument of saving Good to a Number of them. He was several Years ago ordained to the sacred Ministry by the Reverend Presbytery of *Suffolk* County on said Island; and has done well, so far as I have heard, as a Missionary to the *Oneida* Nation, for two Years past. May God mercifully preserve him, amidst loud Applauses, from falling into the Snare and Condemnation of the Devil!—I say, after seeing the Success of this Attempt, I was more encouraged to hope that such a Method might be very successful.

WITH these Views of the Case, and from such Motives as have been mentioned, above Eight Years ago I wrote to the Reverend *John Brainerd*, Missionary in *New-Jersey*, desiring him to send me two likely Boys for this Purpose, of the *Delaware* Tribe: He accordingly sent me *John Pumshire* in the 14th, and *Jacob Woolley* in the 11th Years of their Age; they arrived here *December* 18th, 1754 and behaved as well as could be reasonably expected; *Pumshire* made uncommon Proficiency in Writing. They continued with me till they had made considerable Progress in the Latin and Greek Tongues; when *Pumshire* began to decline, and by the Advice of Physicians,

I sent him back to his Friends, with Orders, if his Health would allow it, to return with two more of that Nation, whom Mr. *Brainerd* had at my Desire provided for me. *Pumshire* set out on his Journey, *November* 14th, 1756 and got Home, but soon died. And on *April* 9th, 1757 *Joseph Woolley* and *Hezekiah Calvin* came on the Horse which *Pumshire* rode.

THE Decline and Death of this Youth was an instructive Scene to me, and convinced me more fully of the Necessity of special Care respecting their Diet; and that more Exercise was necessary for them, especially at their first coming to a full Table, and with so keen an Appetite, than was ordinarily necessary for *English* Youth. And with the Exercise of such Care, as one who understands the Case, and is willing to take the Trouble of it, may use, I am persuaded there is no more Danger of their Studies being fatal to them, than to our own Children. There have been several long Fits of Sickness of one and another in this School, with a nervous Fever, Pleurisies, Dysenteries, &c. but perhaps not more than have been among so large a Number of common labouring People in so long a Time.

SOMETIME after those Boys came, the Affair appearing with an agreeable Aspect, it being then a Time of profound Peace in this Country, I represented the Affair to Colonel *Elisha Williams*, Esq.; late Rector of *Yale-College*, and to the Rev'd Messieurs *Samuel Moseley* of *Windham*, and *Benjamin Pomeroy* of *Hebron*, and invited them to join me; they readily accepted the Invitation; and a Gentleman learned in the Law supposed there might be such an Incorporation among ourselves as might fully answer our Purpose. And Mr. *Joshua Moor*, late of *Mansfield*, deceased, appeared to give a small Tenement in this Place, for the Foundation, Use and Support of a Charity-School, for the Education of *Indian* Youth, &c. But it pleased God to take the good Colonel from an unthankful World soon after the Covenant was made and executed, and thus deprived us of the Benefit of his singular Learning, Piety and Zeal in the Affair. Notwithstanding, a Subscription was soon made of near £500 lawful Money, towards a Fund for the Support of it at 6 percent. But several Gentlemen of the Law, doubting of the Validity and Sufficiency of such an Incorporation; several Steps were taken to obtain the Royal Favour of a Charter, but none effectual. The War soon commenced, and the Reports from Day to Day of the Ravages made, and Inhumanities and Butcheries committed by the Savages on all Quarters, raised in the Breasts of great Numbers, a Temper so warm, and so contrary to Charity, that I seldom thought it prudent so much as to mention the Affair. Many advised me to drop it, but it appeared to others so probable to be the very Method which God would own, that I thought better to scrabble along with it, as well as I could, till divine Providence should change the Scene.

THE Prospects, notwithstanding our outward Troubles, seemed to be increasing: Such was the orderly and good Behaviour of the Boys, through the Blessing of

God on Instruction and Discipline, that Enemies could find but little or nothing that was true wherewith they might reproach the Design; and those whose Sentiments were friendly, observed with Pleasure the good Effects of our Endeavours: And the Liberalities, especially of Gentlemen of Character, encouraged me more and more to believe it to be of God, and that he designed to succeed and prosper it, to the Glory of his own great Name; and that I ought in Compliance with such Intimations of Providence from Time to Time, proportionally to increase the Number.

I HAVE had two upon my Hands since *December* 18th, 1754, and Four since *April* 1757, and Five since *April* 1759, and Seven since *November* 1760, and Eleven since *August* 1st, 1761, and after this Manner they have increased as I could obtain those who appeared promising. And for some Time I have had Twenty-five devoted to School as constantly as their Health will allow, and they have all along been so, excepting that in an extraordinary Crowd of Business, I have sometimes required their Assistance. But there is no great Advantage, excepting to themselves, to be expected from their Labour, nor enough to compensate the Trouble of instructing them in it, and the Repair of the Mischiefs they will do, while they are ignorant of all the Affairs of Husbandry, and the Use of Tools. The principal Advantage I have ever had in this Respect has been by *David Fowler* and *Joseph Woolley*, and more by *David* than all the rest: These Lads will likely make good Farmers, if they should ever have the Advantage of Experience in it.

THREE of this Number are *English* Youth, one of which is gone for a Time to *New-Jersey* College, for the sake of better Advantage for some Parts of Learning: He has made some Proficiency in the *Mohawk* Tongue: The other two are sitting for the Business of Missionaries. One of the *Indian* Lads is *Jacob Woolley*, who is now in his last Year at *New-Jersey* College, and is a good Scholar; he is here by the Leave and Order of the President, designing to get some Acquaintance with the *Mohawk* Tongue. Two others are sent here by the Rev. Mr. *Brainerd*, and are designed for Trades; the one for a Blacksmith (a Trade much wanted among the *Indians*) and is to go to his Apprenticeship as soon as a good Place is ready for him; the other is designed for a Carpenter and Joiner, and is to go to an Apprenticeship as soon as he has learned to read and write. Another of the *Indians* is Son to the Sachem at *Mohegan*, and is Heir-apparent; he is somewhat infirm as to his bodily Health: For his Support last Year I have charged nothing more than 10l. lawful Money, granted by the Hon. *London* Commissioners. Several of my Scholars are considerably well accomplished for School-Masters, and 7 or 8 will likely be well fitted for Interpreters in a few Years more. And four of this Number are Girls, whom I have hired Women in this Neighbourhood to instruct in all the Arts of good Housewifery, they attending the School one Day in a Week to be instructed in writing, &c. till they shall be fit for an Apprenticeship, to be taught to make Men's and Women's Apparel, &c. in order to accompany these Boys, when they shall have Occasion for such Assistance in the Business of their Mission. And six of them are *Mohawks*, obtained pursuant and according to the Direction of the Honourable General Assembly of the Province of the *Massachusetts-Bay*, and are learning to speak, write, and read *English*: And the most of them make good Proficiency therein.

I HAVE, by the good Providence of God, been favoured with religious, faithful and learned Masters, in general, from the first setting up of this School, at the Expence of about £56 lawful Money per Annum, i.e. £3 per Month, with their Board, and all Accommodations, and a Horse kept or provided when needed; which I suppose can't be esteemed less than the Sum which I mention: And if this seems to any to be large, I have only this to say, that I could not have the Choice of Masters at less Expence. But the Expence for Tuition will likely be saved for some Time, by the Generosity of a young Gentleman, who proposes to keep it *gratis* a few Months.

THE Method of conducting this School has been, and is designed to be after this Manner, viz. they are obliged to be clean, and decently dressed, and be ready to attend Prayers, before Sun-rise in the Fall and Winter, and at 6 o'Clock in the Summer. A Portion of Scripture is read by several of the Seniors of them: And those who are able answer a Question in the *Assembly's Catechism*, and have some Questions asked them upon it, and an Answer expounded to them. After Prayers, and a short Time for their Diversion, the School begins with Prayer about 9, and ends at 12, and again at 2, and ends at 5 o'clock with Prayer. Evening Prayer is attended before the Day-light is gone. Afterwards they apply to their Studies, &c. They attend the public Worship, and have a Pew devoted to their Use, in the House of God. On Lord's-Day Morning, between and after the Meetings, the Master, or some one whom they will submit to, is with them, inspects their Behaviour, hears them read, catechises them, discourses to them, &c. And once or twice a Week they hear a Discourse calculated to their Capacities upon the most important and interesting Subjects. And in general they are orderly and governable: They appear to be as perfectly easy and contented with their Situation and Employment as any at a Father's House. I scarcely hear a Word of their going Home, so much as for a Visit, for Years together, except it be when they first come.

AND the Success of Endeavours hitherto, the general Approbation of great and good Men, and the Testimonies many have given of it, by their seasonable Liberality towards its Support, have seemed to me such evident Tokens of a Divine Hand in Favour of it, and so plain Intimations of the Divine Will concerning it, that I have, as I said before, thought it Duty, notwithstanding all Discouragements, to pursue the Design, and endeavour to keep Pace with the Providences of God in Favour of it as to their Number, and trust in Him, "whose the Earth is, and the Fullness thereof," for further Supplies. And I have hoped this would be esteemed sufficient to clear me of the Imputation of Presumption and Rashness in risking my own private Interest, as I have done.

Eleazar Wheelock, *A Plain and Faithful Narrative of the Original Design, Rise, Progress and Present State of the Indian Charity-School at Lebanon, in Connecticut* (Boston: Richard and Samuel Draper, 1763), 29–37.

34

The Difference between True and False Religion

Henry Venn

HENRY VENN (1725–97) grew up around London where his father, Richard Venn, served as rector of St. Antholin's Watling Street. Educated at Cambridge University, Henry earned a BA in 1745 and MA in 1749. After his ordination as an Anglican minister in June 1749, he bounced around as a curate in London and Surrey before settling as the curate of Clapham in 1754. While at Clapham, he came into contact with various evangelicals, including the banker John Thornton, George Whitefield, and Selena, Countess of Huntingdon. Later, in 1759, Venn agreed to an appointment as the vicar of Huddersfield in northern England, arranged by the evangelical aristocrat the Second Earl of Dartmouth. There Venn took on the herculean task of preaching between eight and ten sermons weekly in addition to his duties of catechizing parishioners and preparing them for communion. In 1771 Venn moved to Yelling, twelve miles outside of Cambridge, where he persisted as a cleric until shortly before his death in 1797. His proximity to Cambridge allowed him to mentor some of the next generation of evangelical Anglicans, including Charles Simeon.

One of Venn's most popular works was his *Complete Duty of Man* (1763), which he wrote during a time of illness while stationed in Clapham. Venn seemed to have modeled his book on the popular seventeenth-century High Church text, *The Whole Duty of Man*, but from an evangelical perspective. Venn's *Complete Duty of Man* is a devotional consisting of sections on practical divinity followed by short prayers. In one chapter entitled "On the Nature of True and False Repentance: The Reasons Why All Are Commanded to Repent; and the Means of Attaining Repentance," Venn explained the differences between true and false repentance. While it is often assumed that evangelicals bullied audiences into conversion by preaching hellfire-and-brimstone-type sermons, Venn demonstrated that the truly

FIGURE 34.1 Henry Venn (Detail), courtesy of the National Portrait Gallery, London.

penitent are more concerned about sin than fear of hell and damnation. His point is that fear-induced piety is ephemeral by comparison with heartfelt repentance.

The Complete Duty of Man

IT is a truth fully revealed in Scripture, that without repentance no one can enter into life. But the misfortune is, when men are assured it cannot be well with them unless they are found in the exercise of repentance, they determine, with a fatal precipitancy, to call something by this name which bears only a superficial worthless resemblance of it, and then flatter themselves with the vain imagination that this base counterfeit shall yet be entitled to all the blessings promised to the divine original.

To compare therefore and distinguish the true repentance from the false; to shew why every one who will be saved must experience the change it implies; and the way to attain it; will be a subject of great use, through the blessing of God, to discover prevailing errors which lie at the root of all careless and profane living, and to awaken every reader to self-examination on this important point.

First then, let it be observed, that a false repentance flows *only* from a sense of danger and a fear of impending wrath. When the conscience of a sinner is alarmed with a sense of his dreadful guilt and danger, it must of necessity loudly remonstrate against those sins which threaten him with the destruction of hell: hence those frights and terrors which are frequently found amongst men in danger, or under apprehensions of death. At such times their sins, some grosser enormities especially, convince them to their face, and all their aggravations are remembered with bitterness; conscience draws up the indictment, and sets home the charge against them; the law passes the sentence, and condemns them without mercy. And what have they now in prospect? What but a fearful looking-for of fiery indignation to consume them? Now with what distress will they cry out and howl upon their beds for the greatness of their sin? With what amazement will they expect the dreadful issue of their sinful practice? How ready are they now to make resolutions of beginning a humble, watchful, holy life? In this their terror, conscience like a flaming sword keeps them from their former course of impiety and sensuality.

But what is all this repentance more than the fear of the worm that never dieth, and of the fire that never shall be quenched? Let but conscience be pacified, and the tempest of the troubled mind allayed, and this false penitent will return with the dog to his vomit again, till some new alarm revive his convictions of sin and danger, and with them the same process of repentance. Thus too many will sin and repent, and repent and sin all their lives.

Or it may be, distress of conscience makes a deeper impression, and fixes such an abiding dread of particular gross sins, that there appears a visible reformation. Yet in this case the sinner's lusts are only dammed up by his fears; and was the dam broken down, they would immediately run again in their former channel with renewed force. It is true, all this terror is often a preparative to true repentance; but if it proceeds no further, it proves abortive.

Here it is necessary to observe, that though there may be much terror and external reformation without true repentance, yet it is something to be thus far affected; the greater part of true penitents were sometimes under the same distressing circumstances, and at first began out of mere selfishness to fly from the wrath to come. Instead therefore of construing what is said against false repentance, as if all was lost because your repentance is not yet of the right kind; let it work more reasonably, and excite you to prayer, that those terrors and checks which are in themselves no certain proofs of the sincerity of your repentance, may be perfected and issue in what undoubtedly are such proofs.

It was said that false repentance flows only from a sense of danger and a fear of impending wrath. The character of true repentance is quite opposite: here sin itself becomes the greatest burden and object of aversion; sorrow springs from an affecting humbling sense of the dishonour and injury the penitent feels he has done unto God; not only from a selfish concern for his own safety, but from a regard to God, to which he was before a stranger; from a conviction that his whole deportment and the ruling tempers of his heart at all times have been evil and desperately wicked. The language of a true Scripture penitent is such as this: *I acknowledge my transgression, and my sin is ever before me: mine iniquities are gone over my head as a heavy burden; they are too heavy for me. Deliver me from all my transgressions, let not my sins have dominion over me. Innumerable evils have compassed me about, mine iniquities have taken hold upon me, so that I am not able to look up: they are more than the hairs of mine head, therefore my heart faileth me. Be pleased, O Lord, to deliver me. O Lord, make haste to help me.* Here you see the true penitent mourns for all his lusts, and hates them all; he is willing none should be spared, no, not so much as a right hand, or a right eye.

How great and apparent the difference between being struck with fear, restrained by terror, or driven from a course of sinning by the lashes of an awakened conscience! Between this, I say, and loathing ourselves in our own sight for all our iniquities, vehemently desiring grace and strength to conquer and mortify corruption, and to be delivered from the tyrannous rule of sin! The former is merely the sordid fruit of self-love, which compels the soul to fly from danger; the latter, the exercise of a vital principle, which separates the soul from sin, and engages the whole man in a persevering opposition against it...

I would flatter myself that you have an earnest desire to be informed what course you must take to be brought into a state of true repentance: if this is your desire, instead of multiplying directions, it will suffice to press you to observe the few following.

First, Frequently read the Scripture with devout seriousness and unfeigned submission to it, as the method prescribed by God himself for your recovery, and let your thoughts dwell on what immediately respects your own case, that is, the nature and workings of true repentance. The fifty-first *Psalm* will unfold to you the heart of the penitent contrite *David*; and the fifteenth of St. *Luke*, the affecting return of a sinner in your own condition to his much injured Father: and the same inward and entire change of heart is described at large in the fifth chapter of the *Ephesians*, and in the sixth also to the 17th verse. These and similar portions of Scripture it must be your care to read, and to form clear notions of what it is you have been reading. Whilst thus employed you are in the way to receive some enlivening communications, to find desires after God spring up in your soul, and those very dispositions towards him, which you have been seeing with your eyes in his own word, are properties of true repentance.

Secondly, Consider the corruption of your nature, and the many sins you have actually committed. Only commune with your own heart, and you will immediately find your own inclinations are strongly bent to many things which your conscience tells you ought not to be done, and that you have a great aversion to other things which are in themselves excellent, and ought to be done by you: you will observe a miserable confusion and inconsistency in your thoughts, a perverseness in your will, and a prevailing sensuality in your affections.

The fruit of this universal depravity you must also carefully observe, as it has appeared in your multitude of transgressions. Think on the several places you have lived in, and what in each of these your sins have been: take an account of your offences against those with whom you have dealt in a way of trade, conversed with in intimacy and friendship, or those on whom you should have had compassion and exercised the most tender love: mark those sins which have arose from your outward circumstances: and above all reflect deeply on what is, strictly speaking, your own iniquity, the sin to which you are most enslaved, whether passion, envy, unclean desire, pride and self-conceit, lying, the love of money or of esteem: take notice in how many instances it has broke out, so as to leave uneasy impressions on your mind, and yet has been again and again repeated: after this, think how often you have stifled convictions; how often turned away from the offers of grace and calls to repentance: think of your sins against a Redeemer; that you have been willing to live so long in ignorance of his undertaking; have not thought at all of his obedience, though the righteousness of God, nor of his sacrifice, though the blood of God: think of the despite you have done against the Holy Spirit, resisting his motions, and excusing yourself from a compliance with his secret suggestions. And then at the end of all reckon up the several aggravations of your sin, the judgments and afflictions, the mercies and deliverances, the counsels and reproofs, the light and knowledge, the vows and promises you have sinned against.

Thirdly, You must pray to the God of all grace to *give* you repentance unto life. Naturally you suppose you have it in your own power to repent just when you please; at least you suppose the alarming circumstances of sickness and approaching death will of themselves lead you to repent: a proud opinion this, which experience daily proclaims to be an utter falsehood, and the Bible exposes as such to every attentive reader, by calling repentance the gift and the grant of God. For to produce in the ground of the heart an abiding sense of our own vileness and detestation of it, with confidence in the pardoning mercy of God through Christ, with a zeal for his glory expressing itself in newness of life (which alone is what the Bible means by repentance) to produce a change of this nature belongeth only to the effectual working of God's holy Spirit: because self-love and pride with all their force withstand all charges of sinfulness, and every natural inclination of the soul rises up in arms, and opposes with all its might true humiliation: whilst at the same time it is impossible, without divine light and supernatural teaching, to discover any such loveliness in a just and sin-hating God, or in obedience to his law, as to create abhorrence of sinful lusts; those very lusts which have been long, alas! cherished and indulged as the best sources of gratification and pleasure. Therefore it is through the grace of God alone, the fountain from which proceeds every good and perfect gift, that you must receive repentance unto life. It is your part, as a reasonable and immortal creature, to hear the command of God to repent; and, as a helpless sinner insufficient to every good work, to pray for his almighty Spirit, that you may be obedient to it. It is your part meekly to confess your own inability to glorify God by true repentance, and to beg of him, in whose hands are the hearts of all men, that with this sense and resolution you may be turned to him, seeing and bewailing the sin of your nature as well as of your practice, of your heart as well as of your life, and desiring grace to approve yourself to God in newness of spirit a sincere penitent.

Henry Venn, *The Complete Duty of Man: Or a System of Doctrinal and Practical Christianity* (London: J. Newberry, 1763), 87–90, 109–12.

35

Salvation at Sea

John Newton

JOHN NEWTON (1725–1807) is best known for his hymn "Amazing Grace," but his importance to evangelicalism extends much further. Born in London on July 24, 1725, Newton was groomed to follow his father's footsteps as a mariner, taking his first voyage at age eleven. Newton candidly chronicled his early life, including his love for Mary Catlett, his future wife, as well as his Atlantic tours, in a series of letters to the Anglican clergyman Thomas Haweis, later published in 1764 as *An Authentic Narrative of Some Remarkable and Interesting Particulars in the Life of *********. In the *Authentic Narrative*, Newton confessed his blasphemous language and implicit immorality as a seaman in the mid-1740s. While trying to set up a slave-trading business on the Guinea coast of Africa, he suffered from severe bouts of illness, starvation, and humiliation for two years before boarding a ship called the *Greyhound* that traveled to Brazil and Newfoundland, on its way to England. Waking up suddenly during one evening in March 1748, he recounted the severity of a storm that pummeled the *Greyhound* in the north Atlantic. This dramatic scene brought him to a renewed sense of piety as he prayed for the first time in years for his survival.

That fateful evening in March is when Newton dated his conversion. From this point on he diligently read his Bible and other religious texts. The evidence, however, points to a more profound and thoughtful awakening about six months later while on board a slave ship making its way from England to Africa. A violent illness brought Newton to a position of penitence as he prayed for the state of his soul, calling on the atoning work of Christ to save him. Now feeling an inner peace and freedom from sin, he returned to England where he married Mary Catlett on February 12, 1750. For the next four years, Newton made a living as a slave trader before resigning from his unprincipled profession due to health reasons. While it is striking that after he became a Christian he continued to profit unapologetically as a slave trader, it must be remembered that his faith did not mature until after he came into contact with anti-slavery evangelicals like John Wesley. Later in life,

FIGURE 35.1 John Newton (Detail), courtesy of the National Portrait Gallery, London.

Newton turned full circle and publicly declared his abhorrence of the slave trade, supporting the abolitionist efforts of William Wilberforce and penning his own anti-slavery tract in 1787, *Thoughts upon the African Slave Trade*.

Once retiring as a slaver, he took a job as a tide surveyor at Liverpool, beginning in August 1755. In his spare time, he studied Greek, Hebrew, and Syriac (he taught himself Latin while at sea) and became a leading lay evangelical in the Church of England. He found the preaching of George Whitefield, John Wesley, and Henry Venn appealing as he formulated his own moderate Calvinistic beliefs. Finding success as a lay preacher, Newton began seriously considering entering the ministry. The taint of Methodism, however, delayed his ordination into the Anglican Church until 1764. For the next sixteen years, Newton served as the curate to the parish at Olney in Buckinghamshire, England where he worked with the poet William Cowper on a collection of hymns. He finished his career in London, accepting a call in January 1780 to minister at St. Mary Woolnoth. In England's largest city, he established himself as a leading evangelical clergyman in the Anglican Church, counseling such notables as William Wilberforce and preaching to vast crowds. As a theologian, spiritual director, and preacher, Newton's contribution to evangelicalism rests on more than his ability as a hymn writer.

An Authentic Narrative

"Letter VII"

At length, our business finished, we left Cape *Lopez*, and after a few days stay at the island of *Annabona*, to lay in provisions, we sailed homewards, about the beginning of *January* 1748. From *Annabona* to *England*, without touching at any intermediate port, is a very long navigation, perhaps more than seven thousand miles, if we include the circuits necessary to be made on account of the trade winds. We sailed first westward, till near the coast of *Brazil*, then northwards, to the banks of *Newfoundland*, with the usual variations of wind and weather, and without meeting any thing extraordinary. On these banks we stopped half a day to fish for cod: this was then chiefly for diversion; we had provisions enough, and little expected those fish (as it afterwards proved) would be all we should have to subsist on. We left the banks *March* 1, with a hard gale of wind westerly, which pushed us fast homewards. I should here observe, that with the length of this voyage in a hot climate, the vessel was greatly out of repair, and very unfit to support stormy weather: the sails and cordage were likewise very much worn out, and many such circumstances concurred, to render what followed more dangerous. I think it was on the ninth of *March*, the day before our catastrophe, that I felt a thought pass through my mind, which I had long been a stranger to. Among the few books we had on board, one was *Stanhope's Thomas à Kempis*: I carelessly took it up, as I had often done before, to pass away the time; but I had still read it with the same indifference, as if it was entirely a romance. However, while I was reading this time, an involuntary suggestion arose in my mind, What if these things should be true? I could not bear the force of the inference, as it related to myself, and therefore shut the book presently. My conscience witnessed against me once more, and I concluded, that, true or false, I must abide the consequences of my own choice. I put an abrupt end to these reflections, by joining in with some vain conversation or other that came in my way.

But now *the Lord's time was come*, and the conviction I was so unwilling to receive, was deeply impressed upon me, by an awful dispensation. I went to bed that night in my usual security and indifference, but was awakened from a sound sleep by the force of a violent sea, which broke on board us. So much of it came down below, as filled the cabin I lay in with water. This alarm was followed by a cry from the deck, that the ship was going down, or sinking. As soon as I could recover myself, I essayed to go upon deck, but was met upon the ladder by the Captain, who desired me to bring a knife with me. While I returned for the knife, another person went up in my room, who was instantly washed overboard. We had no leisure to lament him, nor did we expect to survive him long; for we soon found the ship was filling with water very fast. The sea had torn away the upper timbers on one side, and made a mere wreck in a few minutes. I shall not affect to describe this disaster in the marine dialect, which would be understood by few; and therefore I can give you but a very inadequate idea of it. Taken in all circumstances it was astonishing, and almost miraculous, that any of us survived to relate the story. We had immediate recourse to the pumps, but the water increased against our efforts: some of us were set to *bailing* in another part of the vessel, that is, to lade it out with buckets and pails. We had but eleven or twelve people to sustain this service; and notwithstanding all we could do, she was full, or very near it; and then with a common cargo she must have sunk of course: but we had a great quantity of beeswax and wood on board, which were specifically lighter than the water; and as it pleased God that we received this shock in the very crisis of the gale, towards morning, we were enabled to employ some means for our safety, which succeeded beyond hope. In about an hour's time the day began to break, and the wind abated. We expended most of our clothes and bedding to stop the leaks (though the weather was exceeding cold, especially to us, who had so lately left a hot climate), over these we nailed pieces of boards, and at last perceived the water abate. At the beginning of this hurry I was little affected; I pumped hard, and endeavoured to animate myself and my companions: I told one of them, that in a few days this distress would serve us to talk of over a glass of wine: but he being a less hardened sinner than myself, replied with tears, "No, it is too late now." About nine o'clock, being almost spent with cold and labour, I went to speak with the Captain, who was busied elsewhere, and just as I was returning from him, I said, almost without any meaning, "If this will not do, the Lord have mercy upon us." This, (though spoken with little reflection) was the first desire I had breathed for mercy for the space of many years. I was instantly struck with my own words, and as *Jehu* said once, *What hast thou to do with peace?* So it directly occurred, *What mercy can there be for me?* I was obliged to return to the pump, and there I continued till noon, almost every passing wave breaking over my head; but we made ourselves fast with ropes, that we might not be washed away. Indeed I expected, that every time the vessel descended in the sea, she would rise no more; and though I dreaded death *now*, and my heart foreboded the worst, if the scriptures, which I had long since opposed, were indeed true; yet still I was but half convinced, and remained for a space of time in a sullen frame, a mixture of despair and impatience. I thought, if the Christian religion was true, I could not be forgiven; and was therefore expecting, and almost, at time, wishing to know the worst of it...

"Letter VIII"

THE 10th (that is in the present style the 21st) of *March*, is a day much to be remembered by me, and I have never suffered it to pass wholly unnoticed since the year 1748. On that day the Lord sent from on high and delivered me out of deep waters.—I continued at the pump from *three* in the *morning* till near *noon*, and then I could do no more. I went and lay down upon my bed, uncertain, and almost indifferent, whether I should rise again. In an hour's time I was called, and not being able to pump, I went to the helm, and steered the ship till midnight, excepting a small interval for refreshment. I had here leisure and convenient opportunity for reflection: I began to think of my former religious professions, the extraordinary turns in my life; the calls, warnings, and deliverances I had met with, the licentious course of my conversation, particularly my unparalleled effrontery in making the gospel history (which I could not now be sure was false, though I was not as yet assured it was true) the constant subject of profane ridicule. I thought, allowing the scripture premises, there never was nor could be such a sinner as myself, and then comparing the advantages I had broken through, I concluded at first that my sins were too great to be forgiven. The scripture likewise seemed to say the same, for I had formerly been well acquainted with the Bible, and many passages upon this occasion returned upon my memory, particularly those awful passages, *Proverbs* 1:24–31; *Hebrews* 6:4, 6; and 2 *Peter* 2:20, which seemed so exactly to suit my case and character, as to bring with them a presumptive proof of a divine original. Thus, as I have said, I waited with fear and impatience to receive my inevitable doom. Yet though I had thoughts of this kind, they were exceedingly faint and disproportionate; it was not till long after (perhaps several years) till I had gained some clear views of the infinite righteousness and grace of Christ Jesus my Lord, that I had a deep and strong apprehension of my state by nature and practice, and perhaps till then I could not have borne the sight. So wonderfully does the Lord proportion the discoveries of sin and grace, for he knows our frame, and that if he was to put forth the greatness of his power, a poor sinner would be instantly overwhelmed, and crushed as a moth. But to return; when I saw, beyond all probability, there was still hope of respite, and heard about six in the evening, that the ship was freed from water—there arose a gleam of hope. I thought I saw the hand of God displayed in our favour; I began to pray—I could not utter the prayer of faith; I could not draw near to a reconciled God, and call him father. My prayer was like the cry of the ravens, which yet the Lord does not disdain to hear. I now began to think of that *Jesus* whom I had so often derided; I recollected the particulars of his life, and of his death; a death for sins not his *own*, but, as I remembered, for the sake of those who in their distress should put their trust in him. And now I chiefly wanted evidence.—The comfortless principles of infidelity were deeply riveted, and I rather wished than believed these things were real facts. You will please to observe, Sir, that I collect the strain of the reasonings and exercises of my mind in one view, but I do not say that all this passed at one time. The great question now was, how to obtain *faith?* I speak not of an appropriating faith (of which I then knew neither the nature nor necessity), but how I should gain an assurance that the scriptures were of a divine inspiration, and a sufficient warrant for the exercise of trust and hope in God. One of the first helps I received (in consequence of a determination to examine the New Testament more carefully) was from *Luke* 11:13. I had been sensible that to profess faith in Jesus Christ, when in reality I did not believe his history, was no better than a mockery of the heart searching God; but here I found a spirit spoken of which was to be communicated to those who ask it: Upon this I reasoned thus—If this book is true, the promise in this passage must be true likewise: I have need of that very spirit, by which the whole was wrote, in order to understand it aright. He has engaged here to give that spirit to those who ask.—I must therefore pray for it, and if it is of God he will make good his own word. My purposes were strengthened by *John* 7:17. I concluded from thence, that though I could not say from my heart that I believed the gospel, yet I would for the present take it for granted, and that by studying it in this light I should be more and more confirmed in it. If what I am writing could be perused by our modern infidels, they would say (for I too well know their manner) that I was very desirous to persuade myself into this opinion. I confess I was; and so would they be, if the Lord should show them, as he was pleased to show me at that time, the absolute necessity of some expedient to interpose between a righteous God, and a sinful soul: upon the gospel scheme I saw at least a peradventure of hope, but on every other side I was surrounded with black unfathomable despair…

"Letter X"

Who would not expect to hear, that after such a wonderful unhoped-for deliverance as I had received, and after my eyes were in some measure enlightened to see things aright, I should immediately cleave to the Lord and his ways, with full purpose of heart, and consult no more with flesh and blood? But alas it was far otherwise with me; I had learned to pray, I set some value upon the word of God, and was no longer a libertine, but my soul still cleaved to the dust. Soon after my departure from L—, I began to intermit, and grow slack in waiting upon the Lord; I grew vain and trifling in my conversation; and though my heart smote me often, yet my armour was gone, and I declined fast; and by the time we arrived at *Guinea*, I seemed to have forgot all the Lord's mercies, and my own engagements, and was (profaneness excepted) almost as bad as before. The enemy prepared a train of temptations, and I became his easy prey; and, for about a month, he lulled me asleep in a course of evil, of which, a few months before, I could not have supposed myself any longer capable. How much propriety is there in the Apostle's advice, "Take heed lest any of you be hardened through the deceitfulness of sin." O who can be sufficiently upon their guard! Sin first deceives, and then it hardens: I was now fast bound in chains; I had little desire, and no power at all to recover myself. I could not but at times reflect how it was with me; but if I attempted to struggle with it, it was in vain. I was just like *Samson*, when he said, "I will go forth and shake myself as at other times," but the Lord was departed, and he found himself helpless, in the hands of his enemies. By the remembrance of this interval the Lord has often instructed me since, what a poor creature I am in myself, incapable of standing a single hour, without continual fresh supplies of strength and grace from the fountain-head.

At length, the Lord, whose mercies are infinite, interposed in my behalf. My business in this voyage, while upon the coast, was to sail from place to place in the long-boat to purchase slaves. The ship was at *Sierra Leon*, and I then at the *Plantanes*, the scene of my former captivity, where every thing I saw might seem to remind me of my ingratitude. I was in easy circumstances, courted by those who formerly despised me: the *lime-trees* I had planted were growing tall, and promised fruit the following year, against which time I had expectations of returning with a ship of my own. But none of these things affected me, till, as I have said, the Lord again interposed to save me. He visited me with a violent fever, which broke the fatal chain, and once more brought me to myself. But O what a prospect! I thought myself now summoned away—My past dangers and deliverances, my earnest prayers in the time of trouble, my solemn vows before the Lord at his table, and my ungrateful returns for all his goodness, were all present to my mind at once. Then I began to wish that the Lord had suffered me to sink into the ocean, when I first besought his mercy. For a little while I concluded the door of hope to be quite shut; but this continued not long. Weak, and almost delirious, I arose from my bed, and crept to a retired part of the island; and here I found a renewed liberty to pray. I durst make no more resolves, but cast myself before the Lord, to do with me as he should please. I do not remember, that any particular text, or remarkable discovery, was presented to my mind, but in general I was enabled to hope and believe in a crucified Saviour. The burden was removed from my conscience, and not only my peace, but my health was restored; I cannot say instantaneously, but I recovered from that hour, and so fast, that when I returned to the ship two days afterwards, I was perfectly well before I got on board. And from that time, I trust, I have been delivered from the power and dominion of sin, though as to the effects and conflicts of sin dwelling in me, I still "groan, being burthened." I now began again to wait upon the Lord, and though I have often grieved his Spirit, and foolishly wandered from him since (when alas shall I be more wise), yet his powerful grace has hitherto preserved me from such black declensions as this I have last recorded; and I humbly trust in his mercy and promises, that he will be my guide and guard to the end...

"Letter XIV"

One word concerning my views to the *ministry*, and I have done.—I have told you that this was my dear mother's hope concerning me; but her death, and the scenes of life in which I afterwards engaged, seemed to cut off the probability. The first desires of this sort in my own mind, arose many years ago, from a reflection on *Galatians* 1:23–4. I could not but wish for such a public opportunity to testify the riches of divine grace. I thought I was, above most living, a fit person to proclaim that faithful saying, "That Jesus Christ came into the world to save the chief of sinners" and as my life had been full of remarkable turns, and I seemed selected to shew what the Lord could do, I was in some hopes that perhaps sooner or later he might call me into this service.

I believe it was a distant hope of this that determined me to study the original scriptures; but it remained an imperfect desire in my own breast, till it was recommended to me by some Christian friends. I started at the thought, when first seriously proposed to me; but afterwards set a part some weeks to consider the case, to consult my friends, and to entreat the Lord's direction—The judgment of my friends, and many things that occurred, tended to engage me. My first thought was to join the dissenters, from a presumption that I could not honestly make the required subscriptions: but Mr. C—, in a conversation upon these points, moderated my scruples; and preferring the established church in some other respects, I accepted a title from him some months afterwards, and solicited ordination from the late Archbishop of *York*; I need not tell you I met a refusal, nor what steps I took afterwards to succeed elsewhere. At present I desist from any applications. My desire to serve the Lord is not weakened; but I am not so hasty to push myself forward as I was formerly. It is sufficient that he knows how to dispose of me, and that he both can and will do what is best. To him I commend myself: I trust that his will and my true interest are inseparable. To his name be glory forever. And thus I conclude my story, and presume you will acknowledge I have been particular enough.

John Newton, *An Authentic Narrative of Some Remarkable and Interesting Particulars in the Life of* ******** (London: J. Johnson, 1764), 106–19, 144–9, 206–8.

36

An Anglican Minister Describes Faith

William Romaine

WILLIAM ROMAINE (1714–95) was born on September 25, 1714, in Hartlepool, in the county of Durham, England. His father, a Huguenot merchant, had emigrated to Britain in the aftermath of Louis XIV's revocation of the edict of Nantes in 1685 and soon joined the Church of England. Romaine graduated from Christ Church, Oxford, with a BA in 1734 and MA in 1737, and was ordained a deacon in the Anglican Church in 1736 and a minister two years later. In the early part of his career, he held a number of clerical appointments, including curate at Banstead, Surrey; chaplain to Sir Daniel Lambert; lecturer at St. Botolph's, Billingsgate; and lecturer at St. Dunstan-in-the-West, Fleet Street before taking on minor appointments in London as assistant morning preacher at St. George's, Hanover Square, from 1750 to 1755; chaplain to Selena, Countess of Huntingdon from 1755 to 1781; curate and morning preacher at St. Olave's, Southwark, from 1756 to 1759; curate and morning preacher at St. Bartholomew-the-Great, West Smithfield, from 1759 to 1761; and morning preacher and lecturer at Westminster Chapel in 1761. Through Lady Huntingdon's influence, Romaine eventually gained the living of the parish of St. Andrew-by-the Wardrobe with St. Anne, Blackfriars, in 1766, filling the pulpit there until his death in 1795. As the only beneficed evangelical clergyman in London prior to John Newton's arrival in 1780, Romaine stood out in the city, drawing large crowds to hear him preach while also taking fire from critics who ridiculed his doctrines.

Although at Oxford University at roughly the same time as John and Charles Wesley and George Whitefield, Romaine's association with evangelicals came later in his life. As a young cleric, he described himself as prideful, and despite his success as a preacher and noted Hebrew scholar, he felt spiritually troubled until his conversion around midcentury. Theologically, he adhered to a moderate form of Calvinism, championing the doctrine of election and rejecting the Arminianism of Wesleyan Methodism, though he kept an amiable relationship with the Wesley brothers. Romaine's most important works were *The Life of Faith* (1764), *The Walk*

figure 36.1 William Romaine (Detail), courtesy of the National Portrait Gallery, London.

of Faith (1771), and *The Triumph of Faith* (1795), which formed a trilogy on Christian spirituality. Within these treatises, he analyzed the notion of evangelical faith from a Reformed perspective. While arguing that faith is a divine gift that cannot be earned, in the following excerpt from his *Life of Faith*, he strongly urged his reader to pursue a life of holiness which would bring peace and happiness to the steadfast believer.

The Life of Faith

There are two things spoken of faith in scripture, which highly deserve the attention of every true believer. The one is the state of safety, in which he is placed by faith, being delivered from every evil and danger in time and in eternity, to which sin had justly exposed him; and the other is the happiness of this state, consisting in an abundant supply of all spiritual blessings freely given to him in Christ, and received, as they are wanted, by the hand of faith out of the fullness of Christ. By which means whoever has obtained this precious faith has a quiet conscience at peace with God, and need not fear any manner of evil, how much soever it be deserved, and thereby he may at all times come boldly to the throne of grace to receive whatever is necessary for his comfortable walk heavenwards. Every grace, every blessing promised in scripture, is his, and he may and does enjoy them so far as he lives by faith upon the Son of God: so far his life and conversation are well ordered, his walk is even, his spiritual enemies are conquered, the old man is mortified with his affections and lusts, and the new man is renewed day by day after the image of God in righteousness and true holiness. And from what he already enjoys by faith, and from the hopes of a speedy and perfect enjoyment, he rejoices in the Lord with joy unspeakable and full of glory.

It is much to be lamented, that few live up to these two privileges of faith. Many persons, who are truly concerned about the salvation of their souls, live for years together full of doubts and fears, and are not established in the faith, that is in Christ Jesus; and several who are in a good measure established, yet do not walk happily in an even course, nor experience the continual blessedness of receiving by faith a supply of every want out of the Saviour's fullness. These things I have long observed, and what I have been taught of them from the scripture and from the good hand of God upon me I have put together, and throw it as a mite into the treasury. I am sure it was never more wanted, than at present. May the good Lord accept the poor offering, and bless it to the hearts of his dear people to the praise of the glory of his own grace.

For the clearer understanding of what shall be spoken upon the life of faith, it will be needful to consider first what faith is: for a man must have faith before he can make use of it. He must be in Christ, before he can live upon Christ. Now faith signifies the believing [of] the word of God. It relates to some word spoken or to some promise made by him, and it expresses the belief which a person who hears it has of its being true. He assents to it, relies upon it, and acts accordingly. This is faith. And the whole word of God, which is the ground of faith, may be reduced to two points, namely, to what the law reveals concerning the justification of a righteous man, and to what the gospel reveals concerning the salvation of a sinner. A short examination of these points will discover to us a great number of persons, who have no faith at all in the word of God.

First, Every man in his natural state before the grace of Christ, and the inspiration of his Spirit has no faith. The scripture says, God hath shut up all that are in this state in unbelief: and when the Holy Spirit awakens any one of them, he convinces him of sin, and of unbelief in particular. When the comforter is come, says Christ, he shall convince the world of sin, because they believe not in me.

Secondly, A man who lives careless in sin has no faith. He does not believe one word, that God says in his law. Let it warn him of his guilt, and shew him his great danger, yet he sets at naught the terrors of the Lord. He acts as if there was no day of judgment, and no place of eternal torments. He has no fear of God before his eyes. How can such a practical Atheist as this have any faith?

Thirdly, The formalist has no faith. He is content with the form of godliness, and denies the power of it. The veil of unbelief is upon his heart, and the pride of his own good works and duties is ever before his eyes, that he finds no want of the salvation of Jesus, and is averse to the grace of the gospel. All his hopes arise from what he is in himself, and from what he is able to do for himself. He neither believes God speaking in the law, nor in the gospel. If he believed his word in the law, it would convict him of sin and forbid him to go about to establish a righteousness of his own; because by the works of the law shall no flesh living be justified, yet this he does not believe. If he believed the word of God in the gospel, it would convince him of righteousness, of an infinitely perfect righteousness wrought out by the God-man Christ Jesus, and imputed to the sinner without any works of his own: for unto him that worketh not, but believeth on him that justifieth the ungodly, his faith is imputed for righteousness. To this he dare not trust wholly for his acceptance before God, therefore he has no faith.

Fourthly, A man may be so far enlightened as to understand the way of salvation, and yet have no faith. This is a possible case. The apostle states it, 1 *Corinthians* 13:2: "Though I understand all mysteries, and all knowledge, yet I may be nothing." And it is a dangerous case, as *Hebrews* 10:26: "If we sin willfully after that we have received the knowledge of the truth, there remaineth no more sacrifice for sins." Here was such a knowledge of the truth as left a man to perish without the benefit of Christ's sacrifice, therefore he wanted that faith, which whosoever hath shall be saved…

For want of attending to the important truths already considered, and of bringing them into constant use and exercise, young believers fall into another great mistake, which keeps their faith weak, and stops its growth, namely a hearkening to sense, and trusting to its reports, which is the fifth general head I purposed to consider.

They are seeking to be established, and they think, that they should have no doubt of their being true believers, if they had but the testimony of sense, and comfortable feelings to assure them of it. And being used to judge in this way in other matters, for it is our strongest evidence in natural things, they are disposed to expect the same in spiritual; and they are the rather disposed to it, because sensible comforts are promised in scripture: which being very desirable and pleasing to nature, they are apt to covet them too much, and from not regarding what the scripture says about them, they are apt to seek them in a wrong way, and for a wrong end. Sense judges from what it sees, and draws its inferences from what it feels: so that its report to the conscience, either of a believer's state or of his growth in it, is not from unchangeable things, which would settle the conscience in peace, but from changeable things, which leave room for continual doubting. Sense also looks at the fruits of faith more than at the object of it, and if the believer has been misled and taught to confound these two together, he will be at great uncertainty in judging of his state: for instead of making the word of God, he will make his comforts the ground of his faith, and as these are more or less, so will his faith be. When he has comfortable feelings, then he will think himself a believer, and when he has none, then he will think himself an unbeliever, changing as his feelings do like the wind, and varying as his comforts do like the weather. This is a common case. I have seen the sad effects of it in the lives of many of my acquaintance, who from being taught thus to judge of themselves, were tossed about for several years, up and down, now comforted, then doubting, and could not get any solid establishment, till the word and Spirit of God convinced them, that sense was not to be the ground of their believing, nor the object to which they were to look. Sense judges by feeling and reports what it sees. Sense says, now I am in the favour of God: for I feel it. Now he is my God: for I find him so, I am comforted. Now he demonstrates it to me: for I feel nearness to him in prayer and sweet answers. Now I am sure my duties and services are acceptable: for I am quite lively in them, and come from them with warm affections. Now I cannot doubt: for I feel the assurance of his love to me. And when sense has lost those comfortable feelings, then it draws contrary inferences—Now I am not in the favour of God: for I don't feel it. Now he is not my God: for I don't find him so, I am not comforted, &c. What can be the issue of this, but continual wavering and changing? For our feelings are sometimes more, sometimes less, as every believer experiences. What a state then must he be in, who has no way to judge of himself, but by those changeable things? What room does he leave for continual doubting, and what trouble and misery does he thereby bring upon himself, as well as dishonour, to the unchangeableness of God in his nature and promises?

If the poor weak believer should say, I am convinced of this, and I should be glad to have my faith fixed upon such a foundation as changeth not. Then let it rest upon the word of God, which is the only ground of believing, and is therefore called the word of faith, upon which faith is built, and by which it is nourished and grows up. It is the work of faith to believe what God hath spoken, and because he hath spoken it: for his word changeth not. It abideth the same for ever; therefore what it truly reports, stands upon an immoveable rock. Sense and feeling may report things contrary to it, but the believer can silence them with *God hath spoken it*: for his faith has evidence of things not seen, and does not form its judgment by the things which are seen, but by the things which are not seen. Generally speaking faith judges the very contrary to what sense does, and will not believe what sense perceives. Abraham against hope believed in hope, so do all his children. They believe the pardon of sin, victory over sin, and the death of sin, the immortality of the body, though crumbled to dust and atoms, the second coming of Christ, and the eternal state of happiness or misery. Faith looks at God's word, calling the things which be not, as though they were, and is commonly forced to contradict sense. Sense judges from what it sees—Faith from what God says. Sense is governed by what appears—Faith by what God says shall be. Sense looks inward—Faith looks outward. Faith can answer the seeming contradictions, which sense opposes to it, from the word of God which cannot be broken. And when sense is ready to despair, and all its fine frames and feelings are gone, then the believer can still trust the Lord, and have a good hope because of the word of his grace.

But perhaps thou art ready to say, it is written, that there is great joy and peace in believing, yea, joy, unspeakable and full of glory. True, these are what faith produces, and not what it is. These are the fruits of faith which it brings forth in most abundance, when it is kept distinct from sense. The more simple faith is, the more it eyes Christ the object of faith, and the word the ground of faith, the more clear and distinct will its actions be, and consequently it will bring greater peace into the conscience, and more joy into the affections. But still these fruits are not faith; no more than the fruit is the tree. The fruits do not go before faith, but follow it, and grow from it. This is God's order. He gives us his word to be the ground of our believing, and by believing all things promised in the word are made ours, then we go on comfortably, and are happy; but when sense is put in the place of the word, then the consequence is, that weak believers have got a changeable rule to judge of themselves by, which hinders them from being established in believing, and from attaining the promised peace and joy.

William Romaine, *A Treatise upon the Life of Faith* (London: J. Worrall, 1764), 25–33, 148–58.

37

Faith Restricted to the Mind

John Erskine

AFTER WITNESSING THE remarkable revivals at Cambuslang and Kilsyth in the summer and autumn of 1742, John Erskine (1721–1803) made a commitment to enter the ministry. His decision, however, was not warmly affirmed by his immediate family. His father, John Erskine, professor of municipal law at Edinburgh University, and his grandfather, Colonel John Erskine, lieutenant governor of Stirling Castle and laird of estates in Carnock and Cardross, had high hopes that the young Erskine would become a barrister and live life as a gentleman of leisure. But the revivals of 1742, and in particular seeing ministers like George Whitefield and Scottish divines such as Thomas Gillespie, John Maclaurin, and Alexander Webster preach to the emotionally responsive crowds in western Scotland, convinced Erskine of his calling. Once licensed to preach in 1743, Erskine moved up the ranks within the Church of Scotland, serving the rural parishes of Kirkintilloch and Culross before translating to Edinburgh, where he preached at New Greyfriars and then ended his career at Old Greyfriars. Erskine co-ministered at Old Greyfriars with the renowned historian William Robertson, his classmate during his days at Edinburgh University and his ecclesiastical rival. As leader of the so-called Moderate literati, Robertson opposed the perceived "enthusiasm" of revivalist preaching, especially by George Whitefield. Robertson and the other Moderate ministers in Scotland sought to strengthen the ministry by promoting gentility and polite preaching, rather than traditional doctrines and the necessity of the new birth that evangelicals like Erskine viewed as essential material for the pulpit. Although opposing each other in the ecclesiastical courts, Erskine and Robertson maintained a cordial relationship that continued until the latter's death in 1793.

Once introduced to a network of evangelicals that supported the revivals in America, Britain, and Europe, Erskine corresponded with Joseph Bellamy, Aaron Burr, Sr., Benjamin Colman, Samuel Davies, Jonathan Dickinson, Timothy Dwight, Jonathan Edwards, Jonathan Edwards, Jr., Samuel Finley, Samuel Hopkins,

FIGURE 37.1 John Erskine (Detail), courtesy of the National Portrait Gallery, London.

Jedidiah Morse, Charles Nisbet, Thomas Prince, and Eleazar Wheelock in America; the English Baptists Andrew Fuller and John Ryland Jr.; and Christians living in Holland like Hugh Kennedy and Gijsbert Bonnet of Utrecht. Erskine's friendship with Edwards is especially noteworthy. Not only did Erskine send Edwards hundreds of books to help feed a hungry theologian's appetite for knowledge, but the Scottish evangelical also took the lead role in publishing many of Edwards's posthumous works, including *A History of the Work of Redemption* (1774), *Practical Sermons* (1788), *Miscellaneous Observations on Important Theological Subjects* (1793), and *Remarks on Important Theological Controversies* (1796). But Erskine was no Edwardsian. Although appreciating Edwards as a theological genius who bolstered evangelical Christianity, Erskine disagreed with his American friend on the nature of salvation. Whereas Edwards determined that God's grace enlivened one's affections—or the whole being of a person including one's intellect and will—Erskine took a more rationalistic approach. In his theological treatise, *The Nature of Christian Faith* (1765), he argued that faith was simply the revelation of divine knowledge. From studying John Locke's philosophy, Erskine came to the conclusion that true believers had received supernatural sight by God's Spirit whereby they could now see the truth: that Jesus Christ was the Son of God and the only means of salvation. The revelation of this knowledge was so powerful that one's rational faculties could not deny its veracity. For Erskine, faith had nothing to do with the will, as Edwards had proposed, but instead was limited to the mind's experience of truth.

The Nature of Christian Faith

FAITH or Belief, in strict propriety of speech, is that credit we give to the testimony of one, in whose knowledge of what he testifies, and in whose integrity we confide. Though often it is used in a sense less proper, and denotes in general persuasion or assent, whether founded upon testimony or intrinsic evidence.

The Holy Ghost in the sacred oracles means to be understood, and therefore speaks to men in their own language, and uses words in their common acceptation. Faith therefore in the Scripture does not signify, choice, affection, temper, or behaviour; for, in common language, it does not signify these: but merely persuasion or assent, and commonly a persuasion founded on testimony...

That saving faith is properly an assent, is further evident, because it is often termed knowledge: Isaiah 53:11. By his knowledge shall my righteous servant justify many. John 17:3. This is life eternal, to know thee the only true God, and Jesus Christ whom thou has sent. 1 Timothy 2:4. Who will have all men to be saved, and to come to the knowledge of the truth. 2 Peter 1:2–3. Grace and peace be multiplied unto you, through the knowledge of God, and of Jesus our Lord; according as his divine power hath given unto us all things that pertain to life and godliness, through the knowledge of him that hath called us to virtue and glory. In these passages knowledge must mean faith, because the distinguishing properties, attendants, and consequences of faith, are ascribed to it, in them. In other Scriptures, knowledge means a clear undoubted persuasion. Thus, 2 Corinthians 5:11. Knowing therefore the terror of the Lord, we persuade men. 1 Thessalonians 5:2. For yourselves know perfectly, that the day of the Lord so cometh, as a thief in the night. 2 Timothy 1:12. I know whom I have believed, and I am persuaded that he is able to keep that which I have committed unto him against that day. 1 John 2:21. I have not written unto you, because ye know not the truth: but because ye know it, and that no lie is of the truth. Why then should not knowledge mean persuasion, in the Scriptures, where it is put for faith?

Other ideas of faith, substituted in the place of persuasion, are better calculated to flatter the pride of man, that his acceptance with God is founded on something worthy and excellent in the frame of his mind, in the choice of his will, and in the bias of his affections. For that very reason, these ideas must be false. The office assigned to faith in the plan of salvation, is assigned it for this purpose, that all pretences to merit may be borne down, and the sovereignty and freedom of God's grace in bestowing salvation may appear. Romans 4:16. "Therefore it is of faith, that it might be by grace." Faith has no moral efficacy towards procuring our pardon and acceptance.

To this reasoning an able writer has objected, that a self-righteous heart may make a righteousness of a passive, as well as of an active faith, and be as proud of his passivity, as the Pharisee was of his fasting twice in the week.—But, is there not a mighty difference, between fasting, in which you abstain from what is desirable, or suffer what is painful, from a free choice which you imagine virtuous; and the assenting to a truth, when that assent is constrained by evidence. If one is proud of the last, may he not with equal reason be proud, that he believes the sun is in the firmament, when his eyes are struck with the meridian splendor of that glorious luminary?

Assent or persuasion is the only notion of faith, which, without straining, will apply to every Scripture, where any kind of faith is mentioned. Let the unbiased reader consult his Bible, and judge for himself.

To leave no room for dispute, an inspired author has given us a description of the faith by which the just shall live. Hebrews 11:1. "Now faith is the substance of things hoped for, the evidence of things not seen." While worldly men see through a false medium, even things present and visible, and are blind to their true nature and consequences; faith renders invisible things visible, and absent things present. It gives so lively and realizing a representation of things hoped for, that they seem, as it were, actually existing before us. Our persuasion of them is as undoubted, as if we saw them with our bodily eyes, or had a mathematical demonstration of their reality. With Stephen, faith sees the heavens open, and Jesus standing at the right-hand of God: nay, with Paul, it is caught up into the third heaven, and hears the praises of the redeemed. Its piercing eyes penetrate into that within the veil, whether the Forerunner has for us entered: and there behold the King in his beauty, and the land that is yet afar off. Nor is there in this any thing incredible. When we are firmly persuaded of any thing, in its own nature important and affecting, and appearing so to us, the mind is naturally led to contemplate it so steadily, that it impresses us, in some measure, as if it were already existing, present with us, and visible to our bodily eye. Faith is like those glasses, which give important and undoubted, though not full and distinct discoveries of objects, which our sight, without such assistance, could not perceive...

BUT does the faith of God's elect differ from that of others, only in the thing assented to?—By no means. The nature and foundation of the assent in him who has saving faith, is specifically different from the nature and foundation of the assent in self-deceivers.

Self-deceivers may have orthodox sentiments of religion. They may understand all mysteries and all knowledge, and yet want charity, 1 Corinthians 13:2. And what they thus understand, they may also believe, being convinced by miracles and other external evidences, that these mysteries are indeed a divine revelation. Many believed in Christ's name, when they saw the miracles which he did, to whom Jesus would not commit himself, because he knew all men. John 2:23–24.

Shall we then say, that saving faith is not founded upon evidence, and that it assents to truth it knows not why?—That would contradict the apostle's assertion, Hebrews 11:1 that faith is the evidence...of things not seen, i.e. furnishes the mind with convincing evidence of objects invisible to the bodily eye: and Christ's promise, that the Spirit shall convince...the world of sin, of righteousness, and of judgment. John 16:8. The word signifies to convince by way of demonstration, or so to manifest the evidence of a truth, that it shall appear unreasonable to entertain the least doubt of it...The Spirit takes from the scripture, the grand evidence of faith which he had lodged there, and carries it to the hearts of the elect, and then the light and power of divine truth so apprehends and overcomes the soul, that it can no longer resist.

That triumphant evidence, is no other than the glory and excellency of the gospel scheme of revelation, manifested by the Holy Spirit in such a manner, as produces full conviction, that a scheme so glorious could have none but God for its author. If the gospel be hid, and men perish thro' unbelief, it is hid from those, whose minds the God of this world hath blinded, least the light of the glorious gospel of Christ should shine unto them. 2 Corinthians 4:4. Where the gospel is discerned in its native lustre and glory, unbelief cannot remain, and souls cannot perish. God begins a saving change on the heart, by shining into it, to give the light of the knowledge of his glory in the face of Jesus Christ...

It is no objection against what I have said, that many discern no such glory in the gospel, as indicates its divine original. Truths wholly unknown to some, may be as intuitively evident to others, as general maxims are to all. A connoisseur can discern beauties in a fine picture or statue, which wholly escape the vulgar eye. White and black, sweet and bitter are different, and the difference is extremely perceptible, tho' the blind and tasteless perceive it not. Minds enlightened by the Spirit, can clearly discern the rays of divinity in the sacred oracles. If others are incapacitated by mental blindness from thus discerning them, that does not diminish their native brightness. The word of God's grace falls with such power and evidence on the soul of the enlightened sinner, that he can no more withhold his assent, than one who has his eyes open and sound, can hinder himself from seeing light at noon day, or than a philosopher can restrain his assent from a mathematical theorem, when his understanding is overpowered by demonstration. As even in these lower cases, the soul is merely passive, it must be much more so here, when a divine power concurs with convincing light, and wherever it comes, perfectly subdues...

I have said nothing of another ground of certainty, that Jesus is the Christ the Son of the living God, peculiar to true believers: I mean, their experiencing that he is the Christ, by his enlightening their understandings as a prophet, speaking peace to their consciences as a priest, and renewing their wills as a king. They cannot doubt that he is the God of Israel who hath done for them these wondrous works. Psalm 72:18. God's Son is revealed in them, Galatians 1:16 and by his operations on their hearts, shews himself the Son of God. Hence God promises, Hosiah 2:20. "I will betroth thee unto me in faithfulness, and thou shalt know the Lord." There is evidently a knowledge of God, and faith in him, which precedes in order of nature man's being betrothed unto God. But then there is another knowledge of God, posterior to our spiritual espousals, even a knowledge that God is faithful to his promises, by feeling these promises accomplished to us in particular. But this evidence of God's faithfulness, cannot be the primary foundation of faith, because believing goes before it. It is after we have believed, that we are sealed with the Holy Spirit of promise, Ephesians 1:13. And indeed, this is rather a certainty from our own feelings, than a crediting the divine testimony, that Jesus is the Christ: an assurance of sense, not of faith: and an assurance not only of the truth of the gospel, but of a fact no where revealed there, our own particular interest in God's favour, and in the operations of his sanctifying spirit.

John Erskine, *Theological Dissertations* (London: Edward and Charles Dilly, 1765), 139–43, 176–9, 181–2, 185–6.

38

Advice to Women on Chastity, Poverty, and Obedience

Mary Fletcher

ONE OF THE most influential Methodist women of the eighteenth century was the humble and austere Mary Fletcher (1739–1815). Born into the wealthy and power-ful Bosanquet family of London, Mary renounced her lavish upbringing, leaving home in 1760 and soon joined the Methodists at the London Foundry Society. After experiencing the raptures of a revival in 1761–62, Mary established a Christian society to help the poor northeast of London at Leytonstone in 1763. On Thursday evenings, she read Bible passages at Methodist class meetings that attracted some three dozen adults and an equal number of children until 1768 when the group moved to Morley, south of Leeds. On March 18, 1769, Wesley wrote a letter to Mary's companion and co-worker, Sarah Crosby, suggesting that women should not expound upon the scriptures, since he believed that honor was reserved for men. But in February 1773 Mary determined to chart a different course and for the first time in public, referenced a biblical passage. Mary wed Wesley's lieutenant, John William Fletcher, vicar of Madeley, on November 12, 1781. Fletcher had a deep respect for Mary's piety and once married, the two sustained a dynamic ministry in Madeley witnessing to the colliers and lower ranks in the parish. The marriage ended abruptly, however, when John died of a fever in August 1785. Heartbroken, Mary managed to continue her ministry at Madeley, preaching as much as five times a week shortly before her death in 1815.

FIGURE 38.1 Mary Fletcher (Detail), courtesy of the National Portrait Gallery, London.

Jesus, Altogether Lovely

Hoxton, *March* 10, 1763

My dear Sisters,

SINCE the time my heavenly father hath been pleased to discover to me, it was his will to call me from you to another place, this thought has often occurred to my mind, "Have I discharged my duty faithfully towards them? Have I strove to discern their every danger, and to warn them of it, as if it were my own soul? And have I from time to time, not failed to declare unto them whatever has appeared to me a more excellent way?" As I looked back, I found I was dissatisfied, and many things arose in my mind, as necessary to be spoken, before I could be content to part with you. Again, I thought, though I should speak them now, yet after a little time, I shall feel a desire of repeating them. This consideration induced me to write a few lines to each of you, that I may be clear of your blood.

My desire and prayer to God for you is, that you may every moment behold Jesus, as *altogether lovely!* The infinite consequence this is of to your soul, has often been the subject of our conversation. That there is but one way of beholding him now, and that this way is by faith, we all know; but how to keep this eye of the soul always clear and unsullied, like the finest glass, free from every speck and flaw, is the point we want to be instructed in. Let us therefore simply draw near to him who will give us wisdom liberally, because we need it; and who while we serve him in uprightness, will not lay folly to our charge.

Our grand enemy, well knowing that nothing can hurt the soul, while its eye is simply fixed on Jesus, makes his continual attack here: sometimes by pleasing, sometimes by painful objects, which he is always presenting to the mind, hoping to turn away its eye from him, who alone is lovely; and because this roaring lion is always watching for our destruction, and every object round us tends to the same end, our Lord hath strictly commanded all who would follow him, 1st. To take up their cross daily, and 2dly. To deny themselves.

It is by a life of self-denial alone, that the eye of our faith can be kept clear. I was not a little blessed the other day with the words of a good man, expressing his desire of being devoted to God, in a solemn observance of *chastity, poverty,* and *obedience.* The words struck me much, and appeared to contain the whole of a Christian life. The Lord was pleased to apply them close to my soul: and I will endeavour simply to relate what then occurred on each head. Indeed I know not since our lot has been cast together that I have ever received any blessing but what, with God's help I have strove to communicate to you.

I. *On* CHASTITY

Blessed are the pure in heart, for they shall see God.

THEIR Eye being unclouded, doth behold the *Invisible* in every thing. Heaven above, and Earth beneath, all to them is full of God. Their understanding, being no longer darkened with any pollution of flesh or spirit, they continually, as a clear mirror, reflect the glorious image of Him, whom beholding, they are constrained to cry out, "My beloved is fairer than ten thousand, and *altogether lovely.*" And while we are speaking of Chastity in its first sense (I mean with reference to Jesus and the soul) we shall easily discern that every deviation from him, is a degree of spiritual adultery. Is he the God of our body, and not of our soul? Doth he require us to keep our garments unspotted, and doth he not require purity in the inward parts? Surely he doth; for *without holiness* of heart, *no man shall see the Lord.* And however fair and beautiful our outward life may appear, unless our heart is kept unpolluted, Jesus will not come and make his abode with us. Now what outward sin does to the body, thoughts do to the soul; and as a wife treacherously depart-ing from her husband, divorces herself from him according to the law of God; so the soul embracing any imagination or idea, contrary to the purity of her heavenly bridegroom, dissolves the union subsisting between them...

My business with *you* is, only to guard you against those snares, which *Satan* will assuredly lay for your feet.

The first, and indeed the most dangerous snare he can throw in your way is, any kind or degree of intimacy with single men. Indeed I would wish you to be very sparing in your conversation with any man; but more especially with those that are single. All familiarity with these ought to be avoided; even with the most devout; "for the most innocent commerce with them, if it wounds not our con-science, leaves a stain on our reputation; and the smoke blackens, when the fire does not burn us."

The second stratagem of *Satan* will be, to overcloud your light, and lead you to dwell, in your mind, on the advantages you might meet with in another way of life; and if once he can get you so far, he will soon draw a curtain over those delightful views; stop those sweet breathings of your soul after Jesus, which once you enjoyed in the days of your simplicity, when your soul was a stranger to any other language, than

"Jesus, thee *alone* I know
Monarch of my simple heart."

To avoid this, you must stand all the day long on your watch-tower, fixing it in your mind,—I have given myself wholly unto thee; and "will know no other love than thine": and every thought to the contrary, however innocent in its appearance, however reasonable or profitable, must be cast into that fire of Jesu's love burning on your heart! What to another woman may be innocent, to *you* would be pollution: that which to a free woman might be even commendable, to her that is bound to an husband, would be a degree of adultery. Leave not then your heavenly Bridegroom; no not for one moment; not even in thought: but lean your feeble soul continually on him, who even in this life is *able to keep you from falling* and to preserve you *faultless in the presence of his glory with exceeding joy*...

II. *On* POVERTY

But is this poverty in temporal things all which God requires? Surely, no. It is the *poor in spirit* our Lord hath pronounced blessed; and declares, that theirs is the kingdom of heaven. But that we may the more closely apply it to ourselves, let us 1st consider, what this poverty of spirit does not, 2dly what it does consist in; and 3dly, what are the fruits we may expect from it?

1st, It does not consist in lowly words, in saying, God hath done nothing for us, when we know he hath wrought many and great deliverances; or, in at all denying what he hath done for our souls.

2dly, It does not consist in so becoming all things to all men, as to hurt our own souls; to countenance sin; or to be backward in testifying our Saviour openly.

But it consists in the *true* knowledge of ourselves, from the light of God shining on our hearts, by faith. And this knowledge is the ground and foundation of all religion. This is the substance of that text, "Learn of me to be meek and lowly, and ye shall find rest to your souls." And verily it is a rest none can conceive but by experience; for it lays a man so low, that every arrow goes over his head; yea, and it raises him so high, that he is out of the reach both of men and devils. For the souls that are truly humble cannot be cast down, since they know no other will but that of God; and being truly mortified, and united to Jesus, with a perfectly disinterested love, they delight as much in God's justice, as in his mercy; being perfectly willing to be visited by him in any manner he sees fit. They know their God is a consuming fire; and they glory in having him so; casting themselves as it were upon it, and rejoicing that all which will not bear this refining flame should be consumed: determined to drink deep into that spirit of humility, which alone can abide the day of his coming, or stand, when he appeareth...

III. *On* OBEDIENCE

TO you who have kept the faith, it will not be grievous to say, Study obedience as the rule of your life. Obedience to God, and to man, for his sake. But what is the obedience we owe to God? *Absolute* and *entire*; in small, as well as great things; and because it is in little things we are most apt to offend, I will speak most particularly of these. This obedience requires us always to have a ready mind, simply determined to follow the light of God, whatever it may cost us; and when we have laid ourselves out, and think to do some great thing for God, and our neighbour, to be equally willing, the end we proposed should be either answered, or frustrated. So likewise when we have proposed to spend a day in such or such a manner, and the providence of God prevents, we should remember, "the hairs of my head are all numbered." And none hath any power against a child of God, but what is given him from above. Therefore submit to it, as the order of that God who hath declared, that in his sight, "obedience is better than sacrifice; and to hearken than the fat of rams." In short we should see God in every thing, and make it our sole business, inwardly to listen to that still small voice, which none but silent souls can hear; and outwardly, to meet him in the order of his providence: remembering we are all his own, and "lying before him as soft wax, ready to be formed into any shape he pleases." And this simple recollecting ourselves in the presence of God, receiving every occurrence as from him; and offering up every action to him, is the spirit and life of true religion. Were we but more perfect in this lesson, we should continually experience the truth of those words, "the Lord is my hiding place and my *castle*, whereunto I may *always* resort?"

Next let us consider, what it is to obey man, for the Lord's sake, and whom we are so to obey?

1st. This obedience does not consist merely in *Affection*, "I will do what such a one orders, because I love him, or because he hath done me much good, and therefore I find great pleasure in obeying him." This is often idolatry rather than obedience.

2dly. Neither does it consist in obeying such or such a person, "because he is very spiritual, and perhaps nearer the heart of Christ, than most others." This is as if I was to throw away the laws of my own king, in order to follow those of another, because I believed him to be a better man...

But who are the persons we are so to obey? St. Paul tells us, *The powers that be are ordained of God.* Those who are at this time set over the country where you dwell; the church you belong to; or the family you live in: All these whether high or low in grace, (as far as you can without sin) you are bound by the laws of God to obey. But more especially those who watch over our souls. Otherwise it is to be feared, he who hath said, *Touch not mine anointed*, should add, *Vengeance is mine, I will repay.*

Mary Fletcher, *Jesus, Altogether Lovely: Or a Letter to Some of the Single Women in the Methodist Society* (London: Robert Hawes, [1766]), 2–8, 10–12.

39

Defending the Doctrine of Christian Perfection

John William Fletcher

METHODISM BEGAN AS a movement of renewal within the Church England in the late 1730s. Over the course of the eighteenth century two identifiable parties developed, one headed by John and Charles Wesley that promoted Arminian beliefs and another led by George Whitefield that held fast to Calvinism. Both were united in their belief in original sin, justification by faith, and the call to a holy life according to the will of God. But soon, the two branches disputed whether God has elected a limited number of persons before the creation of the world to be eternally saved (predestination), whether the Law of God continues to have authority in the life of a Christian believer (antinomianism), and whether Christians can overcome sinful desires and grow into perfect love of God and neighbor (Christian perfection).

John William Fletcher (1729–85), born Jean Guillaume de la Fléchère, from Nyon, Switzerland, became one of the outstanding personalities in the second generation of Methodists. Around 1750, he came to England where he took a position as a tutor to the children of Thomas Hill, MP for Shrewsbury. In the winter 1752–53, he became acquainted with the Methodists, forming close friendships with Charles Wesley as well as Lady Huntingdon. Three years after his ordination as a minister in the Church of England, he left the Hill family in 1760 to become vicar of Madeley in Shropshire, a center of the early industrial revolution in England. He remained vicar of Madeley for the remainder of his life.

Fletcher hoped to keep the peace between the Wesleyans and Calvinists but eventually had to choose sides. When the Methodist preacher Walter Shirley voiced his concern regarding some of the comments made in the Methodist minutes at the 1770 conference, Fletcher felt obliged to correct what he believed were misinterpretations about Wesley's doctrines. Originally a series of private letters written to Shirley, these manuscripts were quickly rushed to the press and published in 1771 as *A Vindication of the Rev. Mr. Wesley's Last Minutes*, later known as the

<small>FIGURE</small> 39.1 John William Fletcher (Detail), courtesy of the National Portrait Gallery, London.

First Check to Antinomianism. Subsequent *Checks to Antinomianism* would soon follow as Fletcher moved on to debate others besides Shirley. In this first polemic, Fletcher provides perhaps his clearest interpretation of Wesleyan theology.

First Check to Antinomianism

Hon. and Rev. Sir,

BEFORE a Judge passes sentence upon a person accused of theft, he hears what his neighbours have to say for his character. Mr. Wesley, I grant, is accused of what is worse than theft, *dreadful heresy*; and I know that whosoever maintains a dreadful heresy is a *dreadful heretic*, and that the church of Rome shews no mercy to such: but may not *real Protestants* indulge with the privilege of a felon one whom they so lately respected as a brother? And may not I, an old friend and acquaintance of his, be permitted to speak a word in his favour, before he is branded in the forehead, as he has already been in the back? ...

When, in an intricate case, a prudent Judge is afraid to pass an unjust sentence, he inquires, as I observed, into the general conduct of the person accused, and by that means frequently finds out the truth which he investigates. As that method may be of service in the present case, permit me, Sir, to lay before you a general view of Mr. W.'s doctrine.

> (1) For above these sixteen years I have heard him frequently in his chapels, and sometimes in my church; I have familiarly conversed and corresponded with him, and have often perused his numerous works in verse and prose: and I can truly say, that during all that time I have heard him, upon every proper occasion, steadily maintain the total fall of man in Adam, and his utter inability

to recover himself, or take any one step towards his recovery, *without the grace of God preventing him that he may have a good will, and working with him when he has that good will.*

The deepest expressions that ever struck my ears, on the melancholy subject of our natural depravity and helplessness, are those which dropped from his lips: and I have ever observed that he constantly ascribes to divine grace, not only the good works and holy tempers of believers, but all the good thoughts of upright Heathens, and the good desires of those professors whom he sees *begin in the Spirit and end in the flesh;* when, to my great surprise, some of those who accuse him of "robbing God of the glory of his grace, and ascribing too much to man's power," directly or indirectly maintain, that Demas and his fellow apostates never had any grace; and that if once they went on far in the ways of God, it was merely by the force of fallen nature; a sentiment which Mr. W. looks upon as diametrically opposite to the humbling assertion of our Lord, *Without me ye can do nothing,* and which he can no more admit than the rankest Pelagianism.

(2) I must likewise testify that he faithfully points out Christ as the only way of salvation; and strongly recommends faith as the only means of receiving him, and all the benefits of his righteous life and meritorious death: and truth obliges me to declare, that he frequently expresses his detestation of the errors of modern Pharisees, who laugh at original sin, set up the powers of fallen man, cry down the operations of God's Spirit, deny the absolute necessity of the blood and righteousness of Christ, and refuse him the glory of all the good that may be found in Jew or Gentile. And you will not without difficulty, Sir, find in England, and perhaps in all the world, a minister who hath borne more frequent testimonies, either from the pulpit or the press, against those dangerous errors. All his works confirm my assertion, especially his sermons on original sin, and salvation by faith, and his masterly refutation of Dr. Taylor, the wisest Arian, Pelagian, and Socinian of our age. Nor am I afraid to have this testimony confronted with his minutes, being fully persuaded that, when they are candidly explained, they rather confirm than overthrow it.

His preaching of the fall and the recovery is attended with a peculiar advantage, it is close and experimental: he not only points out the truth of those doctrines, but presses his hearers to cry to God that they may feel their weight upon their heart. Some open those great truths very clearly, but let their congregations rest, like the stony ground hearers, in the first emotions of sorry and joy which the word frequently excites. Not so Mr. Wesley; he will have true penitents *feel the plague of their own hearts, travel, be heavy laden, and receive the sentence of death in themselves according to the glorious ministration of condemnation:* and *according to the ministration of the spirit which exceeds in glory,* he insists upon true believers know-ing for themselves, that *Jesus hath power on earth to forgive sins,* and asserts that they *taste the good word of God and the powers of the world to come,* and that they *are made partakers of the Holy Ghost and the divine nature; the Spirit itself bearing witness with their spirit that they are the children of God.*

(3) The next fundamental doctrine in Christianity, is that of holiness of heart and life; and no one can accuse here Mr. W. of leaning to the Antinomian delusion, which *makes void the law through* a speculative and barren *faith;* on the contrary, he appears to be peculiarly set for the defence of practical reli-gion: for, instead of representing Christ as the minister of sin with ranters, to the great grief and offence of many, he sets him forth as a complete *Saviour from sin.* Not satisfied to preach holiness begun, he preaches finished holiness, and calls believers to such a degree of heart-purifying faith, as may enable them continually to *triumph in Christ,* as being *made to them of God sanctifica-tion* as well as *righteousness.*

It is, I grant, his misfortune (if indeed it is one) to preach a *fuller salvation* than most professors expect to enjoy here; for he asserts that Jesus can *make clean the inside,* as well as the outside, of his vessels unto honour; that *he hath power on earth to save his people from their sins,* and that *his blood cleanses from all sin,* from the guilt and defilement both of original and actual corruption. He is bold enough to declare with St. John, that *if we say we have no sin,* either by nature or practice, *we deceive ourselves and the truth is not in us; but if we confess our sins, God is faithful and just to forgive us our sins, and to CLEANSE us from all unrighteousness.* He is *legal* enough not to be ashamed of these words of Moses, *The Lord thy God will circumcise thine heart, and the heart of thy seed, to love the Lord thy God with all thine heart, and with all they soul, that thou mayest live.* And he dares to believe that the Lord can perform the words which he spoke to Ezekiel: *I will sprinkle clean water upon you, and you shall be clean; from ALL your filthiness, and from ALL your idols will I cleanse you. A new heart also will I give you; I will take away the stony heart out of your flesh, and I will give an heart of flesh: and I will put my spirit within you, and cause you to walk in my statues; and ye shall keep my judgments and do them. I will also save you from ALL your unclean-ness.* Hence it is that he constantly exhorts his hearers to *grow in grace, and in the knowledge of the Saviour,* till by a strong and lively faith, they can continually *reckon themselves to be dead indeed unto sin, but alive unto God through Jesus Christ our Lord:* he tells them that *he who committeth sin is the servant of sin.*—That *our old man is crucified with Christ that the body of sin might be destroyed, that hence-forth we should not serve sin.*—That *if the Son shall make them free they shall be free indeed.*—And that, although *the law of the spirit of life in Christ Jesus* will not deliver them from the innocent infirmities incident to flesh and blood, it will nevertheless *make them free from the law of sin and death,* and enable them to say with holy triumph, *How shall we that are dead to sin live any longer therein?* In a word, he thinks that God can so *shed abroad his live in our hearts by the Holy Ghost given unto us,* as to *sanctify us wholly, soul, body and spirit*; and enable us to *rejoice evermore, pray without ceasing, and in every thing give thanks.* And he is persuaded that *he who can do far exceeding abundantly above all that we can ask or think,* is able to fill us with the *perfect love which casts out fear;* that *we, being delivered out of the hands of our enemies,* may *have the mind that was in Christ, be righteous as the MAN Jesus was righteous, walk as he also walked;* and *be* in our measure as *he was in the world,* he as the stock of *the tree of righteousness* and we as the branches, *having our fruit from him unto holiness,* and *serving God without fear in true righteousness all the days of our life.*

This he sometimes calls full sanctification, the state of *fathers* in Christ, or *the glorious liberty of the children of God;* sometimes a being *strengthened, established, and settled;* or being *rooted and grounded in love*: but most commonly he calls it Christian *perfection*; a word which, though used by the apostles in the same sense, cannot be used by him without raising the pity or indignation of one half of the religious world; some making it the subject of their pious sneers, and godly lampoons; while others tell you roundly "they abhor it above every thing in the creation."

Tantaene animis coelestibus irae!

On account of this doctrine it is that he is traduced as a Pharisee, a Papist, an Anti-christ; some of his opposers taking it for granted that he makes void the priestly office of Christ, by affirming that his blood can so completely wash us here from our sins, that at death we shall be *sound of him in peace, without spot, wrinkle, or any such thing*; while others, to colour their opposition to the many scriptures which he brings to support this unfashionable doctrine, give it out that he only wants the old man so refined in all his tempers, and regulated in all his outward behaviour as to appear *perfect in the flesh*: or, in other terms, that he sets up pharisaic self, instead of Christ completely *formed in us* as the full *hope of glory.* But I must (for one) do him the justice to say he is misapprehended, and that what he calls perfection, is nothing but the rich cluster of all the spiritual blessings promised to believers in the gospel; and, among the rest, a continual sense of the virtue of Christ's atoning and purifying blood, preventing both old guilt from returning, and new guilt from fastening, upon the conscience; together with the deepest consciousness of our helplessness and nothingness in our best estate, the most endearing discoveries of the Redeemer's love, and the most humbling and yet ravishing views of his glorious fullness; witness these lines which conclude one of his favourite hymns on that subject.

> Confound o'er-power me with thy grace;
>> I would be by myself abhor'd:
> (All might, all majesty, all praise,
>> All glory be to Christ my Lord.)
> O let me gain perfections height,
>> O let me into nothing fall,
> Be less than nothing in my sight,
>> And feel that Christ is all in all.

(4) But this is not all, he holds also general redemption, and its necessary consequences, which some account *dreadful heresies*. He asserts with St. Paul, that *Christ, by the GRACE of God, tasted death for every man*; and this *grace* he calls *free*, as extending itself *freely* to all. Nor can he help expressing his surprise at those pious ministers, who maintain that the Saviour keeps his grace, as they suppose he kept his blood, from the greatest part of mankind, and yet engross to themselves the title of *preachers of free grace*.

He frequently observes with the same Apostle, that *Christ is the Saviour of ALL men, but especially of them that believe*; and that *God will have ALL men to be saved*, consistently with their moral agency, and the tenor of his gospel.

With St. John he maintains that *God is love*, and that *Christ is the propitiation not only for our sins, but also for the sins of the WHOLE world*: with David he affirms that *God's mercy is over all his works*, and with St. Peter, that *the Lord is not willing that any should perish, but that ALL should come to repentance*; yea, that *God*, without hypocrisy, *commandeth ALL men EVERY WHERE to repent*. Accordingly he says with the Son of God, *Whosoever will, let him come, and take of the water of life freely*; and after his blessed example, as well as by his gracious command, he *preaches the gospel to every creature*, which he apprehends would be inconsistent with common honesty, if there was not a *gospel FOR every creature*. Nor can he doubt of it in the least, when he considers that *Christ is a king* as well as a priest, that *we are under a law to Him*, that *those men who will not have him reign over them, shall be brought and fain before him*, yea, that *he shall judge the secrets of men according to St. Paul's Gospel, take vengeance of all them that obey not his own gospel*, and *be the author of eternal salvation to* none but *them that obey him*. With this principle, as with a key given us by God himself, he opens those *things which are hard to be understood in the epistles of St. Paul, and which they that are unlearned and unstable wrest, as they do* some *other scriptures, if* not *to their own destruction*, at least to the *overthrowing of the faith of some* weak Christians, and the hardening of many, very many infidels...

(5) As a consequence of the doctrine of general redemption, Mr. W. lays down two axioms of which he never loses sight in his preaching. The first

is, that ALL OUR SALVATION IS OF GOD IN CHRIST, and therefore OF GRACE; all opportunities, invitations, inclination, and power to believe being bestowed upon us of mere grace—grace most absolutely free: and so far I hope that all who are called gospel-ministers agree with him: but he proceeds farther, for secondly, he asserts with equal confidence, that according to the gospel dispensation, ALL OUR DAMNATION IS OF OURSELVES, by our obstinate unbelief, and avoidable unfaithfulness; as we may *neglect so great salvation, desire to be excused* from coming to the feast of the Lamb, *make light of* God's gracious offers, refuse to *occupy, bury our talent,* and act the part of the *slothful servant;* or in other words, *resist, grieve, do despite to,* and *quench the Spirit* of grace, BY OUR MORAL AGENCY.

John Fletcher, *First Check to Antinomianism: Or, A Vindication of the Rev. Mr. Wesley's Last Minutes...in Five Letters* (Bristol: W. Pine, 1771), 7–15, 17.

40

A Selection of Hymns

William Williams

A SON OF a farmer, William Williams (1717–91) grew up in the parish of Llanfair-ar-y-Bryn, three miles east of Llandovery in Carmarthenshire, Wales. Williams attended a Dissenting academy at Llwyn Llwyd, close to Hay-on-Wye, intending to be a physician, but made a career change after hearing a sermon on God's judgment by the Welsh evangelist Howell Harris in 1738. After his ordination as a deacon at St. David's in August 1740, he served as a curate at Llanwrtyd and Llanddewi Abergwesyn in Brecknockshire but was denied the title of an Anglican minister in 1743 due to his itinerant preaching and support of the ministries of Howell Harris and Daniel Rowland. In the early 1740s, Williams resigned as an Anglican curate to work as Rowland's assistant. Around the same time, Williams's father died and he inherited the family farm at Pantycelyn, which provided a modest living that allowed him to devote more time to itinerate as a Welsh (Calvinistic) Methodist. He traveled throughout Wales at various intervals in the 1740s, preaching and building up societies. When Harris and Rowland grappled over leadership of Welsh Methodism in the mid-1740s Williams eventually had to choose sides. Aligning himself with Rowland, Williams devoted much of the 1750s to reading and writing, which contributed greatly to establishing him as a significant hymnist and theologian. Reconciliation between Harris and Rowland and Williams in the early 1760s coincided with a revival at Llangeitho in 1762. Feeling invigorated by this fresh wind of the Spirit, Williams spent at least some of the 1770s touring western and south Wales as a preacher.

Although contributing greatly to the evangelical revivals in Wales, Williams is best known for his writings, particularly his hymns. Along with *Aleluia* (1744), he published close to one thousand hymns collected in works like the three-part *Hosanna i Fab Dafydd* ("Hosanna to the Son of David"), published in 1751, 1753, and 1754, as well as the later, more refined *Caniadau y rhai sydd ar y Môr o Wydr* ("Those Songs on the Sea of Glass") in 1762, the three-part *Ffarwel Weledig, Croesaw Anweledig Bethau* ("Farewell Visible, Welcome Invisible Things") in 1763,

FIGURE 40.1 William Williams "Pantycelyn" (Detail), National Library of Wales, Aberystwyth.

and the two-part English translation, *Gloria in Excelsis* (1771–72). His most popular hymn, "Guide Me O Thou Great Jehovah," was composed by Williams in Welsh, later appearing in English as a supplement to the nineteenth edition of George Whitefield's *Collection of Hymns for Social Worship* in 1774. Glancing at Williams's hymns, one will notice his ability to combine doctrine with piety, lyrically describing devotion to Christ from the point of view of a thankful believer who has been saved from sin.

Gloria in Excelsis

"HYMN I"

EACH Letter of thy holy Name,
    Sweet JESUS, sounds of Life;
Thy Love and Favour can expel
    All Tumults, Fears and Strife.

Under thy gracious Wings repos'd
    I'd always wish to be,
Renounce all Pleasures for that one
    Of ever loving Thee.

The Earth and Seas, with all their rich
    And unexhausted Store,
Are comprehended in thy Self
    Ten thousand Times and more.

Salvation is my happy Rest,
    Salvation is my Home;
And let Salvation be engrav'd
    Upon my silent Tomb.

From Guilt and Sin, from Death and Hell,
    And every Misery,
Most freely ransom'd, now I taste
    The glorious Liberty.

"HYMN III"

LORD let me gain that happy Rest,
    The Rest I long to see,
And taste the immortal Love divine
    That wholly springs from thee.

Let Cares and Troubles, Fears, and Strife,
    Far from my Thoughts remove,
And let me wander in the Shade
    Of everlasting Love.

Feed me with that delicious Feast,
    That inward Peace and Joy,
Which all my Troubles, Pain, and Woes,
    Shall instantly destroy.

Within the Bounds of dying Love
    Securely let me stray
In endless Mazes, till the Dawn
    Of everlasting Day.

Those Scenes my happy Thoughts shall fill,
    And keep me from the Noise,
The Tumults of the lower Spheres,
    Or its terrestrial Joys.

"HYMN XVI"

BENEATH thy Cross I lay me down,
And mourn to see thy bloody Crown,
Love drops in Blood from every Vein,
Love is the Spring of all his Pain.

Here, JESUS, I shall ever stay,
And spend my longing Hours away,
Think on thy bleeding Wounds and Pain,
And contemplate thy Woes again.

The Rage of Satan and of Sin,
Of Foes without, and Fears within,
Shall ne'er my conq'ring Soul remove,
Or from thy Cross, or from thy Love.

Secur'd from Harms beneath thy Shade,
Here Death and Hell shall ne'er invade,
Nor Sina'h, with its thund'ring Noise,
Shall e'er disturb my happier joys.

O, unmolested happy Rest!
Where inward Fears are all supprest,
Here I shall love, and live secure,
And patiently my Cross endure.

"HYMN XXXVII"

O'ER those gloomy Hills of Darkness
    Look my Soul, be still and gaze,
All the Promises do travel
    On a glorious Day of Grace,
        Blessed Jubil, &c.
        Let thy glorious Morning dawn.
Let the Indian, let the Negro,
    Let the rude Barbarian see
That divine and glorious Conquest
    Once obtain'd on Calvary;
        Let the Gospel, &c.
        Word resound from Pole to Pole.
Kingdoms wide that sit in Darkness,
    Let them have the glorious Light,
And from Eastern Coast to Western
    May the Morning chase the Night,
        And Redemption, &c.
        Freely purchas'd win the Day.

May the glorious Days approaching,
> *From eternal Darkness dawn,*
And the everlasting Gospel
> *Spread abroad thy holy Name.*
>> *Thousand Years, &c.*
>> *Soon appear, make no Delay.*

Lord, I long to see that Morning,
> *When thy Gospel shall abound,*
And thy Grace get full Possession
> *Of the happy promis'd Ground;*
>> *All the Borders, &c.*
>> *Of the great Immanuel's Land.*

Fly abroad, eternal Gospel,
> *Win and conquer, never cease;*
May thy eternal wide Dominions
> *Multiply, and still increase;*
>> *May thy Scepter, &c.*
>> *Sway th' enlight'ned World around.*

O let Moab yield and tremble,
> *Let Philistia never boast,*
And let India proud be scatt'red
> *With their numerable Host;*
>> *And the Glory, &c.*
>> *Jesus only be to thee.*

A Collection of Hymns for Social Worship

SUPPLEMENT

HYMN CXVII

Christ a sure Guide

GUIDE me, O thou great Jehovah,
Pilgrim, through this barren Land,
I am Weak, but thou art Mighty,
Hold me with thy pow'rful Hand,
Bread of Heav'n, Bread of Heav'n,
Feed me till I want no more.

Open now the crystal Fountain
Whence the healing Streams do flow,

Let the fiery cloudy Pillar,
Lead me all my Journey through,
Strong Deliv'rer, Strong Deliv'rer,
Be thou still my Strength and Shield.

When I tread the Verge of Jordon,
Bid my anxious Fear subside;
Death of Deaths, and Hell's Destruction,
Land me safe on Canaan's side,
Songs of Praises, Songs of Praises,
I will ever give to Thee.

William Williams, *Gloria in Excelsis: Or Hymns of Praise to God and the Lamb* (Carmarthem: John Ross, 1772), 3–5, 15, 33–4; George Whitefield, *A Collection of Hymns for Social Worship, More Particularly Designed for the Use of the Tabernacle and Chapel Congregations in London*, nineteenth edition (London: Henry Cock, 1774), 231.

41

Advice on Alcohol

Samson Occom

THE MOHEGAN SAMSON Occom (1723–92) converted to Christianity in 1741 during the Great Awakening. Within three years of his conversion he made his way to Lebanon, Connecticut, to study English, Hebrew, Greek, Latin, and theology under Eleazar Wheelock's tutorship. In the years that followed, Occom was licensed as a Presbyterian minister in 1759 and became a key leader among Native Americans. He served as a schoolmaster and minister and provided legal counsel to the Montauk Indians of Long Island, and as a missionary to the Oneida in New York between 1761 and 1763 until his efforts were disrupted by Pontiac's War. In the mid-1760s, Occom agreed to travel to Britain for two and a half years to raise money for Wheelock's new school for Indians, preaching over 300 sermons to large crowds and collecting some £12,000. His relationship with Wheelock dissolved, however, when Occom returned to America to find out that the money would be put toward establishing Dartmouth College as an elitist school for white males. Near the end of his life, Occom helped to found Brothertown, an independent community of Native American Christians in Oneida territory in New York. He ministered to the Natives there, as well as the neighboring inhabitants at New Stockbridge, until his death on July 14, 1792.

Occom's best-known work was his *Sermon Preached at the Execution of Moses Paul* (1772), which went through at least nineteen editions in the eighteenth century. The sermon addressed the Wampanoag Moses Paul, who had been convicted in New Haven for the murder of a white man named Moses Cook at a tavern in Bethany, Connecticut, in December 1771. Paul was scheduled to be executed in June 1772 but appealed his case to the Connecticut General Assembly and the Superior Court, citing the racial bias of the white jury. After losing his appeal, and with his death imminent, Paul wrote to his fellow Native American asking Occom to deliver his execution sermon. For Occom's sermon preached on September 2, 1772, he employed Romans 6:23, "For the wages of sin is death, but the gift of God is eternal life through Jesus Christ our Lord," as his biblical text. Occom

FIGURE 41.1 Samson Occom (Detail), courtesy of the National Portrait Gallery, London.

intended the sermon to spur the convicted man to search for saving grace in the last remaining minutes of his life, but the message also spoke more generally to the gathered crowd on the power of sin over all humanity. In the final portion of his discourse, Occom offered a critical appraisal of Native American alcohol abuse, imploring his people to seek sobriety in order to avoid poverty and continual exploitation by white Europeans.

A Sermon, Preached at the Execution of Moses Paul

I shall now address myself to the Indians, my brethren and kindred according to the flesh.

My poor kindred,

You see the woeful consequences of sin, by seeing this our poor miserable country-man now before us, who is to die this day for his sins and great wickedness. And it was the sin of drunkenness that has brought this destruction and timely death upon him. There is a dreadful woe denounced from the Almighty against drunkards, and it is this sin, this abominable, this beastly and accursed sin of drunkenness, that has stripped us of every desirable comfort in this life; by this we are poor, miserable and wretched; by this sin we have no name nor credit in the world among polite nations; for this sin we are despised in the world, and it is all right and just, for we despise ourselves more; and if we don't regard ourselves, who will regard us? And it is for our sins, and especially for that accursed, that most devilish sin of drunkenness that we suffer every day. For the love of strong drink we spend all that we have, and every thing we can get. By this sin we can't have comfortable houses, nor any thing comfortable in our houses; neither food nor raiment, nor decent utensils. We are obliged to put up any sort of shelter just to screen us from the severity of the weather; and we go about with very mean, ragged and dirty clothes, almost naked. And we are half starved, for most of the time obliged to pick up any thing to eat.—And our poor children are suffering every day for want of the necessaries of life; they are very often crying for want of food, and we have nothing to give them; and in the cold weather they are shivering and crying, being pinched with cold.—All this is for the love of strong drink. And this is not all the misery and evil we bring on ourselves in this world; but when we are intoxicated with strong drink, we drown our rational powers, by which we are distinguished from the brutal creation; we unman ourselves, and bring ourselves not only level with the beasts of the field, but seven degrees beneath them; yea we bring ourselves level with the devils; I don't know but we make ourselves worse than the devils, for I never heard of drunken devils.

My poor kindred, do consider what a dreadful abominable sin drunkenness is. God made us men, and we choose to be beasts and devils; God made us rational creatures, and we choose to be fools. Do consider further, and behold a drunkard, and see how he looks when he has drowned his reason; how deformed and shameful does he appear? He dis-figures every part of him, both soul and body, which was made after the image of God. He appears with awful deformity, and his whole visage is dis-figured; if he attempts to speak he cannot bring out his words distinct, so as to be understood; if he walks he reals and staggers to and fro, and tumbles down. And see how he behaves, he is now laughing, and then he is crying; he is singing and the next minute he is mourning; and is all love to every one, and anon he is raging, & for fighting, & killing all before him, even the nearest and dearest relations and friends: Yea nothing is too bad for a drunken man to do. He will do that, which he would not do for the world, in his right mind; he may lie with his own sister or daughter as Lot did.

Further, when a person is drunk, he is just good for nothing in the world; he is of no service to himself, to his family, to his neighbours, or his country; and how much more unfit is he to serve God: yet he is just fit for the service of the devil.

Again, a man in drunkenness is in all manner of danger, he may be kill'd by his fellow-men, by wild beasts, and tame beasts; he may fall into the fire, into the water, or into a ditch; or he may fall down as he walks along, and break his bones or his neck; he may cut himself with edge-tools.—Further, if he has any money or any thing valuable, he may loose it all, or may be robb'd, or he may make a foolish bargain, and be cheated out of all he has.

I believe you know the truth of what I have just now said, many of you, by sad experience; yet you will go on still in your drunkenness. Tho' you have been cheated over and over again, and you have lost your substance by drunkenness, yet you will venture to go on in this most destructive sin. O fools when will ye be wise?—We all know the truth of what I have been saying, by what we have seen and heard of drunken deaths. How many have been drowned in our rivers, and how many frozen to death in the winter seasons! Yet drunkards go on without fear and consideration: alas, alas! What will become of all such drunkards? Without doubt they must all go to hell, except they truly repent and turn to God. Drunkenness is so common amongst us, that even our young men and young women are not ashamed to get drunk. Our young men will get drunk as soon as they will eat when they are hungry.—It is generally esteemed amongst men, more abominable for a woman to be drunk, than a man; and yet there is nothing more common amongst us than female drunkards. Women ought to be more modest than men; the holy scriptures recommend modesty to women in particular:—but drunken women have no modesty at all. It is more intolerable for a woman to get drunk, if we consider further, that she is in great danger of falling into the hands of the sons of Belial, or wicked men, and being shamefully treated by them.

And here I cannot but observe, we find in sacred writ, a woe denounced against men, who put their bottles to their neighbours mouth to make them drunk, that they may see their nakedness: and no doubt there are such devilish men now in our day, as there were in the days of old.

And to conclude, consider my poor kindred, you that are drunkards, into what a miserable condition you have brought yourselves. There is a dreadful woe thundering against you every day, and the Lord says, That drunkards shall not inherit the kingdom of God.

And now let me exhort you all to break off from your drunkenness, by a gospel repentance, and believe on the Lord Jesus and you shall be saved. Take warning by this doleful sight before us, and by all the dreadful judgments that have befallen poor drunkards. O let us all reform our lives, and live as becomes dying creatures, in time to come. Let us be persuaded that we are accountable creatures to God, and we must be called to an account in a few days. You that have been careless all your days, now awake to righteousness, and be concerned for your poor and never-dying souls. Fight against all sins, and especially the sin that easily besets you, and behave in time to come as becomes rational creatures; and above all things, receive and believe on the Lord Jesus Christ, and you shall have eternal life; and when you come to die, your souls will be received into heaven, there to be with the Lord Jesus in eternal happiness, with all the saints in glory; which, God of his infinite mercy grant, thro' Jesus Christ our Lord.

Samson Occom, *A Sermon, Preached at the Execution of Moses Paul, an Indian, Who Was Executed at New Haven, on the 2d of September 1772, for the Murder of Mr. Moses Cook* (New Haven, CT: T. & S. Green, [1772]), 28–32.

42

An Argument for the Separation of Church and State

Isaac Backus

FOR MUCH OF his life, the New England Separatist Isaac Backus (1724–1806) actively campaigned to rid America of taxes that supported state churches. Born on January 9, 1724, in Norwich, Connecticut, he ran the family farm and extensive land holdings when his father died in 1740. From hearing the preaching of Eleazar Wheelock and other revivalists during the Great Awakening, Backus experienced conversion in August 1741. He and his mother left the Congregationalist church in Norwich in 1746 to unite with a Separatist evangelical congregation. In the same year, Backus began itinerating throughout New England. Two years later in April 1748 he was ordained as the permanent minister of a Separatist congregation between Bridgewater and Middleborough, Massachusetts. But less than a year later, he was arrested for not paying taxes for the benefit of the state-supported Congregational church. Once freed, he reorganized his congregation into the First Baptist Church of Middleborough on January 16, 1756, having come to the conclusion that infant baptism was unbiblical. For much of the remainder of his life, he banded together with other Baptists who petitioned the government for relief from paying taxes to state churches. His *Appeal to the Public for Religious Liberty* (1773) stressed religious tolerance and equality, arguing that since Christ's kingdom was "not of this world" it would be impossible to recreate the kind of godly commonwealth that many of the New England Puritans had imagined. Accordingly, the more practical and fairest solution would be to allow Americans to attend, and financially back, the church of their choice. But Backus's opinions were ahead of his time, for the disestablishment of the Congregational church in Connecticut did not take place until 1818, and Massachusetts held out even longer, until 1833.

FIGURE 42.1 Isaac Backus (Detail), courtesy the Franklin Trask Library, Andover Newton Theological School.

An Appeal to the Public for Religious Liberty

We are not insensible that an open appearance against any part of the conduct of men in power, is commonly attended with difficulty and danger; and could we have found any way wherein with clearness we could have avoided the present attempt, we would gladly have taken it. But our blessed Lord & only Redeemer, has commanded us, to *stand fast in the liberty where with he has made us free*; and things appear so to us at present that we cannot see how we can fully obey this command, without refusing any active compliance with some laws about religious affairs that are laid upon us. And as those who are interested against us, often accuse us of complaining unreasonably, we are brought under a necessity of laying open particular facts which otherwise we would gladly have concealed: and all must be sensible that there is a vast difference between exposing the faults, either of individuals or communities, when the cause of truth and equity would suffer without it, and the doing of it without any such occasion. We view it to be our incumbent duty, to render unto Caesar the things that are his, but that it is of as much importance not to render unto him any thing that belongs only to God, who is to be obeyed rather than man. And as it is evident to us, that God always claimed it as his sole prerogative to determine by his own laws, what his worship shall be, who shall minister in it, and how they shall be supported; so it is evident that their prerogative has been, and still is, encroached upon in our land. For,

1. Our legislature claim a power to compel every town and parish within their jurisdiction, to set up and maintain a paedobaptist worship among them; although it is well known, that infant baptism is never express'd in the Bible, only is upheld by men's reasonings, that are chiefly drawn from Abraham's

covenant which the Holy Ghost calls, *The covenant of circumcision*, Acts 7:8. And as circumcision was one of the handwriting of ordinances which Christ has *blotted out*, where did any state ever get any right to compel their subjects to set up a worship upon that covenant?

2. Our ascended Lord gives *gifts unto men* in a sovereign way as seems good unto him, and he requires *Every man, as he has received the gift, even so to minister the same*; and he reproved his apostles when they forbid one who was improving his gift, because he followed not them. 1 Peter 4:10–11. Luke 9:49. But the Massachusetts legislature, while they claim a power to compel each parish to settle a minister, have also determined that he must be one, who has either an academic degree, or a testimonial in his favour from a majority of the ministers in the country where the parish lies. So that let Christ give a man ever so great gifts, yet hereby these ministers derive a noble power from the state, to forbid the improvement of the same, if he follows not their schemes. And if the apostles assumed too much in this respect to themselves, even when their Lord was with them, can it be any breach of charity to conclude that ministers are not out of danger of doing the like now, especially if we consider how interest operates in the affair! For,

3. Though the Lord hath *ordained that they which preach the gospel shall live of the gospel*; or by the free *communications to them*, which his gospel will produce. 1 Corinthians 9:13–14. Galatians 6:6–7. Yet the ministers of our land have chosen to *live by the law*; and as a reason therefor, one of their most noted writers [Cotton Mather], instead of producing any truth of God, recites the tradition of man, who said, "Ministers of the gospel would have a poor time of it, if they must rely on a *free contribution of the people* for their maintenance." And he says, "The laws of the province having had the royal approbation to ratify them, they are the king's laws. By these laws it is enacted, that there shall be a public worship of God in every plantation; that the person elected by the majority of the inhabitants to be so, shall be looked upon as the minister of the place; that the salary for him, which they shall agree upon, shall be levied by a rate upon all the inhabitants. In consequence of this, the minister *thus* chosen by the people, is (not only Christ's but also) in reality, the *king's minister*; and the salary raised for him, is raised in the *king's name*, and is the king's allowance unto him."

Now who can hear Christ declare, that his kingdom is, NOT OF THIS WORLD, and yet believe that this blending of church and state together can be pleasing to him? For though their laws call them "orthodox ministers," yet the grand test of their orthodoxy, is the major vote of the people, be they saints or sinners, believers or unbelievers. This appears plain in the foregoing quotation; and another of their learned writers lately says, "It is the congregation in its parochial congregational capacity, that the *law* considers; and this as such does not enough partake of an ecclesiastical nature to be subject to ecclesiastical jurisdiction."

Hence their ministers and churches must become subject to the court, and to the majority of the parish in order to have their salary raised in the *king's name*: But how are either of them in the mean time subject to the authority of Christ in his church? How can any man reconcile such proceedings to the following commands of our Master which is in heaven? Matthew 23:9–10. What matter of grief and lamentation is it, that men otherwise so knowing and justly esteemed, should by the traditions of men be carried into such a *crooked* way as this is! For though there is a shew of equity in allowing every society to choose its own minister; yet let them be ever so unanimous for one who is of a different *mode* from the court, their choice is not allowed. Indeed as to doctrine ministers who preach differently, yea directly contrary to each other, about Christ and his salvation, yet are supported by these laws which at the same time limit the people to one circumstantial mode...

How essentially and how greatly does this constitution differ, and from the institutions established in God's word, both in their nature and effects?

1. In their *nature*. Here you find that every religious minister in that constitution, is called the king's minister, because he is settled by direction of the king's laws, and the tax for such a minister's support is raised in the king's name, and is called the king's dues: whereas no man in the Jewish church might approach to minister at the holy altar, but such as were *called of God, as was Aaron*: and the means of their support, were such things as God required his people to *offer and consecrate to Him*; and when they withheld the same, he says, *ye have robbed* ME, *even this whole nation*; and it is represented as his peculiar work to reward obedience, and to punish disobedience in such affairs. It is evident from sacred record, that good men in every station, used their influence by word and example to stir up their fellow servants to do their duty toward God in these respects; and good rulers, in conjunction with church-officers, took care to have what was offered to him secured and distributed according to God's commandments. But what is there in all this that can give the least countenance to the late method, of men making laws to determine who shall be Christ's ministers, and to raise money for them in their *own name*! Christ said to the Jews, *I am come in my Father's name, and ye receive me not; if another shall come in his own name, him ye will receive. How can ye believe, which receive honor one of another, and seek not the honor that cometh from* GOD ONLY? John 5:43–4...

2. The *effects* of the constitution of our country are such, that as it makes the majority of the people the test or orthodoxy, so it emboldens them to usurp God's judgment seat, and (according to Dr. Mather's own account, which we have often seen verified) they daringly give out their sentence, That for a *few* to

profess a persuasion different from the *majority*, it must be from bad motives; and that, *they know in their conscience* that they do not act by the universal law of equity, if they plead to be exempted from paying the *money* which the *majority* demand of them! And though in our CHARTER the king grants to all protestants *equal liberty of conscience*: yet for above thirty years after it was received, the Congregationalists made no laws to favour the consciences of any men, in this affair of taxes, but their own sect; and it is here called arbitrary power, and even a forbidding that the king should have his dues, if a governor shewed so much regard to the Charter, as to oppose their extorting money from people of the king's denomination, for their Congregational ministers. And perhaps the learned author now referred to, never delivered a plainer truth, than when he said, "The reforming churches flying from Rome, carried some of them more, some of them less, all of them something of Rome with them, especially in that spirit of *imposition* and *persecution* which too much cleaved to them."

Isaac Backus, *An Appeal to the Public for Religious Liberty, Against the Oppressions of the Present Day* (Boston: John Boyle, 1773), 16–24.

43

A Selection of Poems

Phillis Wheatley

KIDNAPPED FROM AN unknown location in Africa, Phillis Wheatley (1753–84) was forced on board a slave ship and sold to the Boston merchant John Wheatley and his wife, Susannah, in 1761. The Wheatleys named Phillis after the vessel that brought her to America and raised her alongside their older twin children, Mary and Nathaniel. From all accounts, the Wheatleys treated Phillis like a daughter, as opposed to a slave or even a servant. They allowed her to mingle socially with visiting guests and did not require her to do the household chores normally reserved for working females. Phillis quickly learned to read and write, displaying an affinity for classical literature and poetry. Growing up in an evangelical home, Phillis embraced Christianity and the revivalist preaching of George Whitefield in particular. Through Susannah's network, Phillis was introduced to American and British evangelicals like Samuel Hopkins, John Moorhead, Samson Occom, Obour Tanner, and the Countess of Huntingdon, many of whom she maintained correspondences with independently.

As Phillis's writing matured, the Wheatleys made arrangements to publish a book of her poetry. With the Countess of Huntingdon patronizing the young author, Archibald Bell of London agreed to publish Wheatley's *Poems on Various Subjects, Religious and Moral* in 1773. The end product, dedicated to Lady Huntingdon, offered nearly forty poems and included a frontispiece portrait of Phillis, a luxury addendum unprecedented at that time for a black author. Much of her work exhibits a Calvinistic dependence on God's grace, deterring her readers from relying on human wisdom alone. In her poem "On Virtue," probably composed in 1766, Phillis argues that classical virtue is incomparable with the kind of morality that authentic Christianity produces. Other poems are linked with specific events, such as "To the King's Most Excellent Majesty," which praises George III for repealing the Stamp Act. Most critics agree that her most notorious poem is "On Being Brought from Africa to America" since at first glance it appears to condone the Atlantic slave trade. In the controversial piece, Wheatley views

<small>FIGURE</small> 43.1 Phillis Wheatley (Detail), courtesy of the Library of Congress, LC-USZC4-5316.

her capture in Africa as providentially providing the means by which she comes to faith in Christianity. Not necessarily justifying slavery, Wheatley was simply claiming that good can come out of evil. Perhaps her most influential work was her elegy of George Whitefield, written only eleven days after his death. Originally published separately in 1770, "On the Death of the Rev. Mr. George Whitefield" went through five editions in the eighteenth century and alerted the transatlantic world to the talents of an aspiring literary genius.

The *Boston Post-Boy* published Wheatley's "A Farewell to America. To Mrs. S.W." while she was traveling to Britain. It appeared again in her *Poems on Various Subjects, Religious and Moral.* The poem recounts a tearful departure between Phillis and Susannah Wheatley and looks forward to time spent in England. There are hints, however, that besides recovering from an apparent physical ailment Phillis might have had plans to gain her freedom in Britain. Wheatley arrived in England on the anniversary of a landmark case in which Lord Chief Justice William Murray, first earl of Mansfield, ruled that the Virginia slave James Somerset could not legally be forced to return to the colonies enslaved. The decision effectively granted freedom to slaves once they stepped foot on English soil. We cannot be sure that Phillis intended self-manumission, but regardless she convinced Nathaniel Wheatley, her traveling companion and the person who ran the family business, to promise her freedom once harboring at Boston in September 1773.

Now on her own, and without the financial support of a master, Phillis found it difficult to provide for herself, even though the Wheatleys most likely permitted her to live with them. But once Susannah died on March 29, 1773, and John, five years later on March 12, 1778, and perhaps in order to gain social stability, Phillis married the purportedly irresponsible free black merchant John Peters. As

Peters dug himself deeper into debt, Phillis and her husband struggled to make ends meet. The poor timing and expensive format of her anticipated second book virtually guaranteed its failure. The 1779 subscription proposal led to nothing, for the book never saw the light of day. Although famous in her lifetime, and achieving great literary success, her final years were obscure and plagued with financial uncertainty. She died on December 5, 1784, and was laid to rest in an unmarked grave in Boston.

"On Virtue"

O Thou bright jewel in my aim I strive
To comprehend thee. Thine own words declare
Wisdom is higher than a fool can reach.
I cease to wonder, and no more attempt
Thine height t' explore, or fathom thy profound.
But, O my soul, sink not into despair,
Virtue is near thee, and with gentle hand
Would now embrace thee, hovers o'er thine head.
Fain would the heav'n-born soul with her converse,
Then seek, then court her for her promis'd bliss.

Auspicious queen, thine heav'nly pinions spread,
And lead celestial Chastity along;
Lo! now her sacred retinue descends,
Array'd in glory from the orbs above.
Attend me, Virtue, thro' my youthful years!
O leave me not to the false joys of time!
But guide my steps to endless life and bliss.
Greatness, or Goodness, say what I shall call thee,
To give an higher appellation still,
Teach me a better strain, a nobler lay,
O thou, enthron'd with Cherubs in the realms of day!

"To the KING's Most Excellent Majesty, 1768"

YOUR subjects hope, dread Sire—
The crown upon your brows may flourish long,
And that your arm may in your God be strong!
O may your sceptre num'rous nations sway,
And all with love and readiness obey!

But how shall we the British king reward!

Rule thou in peace, our father, and our lord!
 Midst the remembrance of thy favours past,
 The meanest peasants most admire the last
 May George, belov'd by all the nations round,
 Live with heav'ns choicest constant blessings crown'd!
 Great God, direct, and guard him from on high,
 And from his head let ev'ry evil fly!
 And may each clime with equal gladness see
 A monarch's smile can set his subjects free!

"On Being Brought from Africa to America"

  'Twas mercy brought me from my Pagan land,
 Taught my benighted soul to understand
 That there's a God, that there's a Saviour too:
 Once I redemption neither sought nor knew.
 Some view our sable race with scornful eye,
 "Their colour is a diabolic die."
 Remember, Christians, Negros, black as Cain,
 May be refin'd, and join th' angelic train.

"On the Death of the Rev. Mr. GEORGE WHITEFIELD, 1770"

  HAIL, happy saint, on thine immortal throne,
 Possest of glory, life, and bliss unknown;
 We hear no more the music of thy tongue,
 Thy wonted auditories cease to throng.
 Thy sermons in unequall'd accents flow'd,
 And ev'ry bosom with devotion glow'd;
 Thou didst in strains of eloquence refin'd
 Inflame the heart, and captivate the mind.
 Unhappy we the setting sun deplore,
 So glorious once, but ah! it shines no more.

  Behold the prophet in his tow'ring flight!
 He leaves the earth for heav'n's unmeasur'd height,
 And worlds unknown receive him from our sight.
 There Whitefield wings with rapid course his way,
 And sails to Zion through vast seas of day.
 Thy pray'rs, great saint, and thine incessant cries

Have pierc'd the bosom of thy native skies.
 Thou moon hast seen, and all the stars of light,
How he has wrestled with his God by night.
He pray'd that grace in ev'ry heart might dwell,
He long'd to see America excel;
He charg'd its youth that ev'ry grace divine
Should with full lustre in their conduct shine;
That Saviour, which his soul did first receive,
The greatest gift that ev'n a God can give,
He freely offer'd to the num'rous throng,
That on his lips with list'ning pleasure hung.

     "Take him, ye wretched, for your only good,
Take him ye starving sinners, for your food;
Ye thirsty, come to this life-giving stream,
Ye preachers, take him for your joyful theme;
Take him my dear Americans, he said,
Be your complaints on his kind bosom laid:
Take him, ye Africans, he longs for you,
Impartial Saviour is his title due:
Wash'd in the fountain of redeeming blood,
You shall be sons, and kings, and priests to God."

     Great Countess, we Americans revere
Thy name, and mingle in thy grief sincere;
New England deeply feels, the Orphans mourn,
Their more than father will no more return.

     But, though arrested by the hand of death,
Whitefield no more exerts his lab'ring breath,
Yet let us view him in th' eternal skies,
Let ev'ry heart to this bright vision rise;
While the tomb safe retains its sacred trust,
Till life divine re-animates his dust.

"A Farewell to AMERICA. To Mrs. S.W."

I.

ADIEU, New-England's smiling meads,
   Adieu, the flow'ry plain:
I leave thine op'ning charms, O spring,
   And tempt the roaring main

II.

In vain for me the flow'rets rise,
And boast their gaudy pride,
While here beneath the northern skies
I mourn for health *deny'd.*

III.

Celestial maid of rosy hue,
O let me feel thy reign!
I languish till thy face I view,
Thy vanish'd joys regain.

IV.

Susannah *mourns, nor can I bear*
To see the crystal show'r,
Or mark the tender falling tear
At sad departure's hour;

V.

Not unregarding can I see
Her soul with grief opprest:
But let no sighs, no groans for me,
Steal from her pensive breast.

VI.

In vain the feather'd warblers sing,
In vain the garden blooms,
And on the bosom of the spring
Breathes out her sweet perfumes,

VII.

While for Britannia's *distant shore*
We sweep the liquid plain,
And with astonish'd eyes explore
The wide-extended main.

VIII.

Lo! Health *appears! celestial dame!*
Complacent and serene,
With Hebe's *mantle o'er her Frame,*
With soul-delighting mein.

IX.

To mark the vale where London *lies*
   With misty vapours crown'd,
Which cloud Aurora's *thousand dyes,*
   And veil her charms around,

X.

Why Phoebus, *moves thy car so slow?*
   So slow thy rising ray?
Give us the famous town to view,
   Thou glorious king of day!

XI.

For thee, Britannia, *I resign*
   New-England's *smiling fields;*
To view again her charms divine,
   What joy the prospect yields!

XII.

But thou! Temptation hence away,
   With all thy fatal train
Nor once seduce my soul away,
   By thine enchanting strain.

XIII.

Thrice happy they, whose heav'nly shield
   Secures their souls from harms,
And fell Temptation *on the field*
   Of all its pow'r disarms!

Phillis Wheatley, *Poems on Various Subjects, Religious and Moral. By Phillis Wheatley, Negro Servant to Mr. John Wheatley, of Boston, in New England* (London: A. Bell, 1773), 13–4, 17–8, 22–4, 119–22.

44

Practical Disinterested Benevolence

Samuel Hopkins

SAMUEL HOPKINS (1721–1803) joins Joseph Bellamy as one of the two lead-ing intellectual disciples of Jonathan Edwards. Hopkins graduated from Yale in 1741 at the peak of the Great Awakening, having been converted as the revival swept across New England and beyond. Moving on from Yale, he studied briefly with Edwards at his household in Northampton to prepare for his ministry as a Congregationalist clergyman. After his private studies with Edwards, Hopkins secured a pastorate at Housatonic (renamed Great Barrington in 1761), in south-western Massachusetts where he ministered for some twenty-five years. Conflict with parishioners over his salary eventually led to his dismissal in early 1769. But he quickly recovered from this setback and in 1770 was invited to become the pas-tor of the First Congregational Church in Newport, Rhode Island, a large port city known for its flourishing slave trade.

Although wanting to be faithful to Edwards's teachings, Hopkins differed with his mentor on some significant theological points. In his posthumous *Dissertation Concerning the Nature of True Virtue* (1765), Edwards had described true virtue as "benevolence to Being in general." Hopkins sought to clarify some of Edwards's seemingly abstract language as well as promote a theology that had a more sig-nificant practical application. In Hopkins's *Inquiry into the Nature of True Holiness* (1773), and in later works, he stressed "disinterested benevolence" whereby a person selflessly submitted to the divine will to the point of being willing to be damned for God's glory. This theory of disinterested benevolence was put to the test when Hopkins relocated to Newport.

Prior to moving to Rhode Island, Hopkins owned a female slave, remaining indifferent to the evils of the slave trade that thrived less than two hundred miles away from Great Barrington. At this time, Newport was the commercial center of the slave trade in New England and the site of three-quarters of the rum distilleries

FIGURE 44.1 Samuel Hopkins (Detail), Print Collection, Miriam and Ira D. Wallach Division of Art, Prints and Photographs, the New York Public Library, Astor, Lenox and Tilden Foundations.

in Rhode Island. Within a few years of his arrival to the city, and after witnessing the brutal conditions of chained Africans bought and sold in plain sight, he changed his mind on slavery, writing his *Dialogue, Concerning the Slave Trade* in the spring of 1776, months before the signing of the Declaration of Independence. In his *Dialogue*, Hopkins put forward what must have been the natural outcome of his theory of disinterested benevolence: love toward all human beings. Although employing patriarchal language, his portrayal of slavery as morally and biblically antithetical to Christian ideals set him apart from many of the city's professing believers.

Hopkins certainly was not the first New Englander to write about the sin of slavery. Around the beginning of the eighteenth century, the Puritans Samuel Sewall and Cotton Mather voiced their concerns in such notable works as *The Selling of Joseph* (1700) and *The Negro Christianized* (1706), respectively; and at midcentury the Quaker John Woolman completed *Some Considerations on the Keeping of Negroes* (1753). Other New Divinity men—Jonathan Edwards Jr. and Levi Hart—also penned antislavery propaganda at about the same time as Hopkins's *Dialogue*. It comes across as surprising then that Hopkins initially felt alone in his struggle against the avaricious trade. Writing to Granville Sharp on January 15, 1789, he bemoaned that early on in his campaign he was, "so far as I then knew, almost alone in my opposition to the slave trade and the slavery of the Africans." Where Hopkins separated himself from the pack is in the thoroughness of his argument against slavery and his use of the concept of disinterested benevolence to draw attention to the selfishness of holding humans in bondage.

A Dialogue, Concerning the Slavery of Africans

A. SIR, What do you think of the motion made by some among us, to free all our
    African slaves?—They say, that our holding these blacks in slavery, as we do,
    is an open violation of the law of God, and is so great an instance of unrigh-
    teousness and cruelty, that we cannot expect deliverance from present calami-
    ties, and success in our struggle for liberty in the *American* colonies, until we
    repent, and make all the restitution in our power. For my part, I think they
    carry things much too far on this head; and if any thing might be done for the
    freedom of our slaves, this is not a proper time to attend to it, while we are in
    such a state of war and distress, and public affairs of much greater importance
    demand all our attention, and the utmost exertion of the public.

B. Sir, I am glad you have introduced this subject, especially, as you own a num-
    ber of these slaves; I shall attend to it with pleasure, and offer my sentiments
    upon it freely, expecting you will as freely propose the objections you shall have
    against any thing I shall advance. And I take leave here to observe, that if the
    slavery in which we hold the blacks, is wrong; it is a very great and public sin;
    and therefore a sin which God is now testifying against in the calamities he
    has brought upon us, consequently must be reformed, before we can reason-
    ably expect deliverance, or even sincerely ask for it. It would be worse than
    madness then, to put off attention to this matter under the notion of attending
    to more important affairs. This is acting like the mariner, who, when his leaky
    ship is filling with water, neglects to stop the leak or ply the pump, that he may
    mend his sails. There are at the lowest computation, 800,000 slaves in *British
    America*, including the *West-India* islands; and above half a million of these
    are in the colonies on the continent. And if this is in every instance wrong,
    unrighteousness and oppression; it must be a very great and crying sin, there
    being nothing of the kind equal to it on the face of the earth. There are but few
    of these slaves indeed in *New-England*, compared with the vast numbers in
    the islands & the southern colonies; and they are treated much better on the
    continent, and especially among us, than they are in the *West-Indies*. But if it
    be all wrong, and real oppression of the poor helpless blacks, we, by refusing
    to break this yoke, and let these injured captives go free, do practically justify
    and support this slavery in general, and make ourselves, in a measure at least,
    answerable for the whole: and we have no way to exculpate ourselves from the
    guilt of the whole, and bear proper testimony against this great evil, but by
    freeing all our slaves. Surely then this matter admits of no delay, but demands
    our first, and most serious attention, and speedy reformation.

A. I acknowledge the *slave trade*, as it has been carried on with the *Africans*, can-
    not be justified. But I am not yet convinced that 'tis wrong to keep those in
    perpetual bondage, who by this trade have been transported from *Africa* to us,

and are become our slaves. If I viewed this in the light you do, I should agree with you that 'tis of the highest importance that they should all be made free without delay; as we could not expect the favor of heaven, or with any consistency ask it, so long as they are held in bondage.

B. I am glad you have attended to the affair so much as to be convinced of the unrighteousness of the slave trade. Indeed, this conviction has been so spread of late, that it has reached at most all men on the continent, except some of those who are too deeply interested in it to admit the light, which condemns it. And it has now but few advocates, I believe, being generally condemned and exploded. And the members of the Continental Congress have done themselves much honor, in advising the *American* colonies to drop this trade entirely; and resolving not to buy another slave, that shall be imported from *Africa*.

But I think it of importance that this trade should not only be condemned as wrong, but attentively considered in its real nature, and in all its shocking attendants and circumstances, which will lead us to think of it with a detestation and horror which this scene of inhumanity, oppression and cruelty, exceeding every thing of the kind that has ever been perpetrated by the sons of men, is suited to excite; and awaken us to a proper indignation against the authors of this violence and outrage done to their fellow men; and to feelings of humanity and pity towards our brethren, who are the miserable sufferers. Therefore, tho' I am not able to paint this horrid scene of barbarity and complicated iniquity, to the life, or even to tell the one half which may be told, in the short time allotted for this conversation; yet I will suggest a few particulars; leaving you, if you please, to consult the authors who have given a more particular description.

Most of the *Africans* are in a state of heathenism; and sunk down into that ignorance and barbarity into which mankind naturally fall when destitute of divine revelation. Their lands are fertile, and produce all the necessaries of life, the inhabitants are divided into many distinct nations or clans; and of course are frequently entering into quarrels, and open war with each other. The *Europeans, English, French, Dutch,* &c. have carried on a trade with them for above 100 years; and have taken advantage of their ignorance and barbarity, to persuade them to enter into the inhuman practice of selling one another to the *Europeans*, for the commodities which they carry to them, most of which, they stand in no real need of: but might live as well, or better without them: particularly spirituous liquors, which have been carried to them in great quantities, by the *Americans*. They by this means have tempted and excited the poor blacks to make war upon one another, in order to get captives, spreading distress, devastation and destruction over a vast country; by which many millions have perished: and millions of others, have been captured, and sold to the *Europeans & Americans*, into a state of slavery, much worse than death. And the inhabitants of the towns near the sea, are taught to exert all the art and power they have to entrap and decoy one another, that they may make slaves of them, and sell them to us for rum, by which they intoxicate them selves, and become more brutish and savage than otherwise they could be, so that there are but few instances of sobriety, honesty, or even humanity, in these towns on the sea, to which the *Europeans* have access: and they who live the furthest from these places, are the least vicious, and much more civil and humane.

They stand in no need of the rum that is carried there in such vast quantities, by which so many thousands have been enslaved, and which has spread such infinite mischief among them. And I leave it with you to consider to what a dreadful degree the *Americans* have by this abominable practice, bro't the curse upon them, pronounced by an inspired prophet; and how very applicable it is to this case. "Woe unto him that giveth his neighbour drink: that puttest thy bottle to him, and makest him drunken also, that thou mayest look on their nakedness." And is not this curse evidently come upon us, in a dreadful degree, in such a way, as to paint itself out, so that he who runs may read it? We have put the bottle to our neighbours mouths, by carrying immense quantities of rum to them, and enticed them to drink, that we might take advantage of their weakness, and thereby gratify our lusts. By this means multitudes of them have been enslaved, and carried to the *West-Indies* islands, there to be kept to hard labour, and treated ten thousand times worse than dogs. In consequence of which, incredible quantities of rum, and molasses which has been distilled into rum among ourselves, have been imported; the most of which is consumed in intemperance and drunkenness in such a dreadful degree, as to exceed any thing of the kind in any part of the world; by which thousands, yea millions, have ruined themselves, body and soul, forever. Let any one consider this, and forbear to confess, if he can, that this woe has fallen heavily upon us, and that in such a way and connection as to point out the sinful cause.

But to return. This trade has been carried on for a century and more, and for many years past, above an hundred thousand have been brought off the coast in a year, so that many, many millions have been torn from their native country, their acquaintance, relations and friends, and most of them put into a state of slavery, both themselves, and their children forever, if they shall have any posterity, much worse than death. When numbers of these wretched creatures are collected by the savages, they are bro't into the public market to be sold, all naked as they were born. The more than savage slave merchant views them, and sends his surgeon, more particularly to examine them, as to the soundness of their limbs, their age, &c. All that are passed as fit for sale, are branded with a hot iron in some part of their body, with the buyers mark; and then confined, crowded together in some close hold, till a convenient time to put them on board a ship. When they are bro't on board, all are immediately put in irons, except some of the women perhaps, and the small children, where they are so crowded together in that hot climate, that commonly a considerable number die on their passage to the West-Indies, occasioned partly by their confinement, partly by the grief and vexation of their minds, from the treatment they receive, and the situation in which they find themselves. And a number commonly die after they arrive at the *West-Indies*, in seasoning to the climate, so that commonly not above seventy in an hundred survive their transportation; by which means about thirty thousand are murdered every year by this slave trade, which amounts to three million in a century. When they are brought to the *West-Indies*, they are again exposed to market, as if they were so many beasts, and sold to the highest bidder; where again they are separated according to the humour of the traders, without any regard to their friendships or relations, of husbands and wives, parents and children, brothers and sisters, &c. being torn from each other, without the least regard to any thing of this kind, and sent to different places, without any prospect of seeing each other again. They are then put under task-masters, by the purchasing planter, who appoints them their work, and rules over them with rigor and cruelty, following them with his cruel whip, or appointing one to do it, if possible, more cruel than himself. The infirm and feeble, the females, and even those who are pregnant, or have infants to take care of, must do their task in the field equally with the rest; or if they fall behind, may be sure to feel the lash of their unmerciful driver. Their allowance of food at the same time is very coarse and scant, and must be cooked by themselves, if cooked at all, when they want to be asleep. And often they have no food but what they procure for themselves, by working on the Sabbath; for that is the only time they have to themselves. And to make any complaint, or petition for relief, will expose them to some severe punishment, if not a cruel death. The least real or supposable crimes in them, are punished in the most cruel manner. And they have no relief; there being no appeal from their master's sentence and will, who commonly are more like savage beasts, than rational, humane creatures. And to petition for liberty, tho' in the most humble and modest terms, is as much as their lives are worth; as few escape the most cruel death, who presume to hint any thing of this kind to their masters: It being a maxim with those more than cruel tyrants, that the only way to keep them under, and prevent their thinking of the sweets of liberty, is punish the least intimation of it in the severest manner, as the most intolerable affront and insult on their masters. Their labour is so hard, and their diet so scant and poor, and they are treated in all respects with such oppression and cruelty, that they do not increase by propagation in the islands, but constantly decrease, so that every planter must every year at least purchase five to every hundred he has on his plantation, in order to keep his number from diminishing.

But it is in vain to attempt a full description of the oppression and cruel treatment these poor creatures receive constantly at the hands of their imperious, unmerciful, worse than *Egyptian*, taskmasters. Words cannot alter it. Volumes might be wrote, and not give a detail of a thousandth part of the shockingly cruel things they have suffered, and are constantly suffering. Nor can they possibly be conceived of by any one, who has not been an eye witness. And how little a part does he see! They who are witnesses to any part of this horrid scene of barbarous oppression, cannot but feel the truth and propriety of *Solomon's* words, "So I returned, and considered all the oppressions that are done under the sun: and behold the tears of the oppressed, and they had no comforter; and on the side of the oppressors there was power; but they had no comforter. Wherefore I praised the dead, which are already dead, more than the living which are yet alive." *Solomon* never saw any oppression like this, unless he looked forward to this very instance in the spirit of prophecy.

A. Sir, There is one important circumstance in favor of the slave trade; or which will at least serve to counterbalance many of the evils you mention, and that is, we bring these slaves from a heathen land, to places of gospel light; and so put them under special advantages to be saved.

B. I know this has been mentioned by many in favor of the slave trade: but when examined, will turn greatly against it. It can hardly be said with truth, that the *West-India* islands are places of gospel light. But if they were, are the Negroes in the least benefitted by it? Have they any access to the gospel? Have they the least instruction, more than if they were beasts? So far from this, that their masters guard against their having any instruction to their utmost; and if any one would attempt any such thing, it would be at the risk of his life. And all the poor creatures learn of Christianity, from what they see in those who call themselves Christians, only serves to prejudice them to the highest degree against the Christian religion. For they not only see the abominably wicked lives of most of those who are called Christians; but are constantly oppressed by them, and receive as cruel treatment from them, as they could from the worst of beings. And as to those who are brought to the continent, in the southern colonies, and even to *New-England*, so little pains are taken to instruct them, and there is so much to prejudice them against Christianity, that it is a very great wonder, and owing to an extraordinary divine interposition, in which we may say, God goes out of his common way, that any of them should think favorably of Christianity, and cordially embrace it. As to the most of them, no wonder they are unteachable, and get no good by the gospel; but have imbibed the deepest prejudices against it, from the treatment they receive from professed Christians; prejudices which most of them are by their circumstances restrained from expressing; while they are fixed in the strongest degree in their minds.

But if this was not the case, and all the slaves brought from *Africa*, were put under the best advantages to become Christians, and they were in circumstances that tended to give them the most favorable idea of Christians, and the religion they profess; and tho' all concerned in this trade, and in slavery in general, should have this wholly in view, viz. their becoming Christians, by which they should be eternally happy; yet this would not justify the slave-trade, or continuing them in a state of slavery: For to take this method to Christianize them, would be a direct and gross violation of the laws of Christ. He commands us to go and preach the gospel to all nations; to carry the gospel to them, and not to go, and with violence bring them from their native country, without saying a word to them, or to the nations from whom they are taken, about the gospel, or any thing that relates to it.

If the *Europeans* and *Americans* had been as much engaged to Christianize the *Africans*, as they have been to enslave them; and had been at half the cost and pains to introduce the gospel among them, that they have to captivate and destroy them; we have all the reason in the world to conclude that extensive country, containing such a vast multitude of inhabitants, would have been full of gospel light, and the many nations there, civilized and made happy; and a foundation laid for the salvation of millions of millions; and the happy instruments of it have been rewarded ten thousand fold for all their labour and expence. But now, instead of this, what has been done on the coast, by those who pass among the Negroes for Christians, has only served to produce and spread the greatest and most deep-rooted prejudices against the Christian religion, and bar the way to that which is above all things desirable, their coming to the knowledge of the truth that they might be saved. So that while, by the murdering or enslaving millions of millions, they have brought a curse on themselves, and on all that partake with them, they have injured in the highest degree innumerable nations, and done what they could to prevent their salvation, and to fasten them down in ignorance and barbarity to the latest posterity!—Who can realize all this, and not feel a mixture of grief, pity, indignation and horror, truly ineffable! And must he not be filled with zeal to do his utmost to put a speedy stop to this seven-headed monster of iniquity, with all the horrid train of evils with which it is attended.

And can any one consider all these things, and yet pretend to justify the slave-trade, or the slavery of the *Africans* in *America*? Is it not impossible, that a real Christian, who has attended to all this, should have any hand in this trade? And it requires the utmost stretch of charity to suppose that any one ever did, or can buy or sell an African slave, with a sincere view to make a true Christian of him.

Samuel Hopkins, *A Dialogue, Concerning the Slavery of the Africans; Shewing it To Be the Duty and Interest of the American Colonies to Emancipate All Their African Slaves* (Norwich: Judah P. Spooner, 1776), 5–14.

45

Amazing Grace (How Sweet the Sound)

John Newton

IN ADDITION TO his preaching, John Newton devoted considerable time to hymn writing. As early as 1763, he began writing lyrics. Once he moved to Olney, he devoted more time to developing his poetic talent. When his friend William Cowper relocated to Olney in 1767, the two commenced working on a collaborative project that they intended to publish one day. Cowper's lyrical contributions diminished, however, when he suffered from a serious bout of depression in 1773. But Newton forged ahead with several of his own hymns which he added to Cowper's earlier compositions, publishing the corpus as *Olney Hymns* in 1779.

Newton's sermons often originated from the lyrics of his hymns. He typically preserved the meters of early eighteenth-century English hymnody representative in the work of Isaac Watts, as opposed to the more radical altercations employed by Charles Wesley and other evangelicals in the latter half of the century. Newton intended to speak to a wide audience and not simply to the elite and highly educated. In his quest to appeal to the masses, he nevertheless hoped that his hymns would not be viewed with disdain by the higher ranks. Newton's hymns also contain a personal element. The use of "I" and "me" sheds light on the struggles and spiritual elations that he experienced at particular points in his life. In "Faith's Review and Expectation," also known as "Amazing Grace," he peppered the six stanzas with personal pronouns that signaled his overwhelming joy for divine grace which saved "a wretch like me" and brought sight to his once spiritually blind eyes. The hymn itself begins with a reference to 1 Chronicles 17:16–7, describing King David's ecstatic response to the Prophet Nathan's announcement that God promised to establish an eternal kingdom from his line. Newton's tone of amazement in God's grace towards him parallels David's experience: both can hardly believe that God singled them out for such divine favor. Although the tune most associated with "Amazing Grace" was added in 1835 and based on the music from a song called "New Britain," Newton can be credited with writing the most recognized folk hymn of all time.

"Faith's Review and Expectation"

1. *Amazing grace (how sweet the sound)*
     That sav'd a wretch like me!
I once was lost, but now am found,
     Was blind, but now I see.

2. *'Twas grace that taught my heart to fear,*
     And grace my fears reliev'd;
How precious did that grace appear,
     The hour I first believ'd!

3. *Thro' many dangers, toils and snares,*
     I have already come;
 'Tis grace has brought me safe thus far,
     And grace will lead me home.

4. *The LORD has promis'd good to me,*
     His word my hope secures;
He will my shield and portion be,
     As long as life endures.

5. *Yes, when this flesh and heart shall fail,*
     And mortal life shall cease;
I shall possess, within the veil,
     A life of joy and peace.

6. *The earth shall soon dissolve like snow,*
     The sun forbear to shine;
But GOD, who call'd me here below,
     Will be for ever mine.

John Newton and William Cowper, *Olney Hymns, in Three Books* (London: W. Oliver, 1779), 53–4.

46

A Baptist's Beliefs

John Ryland Jr.

JOHN RYLAND JR. (1753–1825) is a neglected but important transitional figure among eighteenth-century English Baptists. His father, the English Baptist minister John Collett Ryland, raised his son in the High Calvinist tradition. A precocious boy, the young Ryland reportedly could read parts of the Bible in Hebrew at age five and the entire New Testament in Greek by the time he turned nine. Three years after his baptism at age fourteen, he delivered his first public sermon. In 1781, at the age of twenty-eight, he took on the role of co-pastor at his father's Baptist church in Northampton, England, and in 1786 became the sole minister when his father moved to Enfield, north of London.

The more Ryland studied the scriptures and theology, the more he questioned the High Calvinism of the previous generation of Baptists under the leadership of John Gill and John Brine which taught that the gospel need not be preached to unbelievers since God would convert those he had elected regardless of anyone's evangelization efforts. During his youth, a few key mentors guided him to a more moderate form of Calvinism that stressed the proclamation of the gospel to all people. The Anglican evangelical clergyman John Newton counseled Ryland throughout their running correspondence between 1774 and 1807, and a second mentor came from Robert Hall Sr., the Baptist minister at Arnesby, who argued in his *Help to Zion's Travellers* (1781) that reprobation was not a fixed state, and that anyone could seek eternal salvation. Perhaps the most significant influence on Ryland's theological development came from studying the writings of Jonathan Edwards. In 1784, Ryland received Edwards's *Humble Attempt to Promote the Explicit Agreement and Visible Union of God's People in Extraordinary Prayer* by post from his Scottish correspondent, John Erskine of Edinburgh. From reading Jonathan Edwards, Ryland, along with his Northamptonshire Baptist friends, Andrew Fuller and John Sutcliff, resolved to meet regularly to pray for revival in England and later in 1792 forged the Baptist Missionary Society with the intent of spreading the gospel abroad. In 1793 Ryland relocated to Bristol to become the

FIGURE 46.1 John Ryland, Jr. (Detail), courtesy of the National Portrait Gallery, London.

president of Bristol Baptist Academy as well as minister of Broadmead Baptist Church. As president of a Baptist college, he trained roughly 200 students during his tenure, teaching courses in Hebrew, Greek, Latin, theology, church history, rhetoric, and logic. He remained in Bristol until his death on May 25, 1825.

Ryland published several sermons during his lifetime and was an avid hymn writer. He also left behind a considerable number of manuscripts. One of the manuscripts held at Bristol Baptist College is his "Confession of Faith" which he delivered at his ordination in Northampton at the College Lane Chapel on June 8, 1781. In the twenty-two pages of manuscript text, Ryland argues for the existence of God, the depravity of humanity, the Bible as God's revelation, the Trinity, the sacrificial death of Jesus Christ, communion as a commemorative meal of Christ's sufferings, and baptism by immersion. Although not all eighteenth-century Christians would have agreed with Ryland's Baptist confession, it nevertheless outlines most of the doctrines that early evangelicals believed.

"A Confession of Faith Delivered by John Ryland Junior of Northampton at His Ordination to the Pastoral Care of the Church in College Lane"

I am not convinced of The Existence of God, by the same immediate and sensible Consciousness which convinces me of my own Existence, but yet I am quite as sure of it. And I believe that nothing but a faulty Disposition of heart cou'd prevent any rational creature from perceiving his Excellence, and choosing Him as the supreme Good. But if I had no other proof of my own Depravity and that of Mankind in general than this, that I feel in myself, and perceive in all around me, a native Indisposition to seek after God, it wou'd be a sufficient Evidence of our Sinfulness and Degeneracy from that Estate in which rational Creatures must needs have been originally framed.

This being the Case, tho apostate Rebels cou'd *not* have any Claim upon God for any *Revelation* (except a Revelation of his Wrath and Vengeance) and tho the *Light of Nature* would have been sufficient to leave the whole World *without Excuse*, for their impious Dissaffection to the divine Character and Disobedience to the divine Will, yet I believe that it wou'd have been absolutely impossible for Sinners to have entertained the least well grounded hope of happiness without a Revelation, and I believe that their corrupt Inclinations, sinful Prejudices, and criminal Aversion to retain God in their Knowledge wou'd have dreadfully prevented their entertaining clear, consistent or impressive Ideas of those various Truths which the Works of God, and the exercise of Reason wou'd presently discover to any Creature who was free from a sordid sensual and criminal Bias.

But I rejoice in the firm Belief of the *Scriptures of Truth* being truly and certainly a Revelation from God. I believe that the Inspiration and divine Authority of the Bible is most clearly demonstrated by *external* Evidence, arising from The Miracles wro't in its Confirmation before unnumbered Enemies. The exact and punctual Fulfillment of Prophecies thro successive Ages. The moral Character of the Penmen, and of the incarnate Savior. The wonderful Preservation of these sacred writings amidst the most desperate Attempts to destroy them. The general Enmity and Opposition made to their Authority by bad Men. The blessed Instrumentality thereof in the Conversion of Men's hearts and the Reformation of their lives. The Support and Consolation administered thereby to Millions of the Servants and Martyrs of Christ in Trouble, Persecution and Death. These and a blessed Variety of other Arguments justly confirm my Faith, and fully confute the pretended Arguments of ungrateful Infidels against this God-breath'd Book. But especially the *internal* Evidence of the truth and divinity of the Scripture affords me the highest Satisfaction. Its Sublimity, Consistency and above all its Purity ascertain its Author. The display of the divine Glory, Perfections and Purposes evince it to have been dictated by that Spirit who searcheth all Things even the deep Things of God. Its Discovery of the human heart proves it to be the Production of one whose omniscient Eye reads the secrets of ev'ry Bosom. Its mysterious but transcendently glorious Plan of Redemption, whereby God is so highly glorified in all his harmonizing Perfections, Law honored, Sin condemned, Satan defeated and Sinners bro't back to God and to the Enjoyment of all possible Good cou'd never have been devised by created Wisdom. While the exceeding great and precious Promises afford such abundant Consolation to the Soul, and its holy Precepts cast such divine Light on the whole Path of Duty, that I might more reasonably question whether my food ever yielded nourishment to my body or whether the Sun ever enlightened my Eyes, than whether this is the very Word of God and therefore I cou'd more readily believe that the Devil made the World, or that cunning Men invented the Sun and placed it in the Sky, than that either Men or Devils made the Bible...

I believe that God is a spiritual, eternal, self existent, independent and unchangeable Being—possessed of all possible Excellencies natural and moral—that he is omnipotent, omnipresent and omniscient—infinitely great, glorious and amiable in Holiness, Justice, Goodness and Truth. I believe that he is infinitely blessed, being self-sufficient to his own Happiness—that he is the first Cause and last End of all Things—that he is the supreme Good, and is all sufficient for the Happiness of his Creatures and for the Government of the Universe.

I believe upon his Testimony who is best acquainted with his own Nature, the Unity of the Godhead and at the same Time the true proper and equal Divinity of the FATHER, the SON and the HOLY SPIRIT—ascribing with the Scripture the very same Perfections to the SON and divine SPIRIT in the same Sense and equal Extent as to the FATHER, as well as attributing to them Works equally honorable and glorious. It wou'd ill become me who cannot explain how my Body, Soul and Spirit are one Man, to attempt explaining how the three that bear record in Heaven are one God. But surely I shou'd act a most irrational Part, when there are mysteries to me inexplicable in every creature around me, to refuse my Assent to God's Account of himself because I cannot understand the Essence of my Maker. It seems to me the greatest of Absurdities to suppose there shou'd be nothing mysterious in the Nature of God, when there is so much of Mystery in every thing else...

I believe that the first Man being created in God's own Image, was righteously and graciously appointed the common Head of his Posterity. That the great JeHoVaH had an undoubted Right to establish such a Constitution, it being holy, just and in its own Nature suited to the general Good of Mankind. But our first Father and public Head being left to the Freedom of his own Will violated the Covenant of Works, and forfeited the divine Favor, lost the divine Image and exposed the whole race of his Posterity to the righteous Curse of the Law.

I believe that human Nature is universally and entirely depraved, that we all come into the World under the Guilt of Adam's first sin, devoid of original Righteousness, and of all right Disposition to love and serve God, that we go astray from the Womb, and have no native Inclination to seek after God or return to him but the carnal Mind is enmity against God is not subject to his Law neither indeed can it be. Tho at the same Time we continue to be justly held under the Law, are wholly to blame for our want of conformity to it, nor is there any reason why the Law shou'd be altered or shou'd make any Allowances in our Favor on account of our Disinclination to obey, or the badness of our hearts. Hence I believe that as there is none righteous no not one, so by the deeds of the Law no man can be justified.

I believe that God is *infinitely amiable* in himself, his Character is the Perfection of Beauty without a single Blemish, and at the same Time he is the gracious Giver of unnumber'd Benefits to us all—consequently our obligations to Love and Obedience are *infinite*. And the Violation of those Obligations even by the most secret Disaffection to his Character or the smallest Deviation from his holy Will is *infinitely criminal*. Therefore every Sin deserves a Punishment someway or other *infinitely severe* to bear a Proportion to the real demerit of the Crime. Hence we whose Offenses are innumerable and each offence infinitely aggravated cou'd never any one of us have been sav'd without an Atonement and Satisfaction of infinite Value.

But I believe (and blessed be God that I ever existed to believe it) that the sovereign, unobliged and self-moved Goodness, and the unfathomable Wisdom of God have contrived a Method of Salvation that is not only consistent with the whole assemblage of the divine Perfections, but which displays their unparalleled Glory in a Manner infinitely superior to all the other Works of God. The Plan of this Salvation was laid in that eternal Counsel in which the sovereign Will of Deity engaged the three Persons in God, and in which the honor of the Trinity and of every Perfection thereof was so amply provided for. The Son of God was set up from everlasting as the public head of his People, who were personally and absolutely chosen in him and given to him in the everlasting Covenant, their eternal Felicity being secured by solemn Compact, not without the Oath of the immutable God.

I am fully assured that in order to affect this Salvation, God the SON was manifested in the Flesh, being born of a Virgin in whom he had been conceived by the Power of the Holy Ghost. Thus he who was from Eternity in the form of God assumed in Time the form of a Servant. Uniting absolute Divinity and real Humanity in his Person, he alone was a fit Mediator between God and Man. And thus Immanuel being constituted under the Law, magnify'd it and made it honorable by his complete Conformity to its righteous commands and by freely suffering the whole Curse which was due to our Violation of it. His People's Sins were imputed to him, that his Righteousness might be imputed to them. His *Humiliation and Sufferings* made an infinitely valuable *Satisfaction* to answer those demands of Law *consequent* to Man's breach of it. And his *Obedience and Righteousness* which are *infinitely meritorious* answer the demands of Law which were *prior* to that breach. And thus the righteous *Governor of the Universe* fully discover'd his *infinite Hatred of Sin* in not sparing his own Son but making his Soul an Offering for Sin, being pleased to bruise him and put him to Grief, and on the other hand he who was once deliver'd unto the accursed Death of the Cross for our offences being now raised for our Justification and seated at the right hand of the majesty on high...

I believe that civil Government is an ordinance of God, that temporal Dominion is not founded in Grace, but that Believers ought to be subject to lawful Authority in all civil matters as well as other men—and that honor shou'd be given to whom honor, and tribute is due. But I believe it is God's peculiar Prerogative to govern the Conscience, and that all persecution for the sake of religious principles is unscriptural and iniquitous.

I believe that Jesus Christ the crowned King of Zion is the alone Head of the Church—that neither Kings, Queens, nor Parliaments have any right to determine Controversies about matters of Faith, nor to appoint rites and ceremonies in the Church.

I believe that the Church of Christ on Earth under the Gospel Dispensation is not national as under the Jewish Oeconomy but that it is composed of elect redeemed Souls who are called by divine Grace out of the World and in consequence of that Calling manifested by holiness of Life have a right to divine ordinances; and in order to the regular administration of the word, the positive institutions, and discipline of the Gospel, have sufficient Authority from Christ to form themselves into distinct Societies or congregated Churches each *independent* of others, tho connected by mutual Affection. That the members of every such Church publicly professing the Faith of the Gospel, and assembling in the Name of Christ have an undoubted Right to *choose their own officers* and in Conjunction with them to receive or exclude others from their communion according to the rules of the sacred word...

I believe that the Lord Jesus has prescribed in the New Testament two positive Institutions which are of standing obligation upon his disciples and followers. Baptism or Immersion in Water in the Name of the sacred Three, being design'd as a public acknowledgement of our Faith in the Father, the Son and the Holy Spirit, and as a striking emblem of the death, burial and resurrection of Christ our surety, who cleanses us from sin in the fountain of his blood, and as a solemn avowal of our obligations to die unto sin as buried with him, and to live here in newness of life, while we also expect a future resurrection to eternal Glory. And in the Lord's Supper I believe that by the receiving of bread and wine as appointed by the dear Redeemer we shew forth the Lord's Death, commemorating his sufferings for our sake and being encouraged to expect the communication of all spiritual blessings from him, are edified in the faith and in love to him and to each other as fellow members of his mystical Body. Now I believe that true Faith only gives a right to either of these Ordinances in the sight of God, and that a credible profession thereof gives a right to them in the sight of Men. And for my own part (while I disclaim all right of judging for others) I am obliged to reject the Practice of Infant Baptism and Infant Communion as equally unscriptural...

I am fully assured of the Resurrection of the Bodies of the just and Unjust of the general judgment of all Mankind by the divine Jesus. And of the most righteous tho awful Punishment of the Wicked Body and Soul in an eternal World of Misery; as well as of the everlasting and complete Felicity of all true Believers in the World of Peace and Purity.

Amen.

John Ryland Jr., "Confession of Faith Delivered by John Ryland Junior of Northampton at His Ordination to the Pastoral Care of the Church in College Lane, June 8, 1781," MS Volumes of Miscellaneous Writings, G97a, z.e.12, Bristol Baptist College, 2–7, 9–12, 18–22.

47

A Gospel Call to Sinners

Henry Alline

MOST OF THE attention on early evangelicalism has focused on colonial America and Britain, yet evangelicalism had important pockets of strength in other parts of the world. In Canada, the foremost revivalist was Henry Alline (1748–84). Born in Newport, Rhode Island, in 1748, he emigrated with his parents to Nova Scotia in 1760, settling in Falmouth. Alline learned farming and, later in his twenties, tanning and currying. His path in life changed courses dramatically when he experienced conversion in 1775. Writing in his journal (published posthumously in 1806), Alline described this event in extravagant language, saying that he had been "ravished" by "Divine ecstasy" and was now "married" to his Savior. His own experience convinced him that others should strive for the same kind of soul-defining moment. After his conversion, he itinerated all over Nova Scotia throughout the end of the 1770s and early 1780s, preaching on the necessity of the "new birth." His rhetorical skills were such that contemporaries referred to him as Nova Scotia's George Whitefield. But unlike Whitefield, Alline refused to associate with a particular denomination, wanting to be known as an independent itinerant preacher. In the final months of his life, and dying of tuberculosis, he sailed from Nova Scotia to New England, arriving in Maine in September 1783 and preaching his way southward to North Hampton, New Hampshire, where he died at the house of the Reverend David McClure in early 1784.

While gifted as a speaker and able to draw crowds and charm audiences, Alline's theological writings did not garner the same respect. In his *Two Mites on Some of the Most Important and Much Disputed Points of Divinity* (1781) and *The Anti-Traditionist* (1783), he put forth a strange blend of Calvinism, Arminianism, and mysticism. He made a case for human free will while advocating the Calvinistic notion of the perseverance of the saints, and he tended to read scripture allegorically rather than literally, searching for deep spiritual meanings beyond obvious interpretations. Besides his theological writings, Alline also published two sets of songbooks: his *Hymns and Spiritual Songs on a Variety of Pleasing and Important*

Subjects (1781), with twenty-two songs; and a larger volume of 488 entries entitled *Hymns and Spiritual Songs* (1786). His most significant contribution to evangelicalism was as an evangelist. His itinerate preaching in the 1770s and 1780s initiated a series of revivals in Nova Scotia that spilled over into northern New England. As an evangelist, Alline consistently spoke on the need for the new birth. Denying that individuals were predestined to heaven or hell, he told his listeners that they had the power to choose to follow or reject Christ and would be held accountable for their decisions. Shortly before his death in 1784, he published *A Sermon, Preached at Fort-Midway* (1783), which was reprinted twice in New England as *A Gospel Call to Sinners!* in 1795 and 1797. Alline's published sermon confirms his belief that everyone has the ability to turn from sin and seek eternal salvation.

A Sermon, Preached at Fort-Midway

O! therefore, as you love your own souls, put off a waiting Saviour no longer lest you lose your soul to all eternity. You say you cannot think that God will convert, or bring your soul into liberty this evening, and yet I dare say you expect he will some other time, and this is the very thing still that keeps you from him: For he never can nor never will be your Saviour until you, not only believe he is able and willing, but so far believe it the present moment, that you will cast yourself on him without any expectation of a future opportunity; yea, you must and will be reduced to such extremity, that you can no longer be put off, or any way pacified with or resting upon, what may, or will be done at some other time, or hereafter, but will in immediate extremity, cry like sinking Peter for help now, *Lord I cannot live any longer without thee, save me, yea save me immediately, or I sink forever.* And then my dear hearers, and never till then, will you receive the waiting Saviour; so that by this time, methinks you must be convinced, that you have been (under a pretended reverence and humility) putting off the Lord, like Felix, for a more convenient season; and thereby baring yourself from salvation, and thus saying that you cannot come yet, and cannot believe yet: but you hope you shall by and by, or some other time; which is the strongest terms saying that you will not believe yet, nor you will not come yet; but by and by, or some other time, when you have got some better frame, you will come; but let me tell you my dear hearers wait and try what you will, and as long as you will for a better heart, a softer heart, a loving heart, a humble heart, or a broken heart, and a better frame, you will be after all, but like the woman who was twelve years trying many physicians for a cure till she spent all her living, and instead of growing better grew worse, and was obliged at last to press through the crowd with all her disorders, and touch the hem of Christ's garment, or never be made whole, yea and if ever you are healed, you must like her not only despair of all other helps and physicians; but be reduced to that perishing extremity, that you will press through the crowd of every temptation and disagreeable Fame to Jesus, the last resource, and complete Saviour.

O believe that you are as fit, and as worthy to come to Christ now, as you will be if you labor, and mourn and pray all your days, and that the Lord Jesus Christ is now waiting to receive you! O believe that the great Jehovah offers you salvation this moment as a free gift. *But saith one again, must I come to him just as I am now, with a hard heart, dark mind, and polluted soul?* I answer yes. Nor will it ever be any better until you do. You may court the terrors of the law, and the awful apprehensions of death and the grave, together with a dismal discovery of the pains of hell, and the despairing horrors of the damned, which indeed may alarm some careless sinner that has never been roused scarcely to a thought of his miserable condition before: But those who have been long awakened by the spirit of God, and under a sense of their danger, there is nothing [that] will affect them, but to cast themselves on God and feel his love and goodness. And therefore instead of your going to Mount Sinai to soften the heart after you have seen your lost undone condition, I would point you to that infinite love, and goodness that so freely bled beneath your sins, and threw open the gates of eternal glory for the vilest of the vile; and therefore ye need not go any longer *to the Mount which burneth with blackness, and darkness and tempest, and to such thunderings and lightnings that made even* Moses *and all the Hebrew camp to tremble; which Mount, if so much as a beast touch, was thrust through with a dart:* but ye may and ought to *come to Mount Sion, the city of the living God, the heavenly Jerusalem, and to an innumerable company of angels, to the general assembly and church of the first born which are written in heaven, and to God the Judge of all, and to the spirits of just men made perfect;* And O shall I tell you! *to Jesus the mediator of the new covenant.* Ah, *and to the blood of sprinkling* my dear hearers, *that speaks better things,* yea, far better, *than the blood of Abel;* and all this a free gift to whomsoever will, may enter and enjoy the glorious privileges forever; but these blessings you can never attain, but by venturing on Christ. And now think a moment (ye that mourn a hard heart) that all this was the price of blood for you. Ah! for you in particular; yea and the same friend that has done all this, will do and grant all that you need; yea so willing to make you everlastingly happy, that he not only offers it to you, but his heaviest complaint and greatest grief is, that even after all he has done for you, ye will not believe him, nor enjoy it; and he mourns because of your danger still, or mourns shall I say because his labor is all to you like to be lost, and you after all the pains he has endured, forever abandoned to all that is good, banished from his presence, and lay down in the regions of eternal darkness and despair; but if you cannot believe this, step with me a moment to the gates of that bloody city where you will see him weeping over a people, that by rejecting his grace have chained themselves to irrecoverable ruin and despair, even when thus gone and that against all that he had done, or could, yet he feels their misery, and condoles their state with a bleeding heart, and in words that might cause any hardness but that of sin or final impenitence to melt; *he beheld* saith God, *the city and wept over it.* Ah wept over it indeed! *saying if thou hadst,* or, O that thou hadst! *known at least in this thy day the things that belonged to thy peace, but,* Ah, by rejecting now *they are* to my almost insupportable grief *hid,* forever hid *from thine eyes!*

Yea so great was his pity, that if it had been possible he would yet have brought them to repentance if his laboring years longer would have done it; labored years longer, did I say? Ah, I am so far from charging God as many do, with designing the misery of them that are lost, or consenting to their ruin, that is permit them to be ruined when he could have prevented it, neglecting to save them when he could, I say instead of believing so, I as firmly believe, as I believe there is a God, that his love is so great, his goodness so uncontainable, that if any more of the fallen race, could be redeemed by his suffering more for them, he would with as much freedom as he once gave his life, when no man took it away, enter again into the flesh, and undergo all the unspeakable miseries again even to death, for such is the nature of the divine Being, as can never be roiled, incensed, or stirred up to thirst for revenge, though a truth, which I have been condemned for declaring: yet a truth that I am more and more willing to vindicate by the infallible word; Yea and a truth that I trust, I shall believe and rejoice to all eternity, but saith one of my hearers, *I thought God was nothing else but vengeance against the ungodly, and angry with the wicked every day.* True my dear friends, he is as vengeance to the finally impenitent, because of sin: But you must not imagine this vengeance, or anger so called to be any thing that is so in God, or awoke in God since the sin was committed, or any thing that is wrath or vengeance in itself; but so to the wicked by reason of the infinite contrariety of their guilt and sin; and thus it is, that he is angry with sin from the consequence of his nature, that is and forever was so opposite to sin, that they can no more abide together than light and darkness, heat and cold; but when light scatters darkness, would you imagine therefrom, that the light was possessed of malice, spite or revenge against the darkness? Or when fire dissolves the ice, will you say, that the fire was incensed by the ice? Or mad with the ice? Why then will you imagine, that God is roiled, incensed, or got a wrath & spirit of revenge stirred up in himself against sin, because he hates and abhors sin? Or why would you say that he was possessed of wrath, and vengeance against the sinner because his nature is so to them, while in their sins, when at the same time his nature in itself is all love and goodness? But some may say again, if God is never roiled nor incensed, why does he cast sinners to hell at all? I answer my dear hearers, he never does for they by sin make their own hell and go to their own place.

But perhaps you will say again, I know they so far make and go to their own hell that they justly deserve it, and therefore God's throne is clear of their blood: but yet I think he could still save them if he would: but as they have so often and willfully rejected, he swears they *shall not enter into his rest.* And now, as that is the conception of many, who are called Christians, I shall speak a few words more in answer whereby I shall discover the horrible consequences of that principle, first if that was the truth, then God is changeable, for when he first calls the sinner, he is not got that wrath and vengeance against him; but by the sinners rejecting the calls, he stirs up a wrath and incenses a justice, which never can be appeased or satisfied. Secondly, he is not only less merciful now, than he was before the sinner rejected his mercy; but likewise possessed of something incensed, or some wrath and anger, as long as the sinner lies in hell, which God never would have felt or been possessed of, if the creature had not sinned; so that consequently not only the creature, but God too is injured by sin to all eternity; which you see must be the case (let people twist and turn as much as they will to cover their dark, and unscriptural sentiments). And now what think you my dear hearers of such blasphemous conceptions of the Deity as many have and hold forth as the truths of the everlasting gospel? Yea and will level all their artillery against any one who presumes to believe in any better God, or who discovers the nature of their principles: But blessed be God, I feel more and more delighted with, confirmed in, and impatient to proclaim that glorious truth with the beloved disciple, *God is love,* yea, *he is light,* saith the same John, *and in him is no darkness at all.* O my hearers fall in love with such a God, whose nature is so good as to exclude him from any possibility of feeling or doing any thing but good; Yea a God, that will labor to do good as long as the creature is in a capacity of receiving—nor will ever give the creature up to misery until he is gone beyond recovery; stepping in himself and saying *what could have been done more, that I have not done? ...*

O! why, why will men love darkness, choose their bondage, and labor so hard against all true reason, and divine revelation to reject the truth, keep themselves in blindness, and bind themselves down to perdition? Who out of pretended reverence and (I was about to say bastard) humility will reply! *why God is a sovereign, and therefore has a sovereign right to dispose of us as he pleases, without giving us any account whether he designs us for happiness or misery, we ought not to be too anxious to know if he intends to save us or not, lest we are guilty of presumption: but do the best we can, go trembling all our days with a hope that he will not finally cast us off, and if he does after we have cast ourselves on his mercy, he will be just, and we shall have no cause to complain.*

And thus with all their pretended love, reverence and humility they have brought forth a brat, that if examined, has been an advocate for the powers of darkness, and a supported Antichrist for many centuries, has made God a liar, charged him with cruelty and injustice and sent many thousands of souls to hell: for God has declared, that *he so loved the world that he gave his only begotten Son, that whosoever believeth in him should not perish but have everlasting life:* But some will say (who believe in any arbitrary, partial God) *that is the elect part of the world;* I wish they would let God speak for himself; who not only says for the world, but likewise goes on to tell the reason, why, *that whosoever*, saith he, *believeth on him, should not perish, but have everlasting life*; and then declares, that he would have all men to be saved and come unto the knowledge of the truth; and then, lest we would not yet believe him, or should charge him with neglect, injustice, cruelty and partiality, he swears as he lives (and commands his servants in the same verse to proclaim that oath) that he has no pleasure in the death of the wicked (not the righteous, but the wicked, he saith) but that (repeating over again, who he means) the wicked turn from his way, and live, and then goes on with a repeated call turn ye, turn ye, concluding with an expostulation, for saith he why will ye die? And now dare they say, after all he has declared, that we do not know whether he is willing to save us or not, or call it presumption to claim, an assurance through his word and grace until we leave this life, and with regard to knowing our particular interest in this truth, he declares in positive terms, *ye shall know the truth, and the truth shall make you free*; And declares that he will manifest himself to his children. And pray what is a manifestation, but making a thing known? Yea even your common reason will teach you, that if things are not made known they are not made manifest.

Yea, what happiness, what salvation, what joy, what life, can it be, that a man can have and not know it? How can Christ be a man's friend, companion, and comforter, joy and strength, and the man not know that he has any Christ, friend, joy, life, strength or comforter? But saith John on this point, *hereby know we, that we dwell in him, and he in us, because he hath given us his spirit. And we know that we are of God* and *he that believeth on the son of God hath the witness in himself.* And Job doth not say, I guess, but *I know that my redeemer liveth*, and Paul doth not say, it may be when we leave this world, God will bring us to heaven, but, *we know that if this our earthly house of this tabernacle were dissolved we have a building of God, a house not made with hands eternal in the heavens.* And David not only saith, that God hath made with him an everlasting covenant, but offers to tell how he was brought to the knowledge of it by his conversion; *come* saith he, *all ye that fear God, and I will declare what he hath done for my soul*; and saith the spouse, *my beloved is mine, and I am his.* Yea and so full are the oracles of life of this truth that if it was necessary, I might continue for an hour, repeating such positive demonstrations from him that cannot lie: and yet against it all, how many will labor to spread the cause of Antichrist, and say *we cannot know that we are converted in this life*, and look upon it, as I before observed, that they are doing God honor, when they are saying, they must leave that with God, must walk trembling all their days, and not presume to intrude into the secrets of God, to be so positive, whether or not he intends to save them.

Henry Alline, *A Sermon, Preached at Fort-Midway: On the 19th of February, 1783.* (Dover: Samuel Bragg, 1797), 13–18, 25–7.

48

The Duty to Respond to the Gospel Message

Andrew Fuller

BORN ON FEBRUARY 6, 1754, at Wicken, Cambridgeshire, Andrew Fuller (1754–1815) was raised as a Particular Baptist by parents who worked as dairy farmers. At the age of seven, he and his family relocated to the village of Soham, a few miles away from Wicken. In November 1769 Fuller had a conversion experience, later joining the Particular Baptist church at Soham as a newly baptized member in the spring of 1770. Talented as a preacher and lay theologian, Fuller became the pastor at Soham in May 1775, filling a vacancy that had existed since 1771. After a stint at Soham, Fuller moved his pastoral duties to the Baptist church at Kettering, Northamptonshire in 1782, remaining there for over thirty years until his death. In 1792, while at Northamptonshire, he helped found the Baptist Missionary Society which sponsored William Carey and his work in India. Fuller devoted a significant portion of his final years to missions, acting as the BMS's secretary and traveling throughout Great Britain to raise funds.

During his years at Soham, in 1777, Fuller began studying Jonathan Edwards's *Freedom of the Will*, which liberated him from the vexing determinism that haunted his High Calvinistic heritage. Edwards's theory on natural, versus moral, inability, convinced Fuller that everyone has the duty to respond to the gospel message, even if their sinful desires keep them from believing in Jesus Christ as Savior. From his careful reading of *Freedom of the Will*, Fuller came to the conclusion that Christians must preach the gospel message to all who will hear it, even if only certain people would respond favorably to God's grace. The ideas spawned from his study of Edwards led him later to publish one of his most celebrated works, *The Gospel Worthy of All Acceptation,* in 1785. This monumental literary achievement, however, brought with it severe criticism from High Calvinists such as William Button and John Martin, on one hand, and those who held Arminian beliefs like the General Baptist Dan Taylor, on the other hand. With the publication of *The*

FIGURE 48.1 Andrew Fuller (Detail), courtesy of the National Portrait Gallery, London.

Gospel Worthy of All Acceptation, Fuller established himself as the leading Baptist theologian of his age, going on to write polemics against such controversial authors as Joseph Priestley and Robert Sandeman.

The Gospel Worthy of All Acceptation

Faith appears always to carry in it the idea of *a crediting some testimony where intuitive evidence cannot be obtained.* If that testimony be merely human, we call it human faith; if divine, divine faith. If the testimony be fabulous, then faith in it is false; if authentic, we call it true. If it relates to historical facts, it has been called historical faith; if to a divine power accompanying the primitive disciples, enabling them to work miracles, their faith in that promise we call the faith of miracles. If it relate only to certain circumstances of the gospel, and the bare existence of things, without taking in their nature and qualities, then 'tis partial faith; if to the essence, sum, and substance of the gospel, then 'tis what accompanies salvation. But in all these, faith is the credit of some testimony. True saving faith is no less so than any of the rest. Nothing deserves that name but what is founded on substantial evidence. When the apostle calls the Thessalonians *believers,* he assigns this as the reason, or as what constituted them such, *Our testimony among you was believed.* Perhaps no better definition then can be given of true faith than that which is given by the Holy Ghost himself in 2 Thessalonians 2:13. THE BELIEF OF THE TRUTH. The gospel is here by way of eminence called *the truth.* The apostle knew there was other truth in existence as well as that, but the importance of that was such as to eclipse all the rest. That was it that represented God in his *true* character, and men in *theirs*—that told them the *truth* without falsehood or flattery, concerning the evil of sin, and its just demerit—that gave them a *true* account of their miseries and necessities, and as well exhibited the glorious *realities* of life and immortality to view. That was it which formed the subject matter of the apostles embassy, and in the reception of which he knew men's everlasting interests were concerned. That was it of which the Son of God himself came down to *bear witness*. To acquiesce therein is to view things in measure as God views them, and as Christ viewed them when he offered himself a sacrifice for sin. Never was such *witness borne* to the excellence of God's law and character, to the evil and demerit of sin, and to the worth of the everlasting enjoyment of God as he then bore! To view things then as he viewed them, is to view them as *they are*, and that is the same thing as the apostle calls *the belief of the truth*. It deserves also to be particularly noticed that what is here called the belief of the truth, is peculiar to the *elect*, accompanies *sanctification of the Spirit*, and terminates in *salvation*...

How low and defective soever this definition may seem, perhaps it may be found that every material idea which the scriptures give us of faith, is herein comprehended. However, to avoid obscurity, I shall attempt more fully to explain the terms. And *First*, it is not supposed but that there may be a *cold assent* to many of the general truths of Christianity; so far as that a man may obtain the character of being orthodox, and may really think himself a believer, yea and may be able to defend those truths for which he is an advocate with clearness and energy; and yet be destitute of saving faith. I would not for a world encourage those deceived souls *who receive not the love of the truth*, while it is manifest a lie in their right hand! By *belief*, then, I understand, and I think the apostle understands, a *cordial reception* of the truth as it is in Jesus; or as the Holy Ghost elsewhere speaks, *a believing with all the heart*: and perhaps it may prove, if closely examined, that nothing short of that, *properly and strictly speaking*, deserves the name of faith. Those who received not the *love* of the truth, notwithstanding the *profession* they made, are said... *not to believe the truth at all*. To believe only the *shadow* of truth, without entering into the *spirit* of it, is little more than to believe nothing at all about it. The apostle Paul, notwithstanding his knowledge of, and zeal for, the law, while blind to its *spirituality*, reckons himself to have been *without* the law. The same may be affirmed concerning mere *professing* zealots in Christianity. They tell us they believe the truth, and doubtless think they do; but while they continue blind to its spiritual glory, which will appear by their knowledge having no tendency to transform them into the image of God, they ought to be considered in no other light than as WITHOUT the truth.

Farther, by *truth* I do not mean, and I think the apostle does not mean, barely such general truths of the gospel, as that there was such a person as Jesus Christ— that he was born at Bethlehem—lived and wrought miracles in Judea—was crucified, buried, and raised again from the dead—that he ascended to glory, and will judge the world at the last day.—That he is God and man, and bears the titles of king, priest, and prophet of his church. That there is an eternal election, a particular redemption, an effectual vocation, a final perseverance, &c. &c. &c.—These, no doubt, are truths, and great truths, and what it is allowed may be believed where no saving faith is. But by truth I mean (and I think the apostle means the same) to include with the aforementioned doctrines their *qualities* or *properties*, which make a great, and even an essential part of their truth. It is as true, and as much a part of the record God hath given of his Son, that he is *altogether lovely*, as that he exists at all. The *beauty* of the divine character, the *evil* of sin, and the *excellence* of Christ, are truths independent of our belief of them. It is as true, and as plainly reported in the scriptures that the gospel is intrinsically good, superlatively glorious, infinitely important, and, in one word, *worthy of all acceptation*, as that it has any existence at all. But to believe this is true saving faith...

Prop. I. FAITH IN CHRIST IS COMMANDED IN THE SCRIPTURES TO UNCONVERTED SINNERS

It is here taken for granted, that whatever God commands, is the duty of those to whom it is commanded. If then true faith were not the duty of unconverted sinners, we might expect never to find any injunctions of that nature directed to them in the Holy Scriptures. We might expect God would as soon command them to be angels as Christians, if the latter is no more their duty than the former. But if, on the other hand, we should find him frequently calling upon persons of this character to believe in his Son, or to do that which amounts to the same thing, then it necessarily follows that this is their duty...

Prop. II. EVERY MAN IS BOUND CORDIALLY TO RECEIVE, AND HEARTILY TO APPROVE, WHATEVER GOD REVEALS.

I should think this proposition ought not to be disputed; for if men are not obliged to approve of what God reveals, then they may be right in disapproving it, which to assert would be horrid, and unworthy of a refutation! Now *approbation* of the gospel, or of God's way of salvation is the distinguishing characteristic of true faith...for to think *well*, and *suitably* of Christ, is to think *justly*, that is, to think and believe the *truth* concerning him, and act accordingly. Now, what of all this is any sinner excused from? Is not he bound to think *suitably* of Christ, and to *choose* him? Or is he at liberty to think *unjustly* concerning him, and to *prefer his idols before him*? Or to *set up another way* of salvation than that which God hath appointed, in opposition to him? It is easy to conceive of mankind being so full of prejudice, and aversion to Christ, that *they cannot think well of him*; yea, and this aversion, being so deeply rooted in them, that nothing short of *almighty power* can bring them to be of a right spirit; but to imagine that they OUGHT NOT to think so much as A GOOD THOUGHT of him, but *are right* in judging him to have *no form nor comeliness, nor beauty that they should desire him*, one should think must shock every sentiment of love and loyalty in an upright heart! I know very well this was once my condition, but it now appears to me to be that of which I have reason to be greatly ashamed. Instead of justifying myself in it, by maintaining that *it was not my duty at that time to think otherwise of him than I did*, I ought to take shame to myself, to *look upon him whom* thus *I pierced, and mourn, as one mourneth for an only son; and be in bitterness, as one that is in bitterness for his first born* . . .

And now, are not true *believers*, to whom *Christ is precious*, here opposed to unbelievers, who are said to *disallow* of him, and to be *disobedient* therein? And does not the apostle speak as if he knew no medium between being a true believer, and a *disobedient* unbeliever? Farther, what medium can there be in this case? Does not every one who has heard of Jesus Christ by the gospel report, either *allow* or *disallow* of him? And is it not impossible, in the nature of things, that he should do otherwise? If our Lord's doctrine be true, there is no such thing as a state of *neutrality* in real religion. Every man is either for him, or against him. Not to allow here, is to disallow. It is then every one's duty either to *allow* of Christ, or it is not. If it is, this is the same thing as its being his duty to believe in him with a saving faith, for those who are here supposed to allow of Christ, are said to *believe* in him; and to them, it is added, *he is precious*. If it is not, then there is nothing wrong, but right in men's *disallowing* of him, *stumbling at the stumbling-stone, stumbling at the word*, although in so doing they are expressly said to be *disobedient* . . .

Prop. III. THE GOSPEL, THOUGH IT BE NO LAW, BUT A MESSAGE OF PURE GRACE, YET VIRTUALLY REQUIRES SUCH AN OBEDIENCE TO IT, WHICH INCLUDES SAVING FAITH

By the gospel VIRTUALLY REQUIRING OBEDIENCE is meant, that by reason of the dignity of its author, with the excellence and importance of its subject matter, men are required to yield submission to it, and that with all their heart. I suppose it might be taken for granted, that the gospel possesses *some degree* of virtual authority; as it is generally acknowledged, that by reason of the dignity of its author, and importance of its subject matter, it deserves the *audience* and *attention* of all mankind. The law of God requires so much on its behalf. The only question is, *how far that authority reaches*, and how far men are laid under obligation by it? If living faith is not the duty of men in general, then it must be supposed that the gospel contains no such authority as to oblige them to it, and that a bare attendance on it, with a cold assent to its general doctrines, is all that is required. On the other hand, if living faith is the duty of men in general, then we may expect to find the gospel possessed of so much virtual authority as to require it; or in other words, that such is the excellent nature of the gospel, that the law of God, which is the law of reason and equity, requires thus much on its behalf . . .

Prop. IV. THE WANT OF FAITH IN CHRIST IS ASCRIBED IN THE SCRIPTURES TO MEN'S DEPRAVITY, AND IS ITSELF THERE REPRESENTED AS A HEINOUS SIN

It is here taken for granted, that whatever is not a sinner's duty, the omission of it cannot be charged on him as a crime, nor imputed to any depravity in him. If then true faith in Christ is not incumbent on sinners in general, we might expect never to hear the want of it charged on them as a fault, any more than not being *elected*, or *redeemed*, which are acts in all respects peculiar to God, and therefore not their duty. Yes, if so, we must expect to find men's incapacity to believe in Christ purely of a *natural* kind, and to have no more of *moral evil* in it than there is in the incapacity of a lame man to walk, a blind man to see, or an idiot to understand: no more than in the incapacity of an infant to believe as a man, or of a man to understand as an angel. But if, on the other hand, we should find the want of true saving faith charged on men as their sin—if in the scriptures no bar should be found to believing in, or coming to, Christ, but what lies in the depravity of a man's own heart—if ignorance, pride, dishonesty of heart, and aversion to God, should be the causes to which the want of faith is imputed; then it cannot be fairly contended whether the contrary is their duty...

'Tis true, we expressly read elsewhere, that *no man* CAN *come unto Christ except the Father draw him*; but there is nothing inconsistent in this. The *cannot* itself consists in a *will not*, or in other words, in the want of a *heart* to come to Christ, with a settled *aversion* to him. The inability of men to come to Christ is doubtless, by this expression, represented as being *total*, which we never deny; but that is no proof of its being *innocent*, which is the point in question. It being *expressly* said *no man* CAN *come*, no more proves that there is any other bar beside what lies in the wickedness of the heart, than its being *expressly* said of *Joseph's brethren, they* COULD NOT *speak peaceably to him*, proves that they had any other bar than their own pride and revenge. It is *expressly* said of some that they *have eyes full of adultery, and* CANNOT *cease from sin*; but none, I should think, supposes them to have been under any other necessity of sinning than what consisted in the strength of their propensities. So it is *expressly* said, *the carnal mind is not subject to the law of God, neither indeed* CAN *be*, and that *they that are in the flesh* CANNOT *please God*; but are they under any other inability than what lies in the badness of their hearts? Or are they free from all obligation to be *subject to God's law*, and to *please him* on that account? Is God indeed such a hard master that if a man were of ever such a right spirit, yet it would be all in vain?...

Prop. V. GOD HAS THREATENED AND INFLICTED THE MOST AWFUL PUNISHMENTS ON MEN FOR THEIR NOT BELIEVING IN THE LORD JESUS CHRIST

It is here taken for granted that nothing can be the cause of God's inflicting punishment but sin. If then true faith be not the duty of men in general, and the want of it is not their sin, we may certainly conclude we shall never any where in scripture find that assigned as a reason of their punishment. But if, on the contrary, we should find that not believing in Jesus Christ is assigned as a reason of God's inflicting punishment, then may we with certainty conclude that it is their sin, and the contrary their duty...

Prop. VI. SEEING OTHER GRACES, OR SPIRITUAL DISPOSITIONS, WITH WHICH SALVATION IS CONNECTED, ARE REPRESENTED AS THE DUTIES

OF MEN IN GENERAL, THERE IS NO REASON WHY FAITH SHOULD NOT
BE THE SAME

If the former part of this proposition can be proved, I suppose the latter will
not be disputed; for though these controversies have in general been carried on
under the names of *repentance* and *faith*; yet they, in fact, have always extended
to every thing truly and spiritually good. I query if an instance can be found of a
person who allows of carnal men being obliged to do things spiritually good, who
yet denies it to be their duty to believe in Christ. However, if such an instance can
be found it is certainly very rare. In general, those who deny one spiritual disposition being the sinner's duty, deny all; and go upon this principle, "that none can
be obliged to act spiritually but spiritual men." If a person could be brought to
acknowledge one of these dispositions to be incumbent on carnal men, probably
he would soon be brought to acknowledge others. As this then seems to be at the
bottom of the controversy, and is a subject of very great importance, the whole of
God's authority over the *hearts* of men being herein concerned, it must be allowed
to deserve a particular consideration.

Andrew Fuller, *The Gospel of Christ Worthy of All Acceptation: Or the Obligations
of Men Fully to Credit, and Cordially to Approve, Whatever God Makes Known*
(Northampton: T. Dicey, [1785]), 10–13, 37, 49–50, 52, 57, 65–6, 71–2, 74, 79–80.

49

The Ideal Student

Charles Nisbet

THE NATIVE SCOTTISH minister Charles Nisbet (1736–1804) followed in the footsteps of his senior colleague John Witherspoon when he emigrated to America to become a college president. Educated at Edinburgh University and licensed to preach in 1760, Nisbet eventually settled at Montrose, on the northeast coast of Scotland, beginning his long tenure in 1764 as its junior, and later senior, Presbyterian minister. As a clergyman sympathetic to the evangelical party in the Church of Scotland, Nisbet openly opposed patronage appointments to church livings and the emphasis by the Moderate party on polite preaching at the expense of the gospel message. Nisbet's biographer, Samuel Miller, noted that his subject went by the nickname of "the walking library" due to his extraordinary intelligence and capability to recall the content of countless books that he had read.

Consistent with many other Scottish evangelicals at the time of the War of Independence, Nisbet developed sympathy for the American colonists and their grievances with Britain. From the pulpit, Nisbet depicted Britain as a nation consumed with sin that would soon be punished by God for its mistreatment of the American colonists. His growing reputation as an outspoken critic of Britain's overseas policies, and the continual tension between him and the more liberal Moderate party within the Kirk, made him a ripe candidate for emigration to America. Following an invitation by the physician and college trustee, Benjamin Rush, Nisbet accepted the offer to be the first principal of Dickinson College in Carlisle, Pennsylvania. After much indecision on his part, Nisbet and his family arrived in Carlisle in July 1785. But his experience in America did not meet his expectations. His family suffered from severe illness, his eldest son struggled with alcoholism, and he wrangled with the college trustees over the school's curriculum and governance. Despite the difficulties he faced, Nisbet stayed in America for the remainder of his life and became an important transmitter of Scottish Common Sense Realism. His 1786 address represents his vision of an enlightened education for the student body at Dickinson College.

FIGURE 49.1 Charles Nisbet (Detail), courtesy of the Archives and Special Collections, Dickinson College.

An Address to the Students of Dickinson College

MY YOUNG FRIENDS,

AFTER despairing even of life, and renouncing all hopes of being useful to this seminary, it has pleased God to restore me to my former health and office. I hope it will be unnecessary for me to say any thing to convince you of my good will to this country, and to this College in particular. If abandoning an honourable and independent station, and renouncing the society of many valuable and long tried friends; if my crossing the vast Atlantic, and exposing my life to the perils of a new climate, are not sufficient to persuade you of my good wishes, it will be needless to use any words to that purpose.

The troubles and distresses of my family, and the pains I have endured, both in body and mind since my arrival in this country, I shall cheerfully forget, if I shall be enabled to be subservient to the conducting of your studies, and forming your taste and morals, so that you may fulfill the hopes of your parents, and prove useful citizens to your country.

You are here assembled from various parts, and must have different views and expectations in life, but I hope you are all agreed in the desire of learning, and resolve to cultivate the powers of your mind, from a conviction that the knowledge you may acquire here, will enable you to fill with dignity and propriety the several stations to which you may be called; and to contribute your parts to promote the happiness, and to raise the reputation of this new and rising empire.

It is of the utmost consequence to your progress in learning, that you form just notions of its dignity, and importance to the public as well as to yourselves as individuals. It is not to spend your years in idleness and dissipation, or to acquire a superficial tincture of letters, that you have been sent hither with so much trouble and expence by your parents. They expect something more solid and useful in return for their pains and charge on your account.—They hope that you will aspire to excellence and distinction in your studies, and that the honest emulation which a public education produces, will engage you to an useful and diligent employment of your time here. You are now in the most pleasant and the most important time of life: your powers are fresh, and easily susceptible of improvement, and the impressions that you receive at this time must be of the utmost importance in determining your future fates and characters. Your present rank as students is honourable. As candidates for science, fame and consequence, you ought to despise every thing that is mean and dishonourable, and think your time too precious to be spent in trifles or vicious pursuits.

A superficial application to learning is so far from being useful, that it is greatly prejudicial. It fills the mind with confused notions, and sometimes with insufferable vanity; it tends to bring learning into disgrace, and leads the world to form false notions of its tendency and importance. It creates a contempt and aversion to study, and is apt to communicate its baleful influence to future generations. It places the student on a level with the forward smatterer, whose learning is extracted from magazines and reviews, and whose pertness arises only from his ignorance.

It is true that all are not endowed with equal powers for making progress in letters, and that different studies are suited to different tempers and characters: yet diligence, application and constant desire of success, will carry every man as far as nature intended he should go; and the various branches of study in which youth are exercised, will point out to every student what he is best qualified for, and develop the natural bent of his genius, so as to direct him how to employ himself in the future. But without application we can make no discovery of our talents, and the indolent student must continue a child for life...

With regard to your behaviour to us and to one another, we hope your parents have taught you the rudiments of good manners, and that you will not disgrace their instructions and example, by petulance, impertinence or rudeness of any kind.—The child who behaves rudely and improperly to others, dishonours his father's house, and gives others an occasion to believe that he has been ill-educated, or that his parents have set him a bad example. A haughty and quarrelsome temper, a proneness to revenge and mischief, are most fatal to the character and happiness of youth, and afford the most unfavourable prognostic of their riper years. "Men are but children of a larger growth." Those habits that are formed, & those propensities that are discovered in youth, ordinarily prevail through the whole of life. Such students as you are here, such citizens you will prove to the republic. If you now acquire a love of order, justice, decency and obliging behaviour, you will be the delight of your parents, and the ornaments and supports of the state; but if you indulge pride and revenge, if you are prone to quarrel, despise and fight with one another, what else can be expected from the growth of such habits, but that you should become the grief of your parents, a disgrace to your masters, and friends, and the pests and firebrands of every society? Make your choice between these extremes.

We do not indeed expect from your early years, the coolness, the prudence & the gravity of advanced age. Such errors as arise from the natural warmth, the innocent gaiety, and even the levity of youth, may be naturally expected and easily pardoned: but we hope you will consider that you are no longer children, that by your admission into this society, and being engaged in the studies and employ-ments of men, you are considered as subjects of moral government, and suscep-tible of the principles of law and order. You have already in a good measure the command of yourselves, and are capable of discerning and being conscious when you are in the wrong. With these capacities you may avoid the follies of childhood, and contrast those habits of attention and application that are proper for your age, and favourable to your progress in your studies.

Idleness and trifling are the bane of youth, both with respect to learning and morals; these habits prevent progress, excite quarrels, and encourage the grossest corruption of manners. They are the beginning of vices and sorrows, and can not be too much checked and discouraged. Trifling is a perverted activity which in every event leads to evil, and tends either to meanness or malice. Let me warn you especially against one vice which is often prevalent among youth, and indicates or promotes the worst dispositions: we mean the practice of exciting or tempting one another to evil, and prompting them to deeds of malice or revenge.—To sow discord among brethren, to irritate the corruptions and evil passions of men, is the employment of the devil, and ought to be held in the utmost abhorrence by all who would be wise or happy.

Magnanimity and dignity of behaviour are virtues that ought to be in high esteem with youths, as they lay the foundations of a good character, and prevent our age from blushing for the meanness of our early years. But it is of the great-est consequence to form just notions of these virtues, and to be well informed wherein real magnanimity consists. It is not in contempt of others, or proneness to revenge, or being the plague or terror of society. On the contrary a person of true magnanimity will always be just to the merits of others, and will reckon nothing so disgraceful as what is unjust, and injurious to the rights of others; and will be ashamed of every thing that is unworthy of human nature, or hurtful to the order of society: he will be mild and gentle to others, and will abstain from injuring them, for his own sake as well as for theirs. He will not leave it in the power of every one to tempt him to indecent and passionate behaviour, nor disgrace him-self because another is injurious; but despising the ignoble passion of revenge, he will avoid the society of the wicked, and associate with those who are capable of instructing and pleasing him by their example, and incapable of tempting him to indecency by injury.

The most effectual antidote against quarrelling and mean behaviour, is diligence and application to your studies: all the vices and miseries of youth arise uniformly from ignorance and trifling. If you are idle, your lives will be at once unprofitable and unpleasant. As an additional incitement to diligence, we would suggest to you the advantages you enjoy as students of this seminary, and the disadvantages you must labour under from its yet infant state. Both these ought to incite you to diligence, that you may improve the one, and surmount or compensate for the other. At present you have leisure, and opportunity of profiting by books and instructors. But as these can not yet be afforded you in such number and variety as is to be wished, on this account you ought to use more diligence to profit by the opportunities you have; and the fewer these are at present, the more honour will your diligence and success reflect on yourselves, and on this new society.

If you ever hope to prosper in learning, you will not content yourselves with reading those parts only of classic authors that are prelected to you by your masters, and of which you are to give an account to them. By confining yourselves to these, you effectually disappoint their intentions, and render their pains useless to yourselves. By making you acquainted with a part, they intended to make you capable of reading the whole. There is no understanding the merit, nor profiting by the talents of an author, by consulting extracts or detached parts; you can not have time to read all that is excellent in them at school; and I know from experience and observation, that a diligent boy will go through the whole of any author in a shorter time than the unequal abilities of a class will get thro' that part that is taught in public.

Altho' the rules of grammar and construction are necessary in order to understand foreign languages, you must not think you [are] done when you have made yourselves masters of these. It remains to attend to the sense, the history, the sentiment, and the beauties of thought and language; to enter into the scope and spirit of the writer, to discern his excellencies and to detect his weakness, or that of the times in which he lived. The classics are useful, not from their being writ in dead languages, or because it costs a great deal of pains to read them: but they are valuable as models of just thinking, examples of true taste, and monuments of the wisdom and capacity of ancient nations, and have been the delight and wonder of many successive generations.

You ought always to remember that real learning does not consist in acquiring a great many confused and indigested ideas, nor in performing public exercises with such apparent propriety as to persuade others that you are learned: far less does it consist in the use of harsh and uncouth terms, which are not familiar to ordinary understandings, but that it consists in the exercise and application of the powers of the mind, the improvement of our intuitive as well as our active faculties, in the knowledge and discerning of truth, and such an acquaintance with

human nature and its excellencies and defects, its acquisitions and history, as may
fit us for the right conduct of life, and for promoting the happiness of ourselves
and others.

In order to profit by reading, meditation and attention must be joined with it,
we must not pass by any thing that we do not understand, or content ourselves
with a single reading of what is useful, excellent or necessary; and we ought to
labour to retain what we have read, because it is only that which we retain that can
be profitable to us in future. Inattentive and desultory reading is only a more active
idleness, and a more decent mode of trifling. It is better to shut the book as soon
as attention fails, than to accustom ourselves to read without it.

A foolish trusting to public exercises has been the ruin of many students. To
confine ourselves to our prescribed lessons, and our studies to the public hours,
argues a narrow mind, destitute of ambition, and insensible of the excellence and
charms of true learning. Poor and scanty must be the attainments of the pretended student, who feigns attention in public, and is idle and negligent in private!
This is rendering public exercises entirely useless, and thwarting the intention
of your instructors. As that can be done in public is to prescribe general rules,
to remove difficulties, to caution against errors, and suggest useful hints and
directions; but the main business of learning is to be compassed only by private
study and meditation; and the student who does not apply his diligence in private,
misunderstands the true nature and design of public instructions. Those parents
likewise are greatly mistaken who insist that their children should be kept to long
confinement and attendance, so as to leave them neither time, spirits or inclination for private study. It is impossible that any should be made scholars in this
manner. Such injunctions discover a deep ignorance of human nature, as if it
were possible to teach boys against their will, or force them into learning by whip-
ping and imprisonment. These methods may readily produce a rooted aversion
for learning, as it is certain that they render progress in it utterly unattainable and
impracticable; but they will never make boys in love with study, or ambitious to
excel in knowledge. Even in the lowest classes, the student must prepare his lesson at home, if he expects to be able to please his master, or keep up with his class;
but such regulations as leave no time for this, deprive the student of opportunities
of profiting, and oblige the master to labour in vain.

As our public library is as yet but indifferently furnished, and could never supply the necessities of all, and as the procuring a variety of books in a new country
is utterly impossible, you ought to be more diligent in the use of all the books you
can command, especially of such as lead to the knowledge of others. Without a
tolerable acquaintance with literary history, a student can not prosecute his studies, whatever opportunities and helps he may enjoy. He must be at a loss where to
apply for help, unless he knows what authors have treated of the subject in which
he desires information.

In order to discover the genius and capacity of students, and to suggest useful hints for conducting their studies and regulating their conduct, I am convinced that private acquaintance and conversation are of great use. It will therefore be agreeable to me to receive visits from all of the students, as often as their studies and mine will permit, and to suggest to them what may be useful, as well as to resolve their doubts and difficulties, being determined to act as the private preceptor, as well as the public instructor of every student, without exception or respect of persons, who comes to this seminary in quest of useful knowledge.

As concord and order are the soul and strength of every society, and peculiarly necessary in a seminary for the study of letters, we hope that every student will reckon it his honour to study these with the greatest care; and to attain these you ought to reflect how disgraceful it is to disturb society, and to appear impatient of order and equal society. It will be our part to render all of you equal justice and encouragement, but it will depend on your conduct to render our labours pleasant and profitable. Beware of pride, from which contention cometh; abhor injustice and insulting manners, and avoid all indecent and provoking expressions. Remember that your character as well as your success in learning, depends on your present behaviour, and that if you do not shew yourselves regular, well-bred and peaceable students, there can be little hope of your becoming useful or estimable citizens of the state.

As your time is your greatest treasure, and may be employed to the best account, we would earnestly recommend a prudent and thrifty improvement of it. For this purpose you ought to rise early, and beware of spending too much of it in unnecessary exercises or childish recreations. You have much to do, and unless you apply to your studies betimes, you must be great losers. Besides, sauntering and idleness are inimical to habits of application; and by neglecting to study, you may soon become incapable of it. If you would practice the lesson of Pythagoras, and examine every evening what you have been doing all day, you will discover the value of time, and the folly of idleness, by observing how little you have done, in comparison of what you might have done, which may lead to a better improvement of time for the future.

You ought never to forget that all true learning is subordinate and conducive to morals and usefulness. It is not in order that you may be admired for your talents that your parents have bestowed on you benefits of a liberal education. They expect that you should become virtuous, orderly and useful members of society, that you should know how to esteem true excellence, to revere truth and honour, to form yourselves upon the best models, to despise every thing that is mean and vicious, to delight in promoting the happiness of others, to be lovers of peace, to form friendship with the virtuous and worthy, to avoid the society of the wicked, and to merit and command the esteem of the wiser part of your fellow citizens.

Young people are apt to imagine that they have little to do with religion, and that it is time enough to think of that in mature life; but this is a grievous mistake. "Train up a child," says Solomon, "in the way that he should go, and when he is old, he will not depart from it." Even a child is known by his way, whether it be pure and whether it be right. Young as you are, you have a conscience; you are subjects of moral discipline, and susceptible of good or bad moral characters. You know not whether you may live to mature age, and what shall become of your souls if you die in an ignorant, thoughtless and irreligious state? We presume that your parents have taught you to know and honour the God who made you, to revere his name, and to pray to him daily, for the pardon of your sins, the purifying of your natures, and final happiness and salvation through Jesus Christ. We hope you are instructed in the necessity of holiness and virtue as the only means to fit you for eternal life. It shall be our endeavour to second the lessons and intentions, as well as to fulfill the wishes of your parents, so far as is in our power, by suggesting to you as occasion offers, suitable advices for your moral and religious conduct in life; and in so doing we are sure of pleasing them by endeavouring to promote your real happiness. Even wicked and thoughtless parents would be sorry to see their children growing up in vicious habits; and nothing can exceed the sorrow of virtuous and Christian parents when their children walk not in the ways of God. Give joy to your parents, and to your masters and friends, by an early application to religious knowledge and practice; read the word of God with care, reverence and attention: pray to God for wisdom and spiritual understanding, and ye shall not ask in vain. Be assured that it is your highest honour to honour God, to thank him for his benefits, and keep his commandments; you will be more worthy of the esteem of your neighbours, if you pray to God morning and evening, if you study to please him, and to keep the Sabbath day holy, to abstain from all mean and vicious conduct. You may assure yourselves that such a conduct will contribute no less to your progress in learning than your improvement in virtue. God is the father of our spirits and ought to be acknowledged and worshipped in that character. He made our souls, with all their wonderful powers; and their improvement and exercise must depend on his bounty. The knowledge of the plowman and the mechanic is attributed in scripture to the teaching of God, and that large and comprehensive knowledge which distinguished King Solomon, is expressly said to have been the gift of God. And who else can give it? As in religion, so likewise in learning, though Paul may plant, and Apollos water, it belongs to God only to give the increase. You are grossly mistaken if you imagine that a religious life is melancholy or disagreeable; on the contrary it is the only road to true pleasure and satisfaction. To have God for your friend, your father and defender, is true dignity as well as solid peace and confidence. Come, ye children, hearken unto me: I will teach you the fear of the Lord. What man is he that desireth life and loveth many days, that he may see good? Keep thy tongue from evil, and thy lips from speaking guile, depart from evil and do good: seek peace, and pursue it. The eyes of the Lord are upon the righteous, and his ears are open to their cry. The face of God is against them that do evil, to cut off their memory from the earth. Behold the fear of the Lord, that is wisdom, and to depart from evil is understanding.

Charles Nisbet, *An Address to the Students of Dickinson College* (Carlisle: Kline & Reynolds, [1786]), 2–4, 6–16.

50

The Unlawfulness of Enslaving Humans

Thomas Clarkson

AN ESSAY WRITTEN by Thomas Clarkson (1760–1846) changed his life. Born on March 28, 1760, in Cambridgeshire, England, Clarkson attended the free grammar school at Wisbech where his father was the headmaster and town minister. Tall, heavy, and grave in manner, Clarkson entered St. John's College, Cambridge, in 1779, graduating in 1783 with a BA. After completing his undergraduate degree, he intended to stay at Cambridge to study for the ministry. Having won a Latin essay prize in 1784, he competed for the award again the following year, writing an answer to the 1785 topic: "Is it lawful to enslave the unconsenting?" His research for this essay changed the course of his life. To answer the proposed question, he studied the Atlantic slave trade, reading books on the subject such as the Quaker Anthony Benezet's *Historical Account of Guinea* (1771). After winning the award for his essay, Clarkson experienced conversion, gave up his quest to become a clergyman, and dedicated his life to ending the slave trade. Quaker abolitionists whom he met published his Cambridge essay in 1786 as *An Essay on the Slavery and Commerce of the Human Species*. His influential *Essay* significantly led to a formal anti-slavery lobbying committee spearheaded by William Wilberforce. Once formed, the committee commissioned Clarkson to gather evidence on the atrocities of the slave trade. Over the course of seven years, he traveled some 35,000 miles by horseback collecting information at London, Bristol, Liverpool, Manchester, Bath, Gloucester, Worcester, Chester, Lancaster, and Birmingham. Although not immediately rewarded for his efforts, Clarkson lived long enough to witness legislation passed in Parliament that ended the slave trade in 1807, and later in 1833, the abolishment of slavery throughout the British Empire.

FIGURE 50.1 Thomas Clarkson (Detail), courtesy of the National Portrait Gallery, London.

An Essay on the Slavery and Commerce of the Human Species

If any man had originally been endued with power, as with other faculties, so that the rest of mankind had discovered in themselves an *innate necessity* of obeying this particular person; it is evident that he and his descendants, from the superiority of their nature, would have had a claim upon men for obedience, and a natural right to command: but as the right to empire is *adventitious*; as all were originally free; as nature made every man's body and mind *his own*; it is evident that no just man can be consigned to *slavery*, without his own *consent*.

Neither can men, by the same principles, be considered as lands, goods, or houses, among *possessions*. It is necessary that all *property* should be inferiour to its *possessor*. But how does the *slave* differ from his *master*, but by *chance*? For though the mark, with which the latter is pleased to brand him, shews, at the first sight, the difference of their *fortune*; what mark can be found in his *nature*, that can warrant a distinction?

To this consideration we shall add the following, that if men can justly become the property of each other, their children, like the offspring of cattle, must inherit their *paternal* lot. Now, as the actions of the father and the child must be thus at the sole disposal of the common master, it is evident, that the *authority* of the one, as a *parent*, and the *duty* of the other, as a *child*, must be instantly annihilated; rights and obligations, which, as they are founded in nature, are implanted in our feelings, and are established by the voice of God, must contain in their annihilation a solid argument to prove, that there cannot be any *property* whatever in the *human species*.

We may consider also, as a farther confirmation, that it is impossible, in the nature of things, that *liberty* can be *bought* or *sold!* It is neither *saleable*, nor *purchasable.* For if any one man can have an absolute property in the liberty of another, or, in other words, if he, who is called a *master*, can have a *just* right to command the actions of him, who is called a *slave*, it is evident that the latter cannot be accountable for those crimes, which the former may order him to commit. Now as every reasonable being is accountable for his actions, it is evident, that such a right cannot *justly* exist, and that human liberty, of course, is beyond the possibility either of *sale* or *purchase*. Add to this, that, whenever you sell the liberty of a man, you have the power only of alluding to the *body*: the *mind* cannot be confined or bound: it will be free, though its mansion be beset with chains. But if, in every sale of the *human species*, you are under the necessity of considering your slave in this abstracted light; of alluding only to the body, and of making no allusion to the mind; you are under the necessity also of treating him, in the same moment, as a *brute*, and of abusing therefore that nature, which cannot otherwise be considered, than in the double capacity of *soul* and *body*.

But some person, perhaps, will make an objection to one of the former arguments. "If men, from the *superiority* of their nature, cannot be considered, like lands, goods, or houses, among possessions, so neither can cattle: for being endued with life, motion, and sensibility, they are evidently *superiour* to these." But this objection will receive its answer from those observations which have been already made; and will discover the true reason, why cattle are justly to be estimated as property. For first, the right to empire over brutes, is *natural*, and not *adventitious*, like the right to empire over men. There are, secondly, many and evident signs of the *inferiority* of their nature; and thirdly, their liberty can be bought and sold, because being void of reason, they cannot be *accountable* for their actions.

We might stop here for a considerable time, and deduce many valuable lessons from the remarks that have been made, but that such a circumstance might be considered as a digression. There is one, however, which, as it is so intimately connected with the subject, we cannot but deduce. We are taught to treat men in a different manner from brutes, because they are so manifestly superiour in their nature; we are taught to treat brutes in a different manner from stones, for the same reason; and thus, by giving to every created thing its due respect, to answer the views of Providence, which did not create a variety of natures without a purpose or design.

But if these things are so, how evidently against reason, nature, and every thing human and divine, must they act, who not only force men into *slavery*, against their own *consent*, but treat them altogether as *brutes*, and make the *natural liberty* of man an article of public commerce! And by what arguments can they possibly defend that commerce, which cannot be carried on, in any single instance, without a flagrant violation of the laws of nature and of God?...

It remains only now to examine by what arguments those, who *receive* or *purchase* their fellow-creatures into slavery, defend the *commerce*. Their first plea is, "that they receive those with propriety, who are convicted of crimes, because they are delivered into their hands by *their own magistrates*." But what is this to you *receivers*? Have the unfortunate *convicts* been guilty of injury to *you*? Have they broken *your* treaties? Have they plundered *your* ships? Have they carried *your* wives and children into slavery, that *you* should thus retaliate? Have they offended *you* even by word or gesture?

But if the African convicts are innocent with respect to you; if you have not even the shadow of a claim upon their persons; by what right do you receive them? "By the laws of the Africans," you will say; "by which it is positively allowed." But can *laws* alter the nature of vice? They may give it a sanction perhaps: it will still be immutably the same, and, though dressed in the outward habiliments of *honour*, will still be *intrinsically base*.

But alas! you do not only attempt to defend yourselves by these arguments, but even dare to give your actions the appearance of lenity, and assume *merit* from your *baseness*! And how first ought you particularly to blush, when you assert, "that prisoners of war are only purchased from the hands of their conquerors, *to deliver them from death*." Ridiculous defence! Can the most credulous believe it? You entice the Africans to war; you foment their quarrels; you supply them with arms and ammunition, and all—from the *motives of benevolence*. Does a man set fire to a house, for the purpose of rescuing the inhabitants from the flames? But if they are only purchased, to *deliver them from death*; why, when they are delivered into your hands, as protectors, do you torture them with hunger? Why do you kill them with fatigue? Why does the whip deform their bodies, or the knife their limbs? Why do you sentence them to death, to a death, infinitely more excruciating than that from which you so kindly saved them? What answer do you make to this? For if you had not humanely preserved them from the hands of their conquerors, a quick death perhaps, and that in the space of a moment, had freed them from their pain: but on account of your *favour* and *benevolence*, it is known, that they have lingered years in pain and agony, and have been sentenced, at last, to a dreadful death for the most insignificant offence.

Neither can we allow the other argument to be true, on which you found your merit; "that you take them from their country for their own convenience; because Africa, scorched with incessant heat, and subject to the most violent rains and tempests, is unwholesome, and unfit to be inhabited." Preposterous men! Do you thus judge from your own feelings? Do you thus judge from your own constitution and frame? But if you suppose that the Africans are incapable of enduring their own climate, because you cannot endure it yourselves; why do you receive them into slavery? Why do you not measure them here by the same standard? For if you are unable to bear hunger and thirst, chains and imprisonment, wounds and torture, why do you not suppose them incapable of enduring the same treatment? Thus then is your argument turned against yourselves…

We may add to these observations, from the testimony of those who have written the History of Africa from their own inspection, that no country is more luxurious in prospects, none more fruitful, none more rich in herds and flocks, and none, where the comforts of life can be gained with so little trouble.

But you say again, as a confirmation of these your former arguments, (by which you would have it understood, that the Africans themselves are sensible of the goodness of your intentions) "that they do not appear to go with you against their will." Impudent and base assertion! Why then do you load them with chains? Why keep you your daily and nightly watches? But alas, as a farther, though a more melancholy proof, of the falsehood of your assertions, how many, when on board your ships, have put a period to their existence? How many have leaped into the sea? How many have pined to death, that, even at the expence of their lives, they might fly from your *benevolence?*

Do you call them obstinate then, because they refuse your favours? Do you call them ungrateful, because they make you this return? How much rather ought you receivers to blush? How much rather ought you receivers to be considered as abandoned and execrable; who, when you usurp the dominion over those, who are as free and independent as yourselves, break the first law of justice, which ordains, "that no person shall do harm to another, without a previous provocation;" who offend against the dictates of nature, which commands, "that no just man shall be given or received into slavery against his own consent;" and who violate the very laws of the empire that you assume, by consigning your subjects to misery…

We come now to that other system of reasoning, which is always applied, when the former is confuted; "that the Africans are an inferiour link of the chain of nature, and are made for slavery."

This assertion is proved by two arguments; the first of which was advanced also by the ancients, and is drawn from the *inferiority of their capacities.*

Let us allow then for a moment, that they appear to have no parts, that they appear to be void of understanding. And is this wonderful, when you *receivers* depress their senses by hunger? Is this wonderful, when by incessant labour, the continual application of the lash, and the most inhuman treatment that imagination can devise, you overwhelm their genius, and hinder it from breaking forth?— No,—you confound their abilities by the severity of their servitude: for as a spark of fire, if crushed by too great a weight of incumbent fuel, cannot be blown into a flame, but suddenly expires, so the human mind, if depressed by rigorous servitude, cannot be excited to a display of those faculties, which might otherwise have shone with the brightest lustre.

Neither is it wonderful in another point of view. For what is it that awakens the abilities of men, and distinguishes them from the common herd? Is it not often the amiable hope of becoming serviceable to individuals, or the state? Is it not often the hope of riches, or of power? Is it not frequently the hope of temporary honours, or a lasting fame? These principles have all a wonderful effect upon the mind. They call upon it to exert its faculties, and bring those talents to the public view, which had otherwise been concealed. But the unfortunate Africans have no such incitements as these, that they should show their genius. They have no hope of riches, power, honours, fame. They have no hope but this, that their miseries will be soon terminated by death ...

Let us now follow them to the colonies. They are carried over in the unfavourable situation described. It is observed here, that though their abilities cannot be estimated high, from a want of cultivation, they are yet various, and that they vary in proportion as the nation, from which they have been brought, has advanced more or less in the scale of social life. This observation, which is so frequently made, is of great importance: for if their abilities expand in proportion to the improvement of their state, it is a clear indication, that if they were equally improved, they would be equally ingenious ...

But where these impediments have been removed, where they have received an education, and have known and pronounced the language with propriety, these defects have vanished, and their productions have been less objectionable. For a proof of this, we appeal to the writings of an African girl [Phillis Wheatley], who made no contemptible appearance in this species of composition. She was kidnapped when only eight years old, and, in the year 1761, was transported to America, where she was sold with other slaves. She had no school education there, but receiving some little instruction from the family, with whom she was so fortunate as to live, she obtained such a knowledge of the English language within sixteen months from the time of her arrival, as to be able to speak it and read it to the astonishment of those who heard her. She soon afterwards learned to write, and having a great inclination to learn the Latin tongue, she was indulged by her master, and made a progress. Her Poetical works were published with his permission, in the year 1773. They contain thirty-eight pieces on different subjects ...

To this poetry we shall only add, as a farther proof of their abilities, the Prose compositions of Ignatius Sancho, who received some little education. His letters are too well known, to make any extract, or indeed any farther mention of him, necessary. If other examples of African genius should be required, suffice it to say, that they can be produced in abundance; and that if we were allowed to enumerate instances of African gratitude, patience, fidelity, honour, as so many instances of good sense, and a sound understanding, we fear that thousands of the enlightened Europeans would have occasion to blush.

But an objection will be made here, that the two persons whom we have particularized by name, are prodigies, and that if we were to live for many years, we should scarcely meet with two other Africans of the same description. But we reply, that considering their situation as before described, two persons, above mediocrity in the literary way, are as many as can be expected within a certain period of years; and farther, that if these are prodigies, they are only such prodigies as every day would produce, if they had the same opportunities of acquiring knowledge as other people, and the same expectations in life to excite their genius.

Thomas Clarkson, *An Essay on the Slavery and Commerce of the Human Species, Particularly the African* (London: J. Phillips, 1786), 68–72, 108–11, 113–4, 164–5, 168–9, 171–2, 175–6.

51

An Appeal to the Higher Ranks
of Society

Hannah More

THE FOURTH OF five daughters born to Mary Grace and Jacob More, Hannah More (1745–1833) grew up in a small cottage at Fishponds in Gloucestershire, England, where her father was the master of the free school within the parish of Stapleton, north of Bristol. The Mores lived frugally on Jacob's meager salary but profited from his extensive knowledge. Hannah learned Latin and mathematics from her father at age eight and later picked up French, Italian, and Spanish when she attended a school in Bristol founded by her older sisters in 1758. At age twenty-two, Hannah agreed to marry William Turner, a local gentry twenty years her senior, who resided in the outskirts of Bristol. Turner had two cousins attending the More sisters' school and so probably met Hannah through that connection. Marrying a cultivated and rich gentleman would have been a dream for a girl like Hannah born of humble origin, but the wedding never took place. Humiliating More, Turner postponed the wedding at least three times during the course of six years for reasons not entirely known. Now twenty-eight, Hannah turned her attention to writing, publishing poems, essays, and plays in the 1770s. With the help of her patron, the famous English actor David Garrick, More's play *Percy* became the toast of the town after its London debut at the Covenant Garden Theater on December 10, 1777. With the success of *Percy*, and her subsequent writings, More experienced a meteoric rise in social status, enabling her to mingle freely with literary critics like Samuel Johnson and Elizabeth Montagu, politicians such as Edmund Burke, and other English elites, including Horace Walpole and Sir Charles Middleton.

In the 1780s and 1790s, More veered away from her worldly pursuits and joined the ranks of evangelicals like Thomas Clarkson, Zachary Macaulay, Henry Thornton, and William Wilberforce—members of the so-called Clapham sect—committed to the abolition of the slave trade. More also became involved in setting

FIGURE 51.1 Hannah More (Detail), courtesy of the National Portrait Gallery, London.

up Sunday schools in the county of Somerset. With the assistance of her sister Patty, and financial aid coming from Wilberforce, Hannah established a number of schools in the 1790s within the industrial district of Mendip. In 1795, she organized the Cheap Repository Tracts, which printed inexpensive chapbooks that contained brief religious stories intended for the lower ranks of society. Begun in February, the Cheap Repository had sold an astounding one million tracts by the end of the year. Yet despite More's concern for the laboring poor, she did not turn her back on England's more prominent residents. She maintained contact with aristocrats and gentry, subtly attempting to evangelize many of them, and, through her printed works, hoped to awaken them to their apparent religious complacency. One of More's bestsellers was her *Thoughts on the Importance of Manners of the Great to General Society*, published in March 1788. Appearing at a time when contemporaries perceived Britain as deteriorating morally, and shortly after the humiliating loss of America, *Thoughts on the Importance of Manners* was a call for religious reform from "the Great." More argued that, rather than quietly watch the nation abandon godliness in favor of materialism and vice, the higher ranks should lead by example. Although born in relative poverty, Hannah More ascended to a position where her literary talents and favorable social standing could showcase the strengths of evangelical Christianity to England's fashionable society.

Thoughts on the Importance of the Manners of the Great to General Society

TO a large and honourable class of the community, to persons considerable in reputation, important by their condition in life, and commendable for the decency of their general conduct, these slight hints are respectfully addressed. They are not intended as a satire upon vice, or a ridicule upon folly, being written neither for the foolish nor the vicious. The subject is too serious for ridicule; and those to whom it is addressed are too respectable for satire. It is recommended to the consideration of those who, filling the higher ranks in life, are naturally regarded as patterns, by which the manners of the rest of the world are to be fashioned...

For though outward actions are the surest, and to human eyes, the only evidences of sincerity, yet Christianity is a religion of *motives* and *principles*. The gospel is continually referring to the *heart*, as the source of good; it is to the poor in *spirit*, to the pure in *heart*, that the divine blessing is annexed. A man may correct many improper practices, and refrain from many immoral actions, from merely human motives; but, though this partial amendment is not without its uses, yet this is only attacking symptoms, and neglecting the mortal disease. But to subdue a worldly temper, to control irregular desires, and to have a clean heart, is to extinguish the soul, and spirit, and essence of sin. Totally to *accomplish* this, is, perhaps, beyond the narrow limits of human perfection; but to *attempt* it (with an humble reliance on superior aid), is so far from being an extravagant or romantic flight of virtue, that it is but the common duty of every ordinary Christian. And this perfection is not the less real, because it is a point which seems constantly to recede from our approaches. Our highest attainments, instead of bringing us "to the mark," only teach us to remove the mark to a greater distance, by giving us more humbling views of ourselves, and more exalted conceptions of the state which we are labouring after. Though the progress towards perfection may be perpetual in this world, the actual attainment is reserved for a better. And this restless desire of a happiness which we cannot reach, and this lively idea of a perfection which we cannot attain, are among the many arguments for a future state, which seem to come little short of absolute demonstration...

But after all, is an excessive and intemperate zeal the *common* vice of the times? Is there any *very* imminent danger that the enthusiasm of the great should transport them to dangerous and inconvenient excesses? Are our young men of fashion so *very* much led away by the ardour of piety, that they require to have their imaginations cooled by the freezing maxims of worldly wisdom? Is the spirit of the age so *very* much inclined to catch and to communicate the fire of devotion, as to require to be damped by admonition, or extinguished by ridicule? When the inimitable Cervantes attacked the wild notions and romantic ideas which misled the age in which he lived, he did wisely, because he combated an actually existing evil; but in this latter end of the eighteenth century, there seems to be little more occasion (among persons of rank, I mean) of cautions against enthusiasm than against chivalry; and he who declaims against religious excesses in the company of well bred people, shews himself to be as little acquainted with the manners of the times, as he would do who should think it a point of duty to write another Don Quixote...

It is, perhaps, one of the most alarming symptoms of the degeneracy of morals in the present day, that the distinctions of right and wrong are almost swept away

in polite conversation. The most serious offences are often named with cool indifference; the most shameful profligacy with affected tenderness. The substitution
of the word *gallantry* for that crime which stabs domestic happiness and conju-
gal virtue, is one of the most dangerous of all the modern abuses of language.
Atrocious deeds should never be called by gentle names. This must certainly contribute, more than any thing, to diminish the horror of vice in the rising generation. That our passions should be too often engaged on the side of error, we may
look for the cause, though not for the vindication, in the unresisted propensities
of our constitution: but that our *reason* should ever be employed in its favour, that
our *conversation* should ever be taught to palliate it, that our *judgment* should ever
look on it with indifference, has no shadow of excuse because this can pretend to
no foundation in nature, no apology in temptation, no palliative in passion.

However defective, therefore, our practice may be; however we may be allured
by seduction, or precipitated by passion, let us beware of lowering the STANDARD
OF RIGHT. This induces an imperceptible corruption into the heart, stagnates the
noblest principle of action, irrecoverably debases the sense of moral and religious
obligation, and prevents us from living up to the height of our nature. It cuts off
all communication with virtue, and almost prevents the possibility of a return to
it. If we do not rise as high as we aim, we shall rise the higher for having aimed at
a lofty mark: but where the RULE is low, the practice cannot be high, though the
converse of the proposition is not proportionally true...

I cannot dismiss this part of my subject without animadverting on the too
prompt alacrity, even of worthy people, to disseminate, in public and general
conversation, instances of their unsuccessful attempts to do good. I never hear a
charity story begun to be related in mixed company, that I do not tremble for the
catastrophe, lest it should exhibit some mortifying disappointment, which may
deter the inexperienced from running any generous hazards, and excite harsh sus-
picions, at an age, when it is less dishonourable to meet with a few casual hurts,
and transient injuries, than to go cased in the cumbersome and impenetrable
armour of distrust. The liberal should be particularly cautious how they furnish
the avaricious with creditable pretences for saving their money, as all the instances
of the mortifications of the humane are added to the armory of the covetous man's
arguments, and produced, as defensive weapons, upon every fresh attack on his
heart or his purse.

But I am willing to hope that that uncharitableness which we so often meet
with in persons of advanced years, is not always the effect of a heart naturally
hard. Misanthropy is very often nothing but abused sensibility. Long habits of the
world, and a melancholy conviction how little good he has been able to do in it,
hardens many a tender hearted person. The milk of human kindness becomes
soured by repeated acts of ingratitude. This commonly induces an indifference
to the well-being of others, and a hopelessness of adding to the stock of human

virtue and human happiness. This uncomfortable disease is very fond of spreading its own contagion, which is a cruelty to the healthy of young and uninfected virtue.—For this distemper, generated by a too sanguine disposition, and grown chronic from repeated disappointments, there is but one remedy, or rather one prevention: and this is a genuine principle of piety. He who is once convinced that he is to assist his fellow creatures, because it is the will of God, and one of the conditions of obtaining his favour, will soon get above all uneasiness when the consequence does not answer his expectation. He will soon become only anxious to do his duty, humbly committing events to higher hands. Disappointments will then only serve to refine his motives, and purify his virtue. His charity will then become a sacrifice less unworthy of the altar on which it is offered. His affections will be more spiritualized, and his devotions more intense. Nothing short of such a courageous piety can preserve a heart hackneyed in the world from relaxed diligence, or criminal despair.

People in general are not aware of the mischief of judging of the rightness of any action by its prosperity, or of the excellence of any institution by the abuse of it. We must never proportion our exertions to our success, but to our duty. If every laudable undertaking were to be dropped because it failed in some cases, or was abused in others, there would not be left an Alms-House, a Charity-School, or an Hospital in the land. And if every right practice were to be discontinued because it had been found not to be successful in every instance, this false reasoning pushed to the extreme, might at last be brought as an argument for shutting up our churches, and burning our bibles.

But if, on the one hand, there is a proud and arrogant discretion which ridicules, as Utopian and romantic, every generous project of the active and the liberal; so there is on the other, a sort of popular bounty which arrogates to itself the exclusive name of *feeling*, and rejects with disdain the influence of an higher principle. I am far from intending to depreciate this humane and exquisitely tender sentiment, which the beneficent Author of our nature gave us, as a stimulus to remove the distresses of others, in order to get rid of our own uneasiness. I would only observe, that where not strengthened by superior motives, it is a casual and precarious instrument of good, and ceases to operate, except in the immediate presence, and within the audible cry of misery. This sort of feeling forgets that any calamity exists which is out of its own sight; and though it would empty its purse for such an occasional object as rouses transient sensibility, yet it seldom makes any stated provision for miseries, which are not the less real because they do not obtrude upon the sight, and awaken the tenderness of immediate sympathy. This is a mechanical charity, which requires springs and wheels to set it a going; whereas, real Christian charity does not wait to be acted upon by impressions and impulses...

But though the passive and self-denying virtues are not high in the esteem of mere good sort of people, yet they are peculiarly the evangelical virtues. The world extols brilliant actions; the Gospel enjoins good habits and right motives: it seldom inculcates those splendid deeds which make heroes, or those sounding sentences which constitute philosophers; but it enjoins the harder task of renouncing self, of living uncorrupted in the world, of subduing besetting sins, and of not thinking of ourselves more highly than we ought. The acquisition of glory was the precept of other religions, the contempt of it is the perfection of Christianity.

Let us then be consistent, and we shall never be contemptible, even in the eyes of our enemies. Let not the unbeliever say that we have one set of opinions for our theory, and another for our practice; that to the vulgar:

We shew the rough and thorny way to heav'n,
While we the primrose path of dalliance tread.

It would become our characters as men of sense, of which consistency is a most unequivocal proof, to choose some rule and abide by it. An extempore Christian is a ridiculous character. Fixed principles will be followed by a consistent course of action; while indecision of spirit will produce instability of conduct. If there be a model which we profess to admire, let us square our lives by it. If the Koran of Mahomet, or the Revelations of Zoroaster, be a perfect guide, let us follow one of them. If either Epicurus, Zeno, or Confucius, be the peculiar object of our veneration and respect, let us fashion our conduct by the dictates of their philosophy; and then, though we may be wrong, we shall not be absurd. But if the Bible be in truth the word of God, as we profess to believe, we need look no farther for a consummate pattern. Let us then make it the rule of our practice here, if it is indeed to be the rule of our judgment hereafter...

But vain will be all endeavours after *partial* and *subordinate* amendment. Reformation must begin with the GREAT, or it will never be effectual. *Their* example is the fountain from whence the vulgar draw their habits, actions, and characters. To expect to reform the poor while the opulent are corrupt, is to throw odours into the stream while the springs are poisoned. Even the excellent institution of Sunday Schools for training religious servants, will avail but little, if as soon as the persons there educated, come into the families of the great, they behold practices diametrically opposite to the instructions they have been imbibing. If they fall into the houses of the profligate, they will hear the doctrines which they have been taught to reverence, derided; if into mere worldly families, they will see them neglected: and to the essential principle of vital Christianity, oblivion is scarcely less fatal than contempt...

It was not by inflicting pains and penalties that Christianity first made its way into the world: the divine truths it inculcated received irresistible confirmation from the LIVES, PRACTICES, and EXAMPLES, of its venerable professors. These were arguments which no popular prejudice could resist, no Jewish logic refute, and no Pagan persecution discredit. Had the primitive Christians only *praised* and *promulgated* the most perfect religion the world ever saw, it could have produced but very slender effects on the faith and manners of the people, if the jealous and inquisitive eye of malice could have detected that the DOCTRINES they recommended had not been illustrated by the LIVES they led.

Hannah More, *Thoughts on the Importance of the Manners of the Great to General Society*, second edition (London: T. Cadell, 1788), 1–2, 16–19, 58–60, 63–6, 68–77, 107–10, 114–5, 120–1.

52

Salvation Comes to a Sailor

Olaudah Equiano

IN THE INTERESTING *Narrative of the Life of Olaudah Equiano* (1789), a former slave named Olaudah Equiano (c. 1745–97), also known as Gustavus Vassa, chronicled his life from the time of his abduction as a youth, in what is today southeastern Nigeria, to his status as a celebrity in Britain in the last quarter of the century. Equiano claimed that he had been captured as a boy and sold to English slavers, before being put aboard a ship to the West Indies and later sent to Virginia where a planter purchased him. The planter quickly sold Equiano to Michael Henry Pascal, a lieutenant in the British Royal Navy, who renamed his slave Gustavus Vassa, taking him back to London, probably at the end of 1754. After years of faithful service, Equiano expected Pascal to free him in 1762 but instead was resold to a Quaker named Robert King in the West Indies. Through astute business ventures, Equiano saved enough money to purchase his freedom from King in 1766. The newly freed man earned a living as a sailor and hairdresser for Dr. Charles Irving, a naval surgeon who developed a method for desalinating seawater. In May 1772, Equiano joined an expedition led by Constantine John Phipps toward the North Pole, with the goal of finding a shorter route to India.

Believing that he narrowly escaped death during the Arctic voyage, Equiano searched for spiritual guidance when he returned to London in 1773. He began attending St. James's Anglican parish church at Piccadilly, sometimes two or three times daily. Not satisfied, he looked into Quakerism, Roman Catholicism, and Judaism. At one point he even considered moving to Turkey, perceiving that Muslims were in many cases godlier than most Christians he encountered. In the midst of his despair, he met a pair of silk weavers from Holborn who gave him a copy of Lawrence Harlow's *The Conversion of an Indian* (1774), which tells the story of a man who found Christianity after moving to a foreign land. Equiano came to understand that his ability to keep eight out of the Ten Commandments would not ensure his eternal salvation. He was told that he needed to experience a "new birth" whereby God would offer a pardon of one's sin on the merits of Christ's

FIGURE 52.1 Olaudah Equiano (Detail), courtesy of the National Portrait Gallery, London.

death on the cross. After hearing a sermon by the Reverend Henry Peckwell, a Calvinistic Methodist minister, Equiano desired to partake of the Lord's Supper. But upon examination, Peckwell determined that the young man had not yet experienced conversion.

Needing more income, Equiano left London for the seas again, this time aboard the *Hope* headed to Spain in late 1774. Now more spiritually sensitive, Equiano cringed when he heard the blasphemous language of the sailors. He returned to London where he met the evangelical social reformer George Smith, who gave his new friend a pocket Bible and Joseph Alleine's *An Alarme to Unconverted Sinners* (1673) before Equiano boarded the *Hope* on its way to Cádiz again. While en route, Equiano read from Acts 4:12, later reflecting that on this occasion "the Lord was pleased to break in upon my soul with his bright beams of heavenly light...I saw the Lord Jesus Christ in his humiliation, loaded and bearing my reproach, sin, and shame. I then clearly perceived that by the deeds of the law no flesh living could be justified. I was then convinced that by the first Adam sin came, and by the second Adam (the Lord Jesus Christ) all that are saved must be made alive. It was given me at that time to know what it was to be born again." Equiano had experienced conversion. Returning to London in December, he heard a sermon by the Anglican evangelical William Romaine at Blackfriars Church which affirmed that good deeds could not replace divine grace. An overjoyed Equiano exited the church feeling confident that he was now a child of God.

In the years that followed, Equiano devoted his life to the abolitionist movement in England. In the 1780s, he worked with Thomas Clarkson, William Wilberforce, Granville Sharp, and others in helping to end the Atlantic slave trade in Britain. In 1789, Equiano published his *Interesting Narrative*, which not only made him wealthy but also bolstered the argument of the abolitionists by offering a first-hand account of the treacherous Middle Passage from the perspective of a former slave. At the time of his death on March 31, 1797, the *Interesting Narrative* had gone through eleven editions, making Equiano the best-known person of African descent in the Atlantic world.

The Interesting Narrative of the Life of Olaudah Equiano

In process of time I left my master, Doctor Irving, the purifier of waters. I lodged in Coventry-court, Haymarket, where I was continually oppressed and much concerned about the salvation of my soul, and was determined (in my own strength) to be a first-rate Christian. I used every means for this purpose; and, not being able to find any person amongst those with whom I was then acquainted that acquiesced with me in point of religion, or, in scripture language, that would shew me any good, I was much dejected, and knew not where to seek relief; however, I first frequented the neighbouring churches, St. James's, and others, two or three times a day, for many weeks: still I came away dissatisfied; something was wanting that I could not get at, and I really found more heartfelt relief in reading my bible at home than in attending the church; and, being resolved to be saved, I pursued other methods. First I went among the Quakers, where the word of God was neither read or preached, so that I remained as much in the dark as ever. I then searched into the Roman Catholic principles, but was not in the least edified. I at length had recourse to the Jews, and that availed me nothing, as the fear of eternity daily harassed my mind, and I knew not where to seek shelter from the wrath to come. However this was my conclusion, at all events, to read the four evangelists, and whatever sect or party I found adhering thereto such I would join. Thus I went on heavily without any guide to direct me the way that leadeth to eternal life. I asked different people questions about the manner of going to heaven, and was told different ways. Here I was much staggered, and could not find any at that time more righteous than myself, or indeed so much inclined to devotion. I thought we should not all be saved (this is agreeable to the Holy Scriptures), nor would all be damned. I found none among the circle of my acquaintance that kept wholly the Ten Commandments. So righteous was I in my own eyes, that I was convinced I excelled many of them in that point, by keeping eight out of ten; and finding those who in general termed themselves Christians not so honest or so good in their morals as the Turks, I really thought the Turks were in a safer way of salvation than my neighbours: so that between hopes and fears I went on, and the chief comforts I enjoyed were in the musical French horn, which I then practiced, and also dressing of hair. Such was my situation some months, experiencing the dishonesty of many people here. I determined at last to set out for Turkey, and there to end my days. It was now early in the spring 1774 ...

The next day I took courage, and went to Holborn, to see my new and worthy acquaintance, the old man, Mr. C—; he, with his wife, a gracious woman, were at work at silk weaving; they seemed mutually happy, and both quite glad to see me, and I more so to see them. I sat down, and we conversed much about soul matters, &c. Their discourse was amazingly delightful, edifying, and pleasant. I knew not at last how to leave this agreeable pair, till time summoned me away. As I was going they lent me a little book, entitled "The Conversion of an Indian." It was in questions and answers. The poor man came over the sea to London, to inquire after the Christian's God, who, (through rich mercy) he found, and had not his journey in vain. The above book was of great use to me, and at that time was a means of strengthening my faith; however, in parting, they both invited me to call on them when I pleased. This delighted me, and I took care to make all the improvement from it I could; and so far I thanked God for such company and desires. I prayed that the many evils I felt with might be done away, and that I might be weaned from my former carnal acquaintances. This was quickly heard and answered, and I was soon connected with those whom the scripture calls the excellent of the earth. I heard the gospel preached, and the thoughts of my heart and actions were laid open by the preachers, and the way of salvation by Christ alone was evidently set forth. Thus I went on happily for near two months; and I once heard, during this period, a reverend gentleman speak of a man who had departed this life in full assurance of his going to glory. I was much astonished at the assertion; and did very deliberately inquire how he could get at this knowledge. I was answered fully, agreeable to what I read in the oracles of truth; and was told also, that if I did not experience the new birth, and the pardon of my sins, through the blood of Christ, before I died, I could not enter the kingdom of heaven. I knew not what to think of this report, as I thought I kept eight commandments out of ten; then my worthy interpreter told me I did not do it, nor could I; and he added, that no man ever did or could keep the commandments, without offending in one point. I thought this sounded very strange, and puzzled me much for many weeks; for I thought it a hard saying. I then asked my friend, Mr. L—d, who was a clerk in a chapel, why the commandments of God were given, if we could not be saved by them? To which he replied, "The law is a schoolmaster to bring us to Christ," who alone could and did keep the commandments, and fulfilled all their requirements for his elect people, even those to whom he had given a living faith, and the sins of those chosen vessels *were already* atoned for and forgiven them whilst living; and if I did not experience the same before my exit, the Lord would say at that great day to me "Go ye cursed," &c. &c. For God would appear faithful in his judgments to the wicked, as he would be faithful in shewing mercy to those who were ordained to it before the world was; therefore Christ Jesus seemed to be all in all to that man's soul. I was much wounded at this discourse, and brought into such a dilemma as I never expected. I asked him, if *he* was to die that moment, whether he was sure to enter the kingdom of God, and added, "Do you *know* that your sins are forgiven you?" He answered in the affirmative. Then confusion, anger, and discontent seized me, and I staggered much at this sort of doctrine; it brought me to a stand, not knowing which to believe, whether salvation by works or by faith only in Christ. I requested him to tell me how I might know when my sins were forgiven me. He assured me he could not, and that none but God alone could do this. I told him it was very mysterious; but he said it was really matter of fact, and quoted many portions of scripture immediately to the point, to which I could make no reply. He then desired me to pray to God to shew me these things. I answered, that I prayed to God every day. He said, "I perceive you are a churchman." I answered I was. He then entreated me to beg of God to shew me what I was, and the true state of my soul. I thought the prayer very short and odd; so we parted for that time. I weighed all these things well over, and could not help thinking how it was possible for a man to know that his sins were forgiven him in this life. I wished that God would reveal this self same thing unto me. In a short time after this I went to Westminster chapel; the Rev. Mr. P—preached, from Lamentations 3:39. It was a wonderful sermon; he clearly shewed that a living man had no cause to complain for the punishment of his sins; he evidently justified the Lord in all his dealings with the sons of men; he also shewed the justice of God in the eternal punishment of the wicked and impenitent. The discourse seemed to me like a two-edged sword cutting all ways; it afforded me much joy, intermingled with many fears, about my soul; and when it was ended, he gave it out that he intended, the ensuing week, to examine all those who meant to attend the Lord's Table. Now I thought much of my good works, and at the same time was doubtful of my being a proper object to receive the sacrament; I was full of meditation till the day of examining. However, I went to the chapel, and, though much distressed, I addressed the reverend gentleman, thinking, if I was not right, he would endeavour to convince me of it. When I conversed with him, the first thing he asked me was, what I knew of Christ? I told him I believed in him, and had been baptized in his name. "Then," said he, "when were you brought to the knowledge of God, and how were you convinced of sin?" I knew not what he meant by these questions; I told him I kept eight commandments out of ten; but that I sometimes swore on board a ship, and sometimes when on shore, and broke the Sabbath. He then asked me if I could read? I answered, "Yes."—"Then," said he, "do you not read in the bible, he that offends in one point is guilty of all?" I said, "Yes." Then he assured me, that one sin unatoned for was as sufficient to damn a soul as one leak was to sink a ship. Here I was struck with awe; for the minister exhorted me much, and reminded me of the shortness of time, and the length of eternity, and that no unregenerate soul, or any thing unclean, could enter the kingdom of Heaven. He did not admit me as a communicant; but recommended me to read the scriptures, and hear the word preached, not to neglect fervent prayer to God, who has promised to hear the supplications of those who seek him in godly sincerity; so I took my leave of him, with many thanks, and resolved to follow his advice, so far as the Lord would condescend to enable me. During this time I was out of employ, nor was I likely to get a situation suitable for me, which obliged me to go once more to sea. I engaged as steward of a ship called the Hope, Capt. Richard Strange, bound from London to Cadiz in Spain. In a short time after I was on board I heard the name of God much blasphemed, and I feared greatly, lest I should catch the horrible infection. I thought if I sinned again, after having life and death set evidently before me, I should certainly go to hell. My mind was uncommonly chagrined, and I murmured much at God's providential dealings with me, and was discontented with the commandments, that I could not be saved by what I had done; I hated all things, and wished I had never been born; confusion seized me, and I wished to be annihilated. One day I was standing on the very edge of the stern of the ship, thinking to drown myself; but this scripture was instantly impressed on my mind—"that no murderer hath eternal life abiding in him," 1 John 3:15. Then I paused, and thought myself the unhappiest man living. Again I was convinced that the Lord was better to me than I deserved, and I was better off in the world than many. After this I began to fear death; I fretted, mourned, and prayed, till I became a burden to others, but more so to myself. At length I concluded to beg my bread on shore rather than go again to sea amongst a people who feared not God, and I entreated the captain three different times to discharge me; he would not, but each time gave me greater and greater encouragement to continue with him, and all on board shewed me very great civility: notwithstanding all this I was unwilling to embark again. At last some of my religious friends advised me, by saying it was my lawful calling, consequently it was my duty to obey, and that God was not confined to place, &c. &c. particularly Mr. G.S. the governor of Tothil-fields Bridewell, who pitied my case, and read the eleventh chapter of the Hebrews to me, with exhortations. He prayed for me, and I believed that he prevailed on my behalf, as my burden was then greatly removed, and I found a heartfelt resignation to the will of God. The good man gave me a pocket Bible and Alleine's Alarm to the Unconverted. We parted, and the next day I went on board again. We sailed for Spain, and I found favour with the captain. It was the fourth of the month of September when we sailed from London; we had a delightful voyage to Cadiz, where we arrived the twenty-third of the same month. The place is strong, commands a fine prospect, and is very rich. The Spanish galloons frequented that port, and some arrived whilst we were there. I had many opportunities of reading the scriptures. I wrestled hard with God in fervent prayer, who had declared in his word that he would hear the groanings and deep sighs of the poor in spirit. I found this verified to my utter astonishment and comfort in the following manner:

On the morning of the 6th of October, (I pray you to attend) or all that day, I thought that I should either see or hear something supernatural. I had a secret impulse on my mind of something that was to take place, which drove me continually for that time to a throne of grace. It pleased God to enable me to wrestle with him, as Jacob did: I prayed that if sudden death were to happen, and I perished, it might be at Christ's feet.

In the evening of the same day, as I was reading and meditating on the fourth chapter of the Acts, twelfth verse, under the solemn apprehensions of eternity, and reflecting on my past actions, I began to think I had lived a moral life, and that I had a proper ground to believe I had an interest in the divine favour; but still meditating on the subject, not knowing whether salvation was to be had partly for our own good deeds, or solely as the sovereign gift of God; in this deep consternation the Lord was pleased to break in upon my soul with his bright beams of heavenly light; and in an instant as it were, removing the veil, and letting light into a dark place, I saw clearly with the eye of faith the crucified Saviour bleeding on the cross on mount Calvary: the scriptures became an unsealed book, I saw myself a condemned criminal under the law, which came with its full force to my conscience, and when "the commandment came sin revived, and I died." I saw the Lord Jesus Christ in his humiliation, loaded and bearing my reproach, sin, and shame. I then clearly perceived that by the deeds of the law no flesh living could be justified. I was then convinced that by the first Adam sin came, and by the second Adam (the Lord Jesus Christ) all that are saved must be made alive. It was given me at that time to know what it was to be born again, John 3:5. I saw the eighth chapter to the Romans, and the doctrines of God's decrees, verified agreeable to his eternal, everlasting, and unchangeable purposes. The word of God was sweet to my taste, yea sweeter than honey and the honeycomb. Christ was revealed to my soul as the chief among ten thousand. These heavenly moments were really as life to the dead, and what John calls an earnest of the Spirit. This was indeed unspeakable, and I firmly believe undeniable by many. Now every leading providential circumstance that happened to me, from the day I was taken from my parents to that hour, was then in my view, as if it had but just then occurred. I was sensible of the invisible hand of God, which guided and protected me when in truth I knew it not: still the Lord pursued me although I slighted and disregarded it; this mercy melted me down. When I considered my poor wretched state I wept, seeing what great debtor I was to sovereign free grace. Now the Ethiopian was willing to be saved by Jesus Christ, the sinner's only surety, and also to rely on none other person or thing for salvation. Self was obnoxious, and good works he had none, for it is God that worketh in us both to will and to do. The amazing things of that hour can never be told—it was joy in the Holy Ghost! I felt an astonishing change; the burden of sin, the gaping jaws of hell, and the fears of death, that weighed me down before, now lost their horror; indeed I thought death would now be the best earthly friend I ever had. Such were my grief and joy as I believe are seldom experienced. I was bathed in tears, and said, What am I that God should thus look on me the vilest of sinners? I felt a deep concern for my mother and friends, which occasioned me to pray with fresh ardour; and, in the abyss of thought, I viewed the unconverted people of the world in a very awful state, being without God and without hope.

It pleased God to pour out on me the Spirit of prayer and the grace of supplication, so that in loud acclamations I was enabled to praise and glorify his most holy name. When I got out of the cabin, and told some of the people what the Lord had done for me, alas, who could understand me or believe my report!—None but to whom the arm of the Lord was revealed. I became a barbarian to them in talking of the love of Christ: his name was to me as ointment poured forth; indeed it was sweet to my soul, but to them a rock of offence. I thought my case singular, and every hour a day until I came to London, for I much longed to be with some to whom I could tell of the wonders of God's love towards me, and join in prayer to him whom my soul loved and thirsted after. I had uncommon commotions within, such as few can tell aught about. Now the bible was my only companion and comfort; I prized it much, with many thanks to God that I could read it for my self, and was not left to be tossed about or led by man's devices and notions. The worth of a soul cannot be told.—May the Lord give the reader an understanding in this. Whenever I looked in the bible I saw things new, and many texts were immediately applied to me with great comfort, for I knew that to me was the word of salvation sent. Sure I was that the Spirit which indicted the word opened my heart to receive the truth of it as it is in Jesus—that the same Spirit enabled me to act faith upon the promises that were so precious to me, and enabled me to believe to the salvation of my soul...

During this period we remained at Cadiz until our ship got laden. We sailed about the fourth of November; and, having a good passage, we arrive in London the month following, to my comfort, with heartfelt to God for his rich and unspeakable mercies. On my return I had but one text which puzzled me, or that the devil endeavoured to buffet me with, viz. Romans 11:6. And, as I had heard of the Reverend Mr. Romaine, and his great knowledge in the scriptures, I wished much to hear him preach. One day I went to Blackfriars Church, and, to my great satisfaction and surprise, he preached from that very text. He very clearly shewed the difference between human works and free election, which is according to God's sovereign will and pleasure. These glad tidings set me entirely at liberty, and I went out of the church rejoicing, seeing my spots were those of God's children. I went to Westminster Chapel, and saw some of my old friends, who were glad when they perceived the wonderful change that the Lord had wrought in me, particularly Mr. G—S—, my worthy acquaintance, who was a man of a choice spirit, and had great zeal for the Lord's service. I enjoyed his correspondence till he died in the year 1784. I was again examined at that same chapel, and was received into church fellowship amongst them: I rejoiced in spirit, making melody in my heart to the God of all my mercies. Now my whole wish was to be dissolved, and to be with Christ—but alas! I must wait mine appointed time.

Olaudah Equiano, *The Interesting Narrative of the Life of Olaudah Equiano, or Gustavus Vassa, the African*, vol. 2 (London: Printed for and sold by the author, [1789]), 116–9, 133–54.

53

Journal of an American Methodist

Francis Asbury

BORN IN A small village outside of Birmingham, England, Francis Asbury (1745–1816) apprenticed as a metalworker before dedicating his life to winning souls for Christ. As a youth, Asbury found the animated worship services of English evangelicals endearing, especially the sermons of John Fletcher, Thomas Haweis, Benjamin Ingham, Henry Venn, and George Whitefield. After his conversion, Asbury joined a Methodist class meeting at West Bromwich and began preaching at age seventeen. Later, in 1767, he became one of a hundred or so Methodist circuit riders traveling throughout Scotland, England, and Ireland. At the 1771 annual Methodist conference, Wesley asked for volunteers to support the work of Richard Boardman, John King, Joseph Pilmore, and Robert Williams in America. Of the five volunteers, Wesley appointed Asbury and Richard Wright to aid the other American Methodist preachers.

Arriving at Philadelphia on October 27, 1771, Asbury was disheartened by the segregation between northern and southern Methodists. Pilmore and Boardman remained content in limiting their ministry to Philadelphia and New York, leaving the South in the hands of King and Williams. Asbury spent much of his initial years trying to fix the organizational problems that plagued American Methodism and help bridge the social divide that split northern itinerants from their southern counterparts. Many obstacles stood in the way of reaching his goals. In the Chesapeake region, he had to contend with the sometimes hostile Anglican clergymen who viewed Methodists as uneducated enthusiasts bent on invading the South. Operationally, Asbury was forced to submit to Thomas Rankin, who Wesley had appointed as head of the American faction in 1773. Like Wesley, but different from Asbury, Rankin pledged unswerving loyalty to the Church of England and vehemently criticized American patriots for rebelling against Britain. Wesley's anti-American *Calm Address to Our American Colonies* (1776) proved especially difficult for Asbury when trying to convince the colonists that not all Methodists were loyalists. Once the conflict between America and Britain erupted into a full-scale

FIGURE 53.1 Francis Asbury (Detail), courtesy of the Library of Congress, LC-USZC4-6153.

war, all the licensed Methodist missionaries, except Asbury, returned to England. The lone Methodist leader simply could not justify deserting his flock. Yet it was this stubbornness that contributed to the eventual success of Methodism as a movement in the aftermath of the Revolutionary War.

Asbury's legacy rests on his tireless commitment as a restless itinerant and in the organizational structure that he built which sustained American Methodism for subsequent generations. Asbury rode approximately 130,000 miles on horseback, delivered roughly 10,000 sermons, and ordained between 2,000 and 3,000 preachers. In 1771, when he arrived in America, hardly a few hundred Methodists could be numbered. But in 1816, the year that Asbury died, more than 200,000 would claim the name Methodist. Asbury led by example, living an ascetic life, never marrying or owning a home, eating very little, giving away practically all his income, and rising at 4 or 5 o'clock in the morning to pray before starting the day's business. Most importantly, Asbury connected with ordinary folk. He forged lasting friendships with commoners who became the backbone of the middling constituency for the new republic's largest denomination.

An Extract from the Journal of Francis Asbury

I remember when I was a small boy and went to school, I had serious thoughts, and a particular sense of the being of a GOD; and greatly feared both an oath and a lie. At twelve years of age the Spirit of GOD strove frequently and powerfully with me: but being deprived of proper means and exposed to bad company, no effectual impressions were left on my mind. And, though fond of what some call innocent diversions, I abhorred fighting and quarreling: when any thing of this sort happened, I always went home displeased. But I have been much grieved to think that so many Sabbaths were idly spent, which might have been better improved. However, wicked as my companions were, and fond as I was of play, I never imbibed their vices. When between thirteen and fourteen years of age, the Lord graciously visited my soul again. I then found myself more inclined to obey; and carefully attended preaching in West-Bromwick; so that I heard *Stillingfleet, Bagnel, Ryland, Anderson, Mansfield,* and *Talbott,* men who preached the truth. I then began to watch over my inward and outward conduct; and having a desire to hear the *Methodists,* I went to *Wednesbury,* and heard Mr. *F.* and Mr. *I.* but did not understand them, though one of their subjects is fresh in my memory to this day. This was the first of my hearing the *Methodists.* After that, another person went with me to hear them again: the text was, *The time will come when they will not endure sound doctrine.* My companion was cut to the heart, but I was unmoved. The next year Mr. M—r came into those parts. I was then about fifteen; and young as I was, the word of GOD soon made deep impressions on my heart, which brought me to Jesus Christ, who graciously justified my guilty soul through faith in his precious blood: and soon shewed me the excellency and necessity of holiness. About sixteen I experienced a marvelous display of the grace of GOD, which some might think was full sanctification; and was indeed very happy though in an ungodly family. At about seventeen I began to hold some public meetings; and between seventeen and eighteen began to exhort and preach. When about twenty-one I went through *Staffordshire* and *Gloucestershire,* in the place of a travelling preacher; and the next year through *Bedfordshire, Suffex,* &c. In 1769 I was appointed assistant in *Northamptonshire;* and the next year travelled in *Wiltshire.* September 3, 1771, I embarked for *America,* and for my own private satisfaction, began to keep an imperfect journal...

ON the 7th of August 1771, the conference began at *Bristol* in *England.* Before this I had felt for half a year strong intimations in my mind, that I should visit *America;* which I laid before the Lord, being unwilling to do my own will, or to run before I was sent. During this time my trials were very great, which the Lord, I believe, permitted to prove and try me, in order to prepare me for future usefulness. At the conference it was proposed that some preachers should go over to the *American* continent. I spoke my mind, and made an offer of myself. It was accepted by Mr. *Wesley* and others, who judged I had a call. From *Bristol* I went home to acquaint my parents with my great undertaking, which I opened in as gentle a manner as possible. Though it was grievous to flesh and blood, they consented to let me go. My mother is one of the tenderest parents in the world: but, I believe, she was blessed in the present instance with divine assistance to part with me. I visited most of my friends in *Staffordshire, Warwickshire,* and *Gloucestershire,* and felt much life and power among them. Several of our meetings were indeed held in the spirit and life of GOD. Many of my friends were struck with wonder, when they heard of my going, but none opened their mouths against it, hoping it was of GOD. Some wished that their situation would allow them to go with me.

I returned to *Bristol* in the latter end of August, where *R. W.* was waiting for me, to sail in a few days for *Philadelphia*. When I came to *Bristol* I had not one penny of money: but the Lord soon opened the hearts of friends who supplied me with clothes and ten pounds: thus I found by experience, that the Lord will provide for those who trust in him.

On Wednesday, September 2, we set sail from a port near *Bristol*; and having a good wind soon past the channel. For three days I was very ill with the sea-sickness: and no sickness I ever knew was equal to it. The captain behaved well to us. On the Lord's Day, September 8, Brother *W.* preached a sermon on deck, and all the crew gave attention.

Thursday 12th. I will set down a few things that lie on my mind. Whither am I going? To the new world. What to do? To gain honour? No, if I know my own heart. To get money? No, I am going to live to GOD, and to bring others so to do. In *America*, there has been a work of GOD: some moving first amongst the Friends, but in time it declined: likewise by the Presbyterians, but amongst them also it declined. The people GOD owns in *England*, are the Methodists. The doctrines they preach, and the discipline they enforce, are, I believe, the purest of any people now in the world. The Lord has greatly blessed these doctrines and this discipline in the three kingdoms: they must therefore be pleasing to him. If GOD does not acknowledge me in *America*, I will soon return to *England*. I know my views are upright now—May they never be otherwise!...

The Lord's-day [November] 18, [1771] I found a day of rest to my soul. In the morning I was much led out with a sacred desire. Lord, help me against the mighty. I feel a regard for the people, and I think the *Americans* are more ready to receive the Word than the *English*: and to see the poor negroes so affected is pleasing: to see their sable countenances in our solemn assemblies, and to hear them sing with cheerful melody their dear Redeemer's praise, affected me much, and made me ready to say, *of a truth I perceive GOD is no respecter of persons.*

Tuesday 20, I remain in *York*, though unsatisfied with our being both in town together. I have not yet the thing which I seek—a circulation of preachers to avoid partiality and popularity. However, I am fixed to the Methodist plan, and do what I do faithfully as to GOD. I expect trouble is at hand. This I expected when I left *England*, and I am willing to suffer, yea, to die sooner than betray so good a cause by any means. It will be a hard matter to stand against all opposition as an iron pillar strong, and steadfast as a wall of brass: but through Christ strengthening me, I can do all things.

Thursday 22. At present I am dissatisfied. I judge we are to be shut up in the cities this winter. My brethren seem unwilling to leave the cities, but I think I shall shew them the way. I am in trouble, and more trouble is at hand, for I am determined to make a stand against all partiality. I have nothing to seek but the glory of GOD, nothing to fear but his displeasure. I am come over with an upright intention, and through the grace of GOD I will make it appear: and I am determined that no man shall bias me with soft words and fair speeches: nor will I ever fear (the Lord helping me) the face of man, or know any man after the flesh, if I beg my bread from door to door; but whomsoever I please or displease, I will be faithful to GOD, to the people, and to my own soul...

Friday [December] 12 [1772]. Went 12 miles into Kent County, and had many great people to hear me. But before preaching, one Mr. *R.* a church-minister came to me and desired to know who I was, and whether I was licensed. I told him who I was. He spoke great swelling words, and told me he had authority over the people, and was charged with the care of their souls. He also told me that I could not and should not preach; and if I did, he would proceed against me according to law. I let him know that I came to preach, and preach I would; and farther asked him if he had authority to bind the consciences of the people, or if he was a justice of the peace; and told him I thought he had nothing to do with me. He charged me with making a schism. I told him that I did not draw the people from the church; and asked him if his church was then open? He told me that I hindered people from their work; but I asked him if fairs and horse-races did not hinder them? And farther told him that I came to help him. He said, he had not hired me for an assistant, and did not want my help. I told him, if there were no swearers or other sinners, *he* was sufficient. But, said he, what did you come for? I replied, to turn sinners to GOD. He said, cannot I do that as well as you? I told him that I had authority from GOD. He then laughed at me, and said you are a fine fellow indeed! I told him I did not do this to invalidate his authority, and also gave him to understand that I did not wish to dispute with him, but he said he had business with me, and came into the house in a great rage. I began to preach, and urged the people to repent and turn from all their transgressions, so iniquity should not prove their ruin. After preaching the parson went out and told the people, they did wrong in coming to hear me; and said I spoke against learning. Whereas, I only spoke to this purpose,—when a man turned from all sin, he would adorn every character in life, both in church and state...

Thursday [July] 14 [1774]. My mind is in peace. I have now been sick near ten months; and many days closely confined. Yet I have preached about three hundred times, and rode near two thousand miles in that time: though very frequently in a high fever. Here is no ease, worldly profit, or honor. What then, but the desire of pleasing God and serving souls, could stimulate to such laborious and painful duties? O that my labor may not be in vain! That the Lord may give me to see fruit of these weak, but earnest endeavors, many days hence!...

From the 23rd of January [1775] till the first of February, my affliction was so severe that I was not able to write. There were several small ulcers on the inside of my throat; and the pain of the gatherings was so severe, that for two weeks I could not rest of nights. My friends were very kind, and expecting my death, they affectionately lamented over me. But on the 29th of January I was happily relieved by the discharge of near a pint of white matter. For a while my mind was in great heaviness; but after some severe conflicts with the powers of darkness; I was calmly resigned to the will of a wise and gracious GOD. O Lord! How wonderful are thy works! It is my desire to know the cause of this affliction; that, if it is in my power, I may remove it. Is it that I may know more of myself and lie in the dust? Or, for my past unfaithfulness? But whatever may be the cause, I humbly hope that all those painful dispensations will work together for my good. In the course of this affliction I found that when my spirit was broken, and brought to submit with cheerfulness to the will of GOD, then the disorder abated, and I began to recover; though Satan was very busy, and like *Job*'s impious wife, suggested to my mind, that I should curse GOD and die; nevertheless, through grace, I am more than conqueror, and can give glory to GOD. The gargle which I used first, to scatter, if possible, the inflammation, was sage tea, honey, vinegar, and mustard; then that which was used to accelerate the gathering, was mallows with a fig cut in pieces: and lastly, to strengthen the part, we used a gargle of sage tea, alum, rose leaves, and loaf sugar...

Monday [August] 7 [1775]. I received a letter from Mr. *T.R.* in which he informed me that himself, Mr. *R.* and Mr. *D.* had consulted, and deliberately concluded, it would be best to return to *England*. But I can by no means agree to leave such a field for gathering souls to Christ, as we have in *America*. It would be an eternal dishonour to the Methodists, that we should all leave three thousand souls who desire to commit themselves to our care; neither is it the part of a good shepherd to leave his flock in time of danger: therefore, I am determined, by the grace of GOD, not to leave them, let the consequence be what it may. Our friends here appeared to be distressed above measure, as the thoughts of being forsaken by the preachers. So I wrote my sentiments both to Mr. *T.R.* and Mr. *G.S.*...

Tuesday [March] 19 [1776]. Under the divine protection, I came safe to *Philadelphia*, having rode about 3000 miles since I left it last...I also received an affectionate letter from Mr. *Wesley*, and am truly sorry that the venerable man ever dipped into the politics of *America*. My desire is to live in love and peace with all men, to do them no harm, but all the good I can. However, it discovers Mr. *Wesley*'s conscientious attachment to the government under which he lived. Had he been a subject of *America*, no doubt but he would have been as zealous an advocate of the *American* cause. But some inconsiderate persons have taken occasion to censure the *Methodists* in *America*, on account of Mr. *Wesley*'s political sentiments...

Lord's-day [July] 28 [1776]. My soul has lately been much drawn out towards GOD in reading the life of Mr. *Brainerd*, and longs to be like him and every other faithful follower of Jesus Christ.

Monday 29. My present mode of conduct is as follows—to read about a hundred pages a day; usually to pray in public five times a day; to preach in the open air every other day; and to lecture in prayer-meeting every evening. And if it were in my power, I would do a thousand times as much for such a gracious and blessed Master. But in the midst of all my little employments, I feel myself as nothing, and Christ to me is all in all.

Francis Asbury, *An Extract From the Journal of Francis Asbury, Bishop of the Methodist-Episcopal Church in America, From August 7, 1771, to December 29, 1778,* vol. 1 (Philadelphia: Joseph Crukshank, 1792), 3–5, 10–11, 56–7, 134, 136–7, 163–4, 185, 205–6, 226.

54

Guidelines for American Methodists

Francis Asbury and Thomas Coke

FRANCIS ASBURY FACED many challenges at the time of the Methodist General Conference at Baltimore in November 1792. The 1780s had been a remarkable decade for American Methodism. After narrowly avoiding a schism in 1780 between northerners and southerners, Asbury was appointed by Wesley in October 1783 as general assistant, the highest rank for an American preacher. Methodist membership rose dramatically in the 1780s, expanding from 8,500 at the start of the decade to over 57,000 by 1790. The number of preaching circuits also increased, from twenty-one to ninety-eight in the same period. By 1784, Wesley finally made provision for American Methodist preachers to be ordained, conceding that the Anglican Church had failed to supply enough priests to meet the needs of the new nation's exploding population. Wesley proceeded to ordain Richard Whatcoat and Thomas Vasey, followed by Thomas Coke (1747–1814), who was placed as a superintendent over America. Wesley further gave Coke instructions to ordain Asbury as co-superintendent. Now Asbury had to share authority with an Englishman of a different temperament in this essentially newly formed independent church.

As opposed to the relatively uneducated Asbury, the urbane Coke attended Jesus College, Oxford, earning a BA and doctorate in civil law. Coke's highbrow upbringing and sophisticated manners brought refinement to American Methodism in a way that Asbury could not. But besides relating to the middling ranks, Asbury had the additional advantage of residing in America, demonstrating a firm commitment to his position. By contrast, Coke struggled to gain the trust and respect of Americans since he kept one foot in the new republic and a second in Britain, traveling back and forth during his tenure. Asbury seized the moment by having his title changed from superintendent to bishop in 1786 (much to Wesley's chagrin) and benefited when American Methodist preachers blocked the ordination of Richard Whatcoat as an additional superintendent. But neither Asbury nor Coke could stop the breach that James O'Kelly generated when he and his followers withdrew from the 1792 conference in protest (eventually forming a separate church) after losing a vote which would have allowed preachers the right to appeal unwanted circuit appointments.

The Doctrines and Disciplines of the Methodist Episcopal Church in America (1792) represents a high water mark for American Methodism, in terms of showcasing its organizational strength, while at the time serves as a reminder of the difficulties at the 1792 conference. Whereas in the 1770s American Methodism struggled to survive, the 1780s brought with it a resurgence of growth that escalated throughout the decade. Yet as it progressed, new problems emerged that leaders like Asbury would have to resolve.

The Doctrines and Disciplines of the Methodist Episcopal Church in America

Of the Trial of Those Who Think They Are Moved by the Holy Ghost to Preach

Question 1. HOW shall we try those who profess to be moved by the Holy Ghost to preach?

Answer 1. Let them be asked the following questions, *viz.* Do they know God as a pardoning God? Have they the love of God abiding in them? Do they desire and seek nothing but God? And are they holy in all manner of conversation?

Answer 2. Have they gifts (as well as grace) for the work? Have they (in some tolerable degree) a clear, sound understanding, a right judgment in the things of God, a just conception of salvation by faith? And has God given them any degree of utterance? Do they speak justly, readily, clearly?

Answer 3. Have they fruit? Are any truly convinced of sin, and converted to God by their preaching?

As long as these three marks concur in any one, we believe he is called of God to preach. These we receive as sufficient proof that he is moved by the Holy Ghost.

Of the Matter and Manner of Preaching, and of Other Public Exercises

Question 1. WHAT is the best general method of preaching?

Answer. To convince, 2. To offer Christ: 3. To invite: 4. To build up: And to do this in some measure in every sermon.

Question 2. What is the most effectual way of preaching Christ?

Answer. The most effectual way of preaching Christ is to preach him in all his offices; and to declare his law, as well as his gospel, both to believers and unbelievers. Let us strongly and closely insist upon inward and outward holiness in all its branches.

Question 3. Are there any smaller advices, which might be of use to us?

Answer. Perhaps these: 1. Be sure never to disappoint a congregation. 2. Begin at the time appointed. 3. Let your whole deportment be serious, weighty, and solemn. 4. Always suit your subject to your audience. 5. Choose the plainest text you can. 6. Take care not to ramble, but keep to your text, and make out what you take in hand. 7. Take care of anything awkward or affected, either in your gesture, phrase, or pronunciation. 8. Print nothing without the approbation of the Conference, or of one of the Bishops. 9. Do not usually pray *ex tempore* above eight or ten minutes (at most) without intermission. 10. Frequently read and enlarge upon a portion of scripture; and let young preachers often exhort without taking a text. 11. Always avail yourself of the great festivals, by preaching on the occasion.

The Nature, Design, and General Rules of the United Societies

1. IN the latter end of the year 1739, eight or ten persons came to Mr. Wesley in London, who appeared to be deeply convinced of sin, and earnestly groaning for redemption. They desired (as did two or three more the next day) that he would spend some time with them in prayer, and advise them how to flee from the wrath to come; which they saw continually hanging over their heads. That he might have more time for this great work, he appointed a day when they might all come together, which from thence forward they did every week, namely on *Thursday* in the evening. To these, and as many more as desired to join with them (for their number increased daily) he gave those advices from time to time which he judged most needful for them; and they always concluded their meeting with prayer suited to their several necessities.

2. This was the rise of the UNITED SOCIETY, first in *Europe* and then in *America.* Such a society is no other than *"a company of men* having the form and seeking the power *of godliness, united in order to pray together, to receive the word of exhortation, and to watch over one another in love, that they may help each other to work out their salvation."*

3. That it may the more easily be discerned, whether they are indeed working out their own salvation, each society is divided into smaller companies, called Classes, according to their respective places of abode. There are but twelve persons in every class; one of whom is styled *The Leader.*—It is his duty,

I. To see each person in his class once a week at least, in order,

   1. To enquire how their souls prosper.

   2. To advise, reprove, comfort, or exhort, as occasion may require;

   3. To receive what they are willing to give, towards the relief of the Preachers, Church and Poor.

II. To meet the Minister and the Stewards of the society once a week; in order,

   1. To inform the Minister of any that are sick, or of any that walk disorderly, and will not be reproved.

   2. To pay to the Stewards what they have received of their several classes in the week preceding.

   3. There is one only condition previously required of those who desire admission into these societies, *a desire to flee from the wrath to come, and to be saved from their sins.* But wherever this is really fixed in the soul, it will be shewn by its fruits. It is therefore expected of all who continue therein, that they should continue to evidence their desire of salvation,

First, By doing no harm, by avoiding evil of every kind; especially that which is most generally practiced, Such as:

> Taking the name of God in vain:
>
> The profaning the day of the Lord, either by doing ordinary work thereon, or by buying or selling:
>
> Drunkenness: or drinking spirituous liquors, unless in cases of necessity:
>
> *The buying or selling of men, women, or children, with an intention to enslave them:*
>
> *Fighting,* quarrelling, brawling; brother *going to law* with brother; returning evil for evil; or railing for railing: the *using many words* in buying or selling:
>
> The *buying or selling goods that have not paid the duty:*
>
> The *giving or taking things on usury,* i.e. unlawful interest:
>
> *Uncharitable* or *unprofitable* conversation: particularly speaking evil of Magistrates or of Ministers:
>
> Doing to others as we would not they should do unto us:
>
> Doing what we know is not for the glory of God: As
>
> The *putting on of gold and costly apparel:*
>
> The *taking such diversions* as cannot be used in the name of the Lord Jesus:
>
> The *singing* those *songs,* or *reading* those *books,* which do not tend to the knowledge or love of God:
>
> Softness and needless self-indulgence:
>
> Laying up treasure upon earth:
>
> Borrowing without a probability of paying; or taking up goods without a probability of paying for them.

4. It is expected of all who continue in these societies that they should continue to evidence their desire of salvation.

Secondly, By doing good, by being in every kind, merciful after their power, as they have opportunity, doing good of every possible sort, and, as far as is possible, to all men:

To their bodies, of the ability which God giveth, by giving food to the hungry, by clothing the naked, by visiting or helping them that are sick or in prison.

To their souls, by instructing, reproving, or exhorting all we have any intercourse with; trampling under foot that enthusiastic doctrine, that "we are not to do good, unless *our hearts be free to it.*"

By doing good, especially to them that are of the household of faith, or groaning so to be; employing them preferably to others, buying one of another, helping each other in business: and so much the more, because the world will love its own, and them *only.*

By all possible *diligence* and *frugality*, that the gospel be not blamed.

By running with patience the race that is set before them, *denying themselves, and taking up their cross daily*: submitting to bear the reproach of Christ, to be as the filth and off-scouring of the world; and looking that men should *say all manner of evil of them falsely for the Lord's sake.*

5. It is expected of all who desire to continue in these societies, that they should continue to evidence their desire of salvation, Thirdly, By attending upon all the ordinances of God: such are

The public worship of God;

The ministry of the word, either read or expounded;

The supper of the Lord;

Family and private prayer;

Searching the scriptures; and Fasting or abstinence.

6. These are the general rules of our societies, all which we are taught of GOD to observe, even in his written word, which is the only rule, and the sufficient rule both of our faith and practice. And all these we know his Spirit writes on truly awakened hearts. If there be any among us who observe them not, who habitually break any of them, let it be known unto them who watch over that soul, as they that must give an account. We will admonish him of the error of his ways. We will bear with him for a season.—But then, if he repent not, he hath no more place among us. We have delivered our own souls.

The Doctrines and Discipline of the Methodist Episcopal Church in America, Revised and Approved at the General Conference Held at Baltimore, in the State of Maryland, in November, 1792: In which Thomas Coke, and Francis Asbury, Presided, eighth edition (Philadelphia: Parry Hall, 1792), 27–8, 45–9.

An Argument for Overseas Missionary Work

William Carey

THE ELDEST OF five children, William Carey (1761–1834) was born on August 17, 1761, at Paulerspury, Northamptonshire, in England. At age fifteen, he began an apprenticeship as a shoemaker, which supplemented his income later when he decided to enter the ministry. Joining the Baptists in 1783, he took on the dual role of shoemaker and minister at Earls Barton and Moulton in Northamptonshire in the 1780s, studying Latin, Greek, and Hebrew when time permitted. At Moulton, and after reading about the voyages of Captain James Cook, Carey started work on a pamphlet that he finished after accepting a pastorate at Leicester in 1789. In his *Enquiry into the Obligations of Christians, to Use Means for the Conversion of the Heathens* (1792), he made a strong argument for overseas missionary work as a fulfillment of the Great Commission. From examining the Bible, he found scripture passages which justified the evangelization of non-European nations. Shortly after the publication of the *Enquiry*, Carey and other Northamptonshire Baptists teamed up to establish the Particular Baptist Society for Propagating the Gospel among the Heathen, better known as the Baptist Missionary Society. In 1793 Carey volunteered as a missionary to India, arriving with his family in Bengal in November of that year. Although gaining very few converts during his years as a missionary, Carey made an enormous impact as an educator, working closely with locals to translate the Bible into the Indian languages of Bengali, Oriya, Sanskrit, Hindi, Marathi, and Assamese and producing several grammars. His expertise in foreign languages led to his appointment in 1801 as professor of Sanskrit, Marathi, and Bengali at Fort William College in Calcutta.

FIGURE 55.1 William Carey (Detail), courtesy of the National Portrait Gallery, London.

An Enquiry into the Obligations of Christians, to Use Means for the Conversion of the Heathens

OUR Lord Jesus Christ, a little before his departure, commissioned his apostles to *Go*, and *teach all nations*; or, as another evangelist expresses it, *Go into all the world, and preach the gospel to every creature*. This commission was as extensive as possible, and laid them under obligation to disperse themselves into every country of the habitable globe, and preach to all the inhabitants, without exception, or limitation. They accordingly went forth in obedience to the command, and the power of God evidently wrought with them. Many attempts of the same kind have been made since their day, and which have been attended with various success; but the work has not been taken up, or prosecuted of late years (except by a few individuals) with that zeal and perseverance with which the primitive Christians went about it. It seems as if many thought the commission was sufficiently put in execution by what the apostles and others have done; that we have enough to do to attend to the salvation of our own countrymen; and that, if God intends the salvation of the heathen, he will some way or other bring them to the gospel, or the gospel to them. It is thus that multitudes sit at ease, and give themselves no concern about the far greater part of their fellow-sinners, who to this day, are lost in ignorance and idolatry. There seems also to be an opinion existing in the minds of some, that because the apostles were extraordinary officers and have no proper successors, and because many things which were right for them to do would be utterly unwarrantable for us, therefore it may not be immediately binding on us to execute the commission, though it was so upon them. To the consideration of such persons I would offer the following observations.

FIRST, If the command of Christ to teach all nations be restricted to the apostles, or those under the immediate inspiration of the Holy Ghost, then that of baptizing should be so too; and every denomination of Christians, except the Quakers, do wrong in baptizing with water at all.

SECONDLY, If the command of Christ to teach all nations be confined to the apostles, then all such ordinary ministers who have endeavoured to carry the gospel to the heathens, have acted without a warrant, and run before they were sent. Yea, and though God has promised the most glorious things to the heathen world by sending his gospel to them, yet whoever goes first, or indeed at all, with that message, unless he have a new and special commission from heaven, must go without any authority for so doing.

THIRDLY, If the command of Christ to teach all nations extend only to the apostles, then, doubtless, the promise of the divine presence in this work must be so limited; but this is worded in such a manner as expressly precludes such an idea. *Lo, I am with you always, to the end of the world.*

That there are cases in which even a divine command may cease to be binding is admitted—As for instance, if it be *repealed*, as the ceremonial commandments of the Jewish law; or if there be *no subjects* in the world for the commanded act to be exercised upon, as in the law of septennial release, which might be dispensed with when there should be no poor in the land to have their debts forgiven. Deuteronomy 15:4. or if, in any particular instance, we can produce a *counter-revelation*, of equal authority with the original command, as when Paul and Silas were forbidden of the Holy Ghost to preach the word in Bithynia. Acts 16:6–7. or if, in any case, there be a *natural impossibility* of putting it in execution. It was not the duty of Paul to preach Christ to the inhabitants of Otaheite [Tahiti], because no such place was then discovered, nor had he any means of coming at them. But none of these things can be alleged by us in behalf of the neglect of the commission given by Christ. We cannot say that it is repealed, like the commands of the ceremonial law; nor can we plead that there are no objects for the command to be exercised upon. Alas! the far greater part of the world, as we shall see presently, are still covered with heathen darkness! Nor can we produce a counter-revelation, concerning any particular nation, like that to Paul and Silas, concerning Bithynia; and, if we could, it would not warrant our sitting still and neglecting all the other parts of the world; for Paul and Silas, when forbidden to preach to those heathens, went elsewhere, and preached to others. Neither can we allege a natural impossibility in the case. It has been said that we ought not to force our way, but to wait for the openings, and leadings of Providence; but it might with equal propriety be answered in this case, neither ought we to neglect embracing those openings in providence which daily present themselves to us. What openings of providence do we wait for? We can neither expect to be transported into the heathen world without ordinary means, nor to be endowed with the gift of tongues, &c. when we arrive there. These would not be providential interpositions, but miraculous ones. Where a command exists nothing can be necessary to render it binding but a removal of those obstacles which render obedience impossible, and these are removed already. Natural impossibility can never be pleaded so long as facts exist to prove the contrary. Have not the popish missionaries surmounted all those difficulties which we have generally thought to be insuperable? Have not the missionaries of the *Unitas Fratrum*, or Moravian Brethren, encountered the scorching heat of Abyssinia, and the frozen climes of Greenland, and Labrador, their difficult languages, and savage manners? Or have not English traders, for the sake of gain, surmounted all those things which have generally been counted insurmountable obstacles in the way of preaching the gospel? Witness the trade to Persia, the East-Indies, China, and Greenland, yea even the accursed Slave-Trade on the coasts of Africa. Men can insinuate themselves into the favour of the most barbarous clans, and uncultivated tribes, for the sake of gain; and how different soever the circumstances of trading and preaching are, yet this will prove the possibility of ministers being introduced there; and if this is but thought a sufficient reason to make the experiment, my point is gained.

It has been said that some learned divines have proved from Scripture that the time is not yet come that the heathen should be converted; and that first the *witnesses must be slain*, and many other prophecies fulfilled. But admitting this to be the case (which I much doubt) yet if any objection is made from this against preaching to them immediately, it must be founded on one of these things; either that the secret purpose of God is the rule of our duty, and then it must be as bad to pray for them, as to preach to them; or else that none shall be converted in the heathen world till the universal down-pouring of the Spirit in the last days. But this objection comes too late; for the success of the gospel has been very considerable in many places already.

It has been objected that there are multitudes in our own nation, and within our immediate spheres of action, who are as ignorant as the South-Sea savages, and that therefore we have work enough at home, without going into other countries. That there are thousands in our own land as far from God as possible, I readily grant, and that this ought to excite us to ten-fold diligence in our work, and in attempts to spread divine knowledge amongst them is a certain fact; but that it ought to supersede all attempts to spread the gospel in foreign parts seems to want proof. Our own countrymen have the means of grace, and may attend on the word preached if they choose it. They have the means of knowing the truth, and faithful ministers are placed in almost every part of the land, whose spheres of action might be much extended if their congregations were but more hearty and active in the cause: but with them the case is widely different, who have no Bible, no written language, (which many of them have not) no ministers, no good civil government, nor any of those advantages which we have. Pity therefore, humanity, and much more Christianity, call loudly for every possible exertion to introduce the gospel amongst them...

THE impediments in the way of carrying the gospel among the heathen must arise, I think, from one or other of the following things;—either their distance from us, their barbarous and savage manner of living, the danger of being killed by them, the difficulty of procuring the necessaries of life, or the unintelligibleness of their languages.

FIRST, As to their distance from us, whatever objections might have been made on that account before the invention of the mariner's compass, nothing can be alleged for it, with any colour of plausibility in the present age. Men can now sail with as much certainty through the Great South Sea, as they can through the Mediterranean, or any lesser Sea. Yea, and providence seems in a manner to invite us to the trial, as there are to our knowledge trading companies, whose commerce lies in many of the places where these barbarians dwell. At one time or other ships are sent to visit places of more recent discovery, and to explore parts the most unknown; and every fresh account of their ignorance, or cruelty, should call forth our pity, and excite us to concur with providence in seeking their eternal good. Scripture likewise seems to point out this method, *Surely the Isles shall wait for me; the ships of Tarshish first, to bring my sons from far, their silver, and their gold with them, unto the name of the Lord, thy God.* Isaiah 60:9. This seems to imply that in the time of the glorious increase of the church, in the latter days, (of which the whole chapter is undoubtedly a prophecy) commerce shall subserve the spread of the gospel. The ships of Tarshish were trading vessels, which made voyages for traffic to various parts; thus much therefore must be meant by it, that *navigation*, especially that which is *commercial*, shall be one great mean of carrying on the work of God; and perhaps it may imply that there shall be a very considerable appropriation of wealth to that purpose.

SECONDLY, As to their uncivilized, and barbarous way of living, this can be no objection to any, except those whose love of ease renders them unwilling to expose themselves to inconveniences for the good of others.

It was no objection to the apostles and their successors, who went among the barbarous *Germans* and *Gauls*, and still more barbarous *Britons*! They did not wait for the ancient inhabitants of these countries, to be civilized, before they could be Christianized, but went simply with the doctrine of the cross; and TERTULLIAN could boast that "those parts of Britain which were proof against the Roman armies, were conquered by the gospel of Christ"—It was no objection to an ELLIOT, or a BRAINERD, in later times. They went forth, and encountered every difficulty of the kind, and found that a cordial reception of the gospel produced those happy effects which the longest intercourse with Europeans, without it could never accomplish. It *is* no objection to commercial men. It only requires that we should have as much love to the souls of our fellow-creatures, and fellow sinners, as they have for the profits arising from a few otter-skins, and all these difficulties would be easily surmounted.

After all, the uncivilized state of the heathen, instead of affording an objection *against* preaching the gospel to them, ought to furnish an argument *for* it. Can we as men, or as Christians, hear that a great part of our fellow creatures, whose souls are as immortal as ours, and who are as capable as ourselves, of adorning the gospel, and contributing by their preaching, writings, or practices to the glory of our Redeemer's name, and the good of his church, are enveloped in ignorance and barbarism? Can we hear that they are without the gospel, without government, without laws, and without arts, and sciences; and not exert ourselves to introduce amongst them the sentiments of men, and of Christians? Would not the spread of the gospel be the most effectual mean of the civilization? Would not that make them useful members of society? We know that such effects did in a measure follow the aforementioned efforts of *Elliot, Brainerd*, and others amongst the American Indians; and if similar attempts were made in other parts of the world, and succeeded with a divine blessing (which we have every reason to think they would) might we not expect to see able Divines, or read well-conducted treatises in defence of the truth, even amongst those who at present seem to be scarcely human?

THIRDLY, *In respect to the danger of being killed by them*, it is true that whoever does go must put his life in his hand, and not consult with flesh and blood; but do not the goodness of the cause, the duties incumbent on us as the creatures of God, and Christians, and the perishing state of our fellow men, loudly call upon us to venture all, and use every warrantable exertion for their benefit? PAUL and BARNABAS, who *hazarded their lives for the name of our Lord Jesus Christ*, were not blamed as being rash, but commended for so doing, while JOHN MARK, who through timidity of mind deserted them in their perilous undertaking, was branded with censure. After all, as has been already observed, I greatly question whether most of the barbarities practiced by the savages upon those who have visited them, have not originated in some real or supposed affront, and were therefore, more properly, acts of self-defence, than proofs of ferocious dispositions. No wonder if the imprudence of sailors should prompt them to offend the simple savage, and the offence be resented; but *Elliot, Brainerd*, and the *Moravian missionaries*, have been very seldom molested. Nay, in general the heathen have shewed a willingness to hear the word; and have principally expressed their hatred of Christianity on account of the vices of nominal Christians.

FOURTHLY, *As to the difficulty of procuring the necessaries of life*, this would not be so great as may appear at first sight; for though we could not procure European food, yet we might procure such as the natives of those countries which we visit, subsist upon themselves. And this would only be passing through what we have virtually engaged in by entering on the ministerial office. A Christian minister is a person who in a peculiar sense is *not his own*; he is the *servant* of God, and therefore ought to be wholly devoted to him. By entering on that sacred office he solemnly undertakes to be always engaged, as much as possible, in the Lord's work, and not to choose his own pleasure, or employment, or pursue the ministry as a something that is to subserve his own ends, or interests, or as a kind of bye-work. He engages to go where God pleases, and to do, or endure what he sees fit to command, or call him to, in the exercise of his function. He virtually bids farewell to friends, pleasures, and comforts, and stands in readiness to endure the greatest sufferings in the work of his Lord, and Master. It is inconsistent for ministers to please themselves with thoughts of a numerous auditory, cordial friends, a civilized country, legal protection, affluence, splendor, or even a competency. The slights, and hatred of men, and even pretended friends, gloomy prisons, and tortures, the society of barbarians of uncouth speech, miserable accommodations in wretched wildernesses, hunger, and thirst, nakedness, weariness, and painfulness, hard work, and but little worldly encouragement, should rather be the objects of their expectation. Thus the apostles acted, in the primitive times, and endured hardness, as good soldiers of Jesus Christ; and though we living in a civilized country where Christianity is protected by law, are not called to suffer these things while we continue here, yet I question whether all are justified in staying here, while so many are perishing without means of grace in other lands. Sure I am that it is entirely contrary to the spirit of the gospel, for its ministers to enter upon it from interested motives, or with great worldly expectations. On the contrary the commission is a sufficient call to them to venture all, and, like the primitive Christians, go every where preaching the gospel.

It might be necessary, however, for two, at least, to go together, and in general I should think it best that they should be married men, and to prevent their time from being employed in procuring necessaries, two, or more, other persons, with their wives and families, might also accompany them, who should be wholly employed in providing for them. In most countries it would be necessary for them to cultivate a little spot of ground just for their support, which would be a resource to them, whenever their supplies failed. Not to mention the advantages they would reap from each others company, it would take off the enormous expence which has always attended undertakings of this kind, the first expence being the whole; for though a large colony needs support for a considerable time, yet so small a number would, upon receiving the first crop, maintain themselves. They would have the advantage of choosing their situation, their wants would be few; the women, and even the children, would be necessary for domestic purposes; and a few articles of stock, as a cow or two, and a bull, and a few other cattle of both sexes, a very few utensils of husbandry, and some corn to sow their land, would be sufficient. Those who attend the missionaries should understand husbandry, fishing, fowling, &c. and be provided with the necessary implements for these purposes. Indeed a variety of methods may be thought of, and when once the work is undertaken, many things will suggest themselves to us, of which we at present can form no idea.

FIFTHLY, As to *learning their languages*, the same means would be found necessary here as in trade between different nations. In some cases interpreters might be obtained, who might be employed for a time; and where these were not to be found, the missionaries must have patience, and mingle with the people, till they have learned so much of their language as to be able to communicate their ideas to them in it. It is well known to require no very extraordinary talents to learn, in the space of a year, or two at most, the language of any people upon earth, so much of it at least, as to be able to convey any sentiments we wish to their understandings.

The Missionaries must be men of great piety, prudence, courage, and forbearance; of undoubted orthodoxy in their sentiments, and must enter with all their hearts into the spirit of their mission; they must be willing to leave all the comforts of life behind them, and to encounter all the hardships of a torrid, or a frigid climate, an uncomfortable manner of living, and every other inconvenience that can attend this undertaking. Clothing, a few knives, powder and shot, fishing tackle, and the articles of husbandry above-mentioned, must be provided for them; and when arrived at the place of their destination, their first business must be to gain some acquaintance with the language of the natives, (for which purpose two would be better than one) and by all lawful means to endeavour to cultivate a friendship with them, and as soon as possible let them know the errand for which they were sent. They must endeavour to convince them that it was their good alone, which induced them to forsake their friends, and all the comforts of their native country. They must be very careful not to resent injuries which may be offered to them, nor to think highly of themselves, so as to despise the poor heathens, and by those means lay a foundation for their resentment, or rejection of the gospel. They must take every opportunity of doing them good, and labouring and travelling, night and day, they must instruct, exhort, and rebuke, with all long suffering, and anxious desire for them, and, above all, must be instant in prayer for the effusion of the Holy Spirit upon the people of their charge. Let but missionaries of the above description engage in the work, and we shall see that it is not impracticable.

It must likewise be of importance, if God should bless their labours, for them to encourage any appearances of gifts amongst the people of their charge; if such should be raised up many advantages would be derived from their knowledge of the language, and customs of their countrymen; and their change of conduct would give great weight to their ministrations.

William Carey, *An Enquiry into the Obligations of Christians, to Use Means for the Conversion of the Heathens* (Leicester: Ann Ireland, 1792), 7–13, 67–76.

56

The Necessity of Evil

Samuel Hopkins

SAMUEL HOPKINS IS arguably the most creative thinker among Jonathan Edwards's followers. Critics called his innovative modifications to Edwards's thought "Hopkinsianism" in order to differentiate his type of evangelical Calvinism. Rather than define virtue aesthetically as benevolence to "Being in general," as Edwards had done, Hopkins posited true virtue in ethical terms, as love of God and one's neighbor. For Hopkins, true self-love meant being willing to sacrifice personal interests for the greater good of the whole. Wanting nothing to do with self-interested behavior, he promoted the notion of disinterested benevolence whereby a person completely and willingly submitted to the divine will no matter what the cost.

Towards the end of his life, Hopkins penned his magnum opus, *A System of Doctrines* (1793). In this two-volume tome, he produced a systematic theology of the New Divinity movement that identified God as a moral legislator who would not tolerate selfishness. While advocating the complete sovereignty of God, Hopkins needed to present a convincing theodicy. Reiterating a position he had taken earlier in a three-part sermon entitled *Sin, Thro' Divine Interposition, An Advantage to the Universe* (1759), he made a valiant attempt at justifying the existence of evil in his *System of Doctrines*. Rather than distance God from corruption in society, Hopkins embraced sin and misery as an essential feature of the divine plan. According to Hopkins, evil is actually good and necessary to achieve the best possible world. Furthermore, God did not simply tolerate evil but willed the existence of it in order to produce ultimate happiness for humanity. Although infamous for his alterations of Edwardsianism, Hopkins established himself as an independent theologian and patriarch of the New Divinity for generations of New England Calvinists.

System of Doctrines

It is to be considered whether the *evil*, both moral and natural, which has taken place, and may continue without end, be really inconsistent with the decrees of God, foreordaining whatsoever comes to pass.

It is probable that the existence of evil in God's world, and before our eyes, has been with many the chief, if not the only ground of dissatisfaction with this doctrine, and the opposition made to it. If no action or event had taken place, but such as appeared to men perfectly right, wise and good; and therefore most agreeable and desirable, none surely would object against God's ordaining every thing that was to take place, in the best manner possible. But since evil has actually taken place, both sin and suffering; and is like to continue forever, to a dreadful and amazing degree; men have been ready to think and say, "Surely this world had been infinitely better, more desirable and happy, if all evil had been effectually and forever excluded, both moral and natural; and nothing but perfect, eternal holiness and happiness had taken place. This is certainly an imperfect, disorderly, confused system, undesirably marred, and in a great measure ruined, by the rebellion of creatures against their Maker, and their consequent sufferings. How then is it possible that, an infinitely wise, powerful and good God, should decree and foreordain all this? To say he has done it, is rather to represent him as unwise and evil, than wise and good; though this might be done, consistent with the freedom and moral agency of man."

It is of great importance that this difficulty and objection should be removed, if possible; for it is not only an objection against God, foreordaining whatsoever comes to pass; but is equally irreconcilable with his supreme, uncontrolled, wise and good government of the world. This leads to observe,

I. THIS objection does not really lie against those who hold that God has foreordained whatsoever comes to pass, more than against those who do not admit this doctrine. And therefore it is far from being just, or agreeable to truth, to consider and represent it, as militating only, or in a peculiar manner, against such a doctrine. For, if the matter be well considered, it will appear, that the objection may be with equal reason and force urged against the objector himself, or those doctrines which he professes to believe. This difficulty, if it be one, is not peculiar to *predestinarians*, but is common to all, who believe in one supreme, infinitely powerful, wise and good Creator and Governor of the world. It has therefore been represented as *the Gordian Knot* in philosophy and theology, and a question above all others unanswerable, WHENCE COMETH EVIL? God is infinitely good; and therefore could not be willing or consent it should take place: But it could not take place, contrary to his will; for he is infinitely wise; and therefore must know how it might be prevented; and he is almighty, and nothing is impossible with him; therefore he was able to prevent it, if he had pleased to do it. How then is it possible that evil should take place, under the government of this God; while he sits at the head of the universe; has all things in his hand, absolutely dependent upon him, and rules infinitely above all control?

This question cannot be answered, on any plan, to the satisfaction of a rational, inquisitive mind, or the difficulty in any measure solved, unless it be supposed and granted, *That all the evil which does take place, is necessary for the greatest possible general good; and therefore, on the whole, all things considered, wisest and best that it should exist just as it does.*

All who believe the divine foreknowledge, or admit that an infinitely perfect Being made and governs the world, must adopt this solution, and grant that, on the whole, it is best that evil, moral and natural, should take place; or be left wholly without any: And indeed, they do either expressly or implicitly grant it, however they may differ as to the mode of explaining the matter, and the reasons why it is better that evil should exist, than otherwise. They who oppose the doctrine of the divine decrees, and yet allow that God could have prevented evil taking place, had he pleased to do it, cannot account for his not preventing it, unless they allow that he saw it was on the whole best, that it should not be prevented; and therefore it was, on the whole, best it should exist.

And they who suppose that sin could not be prevented, if God made free moral agents, and continued them in the exercise of their freedom; and account for the introduction of evil in this way; yet must grant that, *all things considered*, it was better that there should be sin, rather than that there should be no moral agents; and that the system or plan which includes evil, is the best that was possible. For if God foresaw, that if he made moral agents, vast numbers of them would, in the exercise of their freedom, fall into sin and ruin, he would not have made them, and continued them in the exercise of their liberty, if it were not best, on the whole, that evil should take place; and if this was not preferable to any other possible plan; and he did not, all things considered, choose that evil should exist, just as it does. For to say that God made free moral agents, when he knew that they would sin, if he made them; and yet knew that it was not best, *all things considered*, that moral evil should exist; is to say, that he is neither wise, nor good, as well as not omnipotent. This is so plain that it is needless to say any more to make it intelligible and evident to the lowest capacity.

And the same thing, in effect, must be granted even by them who deny the divine foreknowledge of the actions of creatures made free. For if God knew that sin might possibly take place, if he made moral agents; and at the same time knew that it was not, *all things considered*, best that it should take place; but infinitely to the contrary, it could not be best to make any such creatures, and run this dreadful venture; and open a door for the possible introduction of this infinite evil, which never could be remedied: and therefore it was not consistent with wisdom and goodness to make them free, and continue them so, on this supposition. They must therefore grant that it was, in God's view, on the whole, better that evil should take place, and to have the world fall into sin and ruin, than not to create moral agents, and have no moral kingdom; and that he preferred such a world, and to have sinful miserable creatures, rather than not to create; or they must allow that their God was deceived, and is dreadfully disappointed, and now heartily wishes he had not created; or is neither wise nor good: Which is to have no God, or something infinitely worse! It must therefore be observed,

II. It is abundantly evident, and demonstrably certain, from reason, assisted by divine revelation, that all the sin and sufferings which have taken place, or ever will, are necessary for the greatest good of the universe, and to answer the wisest and best ends; and therefore must be included in the best, most wise and perfect plan.

1. This appears evident and certain from the being and perfections of God. God is omnipotent; his understanding is infinite, and he is equally wise and good. He is infinitely above all dependence and control; and hath done, and can and will do, whatsoever pleaseth him. It hence is certain that he will do no thing, nor suffer any thing to be done, or take place, which is not, on the whole, good, wisest and best, that it should take place; and is not most agreeable to infinite wisdom and goodness. It is impossible it should be otherwise. Therefore, when we find that sin and misery have taken place in God's world, and under his government; we may be as certain that it is, on the whole, best it should be so; and that all this evil is necessary in order to answer the best ends, the greatest good of the universe, as we can be, that there is a God, omnipotent, and possessed of infinite wisdom, rectitude and goodness; and he who denies or doubts of the former, equally questions and opposes the latter. If it be once admitted that any evil, or the least event may, or can take place, which is not, on the whole, best, and therefore not desirable that it should be, it must, with equal reason be granted, that nothing but evil, and what is, on the whole, undesirable, may take place; and that the universe may become wholly evil, or infinitely worse than nothing: And all would be left without any ground or reason to trust in God, or any thing else, for the least good for himself, or any other being. The divine perfections and character, are the only security against this, and are the ground of an equal certainty that nothing has taken place, or ever will, which is not on the whole best, or necessary for the greatest good of the whole. And this is a sure ample foundation for the trust, confidence, comfort and joy of him who is a true friend to God, and desires the greatest good of the whole; and consequently is irreconcilably opposed to every event which

is not, on the whole, wisest and best. If *this foundation* were taken away and destroyed, what could the righteous, the truly pious and benevolent do? They must be left without any possible support, and sink into darkness and woe!

There can nothing take place under the care and government of an infinitely powerful, wise and good Being, that is not on the whole wisest and best; that is, for the general good; therefore, though there be things which are *in themselves evil*, even in their own nature and tendency; such are sin and misery; yet considered in their connection with the whole, and as they are necessary in the best system, to accomplish the greatest good, the most important and best ends, they are, in this view, desirable, good, and not evil. And in this view, "There is no *absolute evil* in the universe." There are evils, *in themselves considered*; but considered as connected with the whole, they are not evil, but good. As *shades* are necessary in a picture, to render it most complete and beautiful, they are, in this view and connection, desirable; and the picture would be imperfect and marred, were they not included in it; yet considered separately, and unconnected with the whole, they have no beauty, but deformity, and are very disagreeable: So moral evil is, in itself considered, in its own nature and tendency, most odious, hurtful and undesirable; but in the hands of omnipotence, infinite wisdom and goodness, it may be introduced into the most perfect plan and system, and so disposed, and counteracted in its nature and tendency, as to be a necessary part of it, in order to render it most complete and desirable.

Samuel Hopkins, *The System of Doctrines, Contained in Divine Revelation, Explained and Defended* (Boston: Isaiah Thomas and Ebenezer T. Andrews, 1793), vol. 1, 135–41.

57

Godly Living in a New England Town

Timothy Dwight

TIMOTHY DWIGHT (1752–1817) descended from two prominent New England families. His father Timothy, son of the wealthy and powerful Colonel Timothy Dwight of Northampton, wed Jonathan Edwards's daughter Mary on November 8, 1750. Two years later Mary gave birth to a son. A precious boy, young Timothy learned to read Latin by age eight and in 1769 graduated from Yale College, becoming the youngest member of his class. While at college, Dwight rose early in the morning to study, competing with Nathan Strong as the best student of his class. After graduating with a BA, Dwight remained at Yale for two years, earning his MA in 1771 and then serving as a college tutor. For an undisclosed number of months in 1776 and 1777 he studied with his uncle, Jonathan Edwards Jr., who taught his nephew to appreciate the finer points of Edwardsian theology. On November 5, 1783, Dwight accepted a pastorate at the Congregational Church in Greenfield, Connecticut, where he started a grammar school. Gaining a name as a powerful preacher and head of an academy at Greenfield, he responded favorably to an offer in 1795 to become the president of Yale. During his long tenure as president, Dwight was remembered by former students, such as Lyman Beecher, as inaugurating a period of religious reform at the college and as a pivotal leader during the Second Great Awakening.

In addition to his talents as a preacher and prestige as a college president, Dwight was a prolific author whose literary corpus is as extensive as it is diverse. Besides publishing a number of sermons and theological treatises, he composed a series of poetical works, including *America: Or, a Poem on the Settlement of the British Colonies* (1780), *The Conquest of Canäan* (1785), *The Triumph of Infidelity* (1788), and *Greenfield Hill* (1794). The latter, dedicated to John Adams, describes the town of Greenfield, Massachusetts, and New England in general, as the ideal godly environment for fostering piety. In part five of the poem, Dwight takes on the role of a wise old pastor who advises the townsfolk on how to avoid the pitfalls of sin while encouraging them in godly living.

FIGURE 57.1 Timothy Dwight by John Trumbull (Detail), Yale University Art Gallery, gift of the class of 1817.

Greenfield Hill: A Poem, in Seven Parts

Where western Albion's happy climb
Still brightens to the eye of time,
A village lies. In all his round,
The sun a fairer never found.
The woods were tall, the hillocks green,
The valleys laugh'd the hills between,
Thro' fairy meads the rivers roll'd,
The meadows flower'd in vernal gold,
The days were bright, the mornings fair,
And evening lov'd to linger there.
There, twinn'd in brilliant fields above,
Sweet sisters! sported Peace and Love;
While Virtue, like a blushing bride,
Seren'd, and brighten'd, at their side.
    At distance from that happy way,
The path of sensual Pleasure lay,
Afar Ambition's summit rose,
And Avarice dug his mine of woes.
    The place, with east and western sides,
A wide and verdant street divides:
And here the houses fac'd the day,
And there the lawns in beauty lay.
There, turret-crown'd, and central, stood
A neat, and solemn house of God.
Across the way, beneath the shade,

Two elms with sober silence spread,
The Preacher liv'd. O'er all the place
His mansion cast a Sunday grace;
Dumb stillness fate the fields around;
His garden seem'd a hallow'd ground;
Swains ceas'd to laugh aloud, when near,
And school-boys never sported there.

     In the same mild, and temperate zone,
Twice twenty years, his course had run,
His locks of flowing silver spread,
A crown of glory o'er his head.
His face, the image of his mind,
With grave, and furrow'd wisdom shin'd;
Not cold; but glowing still, and bright;
Yet glowing with October light:
As evening blends, with beauteous ray,
Approaching night with shining day.

     His Cure his thoughts engross'd alone:
For them his painful course was run:
To bless, to save, his only care;
To chill the guilty soul with fear;
To point the pathway to the skies,
And teach, and urge, and aid, to rise;
Where strait, and difficult to keep,
It climbs, and climbs, o'er Virtue's steep.

     As now the evening of his day,
Retiring, smil'd its warning ray;
He heard, in angel-whispers, come,
The welcome voice, that call'd him home.
The little flock he nurs'd so long,
And charm'd with mercy's sweetness song,
His heart with strong affections warm'd,
His love provok'd, his fears alarm'd—
Like him, who freed the chosen band,
Like him, who op'd the promis'd land,
His footsteps verging on the grave,
His blessing thus the Prophet gave.

     "O priz'd beyond expression here,
As sons belov'd, as daughters dear,
Your Father's dying voice receive,
My counsels hear, obey, and live!"

"For you my ceaseless toils ye know,
My care, my faithfulness, and woe.
For you I breath'd unnumber'd prayers;
For you I shed unnumber'd tears;
To living springs the thirsty led,
The hungry cheer'd with living bread;
Of grief allay'd the piercing smart,
And sooth'd with balm the doubting heart;
The wayward flock forbade to roam,
And brought the wandering lambkin home."

"And now, my toils, my duties done,
My crown of endless glory won,
Ev'n while, invited to the skies,
My wing begins through heaven to rise,
One solemn labour still is due,
To close a life, consum'd for you."

"Say, what the gain? Oh search, and say!—
To tread the fatal, sensual way?
To bristle down in pleasure's stye?
To heap up silver, mountains high?
With guilt to climb, with anguish keep,
Ambition's proud, and painful steep?
Should earth for your enjoyment roll,
Can earth redeem the deathless soul?"

"This little life, my children! say,
What is it? A departing day;
An April morn, with frost behind;
A bubble, bursting on the wind;
A dew, exhal'd beneath the sun;
A tale rehears'd; a vision gone."

"How oft too, in the bright career,
Which Pride, and Pleasure wanton here,
While Hope expands her painted wing,
And all around is health, and spring;
How oft resounds the awful knell,
That seals to life a long farewell,
'Thou fool! dissolv'd in guilt and sense,
This night, thy soul is summon'd hence.'"

"Yet on this little life depend
Blessings, and woes, which cannot end.
For Faith and Penitence below,

Immortal life and rapture glow;
For harden'd guilt, eternal ire,
And waves, that surge unfathom'd fire."
            "Then rise from death's benumbing sleep!
See, spread beneath the yawning deep!
Oh rise! and let salvation call
Your time, your thoughts, and talents all."
            "Two only paths before you spread;
And long the way, your feet must tread.
This strait, and rough, and narrow, lies
The course direct to yonder skies.
And now o'er hills, on hills, you climb,
Deserted paths, and cliffs sublime;
And now thro' solitudes you go,
Thro' vales of care, and streams of woe.
Tho' oft you wander sad, forlorn,
The mark of spite, the butt of scorn;
Yet your's the sweets, that cannot cloy,
The SAVIOUR's peace, the Seraph's joy;
While nurture HEAVEN itself supplies,
And fruits depend, and springs arise;
And Health and Temperance, sisters gay,
Despise the lessening length of way;
And sweet, tho' rare, companions smile,
Deceive the road, and lose the toil;
And Hope still points th' approaching goal,
As magnets tremble to the pole."
            "As now at hand the realm appears,
Where pains retire, and cares, and tears,
Then smooths the rough, the rude refines,
The desert blooms, the steep declines;
Then bright, and brighter, spreads the plain,
Where Love begins her vernal reign.
And sweet as music of the skies,
When hymns of bless'd Redemption rise,
Your FATHER's welcome hails you home;
The LAMB, the SPIRIT bid you come;
And all the Family around
Salute you to the blissful ground,
The heirs of life, the sons of God,
And trophies of their SAVIOUR's blood."

"Full wide the other path extends,
And round, and round, serpentine bends.
To sense, bewitching flow'rets bloom,
And charm, and cheat, with strange perfume;
Fruits hang dissolving poison nigh,
And purpling death enchants the eye.
Companions, frolicsome and gay,
Laugh jocund on the downward way,
With wiles entice a thoughtless throng,
And, blinded, lead the blind along,
Where smooth, and treacherous, and steep,
It slides, impending, to the deep."

"At length, where Death dominion holds,
A wide and gloomy gate unfolds—
Thro' solitudes immensely spread,
The mourning mansions of the dead,
A dreary tomb, that knows no bound,
A midnight hung eternal round,
Their journey winds—No friend appears
To dry the stream of endless tears.
Sweet Hope, that sooth'd their pains before,
Returns to soothe their pains no more.
Thro' the long night, the eye looks on,
But meets with no returning sun;
While Peace resigns to blank Despair,
And light is chang'd to darkness there."

"Then rise, and let salvation call
Your time, your thoughts, your talents all!"

"For this, the sacred page explore,
Consult, and ponder, o'er and o'er;
The words of endless life discern;
The way, the means, the motives, learn;
The hopes, the promises, enjoy,
That ne'er deceive, that cannot cloy;
Alarms to Guilt's obdurate mind;
Perennial bliss to Faith assign'd;
The precepts, by MESSIAH given;
His life, the image bright of Heaven;
His death, self-ruin'd man to save;
His rise, primitial, from the grave;
Beyond all other love, his love;

His name, all other names above.
All duties to be learn'd, or done,
All comforts to be gain'd, or known,
To do, to gain, unceasing strive,
The book of books explore, and live."
           "When smiles the Sabbath's genial morn,
Instinctive to the Temple turn;
Your households round you thither bring,
Sweet off'ring to the SAVIOUR KING.
There, on the mercy-seat, he shines,
Receives our souls, forgets our sins,
And welcomes, with resistless charms,
Submitting rebels to his arms."

Timothy Dwight, *Greenfield Hill: A Poem, in Seven Parts* (New York: Childs and Swaine, 1794), 110–5.

58

Debunking Racial Stereotypes

Richard Allen

THROUGH HARD WORK and determination Richard Allen (1760–1831) achieved his dream of freedom and prosperity in America. The son of a female slave, Allen was born on February 14, 1760. His owner, Benjamin Chew, an affluent Philadelphian, sold Allen in 1768 to a Delaware farmer named Stokeley Sturgis. Allen wrote very little about his early life in bondage, except famously referring to slavery as "a bitter pill" in his posthumous autobiography, *The Life, Experience, and Gospel Labors of the Rt. Rev. Richard Allen*. In 1777 Allen came to faith after hearing an evangelical preacher near Sturgis's farm. Not long after his conversion, Allen started attending a Methodist class meeting and began exhorting. Two years later in 1779, he arranged for the Methodist itinerant Freeborn Garrettson to speak to Sturgis at his home. Employing the biblical text of Daniel 5:27, Garrettson shamed Sturgis into working out an agreement with Allen whereby he could pay for his freedom over the course of five years. The eager young man paid off his debt of $2,000 in 1783 after three and a half years of back-breaking work, chopping wood and performing odd jobs in his spare time. Now free, Allen started exhorting as a Methodist in Delaware, New Jersey, and Maryland before settling permanently in Philadelphia in 1786.

Initially serving the black community that attended St. George's Episcopal Church in the City of Brotherly Love, Allen and fellow black preacher Absalom Jones led a mass exodus to found the black Methodist Bethel Church. As an assiduous entrepreneur, he accumulated enough money from his profitable chimneysweep business and other ventures to purchase land and a former blacksmith shop that became Bethel Church, which ceremonially opened its doors in July 1794. The determined Allen, through litigation, strategic planning, and sheer willpower shielded Bethel in the subsequent decades from being taken over by white leadership within the Methodist Church. After securing Bethel's independence, he united with other Atlantic black leaders to form the African Methodist Episcopal Church in 1816, becoming the denomination's first bishop. As the most

FIGURE 58.1 Richard Allen (Detail), courtesy of the Historical Society of Pennsylvani.

influential black leader in his day, he used his prominent role to denounce slavery and defend the reputation of African Americans as moral and upright citizens of the United States.

Allen's uplifting opinion on the potential of black Americans can be seen in his "Address to Those Who Keep Slaves and Approve the Practice," first published as an addendum to a pamphlet that he coauthored with Absalom Jones in 1794. Solely authored by Allen, the "Address" to slaveholders sought to dispel racial stereotypes of blacks as intellectually incapable of thriving in western lands. Opposing a multitude of skeptics, he argued that if people of African descent were set free and educated they would surely succeed in the new republic. Drawing from the biblical narrative of Moses and the Exodus, Allen reminded his readers that God favored the oppressed and, if necessary, would pour out his wrath on those who enslaved his people.

"An Address to Those Who Keep Slaves, and Approve the Practice"

THE judicious part of mankind will think it unreasonable, that a superior good conduct is looked for, from our race, by those who stigmatize us as men, whose baseness is incurable, and may therefore be held in a state of servitude, that a merciful man would not doom a beast to; yet you try what you can to prevent our rising from the state of barbarism, you represent us to be in, but we can tell you, from a degree of experience, that a black man, although reduced to the most abject state human nature is capable of, short of real madness, can think, reflect, and feel injuries, although it may not be with the same degree of keen resentment and revenge, that you who have been and are our great oppressors, would manifest if reduced to the pitiable condition of a slave. We believe if you would try the experiment of taking a few black children, and cultivate their minds with the same care, and let them have the same prospect in view, as to living in the world, as you would wish for your own children, you would find upon the trial, they were not inferior in mental endowments.

We do not wish to make you angry, but excite your attention to consider, how hateful slavery is in the sight of that God, who hath destroyed kings and princes, for their oppression of the poor slaves; Pharaoh and his princes with the posterity of King Saul, were destroyed by the protector and avenger of slaves. Would you not suppose the Israelites to be utterly unfit for freedom, and that it was impossible for them to attain to any degree of excellence? Their history shews how slavery had debased their spirits. Men must be willfully blind and extremely partial, that cannot see the contrary effects of liberty and slavery upon the mind of man; we freely confess the vile habits often acquired in a state of servitude, are not easily thrown off; the example of the Israelites shews, who with all that Moses could do to reclaim them from it, still continued in their former habits more or less; and why will you look for better from us? Why will you look for grapes from thorns, or figs from thistles? It is in our posterity enjoying the same privileges with your own, that you ought to look for better things.

When you are pleaded with, do not you reply as Pharaoh did, "wherefore do ye Moses and Aaron, let the people from their work, behold the people of the land, now are many, and you make them rest from their burdens." We wish you to consider, that God himself was the first pleader of the cause of slaves.

That God who knows the hearts of all men, and the propensity of a slave to hate his oppressor, hath strictly forbidden it to his chosen people, "thou shalt not abhor an Egyptian, because thou was a stranger in his land. Deuteronomy 23:7." The meek and humble Jesus, the great pattern of humanity, and every other virtue that can adorn and dignify men, hath commanded to love our enemies, to do good to them that hate and despitefully use us. We feel the obligations, we wish to impress them on the minds of our black brethren, and that we may all forgive you, as we wish to be forgiven; we think it a great mercy to have all anger and bitterness removed from our minds; we appeal to your own feelings, if it is not very disquieting to feel yourselves under the dominion of a wrathful disposition.

If you love your children, if you love your country, if you love the God of love, clear your hands from slaves, burden not your children or country with them. Our hearts have been sorrowful for the late bloodshed of the oppressors, as well as the oppressed, both appear guilty of each others blood, in the sight of him who said, "he that sheddeth man's blood, by man shall his blood be shed."

Will you, because you have reduced us to the unhappy condition our colour is in, plead our incapacity for freedom, and our contented condition under oppression, as a sufficient cause for keeping us under the grievous yoke? We have shewn the cause of our incapacity, we will also shew, why we appear contented; were we to attempt to plead with our masters, it would be deemed insolence, for which cause they appear as contented as they can in your sight, but the dreadful insurrections they have made, when opportunity has offered, is enough to convince a reasonable man, that great uneasiness and not contentment, is the inhabitant of their hearts.

God himself hath pleaded their cause, he hath from time to time raised up instruments for that purpose, sometimes mean and contemptible in your sight; at other times he hath used such as it hath pleased him, with whom you have not thought it beneath your dignity to contend, many have been convinced of their error, condemned their former conduct, and become zealous advocates for the cause of those, whom you will not suffer to plead for themselves.

Absalom Jones and Richard Allen, *A Narrative of the Proceedings of the Black People, during the Late Awful Calamity in Philadelphia, in the Year 1793: And a Refutation of the Censures, Thrown upon Them in Some Late Publications* (Philadelphia: William W. Woodward, 1794), 23–6.

59

An Anglican Evangelical's Sermon

Charles Simeon

A PROMINENT EVANGELICAL in the late eighteenth and early nineteenth century, Charles Simeon (1759–1836) made a lasting impression at Cambridge, England, through his ministry as a preacher and fellow at the university. While an undergraduate at King's College, Simeon wrestled with doubts about his worthiness to receive communion, which culminated in a conversion experience that freed him of his guilt. After graduating and receiving ordination as an Anglican minister in 1783, Simeon came into contact with a group of evangelicals that regularly gathered at Cambridge, including John Venn, rector of Clapham and son of the Anglican evangelical patriarch Henry Venn of nearby Yelling. Simeon became the vicar of Holy Trinity Church at Cambridge in 1783, serving the church for the remainder of his life.

Simeon gained a reputation for extreme piety. He purportedly rose daily at 4 o'clock in the morning for private prayer, spiritual self-examination, and Bible reading. He actively supported missions, helped to found the Church Missionary Society in 1799, and became involved with the Religious Tract Society, the Colonial and Continental Church Society, the British and Foreign Bible Society, and the London Society for Promoting Christianity among the Jews. As an evangelical clergyman, he regularly preached the gospel message with the hope that his sermon would humble the sinner, exalt the Savior, and promote holiness. His zeal for the saving of souls led him to securing church patronages, which by law could be transferred as a gift or by sale. By the time of his death, Simeon and other likeminded trustees controlled twenty-one church livings in Cheltenham, Bath, Bridlington, Northampton, Birmingham, Bradford, and elsewhere. With control over a number of churches, Simeon appointed evangelical ministers to pulpit vacancies, thus ensuring that future generations of parishioners would hear the gospel message.

FIGURE 59.1 Charles Simeon (Detail), courtesy of the National Portrait Gallery, London.

The Gospel Message

Mark 16:15–16. HE SAID UNTO THEM, GO YE INTO ALL THE WORLD, AND PREACH THE GOSPEL TO EVERY CREATURE: HE THAT BELIEVETH AND IS BAPTIZED SHALL BE SAVED, BUT HE THAT BELIEVETH NOT SHALL BE DAMNED.

IT is to be lamented that an unhappy prejudice subsists in the Christian world against the peculiar and most essential doctrines of our holy religion; and that, while ministers defend with zeal and ability the outworks of Christianity, they are at little pains to lead their hearers within the veil, and to unfold to them those blessed truths whereon their salvation depends. Under the idea that moral discourses are most accommodated to the comprehensions of men, and more influential on their practice, they wave all mention of the sublime mysteries of the gospel, and inculcate little more than a system of heathen ethics. They would be ashamed and almost afraid to make such a passage as this the groundwork of their discourse, lest they should be thought to be contending for some uncertain, unimportant tenets, instead of promoting the interests of piety and virtue. But can any one read such a solemn declaration as that in the text, and account it unworthy of his notice? Can any one consider the circumstances under which it was uttered, or the authoritative manner in which the Apostles were commanded to publish it to the world, and yet think himself at liberty to disregard it? Shall the very recital of it beget suspicion, as though nothing were desired but to establish the Shibboleth of a party? Let us put away such unbecoming jealousies, and enter in a fair and candid manner into the investigation of the words before us: let us consider that they were among the last words of our blessed Lord while he sojourned upon the earth; that they contain his final commission to his Apostles, and, in them, to all succeeding pastors of his church; that they are distinguished by our Lord himself by that honourable appellation, "the Gospel," or Glad Tidings; and that they were delivered by him not only as the rule of our faith, but as the rule of his procedure in the day of Judgment: let us, I say, consider the words in this view, and, with hearts duly impressed and open to conviction, attend to what shall be spoken, while we endeavour to explain the import—vindicate the reasonableness—and display the excellency—of this divine message: and the Lord grant, that, while we are attending to these things, the "word may come, not in word only, but in power, and in the Holy Ghost, and in much assurance."

1. In explaining the import of our text, we shall have little more to do than to ascertain the meaning of the different terms; for the sense of them being once fixed, the import of the whole will be clear and obvious.

Salvation can mean nothing less than the everlasting happiness of the soul. To limit the term to any temporal deliverance would be to destroy utterly the truth as well as the importance of our Lord's declaration: for though it is true, that they, who believed his prophecies relative to the destruction of Jerusalem, escaped to Pella, and were rescued from the misery in which the Jewish nation was involved, yet the followers of our Lord in that and every age have been subjected to incessant persecutions, and cruel deaths; nor was that deliverance either of so great or so general concern that the Apostles needed to go forth "into all the world," or to preach it to "every creature." Our Lord "came to seek and to save that which was lost;" he came to open a way for the recovery of our fallen race, and to restore men to the happiness which they had forfeited by their iniquities: this is the salvation spoken of in the text, and justly termed, a "salvation which is in Christ Jesus with eternal glory."

This salvation is to be obtained by faith; "he that believeth shall be saved." By the term "believing" we are not to understand a mere assent given to any particular doctrine; for there is not any particular doctrine to which the most abandoned sinner, or even the devils themselves may not assent: in this sense of the word, St. James says "the devils believe, and tremble." The faith intended in the text is far more than an acknowledgement of the truth of the gospel; it is an approbation of it as excellent, and an acceptance of it as suitable. Assent is an act of the understanding only: but true faith is a consent of the will also, with the full concurrence of our warmest affections. It is called in one place a "believing with the heart;" and in another a "believing with all the heart." In few words, faith is a new and living principle, whereby we are enabled to rely upon the Lord Jesus Christ for all the ends and purposes for which he came into the world; a principle, which, at the same time that it takes us off from all self-dependence, leads us to purify our hearts from the love and practice of all sin. To such faith as this our Lord frequently annexes a promise of eternal salvation: in his discourse with Nicodemus he says, "As Moses lifted up the serpent in the wilderness, even so much the Son of man be lifted up, that whosoever *believeth in him* should not perish, but have everlasting life. For God so loved the world, that he gave his only begotten Son, that whosoever *believeth in him* should not perish, but have everlasting life. He that *believeth on him* is not condemned; but he that *believeth not* is condemned already, *because he hath not believed* in the name of the only begotten Son of God." And in the close of that chapter it is added, "he that *believeth not the Son*, shall not see life, but the wrath of God abideth on him." Not that there is any thing meritorious in this grace more than in any other; for, as a grace, it is inferior to love; but salvation is annexed to this rather than to any other, because this alone unites us to the Lord Jesus Christ, in whom we are accepted, and by whose merits we are saved.

To the term Salvation is opposed another of a most awful import, namely, Damnation: as the former can not be limited to any temporal deliverance, so neither can this be limited to any temporal judgment: for, not to mention the express and repeated declarations that the punishment of the wicked will be as "a worm that dieth not, and a fire that is not quenched," our Lord, in the very words before us, contrasts the consequences of unbelief with the consequences of faith; thereby manifesting, that they were to be considered by us as of equal magnitude and duration: and, in his account of the final sentence which he will pass upon the righteous and the wicked in the day of judgment, he describes the happiness of the one and the misery of the other by the very same epithet, in order to cut off all occasion of doubt respecting the continuance of either: "these shall go away into everlasting punishment, but the righteous into life eternal." We are constrained therefore to acknowledge, that the threatening in the text includes nothing less than the everlasting misery of the soul, under the wrath and indignation of God.

This, tremendous as it is, will be the fruit of unbelief; "he that believeth not shall be damned." We must not suppose that the unbelief here spoken of characterizes only professed infidels, who openly avow their contempt of Christianity; for then it would by no means afford a sufficient line of distinction between those that shall be saved, and those that shall perish; seeing that there are many who profess to reverence the Christian revelation, while they live in a constant violation of every duty it enjoins. If, the receiving of Christ as he is offered in the gospel, be the faith that saves, then the not receiving of Christ in that manner must be the unbelief that condemns. This observation is of great importance: for the generality seem to have no idea that they can be unbelievers, unless they have formally renounced the Christian faith: their consciences are quite clear on this subject: the guilt of unbelief never caused them one moment's uneasiness. But, can any thing be more plain, than, that the same faith, which is necessary to bring us to salvation, must be also necessary to keep us from condemnation? Indeed it is so self-evident a truth, that the very mention of it appears almost absurd; and yet, it will be well if we admit its full force in the point before us: for, however zealous many are to comprehend holy actions and affections in their definitions of saving faith, they are backward enough to acknowledge that a want of those qualities must evidence them to be in a state of unbelief: Yet, till this truth be felt and acknowledged, there is little hope that the gospel will ever profit them at all.

Charles Simeon, *The Gospel Message* (Cambridge: John Burges, 1796), 5–8.

60

True and False Religion Exposed

William Wilberforce

ON AUGUST 24, 1759, William Wilberforce (1759–1833) was born to a wealthy merchant family from Hull. For two years, beginning in 1767, he attended the town's grammar school where the evangelicals Joseph and Isaac Milner supervised his education. When Wilberforce's father died in 1768, he went to live with an uncle and aunt for two years at their homes in St. James's Place, London, and Wimbledon. Unbeknown to his mother, William was being groomed to appreciate the Calvinistic Methodism of his aunt and uncle. Horrified upon learning this fact, his mother quickly recalled William back to Hull where she designed a reconditioning program, encouraging her son to indulge in the worldly pleasures of the theater and card playing, with the intent of undoing the earlier effects of Methodism. His mother's strategy worked for a while. Wilberforce seemed to have little interest in religion while attending a boarding school from 1771 to 1776 and during his time at St. John's College, Cambridge, where he earned a BA in 1781 and MA in 1788. Even though his father and paternal grandfather had set the pace for William as prosperous merchants, he wanted little to do with the family business, instead pursuing a career in politics, a decision he had made as a student at Cambridge.

Wilberforce's life as a politician began when he was elected MP for Hull in 1780. He held independent views but often supported his college friend William Pitt who rose to the rank of prime minister at the end of 1783. The following year, Wilberforce decided to run as a candidate for Yorkshire, the largest county in England at that time. Although costing him a fortune to run his campaign, he secured a seat as a representative for the prestigious county in 1784. Wilberforce's thoughts turned once again to Christianity in 1785, being convinced of the veracity of orthodox doctrines while traveling abroad with Isaac Milner. In that same year he experienced conversion and contemplated another career, but the Anglican clergyman John Newton counseled Wilberforce that his

FIGURE 60.1 William Wilberforce (Detail), courtesy of the National Portrait Gallery, London.

service to God would be greatest if he stayed the course as a politician. From his friendships with evangelical abolitionists like his relative Henry Thornton, Thomas Clarkson, and Sir Charles and Lady Middleton as well as a momentous conversation on that subject with William Pitt and William Grenville in May 1787, Wilberforce agreed to spearhead parliamentary measures to rid Britain of the slave trade. His spirited speeches on the horrors of slavery and legislative initiatives in the House of Commons at the end of the 1780s and throughout the 1790s, however, led to a series of disappointing votes in Parliament. But Wilberforce did not give up. He redoubled his efforts until his persistence was rewarded in February 1807 when the House of Commons voted to end the British slave trade.

In addition to his interest in the abolition of the slave trade, Wilberforce showed concern for Britain's moral state. In 1793 he began writing on "practical Christianity," later publishing a tome of nearly five hundred pages as *A Practical View of the Prevailing Religious System of Professed Christians* in 1797. In it Wilberforce differentiated between authentic believers and nominal Christians, making a case for the sinful disposition inherited by all humans and the need to acknowledge the salvific benefits of Jesus Christ's death on the cross. From observing the professing Christians of the day, he concluded that most churchgoers assumed that they could make their way to heaven by simple morality and charitable works. Wilberforce's experience as a wayward teenager proved to him the impossibility of Christian living without divine grace and repentance. His widely read *Practical View* came as a clarion call for spiritual reform that was intended to challenge the religious apathy that seemed to be prevalent at that time.

A Practical View of the Prevailing Religious System of Professed Christians

BEFORE we proceed to the consideration of any particular defects in the religious system of the bulk of professed Christians, it may be proper to point out the very inadequate conception which they entertain of the importance of Christianity in general, of its peculiar nature, and superior excellence. If we listen to their conversation, virtue is praised, and vice is censured; piety is perhaps applauded, and profanity condemned. So far all is well. But let any one, who would not be deceived by these "barren generalities" examine a little more closely, and he will find, that not to Christianity in particular, but at best to Religion in general, perhaps to mere Morality, their homage is intended to be paid. With Christianity, as distinct from these, they are little acquainted; their views of it have been so cursory and superficial, that far from discerning its characteristic essence, they have little more than perceived those exterior circumstances which distinguish it from other forms of religion. There are some few facts, and perhaps some leading doctrines and principles, of which they cannot be wholly ignorant; but of the consequences, and relations, and practical uses of these they have few ideas, or none at all.

Does this seem too strong? View their plan of life and their ordinary conduct; and not to speak at present of their general inattention to things of a religious nature, let us ask, wherein can we discern the points of discrimination between them and professed unbelievers? In an age wherein it is confessed and lamented that infidelity abounds, do we observe in them any remarkable care to instruct their children in the principles of the faith which they profess, and to furnish them with arguments for the defence of it? They would blush, on their child's coming out into the work, to think him defective in any branch of that knowledge, or of those accomplishments which belong to his station in life, and accordingly these are cultivated with becoming assiduity. But he is left to collect his religion as he may; the study of Christianity has formed no part of his education, and his attachment to it (where any attachment to it exists at all) is, too often, not the preference of sober reason, but merely the result of early prejudice and groundless prepossession. He was born in a Christian country, of course he is a Christian; his father was a member of the Church of England, so is he. When such is the hereditary religion handed down from generation to generation, it cannot surprise us to observe young men of sense and spirit beginning to doubt altogether of the truth of the system in which they have been brought up, and ready to abandon a station which they are unable to defend. Knowing Christianity chiefly in the difficulties which it contains, and in the impossibilities which are falsely imputed to it, they fall perhaps into the company of infidels; and, as might be expected, they are shaken by frivolous objections and profane cavils, which, had they been grounded and bottomed in reason and argument, would have passed by them "as the idle wind," and scarcely have seemed worthy of serious notice...

From the transient and distant view then, which we have been taking of these assuming Christians, let us approach a little nearer, and listen to the unreserved conversation of their confidential hours. Here, if any where, the interior of the heart is laid open, and we may ascertain the true principles of their regards and aversions; the scale by which they measure the good and evil of life. Here, however, you will discover few or no traces of Christianity. She scarcely finds herself a place amidst the many objects of their hopes, and fears, and joys, and sorrows. Grateful, perhaps, (as well indeed they may be grateful) for health, and talents, and affluence, and other blessings belonging to their persons and conditions in life, they scarcely reckon in the number this grand distinguishing mark of the bounty of Providence; or if they mention it all, it is noticed coldly and formally, like one of those obsolete claims to which, though but of small account in the estimate of our wealth or power, we think it as well to put in our title from considerations of family decorum or of national usage.

But what more than all the rest establishes the point in question: let their conversation take a graver turn: here at length their religion, modest and retired as it is, must be expected to disclose itself; here however you will look in vain for the religion of Jesus. Their standard of right and wrong is not the standard of the gospel: they approve and condemn by a different rule; they advance principles and maintain opinions altogether opposite to the genius and character of Christianity. You would fancy yourself rather amongst the followers of the old philosophy; nor is it easy to guess how any one could satisfy himself to the contrary, unless, by mentioning the name of some acknowledged heretic, he should afford them an occasion of demonstrating their zeal for the religion of their country.

The truth is, their opinions on these subjects are not formed from the perusal of the word of God. The Bible lies on the shelf unopened; and they would be wholly ignorant of its contents, except for what they hear occasionally at church, or for the faint traces which their memories may still retain of the lessons of their earliest infancy.

William Wilberforce, *A Practical View of the Prevailing Religious System of Professed Christians, in the Higher and Middle Classes in this Country, Contrasted with Real Christians*, second edition (London: T. Cadell and W. Davies, 1797), 7–9, 11–2.

61

Godly Government during a Time of Crisis

Lemuel Haynes

THE AMERICAN ABOLITIONIST, revivalist, and theologian Lemuel Haynes (1753–
1833) grew up an indentured servant on the Massachusetts frontier. Little is known
of Haynes's parents, possibly a white New Englander named Alice Fitch and an
unknown black man. Fitch gave birth, perhaps secretly, in the home of Connecticut
resident John Haynes, whose surname was given to Lemuel. Within a few months,
John Haynes indentured the infant to a farmer named David Rose of Granville,
Massachusetts. The young Haynes served out his labor contract as a farmhand until
his release in 1774. Caught up in the patriotism of the day, Haynes joined the min-
utemen in 1774 and marched to Roxbury in the aftermath of the Boston Massacre.
He served as a soldier in the War of Independence, traveling to Ticonderoga in 1776
to help secure the fort that had been captured in 1775 by the British. Tutored after the
War by the New Divinity minister Daniel Farrand of Canaan, Connecticut, Haynes
became a stalwart of evangelical Calvinism. After stints preaching in nearby towns,
he took a post in 1788 at a Congregational church in Rutland, Vermont, where he
served until his dismissal in 1818 (probably because of his opposition to the War of
1812). As a pastor, Haynes distinguished himself as an orthodox preacher, a revivalist, and an adherent of Revolutionary-era republicanism.

Like other New Divinity men, Haynes interpreted the slave trade and slavery as
part of God's providential design. But unlike Jonathan Edwards Jr., Levi Hart, and
Samuel Hopkins, who advocated (though not consistently) the expatriation of freed
blacks to Africa, Haynes argued that in America blacks and whites should live and
work together in unity. In Haynes's mind, true republicanism demanded the eradi-
cation of slavery and the recognition of blacks' equal right to liberty. The Federalist
Party seemed, to Haynes, other New Divinity men, and those like Timothy Dwight
who were sympathetic to the New Divinity, most able to rid the country of slavery as
well as fulfilling the expectation of republican and evangelical Calvinists of a virtuous

FIGURE 61.1 Lemuel Haynes (Detail), courtesy of the Bennington Museum, Bennington, Vermont.

society. Haynes viewed Thomas Jefferson's brand of Democratic Republicanism as a gateway to the unrestrained politics and immoral behavior in the French Revolution. In his 1798 sermon, *The Influence of Civil Government on Religion*, Haynes contrasted a godly American government guided by George Washington and John Adams to the chaotic and sinful French Reign of Terror. The controversial Alien and Sedition Acts of 1798 prompted Haynes to publish in support of the Federalist Party, arguing that such laws were necessary to restrain citizens from destroying the new republic. But both politics and religion would turn against Haynes, and he would find himself without a pulpit after the War of 1812.

The Influence of Civil Government on Religion

THE influence of civil government upon religion and morality, and their connection, is a matter to which our candid attention is called on the present occasion. That God is able to support his cause in the world without the intervention of legislative authority, and that they have no connection, is a sentiment warmly advocated by many; and indeed none can dispute them, without calling in question the power of Omnipotence: but whether it be agreeable to the established constitution of heaven, in ordinary cases, to support religion without civil authority, or whether it be not favorable to virtue, is the inquiry. That God is able to appoint state officers without people's meeting to give their suffrages, is what God has done, and has natural power to do; but none will infer from thence, that such appointment actually will take place without public exertions.

1. CIVIL government was *appointed* by God to regulate the affairs of men. Israel of old received laws, both of a civil and religious nature, from the great Legislator of the universe. This is evident to all who are acquainted with

sacred or profane history. *He removeth kings, and setteth up kings,* Daniel 2:21. *Thou shalt in any wise set him king over thee whom the Lord thy God shall choose,* Deuteronomy 17:15. St. Paul, to enforce obedience to magistracy, points to the origin of civil power, Romans 13. The powers that be are *ordained of God.* Whosoever, therefore, resisteth the power, resisteth the *ordinance of God.*—For he is the minister of God to thee for good. Every appointment of the Deity is favorable to religion, and conducive thereto, as there is no other object worthy [of] divine attention; to suppose otherwise would be an impious reflection on the character of God.

2. WHEN we consider the obvious end for which civil government was instituted, it is easy to see that it is designed as a support to virtue. To suppress vice and immorality—to defend men's lives, religion and properties, are the essential constituents of a good government.

THE wickedness of the human heart is so great, that it needs every restraint. To oppose the impetuous torrent of iniquity; to humanize the soul, and to conduct men in the way of felicity, are objects to which the laws of God and those which are commonly called the laws of men, do mutually point. Without our lives and interests are defended, how can we practice piety? Human laws, as well as divine, do in a sense respect the heart. The criminal is punished for his enormities, by the hand of the civil magistrate, because they are considered as flowing from a bad heart. To say that an institution tends to maintain order, justice, and the rights of men, or that it is favorable to religion, are expressions synonymous. Although the government of a commonwealth has a particular and a more immediate respect to the temporal interests of men, yet there is a higher object to which they stand related, and that renders them important...

4. WERE we to compare those countries and places where wholesome laws exist, and are executed, with those that are without them, we shall find the contrast striking.—Where there are no laws, no subordination, there licentiousness and barbarity hold their empire, and like a malignant fever diffuse their baneful influence without restraint. Every one that is acquainted with sacred or other histories, knows the propriety of the remark. Were we to advert to our own experience, we have the clearest conviction. Is it not the case in general, that a contempt of the good laws of the land, and impiety are inseparable companions?

WE have recent demonstration, that civil authority is in some sense, the basis of religion, and have too much reason to adopt the language in the text, *If the foundations be destroyed, what shall the righteous do!* It is far from my intention to appear in the habit of a partisan, or to stimulate dissension on an occasion like this, while I point you to the unprecedented conduct of a foreign power, as witness to the truth of the topic under consideration. To exaggerate matters I have no inclination, nor to wound the tender feelings of humanity by a tedious detail of French enormities. To pursue their lawless ravages would be to trace the cruel exploits of a blood thirsty Hannibal, or merciless strides of an imperious Alexander. Near twenty villages in Germany have become a sacrifice to the vengeance of a more than savage army. Switzerland, Geneva, (the latter, a place remarkable for their religion and good order) have fallen victims to their cruelties. The soothing words, *liberty* and *equality*, were so dear to us, that we were hoping that true republicanism was their object, and were almost decoyed into their wretched embraces; but they leave not the least traces of it behind them. It is evidently their design, to exterminate order and religion out of the universe, banquet on stolen property, give rules to the world, and so become the tyrants of the earth.

"ECCLESIASTICS, of every description, and particularly the professors of both sexes, (says a late German writer), seem to be the chief objects of republican malevolence, immorality and cruelty; in which the soldiers were led on and encouraged by their officers." That an abolition of religion is an object of French insanity is too evident to be disputed; hence it is that they are so inimical to civil authority, as they view it favorable to morality. We cannot mistake them, when we consider their contempt of the Holy Scriptures, their atheistical decisions, and their more than beastly conduct. Libertinism, and not republicanism, is most certainly their object. It is an inquiry worthy of attention, whether the few years [of] revolution in France has not done more towards promoting infidelity, deism, and all manner of licentiousness, than half a century before. The near connection of religion with wholesome laws, or civil authority, is doubtless an ostensible reason why the latter is so much the object of resentment. The contempt that these states have met with from the French Directory, in their not receiving our Envoys: their insolent and enormous demands on our property—their blind and deceitful intrigues—their lawless depredations on our commerce at sea, are sufficient to shew that it is not peace, liberty and good order they are after, but to make themselves sole arbiters of the world. Many have been caressed with the fascinating yell, *Long live the republican!*—and opened their gates to the French army, but have too late found their tender mercies to be cruelty, and themselves in the hands of a plundering banditti. What outrages have been committed on the persons of old and young! Wives and daughters abused in the presence of their husbands and parents.—Those in sacred orders, notwithstanding their age, illness and profession, dragged from their beds, their houses pillaged, and they have been the chief objects of spite and detestation. Let many villages of Swabia, in Germany, witness to the truth of this observation. Such are the sad effects of no law, no order, no religion; and if the foundations be destroyed, what shall the righteous do?

THE candor and patience of this audience are requested, while a few reflections are deduced from the preceding observations.

1. IT is undoubtedly our duty to become acquainted with the laws of the land. That by which the commonwealth of Israel was governed, was to be well studied by their statesmen, Deuteronomy 17. Especially those who are to be representatives of the people, should well understand the laws of their country: those then of the profession are not disqualified to sit in the seat of government, by virtue of their knowledge in state policy. It is the design of civil government to secure the rights of men, which should be held sacred; it being so nearly connected with religion, renders it important.—It is a subject to which we ought to pay attention, that we may be in a capacity to pursue the best measures to promote it. It is a remark, not without foundation, that they who make the widest mouths against divine revelation, are commonly those who know the least about it, and form their opinion on popular cant. Whether this is not often the case with many who set up against the good laws of the state, is a matter worthy of inquiry. He that can arraign and condemn the constitution and laws of his country, without information, and will judge of a matter before he hears it, in the view of Solomon forfeits the character of a wise man.

2. IS there such a connection between civil and religious order, then we ought to support the former, would we prove ourselves friends to the latter. Indeed he that can oppose and destroy the good laws of his country, his religious character is greatly to be suspected.—He that loves religion, will value and prize that which tends to its support, and feels the influence of the idea in the text, *If the foundations be destroyed, what shall the righteous do?* It is really the character of a good man, that he affords his influence, his property, yea his life in the defence of his country, if called for...

SHOULD the question be asked, how shall we know the man of virtue and patriotism? The answer is obvious, and rationally decided by unerring wisdom, *By their fruit ye shall know them.*

WE infer the integrity of a *Washington*, and an *Adams*, from the invincible attachment they have manifested to the rights of men, through a long series of events, when they had it in their power to sell their country and accumulate millions to themselves. To suppose such men, who have risked their lives, their all, in the cause of freedom for many years, should in the last stage of life turn traitors, when they would have nothing to promise themselves but endless disgrace, confronts every dictate of reason and experience. Perhaps it is not possible for the human mind to have a firmer basis for confidence; and to impeach such characters, without better foundation than ever has appeared, to me, at least appears disingenuous, and argues a jealousy more cruel than the grave.

WHO can reflect on the fatigue, vexation, and hazard to which a WASHINGTON has been exposed in espousing the contested rights of his country, and not feel a sort of indignation to hear his character vilified and impeached without a cause? Are these the returns he is to receive from ungrateful countrymen!—It is true men are not to be idolized, but when we consider them as instruments qualified and raised up by God for great and peculiar service to mankind, it is undoubtedly our duty to love, honor and respect them.

IF I am not mistaken, we live in a day when our liberties are invaded, and the rights of men challenged beyond what we ever experienced, and that under the soothing titles of *Republicanism, Democracy,* &c. These are precious names if well understood; but when they are speciously substituted in the room of *libertinism* and *licentiousness,* they make us sick.

Lemuel Haynes, *The Influence of Civil Government on Religion. A Sermon Delivered at Rutland, West Parish, September 4, 1798. At the Annual Freemen's Meeting* (Rutland: John Walker, 1798), 4–9, 13–4.

62

A Conspiracy Theorist's Theory

Jedidiah Morse

THE CONGREGATIONALIST MINISTER Jedidiah Morse (1761–1826) is known as the "father of American geography," authoring such works as *Geography Made Easy* (1784), *The American Geography* (1789), and *The American Universal Geography* (1793). But he is also remembered as one of America's leading conspiracy theorists. Born in Woodstock, Connecticut, and growing up in the home of a pious family, the sickly Morse was permitted to enroll at Yale College in 1779 rather than fight against the Redcoats. After graduating in 1783, he taught at a girls' school in New Haven while studying divinity under Jonathan Edwards Jr. Morse went on to become the minister of Charlestown's Congregationalist church in 1789 and, in the same year, married Elisabeth Ann Breese, granddaughter of the New Light minister, and former president of the College of New Jersey, Samuel Finley. Their first child, Samuel F. B. Morse, overshadowed his father's importance with his connection to the telegraph.

Jedidiah Morse, like many Americans, rejoiced when France initiated its own revolution in 1789. But as democracy led to increasing bloodshed in the subsequent years, Morse and others gradually distanced themselves from what they now perceived as a godless society bent on spreading hedonism and anarchy throughout the Western world. In the aftermath of the French Revolution, Morse rallied behind the Federalists, the American political party led by Alexander Hamilton that wanted to create a strong central government and an infrastructure that would sustain economic growth. Morse rejected the Democratic-Republicans, and their Francophile leader Thomas Jefferson, believing that the Federalists offered the best hope for maintaining order and traditional Christian values in America.

At the close of the century, Morse came to the conclusion that at the heart of France's irreligion was a grand conspiracy that involved the Illuminati, a German secret society affiliated with the Masons. In his Fast Day sermon on May 9, 1798, Morse declared that the Illuminati had infiltrated the French Jacobin clubs, corrupting the government and promoting infidelity. Having thoroughly permeated

FIGURE 62.1 Jedidiah Morse by Samuel Finley Breese Morse (Detail), Yale University Art Gallery, bequest of Josephine K. Colgate.

France, its surreptitious members were surely turning their attention to the United States and supposedly had already set up branches of the movement within America in the form of democratic societies. Morse did not hesitate in naming the source of his information: *Proofs of a Conspiracy against All the Governments and Religions of Europe* (1797) by the Scottish professor John Robison. Despite the ridicule that he endured from critics such as the Reverend William Bentley of Salem, Massachusetts and the German geographer Christoph Ebeling, Morse continued to warn Americans of this impending threat into the early years of the nineteenth century. But by then Americans had lost interest in the subject of the Illuminati, which proved to be no real threat, and Morse had to endure life in a nation now controlled by the Democratic-Republicans, with Jefferson at the helm.

A Sermon, Delivered at the New North Church in Boston

OUR situation is rendered "hazardous and afflictive," not only from the unfriendly disposition, conduct and demands of a foreign power, which excite painful apprehensions that war may be the consequence, and which render necessary expensive measures of defense; but also and peculiarly from the astonishing increase of *irreligion*. I use this word in a comprehensive sense, and would be understood to mean by it, contempt of all religion and moral obligation, impiety, and every thing that opposeth itself to pure Christianity. *This day is a day of reviling and blasphemy.*

NEVER, at any period, could this be said, in reference to the world at large, with more truth than at the present. Kings, princes, and rulers in all governments; government itself in all, even its mildest, forms; priests and ministers of religion of all denominations; and the institutions of Christianity of all kinds, from the most corrupt to the most pure, are reviled and abused, in a singular manner, in similar language, in all Christian countries, and seemingly by common consent. The existence of a GOD is boldly denied. Atheism and materialism are systematically professed. Reason and Nature are deified and adored. The Christian religion, and its divine and blessed Author, are not only disbelieved, rejected and contemned, but even abhorred, and efforts made to efface their very name from the earth. As the natural fruits of these sentiments, and what we ought to look for where they prevail—fraud, violence, cruelty, debauchery, and the uncontrolled gratification of every corrupt and debasing lust and inclination of the human heart, exist, and are increasing with unaccountable progress. Evidence of the truth of this representation is brought by almost every arrival from Europe, and we have it, in various and convincing forms, before our eyes in our own country.

OUR newspapers teem with slander and personal invective and abuse. Our rulers, grown grey, many of them, in the service of their country; who, in the various dignified and responsible offices they have filled, have discharged their duties with great ability and incorruptible integrity, are yet stigmatized continually, as unfriendly to the rights and liberties of the people, and to the true interests of their country. Our Government itself, the most perfect, the best administered, the least burdensome, and most happyfying to the people of any on earth, is yet steadily opposed in all its important measures, and regular and continual efforts are made to "stop its wheels."

THE Clergy also, who have, according to their influence and abilities supported the Government and vindicated its administration, have received, from the same quarter, a liberal portion of reviling and abuse. And what have the Clergy done to provoke this treatment? Can it be said, with truth, that they are unfriendly to the rights and interests of the people? On what side were they in the year 1775, and during the revolution? What interests can they have separate from that of their people and their country? Are they not connected with both by the tenderest ties? If their people or their country suffer, must they not necessarily suffer with them? Their little all of property stands on the same basis with that of their people, and the same events affect them equally. Could they not subsist in as much ease and affluence as they now do, by other professions? Are their stipends or their prospects of promotion enviable or alluring? Can *they* then be your friends who are continually declaiming against the Clergy, and endeavouring by all means—by falsehood and misrepresentation, to asperse their characters, and to bring them and their profession into disrepute? If the Clergy fall, what will become of your religious institutions? Undoubtedly they must share the same fate. And are they of no value?

WHAT can be the design and tendency of all these things? Have we not reason to suspect that there is some secret plan in operation, hostile to true liberty and religion, which requires to be aided by these vile slanders? Are they not intended

to bring into contempt those civil and religious institutions founded by our venerable forefathers, and to prostrate those principles and habits formed under them,
which are the barriers of our freedom and happiness, and which have contributed
essentially to promote both; and thus to prepare the way among us, for the spread
of those disorganizing opinions, and that atheistical philosophy, which are delug-
ing the Old World in misery and blood?

WE have reason, my brethren, to fear that this preparatory work is already
begun, and made progress among us; and that it is a part of a deep-laid and extensive plan, which has for many years been in operation in Europe. To this plan, as
to its source, we may trace that torrent of irreligion, and abuse of every thing good
and praise-worthy, which, at the present time, threatens to overwhelm the world.
This plan is now unveiled.

IN a work written by a gentleman of literary eminence in Scotland, within the
last year, and just reprinted in this country, entitled, "Proofs of a Conspiracy against
all the Religious and Governments of Europe," we are informed, that a society who
called themselves THE ILLUMINATED has existed for more than twenty years
past in Germany. The express aim of this society is declared to be, "To root out
and abolish Christianity, and overturn all civil government." Their principles are
avowedly atheistical. They abjure Christianity—justify suicide—declare death an
eternal sleep—advocate sensual pleasures agreeably to the Epicurean philosophy—
call patriotism and loyalty narrow minded prejudices, incompatible with universal
benevolence—declaim against the baneful influence of accumulated property, and
in favor liberty and equality, as the unalienable rights of man—decry marriage,
and advocate a promiscuous intercourse among the sexes—and hold it proper to
employ for a good purpose, the means which the wicked employ for bad purposes.

THIS society, under various names and forms, in the course of a few years,
secretly extended its branches through a great part of Europe, and even into
America. Their aim is, to enlist in every country, "such as have frequently declared
themselves discontented with the usual institutions"—to "acquire the direction
of education—of church management—of the professional chair and of the pulpit—to bring their opinions into fashion by every art, and to spread them among
young people by the help of young writers." They are unwearied in their efforts, by
various artifices, to get under their influence the reading and debating societies,
the reviewers, journalists or editors of newspapers and other periodical publications, the booksellers and post-masters; and to insinuate their members into all
offices of instruction, honour, profit and influence, in literary, civil and religious
institutions. The leading members of this Order are men of great talents, zeal and
industry; and governed by their maxim, borrowed from the Jesuits, "that the end
sanctifies the means," they are prevented by none of those religious and moral
principles, which are wont to restrain men when prompted to acts of wickedness,
from pushing their plans by the vilest means.

THIS society, aided by concurrent causes which it has been instrumental in bringing into operation, has already shaken to their foundation, almost all the civil and ecclesiastical establishments in Europe. There is great reason to believe that the French revolution was kindled by the *Illuminati*; and that it has been cherished and inflamed by their principles. The successes of the French armies, many of them, can be traced to the influence and the treacheries of different branches of this society. There are too many evidences that this Order has had its branches established, in some form or other, and its emissaries secretly at work in this country, for several years past. From their private papers which have been discovered, and are now published, it appears, that as early as 1786, they had several societies in America. And it is well known that some men, high in office, have expressed sentiments accordant to the principles and views of this society...

I HOLD it a duty, my brethren, which I owe to God, to the cause of religion, to my country, and to you, at this time, to declare to you, thus honestly and faithfully, these truths. My only aim is to awaken in you and myself a due attention, at this alarming period, to our dearest interests. As a faithful watchman I would give you warning of your present danger.

Jedidiah Morse, *A Sermon, Delivered at the New North Church in Boston*...*May 9th, 1798, Being the Day Recommended by John Adams, President of the United States of America, for Solemn Humiliation, Fasting and Prayer* (Boston: Samuel Hall, 1798), 17–25.

Further Reading

Aalders, Cynthia Y. *To Express the Ineffable: The Hymns and Spirituality of Anne Steele*. Milton Keynes, UK: Paternoster, 2008.

Bebbington, David W. *Evangelicalism in Modern Britain: A History From the 1730s to the 1980s*. London: Unwin Hyman, 1989.

Brekus, Catherine A. *Sarah Osborn's World: The Rise of Evangelical Christianity in Early America*. New Haven, CT: Yale University Press, 2013.

Brooks, Joanna, ed. *The Collected Writings of Samson Occom, Mohegan: Leadership and Literature in Eighteenth-Century Native America*. New York: Oxford University Press, 2006.

Bushman, Richard L., ed. *The Great Awakening: Documents on the Revival of Religion, 1740–1745*. Chapel Hill, NC: University of North Carolina Press, 1989.

Carretta, Vincent. *Equiano the African: Biography of a Self-Made Man*. Athens, GA: University of Georgia Press, 2005.

———. *Phillis Wheatley: Biography of a Genius in Bondage*. Athens, GA: University of Georgia Press, 2011.

Carter, Grayson. *Anglican Evangelicals: Protestant Secessions from the Via Media, c. 1800–1850*. New York: Oxford University Press, 2001.

Chun, Chris. *The Legacy of Jonathan Edwards in the Theology of Andrew Fuller*. Leiden: Brill, 2012.

Coalter, Milton J. *Gilbert Tennent, Son of Thunder: A Case Study of Continental Pietism's Impact on the First Great Awakening in the Middle Colonies*. New York: Greenwood Press, 1986.

Conforti, Joseph A. *Samuel Hopkins and the New Divinity Movement: Calvinism, the Congregational Ministry, and Reform in New England between the Great Awakenings*. Grand Rapids, MI: Eerdmans, 1981.

Evans, Eifion. *Bread of Heaven: The Life and Work of William Williams, Pantycelyn*. Bridgend, UK: Bryntirion Press, 2011.

Fawcett, Arthur. *The Cambuslang Revival: The Scottish Evangelical Revival of the Eighteenth Century*. London: Banner of Truth Trust, 1971.

Fitzmier, John R. *New England's Moral Legislator: Timothy Dwight, 1752–1817.* Bloomington, IN: University of Indiana Press, 1998.

Forsaith, Peter, ed. *Unexampled Labours: Letters of the Revd John Fletcher to Leaders in the Evangelical Revival.* Peterborough, UK: Epworth, 2008.

Grigg, John A. *The Lives of David Brainerd: The Making of an American Evangelical Icon.* New York: Oxford University Press, 2009.

Guelzo, Allen C. *Edwards on the Will: A Century of American Theological Debate.* Middletown, CT: Wesleyan University Press, 1989.

Hall, Timothy D. *Contested Boundaries: Itinerancy and the Reshaping of the Colonial American Religious World.* Durham, NC: Duke University Press, 1994.

Haykin, Michael A. G., and Kenneth J. Stewart, eds. *The Advent of Evangelicalism: Exploring Historical Continuities.* Nashville, TN: B&H Academic, 2008.

Hempton, David. *Methodism: Empire of the Spirit.* New Haven, CT: Yale University Press, 2005.

Hindmarsh, D. Bruce. *The Evangelical Conversion Narrative: Spiritual Autobiography in Early Modern England.* Oxford: Oxford University Press, 2005.

——. *John Newton and the English Evangelical Tradition: Between the Conversions of Wesley and Wilberforce.* Oxford: Oxford University Press, 1996.

Hylson-Smith, Kenneth. *Evangelicals in the Church of England: 1734–1984.* Edinburgh: T&T Clark, 1989.

Jeffrey, David Lyle. *A Burning and Shining Light: English Spirituality in the Age of Wesley.* Grand Rapids, MI: Eerdmans, 1987.

Jones, David Ceri. *"A Glorious Work in the World": Welsh Methodism and the International Evangelical Revival, 1735–1750.* Cardiff, UK: University of Wales Press, 2004.

Karlsen, Carol F., and Laurie Crumpacker, eds. *The Journal of Esther Edwards Burr, 1754–1757.* New Haven, CT: Yale University Press, 1984.

Kidd, Thomas S. *The Great Awakening: The Roots of Evangelical Christianity in Colonial America.* New Haven, CT: Yale University Press, 2009.

Kimbrough, S. T. *The Lyrical Theology of Charles Wesley: A Reader.* Eugene, OR: Cascade Books, 2011.

Lacey, Barbara E., ed. *The World of Hannah Heaton: The Diary of an Eighteenth-Century New England Farm Woman.* DeKalb, IL: Northern Illinois University Press, 2003.

Lambert, Frank. *Inventing the "Great Awakening."* Princeton, NJ: Princeton University Press, 1999.

——. *"Pedlar in Divinity": George Whitefield and the Transatlantic Revivals, 1737–1770.* Princeton, NJ: Princeton University Press, 1994.

Larsen, Timothy, ed. *Biographical Dictionary of Evangelicals.* Downers Grove, IL: InterVarsity Press, 2003.

Le Beau, Bryan F. *Jonathan Dickinson and the Formative Years of American Presbyterianism.* Lexington, KY: University Press of Kentucky, 1997.

Lewis, Donald M., ed. *Dictionary of Evangelical Biography, 1730–1860*. Peabody, MA: Hendrickson, 2004.

McClymond, Michael J., and Gerald R. McDermott. *The Theology of Jonathan Edwards*. New York: Oxford University Press, 2011.

McIntosh, John R. *Church and Theology in Enlightenment Scotland: The Popular Party, 1740–1800*. East Linton, UK: Tuckwell Press, 1998.

McLoughlin, William G. *Isaac Backus and the American Pietistic Tradition*. Boston: Little Brown, 1967.

Marsden, George. *Jonathan Edwards: A Life*. New Haven, CT: Yale University Press, 2004.

——. *A Short Life of Jonathan Edwards*. Grand Rapids, MI: Eerdmans, 2008.

Newman, Richard S. *Freedom's Prophet: Bishop Richard Allen, the AME Church, and the Black Founding Fathers*. New York: New York University Press, 2008.

Noll, Mark A. *The Rise of Evangelicalism: The Age of Edwards, Whitefield and the Wesleys*. Downers Grove, IL: IVP Academic, 2003.

Phillips, Joseph W. *Jedidiah Morse and New England Congregationalism*. New Brunswick, NJ: Rutgers, 1983.

Podmore, Colin. *The Moravian Church in England, 1728–1760*. New York: Oxford Clarendon Press, 1998.

Rack, Henry D. *Reasonable Enthusiast: John Wesley and the Rise of Methodism*. Philadelphia: Trinity Press International, 1989.

Roxburgh, Kenneth B. E. *Thomas Gillespie and the Origins of the Relief Church in Eighteenth-Century Scotland*. New York: Peter Lang, 1999.

Rawlyk, George A., ed. *Henry Alline: Selected Writings*. New York: Paulist Press, 1987.

Saillant, John. *Black Puritan, Black Republican: The Life and Thought of Lemuel Haynes, 1753–1833*. New York: Oxford University Press, 2002.

Schmidt, Leigh Eric. *Holy Fairs: Scotland and the Making of American Revivalism*. Grand Rapids, MI: Eerdmans, 2001.

Smith, John E., Harry S. Stout, and Kenneth P. Minkema, eds. *A Jonathan Edwards Reader*. New Haven, CT: Yale University Press, 2003.

Stout, Harry S. *The Divine Dramatist: George Whitefield and the Rise of Modern Evangelicalism*. Grand Rapids, MI: Eerdmans, 1991.

Streiff, Patrick Philipp. *Reluctant Saint?: A Theological Biography of Fletcher of Madeley*. Peterborough: Epworth, 2001.

Stott, Anne. *Hannah More: The First Victorian*. New York: Oxford University Press, 2004.

Sweeney, Douglas A., and Allen C. Guelzo, eds. *The New England Theology: From Jonathan Edwards to Edwards Amasa Park*. Grand Rapids, MI: Baker Academic, 2006.

Tait, L. Gordon. *The Piety of John Witherspoon: Pew, Pulpit, and Public Forum*. Louisville, KY: Geneva, 2001.

Tomkins, Stephen. *William Wilberforce: A Biography*. Grand Rapids, MI: Eerdmans, 2007.

Tudur, Geraint. *Howell Harris: From Conversion to Separation, 1735–1750*. Cardiff, UK: University of Wales Press, 2000.

Tyson, John R. *Assist Me to Proclaim: The Life and Hymns of Charles Wesley*. Grand Rapids, MI: Eerdmans, 2007.

——. *Charles Wesley: A Reader*. Oxford: Oxford University Press, 1989.

Valeri, Mark. *Law and Providence in Joseph Bellamy's New England: The Origins of the New Divinity in Revolutionary America*. New York: Oxford University Press, 1994.

Ward, W. R. *Early Evangelicalism: A Global Intellectual History, 1670–1789*. Cambridge, UK: Cambridge University Press, 2006.

——. *The Protestant Evangelical Awakening*. Cambridge, UK: Cambridge University Press, 1992.

Westerkamp, Marilyn J. *Triumph of the Laity: Scots-Irish Piety and the Great Awakening, 1625–1760*. New York: Oxford University Press, 1988.

Wigger, John. *American Saint: Francis Asbury and the Methodists*. New York: Oxford University Press, 2009.

Wolffe, John. *The Expansion of Evangelicalism: The Age of Wilberforce, More, Chalmers and Finney*. Downers Grove, IL: IVP Academic, 2007.

Yeager, Jonathan M. *Enlightened Evangelicalism: The Life and Thought of John Erskine*. New York: Oxford University Press, 2011.

CPSIA information can be obtained
at www.ICGtesting.com
Printed in the USA
BVHW031725110422
633984BV00003B/39